Goodman, Asian History

Selected Course Outlines and
Reading Lists from American
Colleges and Universities

Asian History

edited by Grant K. Goodman
UNIVERSITY OF KANSAS

Third Updated and Enlarged Edition

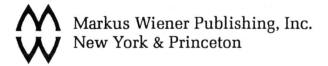 Markus Wiener Publishing, Inc.
New York & Princeton

For information write to: M. Wiener Publishing, Inc.
114 Jefferson Road, Princeton, NJ 08540

Library of Congress Cataloging-in-publication Data

Asian history/Grant K. Goodman, editor.—3rd ed.
    (Selected course outlines from American colleges and
    universities)
        ISBN 1-55876-064-4
        1. Asia—History—Outlines, syllabi, etc. 2. Asia—History—
Bibliography. 3.Asia—History—Study and teaching—United
States. I. Goodman, Grant Kohn, 1924-   . II. Series.
DS33.A87   1992
950—dc20   92-32547
                                                    CIP

Printed in America

TABLE OF CONTENTS

II. CHINESE HISTORY

III. JAPANESE HISTORY

VI. SOUTH ASIAN HISTORY

5

INTRODUCTION

Like the first edition published in 1986, this volume of syllabuses of college and university courses in Asian History is a project of the Conference on Asian History of the American Historical Association. Remarkably, too, because of the superb cooperation of members of the Conference on Asian History, this second edition of ASIAN HISTORY consists entirely of new material. Thus this is not a "revised" edition but rather a truly totally new edition.

This collection is designed, of course, to benefit not only the members of the Conference on Asian History but indeed all of our colleagues who are involved in course work on Asian History throughout academe. The demand for the first edition as well as the impressive scope of the syllabuses contributed to this new edition clearly demonstrate the necessity for and the utility of such a book.

One can not but be profoundly appreciative of the breadth, depth and variety of the syllabuses reprinted here. We are all in the debt of the contributors, and we will all certainly profit from the excellence of their work and from their generosity in sharing their very thoughtful insights with us. As collator of this project on behalf of the Conference on Asian History, it is a pleasure to thank each of the participants and commend their work to all of my colleagues.

Grant   K.   Goodman

Emeritus

University of Kansas

University of Puget Sound
ASIAN STUDIES 144: ASIAN SOCIETIES PAST AND PRESENT
(Twentieth-Century China, India, and Japan in Historical Perspective)

Spring 1992

MWF, 9:00   Jones 202

David Satterwhite (Asian Studies)   Suzanne W. Barnett (History)
Howarth 103B (x3577; home 761-0632)   Library 242 (x3168; home 752-8107)
Office Hours: as posted   Office Hours: as posted

This interdisciplinary course examines the presence of the past in post-
World War II China, India, and Japan. The central assumption of the
course is that each of the major societies of East Asia (China and Japan)
and South Asia (India) is a product of its particular heritage. Despite
their differences, however, these societies have had in common (1) the
need to adjust to a new international order following World War II and
(2) a consequent need to consolidate and define national culture.

The course proceeds on the conviction that the three societies and their
historical experiences are vital parts of our shared present and future
world. The course does not pretend to be a comprehensive survey of any of
the three societies. Rather, it attempts to capture through readings,
lectures, discussions, and writing assignments the current national styles
of the three countries and the historical patterns of their evolution.

The organization of the course avoids a formulaic single approach to the
three countries; still, some central questions apply to all three:

1. What has been the society's central 20th-century experience?
2. What was the society's predisposition to the postwar world?
3. How has the society encountered (a) nationalism, (b) modernization,
    and (c) transition from elitism to popular culture?
4. How do traditional values and cultural experiences inform the
    society's current national style?

Note: Asian Studies 144 meets the Historical Perspective core requirement
       and also counts toward the major/minor in Asian Studies. For the
       core and for major/minor credit, Pass/Fail does not apply; only
       letter grades apply.

Books for purchase (also on library reserve)
    Maurice Meisner, Mao's China and After: A History of the People's
       Republic
    Hugh Tinker, South Asia: A Short History, 2nd edn. (1990)
    Edwin O. Reischauer, The Japanese Today: Change and Continuity
    John Hersey, Hiroshima

    Note: Additional readings include class handouts and some materials
           available only on library reserve under the name of Professor
           Barnett.

Course Requirements
1. Regular class attendance and alert participation
2. Evidence of thoughtful, serious reading of assigned materials
3. Reading cards (due every Friday except Weeks 2, 5, and 15)
4. 1 one-page essay on "Crow Village," due 31 January
5. 2 "hour" exams (essay): 21 February, 25 March
6. 1 paper on Japan past and present, due 27 April
7. Final exam (essay): Tuesday, 12 May, 2-4 p.m.

Grading: Roughly 80% written work, 20% class (as in no. 1 and no. 2 above). As a matter of policy, there should be no extensions on papers, no examinations at other than scheduled times, and no "Incomplete" grades. The "W" grade (for official withdrawal) should apply only when a student has followed official withdrawal procedures by the stated deadline (17 February).

Note: The current Academic Handbook (available from the Registrar's Office) defines University policies and procedures that apply in this course.

Reading cards. On or before Friday of each week except Weeks 2, 5, and 15, you are to turn in a 3x5 "reading card," a brief record of your reading of a newspaper article on China, or India, or Japan, or a combination. Particulars are as follows:

1. Choose an article from one of the following five newspapers only: New York Times, Wall Street Journal, Asian Wall Street Journal, Christian Science Monitor, Washington Post.

2. Choose either a news story or a feature story, from either a current issue of the newspaper or a past issue; you may use library holdings (current issues are on racks in the Periodicals section, back issues are in the basement near the front stairs) or newspapers purchased personally.

3. For the reading card, use a 3x5 card. On the front side, provide a bibliographic reference (author if there is one, title or headline of the article, newspaper title, date, and page number); on the back side, write at least one sentence that captures the content of the article. NOTE: Your sentence(s) must be in your own words.

4. You will want to put your name on the front side of the card, thus to acknowledge your effort; and be sure to put on the card (back side, lower left) the date of your preparation of the card.

5. You may write or type cards, remembering that they will be part of your files for this course.

The primary purpose of this assignment is to introduce contemporary information and interpretations that will complement your assigned reading and enable you better to understand historical perspective.

Written work is vital to learning in this course, and you will do various kinds of writing, both formal and informal. Your instructors expect you to maintain good class notes and notes on your reading assignments (each one!) in order to be able to talk about contents and different authors' points of view. Reading cards provide a regular means of informal presentational writing, and your instructors urge you to use them to work on mastering the art of saying something substantively, accurately, and perhaps even eloquently in short space. The instructors understand that writing is a matter of constant effort (all of us continue to learn to write by writing), but we expect "best effort" and will try to provide useful critique.

Weekly Schedule and Assignments

Week One

W 22 Jan **Overview of the Course** (Barnett, Satterwhite)
Assignment: read syllabus (entire).

F 24 Jan **China: Revolution** (Barnett)
Assignment: Meisner, Prefaces and pp. 3-9

Reading card due

Week Two

M 27 Jan **India and Japan: Independence and economic recovery**
(Satterwhite)
Assignment: Tinker, Preface and pp. 1-27
Reischauer, Preface and pp. 3-36

I. CHINA: THE MANAGED SOCIETY

Plan ahead: One-page essay, double-spaced typewritten, on John Hersey's article (assigned below). Summarize and comment on the issues involved in the process of revolution in rural China in the late 1940s.

Toward the People's Republic of China

W 29 Jan **From "Confucian" to Republican China, and the early Chinese Communist Party** (Barnett)
Assignment: Meisner, pp. 31-51
John Hersey, "The Communization of Crow Village," New Yorker, 22.24:35-41 (July 1946). Class handout.

F 31 Jan **China in revolution and civil war** (Barnett)
DUE (in class): one-page essay on Hersey's article

Week Three   PRC: Early years and revolutionary issues

   Assignment: Meisner, pp. 64-83, 100-112, 140-216

   M 3 Feb Early PRC (Satterwhite)
   W 5 Feb 100 Flowers, Great Leap, crisis (Barnett)
   F 7 Feb China's language, Lo Sun Perry (Foreign Languages and
             Literature)
             Reading card due

Week Four   Ideology and political-economic transition

   Assignment: Meisner, pp. 288-396

   M 10 Feb Cultural Revolution (Satterwhite)
   W 12 Feb Chinese religion and popular culture (Barnett)
   F 14 Feb China's economy, Ernest Combs (Economics)
             Reading card due

Week Five   Beyond the Cultural Revolution: the Dengist era

   Assignment: Meisner, pp. 448-489

   M 17 Feb The current political situation in China, Karl Fields
             (Politics and Government)
   W 19 Feb Wrap-up (Barnett, Satterwhite)
   F 21 Feb CHINA EXAM: Bring bluebooks.

                II: INDIA: THE ELUSIVE UNION

Week Six   India's heritage

   Assignment: Tinker, pp. 28-127
                Class handout on caste in India (from Beatrice Pitney
                Lamb, India: A World in Transition, pp. 140-157)

   M 24 Feb Indian civilization and the British raj (Barnett)
   W 26 Feb Religion and pluralism in India, Christopher Ives (Religion)
   F 28 Feb The Politics of Colonialism, (Satterwhite)
             Reading card due

                            12

<u>Week Seven   Independence</u>

    Assignment: Tinker, pp. 128-218
                  Mohammed Ali Jinnah, from his presidential address
                      at the meeting of the Muslim League, Lahore,
                      March 1940, on Hindus and Muslims as two
                      separate nations (class handout)

  M   2 Mar   **India's political system**, Philip Phibbs (Politics and
            Government)

  W   4 Mar   **Indian nationalism** (Barnett)

  F   6 Mar   **India's leaders:** colonial and post-colonial (Satterwhite)
            Reading card due

<u>Week Eight   Cultural and political change</u>

    Assignment: Tinker, pp. 219-273

  M   9 Mar   **Video:** "Dadi's Family"

  W 11 Mar   **The art of India**, Jean Wetzel (Art)

  F 13 Mar   **Crisis politics** (Satterwhite, Barnett)
            Reading card due

  14-22 March - SPRING RECESS

<u>Week Nine   Transition</u>

  M 23 Mar   **Wrap-up** (Satterwhite, Barnett)

  W 25 Mar   **INDIA EXAM:** Bring bluebooks.

  F 27 Mar   **Introduction to Japan—early history** (Barnett)
            Assignment: Reischauer, part two

            Reading card due

III. JAPAN: THE RESTRAINED DEMOCRACY

Week Ten   War and occupation

Assignment: Reischauer, part three
Hersey, Hiroshima, entire
OPTIONAL. Ian Buruma, "The Devils of Hiroshima," New
York Review of Books, 37.16: 15-19 (25
October 1990). See Suzanne Barnett for a
copy you can borrow.

M 30 Mar   **Nation and Empire from 1868 to 1945** (Satterwhite)

W 1 Apr   **War and Occupation** (Satterwhite)

F 3 Apr   **The Bomb and the Japanese**, Mott Greene (Honors, History)

Reading card due

Week Eleven   Culture and business

Assignment: Reischauer, parts four and five
ON RESERVE: Ezra F. Vogel, "Pax Nipponica?" Foreign
Affairs, 64.4:752-767 (Spring 1986).

M 6 Apr   **Cultural roots of the Japanese work ethic** (Barnett)

W 8 Apr   **Business in Japan**, Denis Umstot (Business and Public
Administration)

F 10 Apr   **Video:** "The Yamaguchi Family"

Reading card due

Plan ahead: Paper on Japan past and present, based on
Reischauer's book The Japanese Today, due Monday, 27 April:
5 pages double-spaced typewritten. Submit original; be sure to
make a copy for yourself.

Give your paper an original and meaningful title. The paper
should provide a lucid, well-argued answer to the following
topical question: What are the ingredients of the Japanese
national character as discussed in historical perspective by
Edwin O. Reischauer in his book The Japanese Today?

Advice: See if you can articulate Reischauer's "image" of the
Japanese as a nation (does that image contrast with those
available from other sources, for example, Vogel's article?).
Keep in the third person (avoid "I," "we") and avoid excursions
and sloppy language. Evaluation will be based on creative,
responsible use of the source material and sophistication of
argument, as well as quality of expression and presentation. Of
course you should show how historical experience contributes to
the definition of contemporary Japanese state and society.

<u>Week Twelve</u>   <u>Stresses in the socio-political realm</u>

   Assignment: Reischauer, part six
                 ENCHI Fumiko, "A Bond for Two Lifetimes--Gleanings"

   M 13 Apr **Literary perspectives on modern Japan** (Barnett)

   W 15 Apr **Japanese language**, Mikiko Ludden (Foreign Languages and
                Literature)

   F 17 Apr **Contemporary Japanese politics** (Satterwhite)

             Reading card due

<u>Week Thirteen</u>   <u>How does Japan's past inform its present?</u>

   M 20 Apr **Recurring themes in Japanese history** (Barnett)

   W 22 Apr **Discussion: Reischauer's thesis** (Satterwhite, Barnett)

                    IV. CHINA, INDIA, AND JAPAN

<u>Weeks Thirteen, Fourteen, and Fifteen</u>   <u>Retrospect and prospect,
                                    commonalities and differences</u>

   Assignment: Handout documents and articles, including the following:
                 MAO Tse-tung, "The Chinese People have Stood Up!" (21
                    September 1949)
                 Jawaharlal Nehru, Speech to the Constituent Assembly,
                    1946
                 KOMURA Jutaro, precis of speech in the Imperial Diet,
                    2 February 1909, on Japan's foreign policy

             DUE: PAPER ON REISCHAUER'S <u>THE JAPANESE TODAY</u> (27
             April). You should hand in the paper in class (or
             after class, provided you were in class) on Monday.

   F 24 Apr **China: Why did China experience revolution?** (Barnett)

             Reading card due

   M 27 Apr **India: What is the quality of India's independence?**
                (Barnett, Satterwhite)

   W 29 Apr **Japan: How does modern Japan differ from other Asian
                societies?** (Satterwhite)

   F 1 May **The tenacity of tradition** (Satterwhite, Barnett)

             Reading card due

   M 4 May **National identity** (Satterwhite)

   W 6 May **Final discussion:** "Asian societies past and present"

READING PERIOD, Thursday through Sunday, 7-10 May - no class.

                 Final Exam (comprehensive):
           Tuesday, 12 May, 2-4 p.m., Jones 202.
                    Bring Bluebooks.
                          15

Asia is enormous, its history long. We can't possibly encounter even the most significant of its cultural monuments in a semester. Rather than seeking to identify famous landmarks spread across great civilizations, this course instead focuses on two themes--Buddhism and warfare--as expressed in texts from the classical flourishing of three Asian civilizations--India, China, and Japan. Speaking historically, Buddhism developed in India about 500 B.C.E., spread to China shortly after the beginning of the Common Era, and thence to Japan half a millennium later. Its flourishing has also been particular to Asia. The study of Buddhism will thus act to tie these Asian civilizations together for us.

By contrast, warfare has occurred in every time and place.

Thus one of our topics seems culturally specific, the other universal. One is apparently religious, the other apparently secular. Beyond this contrast there are other reasons why we might consider these two topics. Both, we will see, are centrally concerned with human suffering, taking a radical position on it--one as a means to inflict it, the other as a means to end it. As extremes, each can be extremely revealing of the cultures in which they occur. We may also be surprised to see combinations of the two. Finally, it turns out that both topics are special interests of mine.

Once the semester is underway, we will break into discussion groups on Wednesday and rejoin for a full class session on Friday. In discussion sections we will engage in close readings of the assigned texts, almost all of which are primary documents from the periods and places we are studying. We'll try to identify their central themes and make connections with other course readings. On Friday I will take these ideas further, bringing in material that is not covered in the readings or offering a framework within which to approach a particular intellectual issue. Attendance is required at all class meetings. More than two unexcused absences will result in a grade penalty.

There will be two five-page papers assigned, each of which will count 15% of your final grade. These will be due on 2 October and 13 November. There will be a ten-page paper due on the date that the final exam would have taken place, which will count for 20% of the grade. In addition we will have frequent short exercises, mostly one-page papers, with an occasional in-class quiz. Some of these will be graded, some will be pass/fail. Whether graded or not, a missed exercise still counts as a zero. Together these will constitute another 20%. The final 20% of your grade is based on class participation. (I know this only adds up to 90%.)

The following books should be available for purchase at the Bookstore. Additionally, there will be a xeroxed sourcebook of readings for the course available for purchase at 38 College Street. Because of the sourcebook, you will not need to use the Reserve Reading Desk at the library.

> Barbara Stoller Miller, tr., *The Bhagavad-Gita*
> Walpola Rahula, *What the Buddha Taught*
> T. P. Kasulis, *Zen Action, Zen Person*
> Victor Mair, tr., *Tao Te Ching*
> Philip Yampolsky, tr., *The Platform Sutra of the Sixth Patriarch*
> William LaFleur, *Buddhism: A Cultural Perspective*

My office is in the Asian Studies and Religion building at 38 College Street, next door to Kappa Sig. Office hours are Tuesday and Wednesday, 3:00 - 4:30 and by appointment. My office phone is -3524.

PART ONE: INDIA

Friday, 30 August: Introduction

Wednesday, 4 September: What is the study of "Asian Civilizations"?

Friday, 6 September: the Hindu tradition
reading (in your sourcebook):
> Jean Varenne, *Yoga and the Hindu Tradition*, pp. 1-51

Wednesday, 11 September: discussion sections
reading:
> Barbara Stoller Miller, tr., *The Bhagavat-Gita* (all)

Friday, 13 September: lecture on the *Gita*

Wednesday, 18 September: Theravada Buddhism-discussion sections
readings:
>LaFleur, *Buddhism: A Cultural Perspective*, pp. 10-44
>Rahula, *What the Buddha Taught* (all)
>"Hinayana" section in your sourcebook (about ten pages)

Friday, 20 September: Theravada/Hinayana Buddhism

The video "Footsteps of the Buddha" will be shown on 23 and 24 September, Monday and Tuesday nights at 7:00 in the Beam Classroom, Visual Arts Center.   Please attend one of these showings.

Wednesday, 25 September: Mahayana discussions (1)
readings:
>Kasulis, *Zen Action, Zen Person*, pp. 16-28
>"Mahayana" section in your sourcebook

Friday, 27 September: lecture on nothing

Wednesday, 2 October: Mahayana discussions (2)
Five page paper due: "What is Buddhism?"

PART TWO: CHINA
Friday, 4 October: The society of ancient China

Wednesday, 9 October: Mencius
readings (in your sourcebook):
>section on Mencius (note: there are two sets of selections)

Friday,11 October: the Confucian world

Wednesday, 16 October: Lao Tzu and Taoism
readings:
>Kasulis, *Zen Action, Zen Person*, pp. 29-38
>Mair, tr., *Tao Te Ching* (all)

Friday, 18 October: the Taoist world

Wednesday, 23 October: Sun Tzu's *Art of War*
readings (in your sourcebook):
>selections from Sun Tzu

Friday, 25 October: lecture on Sun Tzu

Wednesday, 30 October: Ch'an (Zen) Buddhism
reading:
    Yampolsky, *The Platform Sutra of the Sixth Patriarch*, esp. pp. 111-183

PART THREE: JAPAN

Friday, 1 November: Japan and Buddhism

Wednesday, 6 November: Zen
readings:
    Kasulis, *Zen Action, Zen Person*, pp. 39-141
    "Zen" section in your sourcebook

Friday, 8 November: Zen lecture

Wednesday, 13 November: the samurai traditions
readings (in your sourcebook):
    The Sword of No-Sword, pp. 1-57
A five-page paper, drawing on materials from China, is due today.

Friday, 15 November: on the samurai

Wednesday, 20 November: poetry in Chinese and Japanese
Readings:
    LaFleur, *Buddhism: A Cultural Perspective*, pp. 63-76
    Poetry texts from your sourcebook

Friday, 22 November: painting
readings:
    Art texts from your sourcebook

Wednesday, 4 December: Buddhism in America (1)

Friday, 6 December: Buddhism in America (2)
reading:
    Kasulis, *Zen Action, Zen Person*, pp. 142-54

The final exam (take-home) should address Wm LaFleur's *Buddhism*.

University of Wisconsin - Green Bay
Prof. Craig Lockard
MWF 11:15-12:10, WH 116-118

SYLLABUS: History 250
Fall 1991

TRADITIONAL ASIAN CIVILIZATIONS

Food for Thought:

"Only as one looks at the long flow of Asian history can one perceive the direction of its motion and understand what is happening there now."--John K. Fairbank and Edwin O. Reischauer

"We study the past to understand the present. The wisdom of the past is essential to intellectual progress in the future."--Confucius

"I am happy because I am a human and not an animal; a male, and not a female; a Chinese, and not a barbarian; and because I live in Loyang, the most wonderful city in all the world"--Shao Yang (11th century)

"Japan is a world the reverse of Europe. Hardly in anything do their ways conform to ours. They eat and dress...differently.... Their methods of doing business, their manner of sitting down, their buildings, their domestic arrangements...are so unlike ours as to be beyond description or understanding"--Father Alexandro Valignara (Italian Jesuit, 16th century)

"India is a whole world in itself; she is a society of the same magnitude as our Western society."--Arnold Toynbee

"The nature of men is always the same; it is their habits that separate them."--Confucius

Introduction

This course serves as an introduction to Asian history and civilization from early times until about 1800, when Western influence became stronger. The second semester (History 251) will discuss the modern period (since 1800). Because of the pressure of time we will devote much of our attention to China, Japan, and India, but Southeast Asia and Korea will receive some analysis. The course must cover 4,000 years of history of several major culture areas in a very brief time; because of this problem we cannot delve as deeply into any one subject area as many of us would like. Furthermore, we must move through the material rather quickly; it is therefore important to keep up with the readings and lectures. History is woven of many strands, and so we have economic and political history, the study of social structure, of thought, and of art, literature, and music. This course is based on the belief that an introduction to the history of civilization requires a consideration of all of these facets of human activity, a general mapping of the terrain so that students may learn enough to consider where to explore further and gain some idea of the potential rewards for the effort. The first part of the course (6 weeks) concentrates on the development of China's distinctive way of life; there follows a 3 week segment on Korea and Japan. During the last 5 weeks we will discuss South and Southeast Asia, with particular attention to India, Vietnam, Thailand, Java and the Malay World.

The structure and content of the course is based on the following premises: it is impossible to understand the recent history of Asian societies without a detailed examination of major features in traditional society; if you want to understand the politics and economics of a nation, you must also study its cultures; if you want to understand the cultures of a nation, you must also study its politics and economics. Thus, we will take an interdisciplinary "civilizations" approach to Asian history which accords some attention to many aspects of Asian development rather than limiting ourselves to traditional narrative political history. This course has been designed with several purposes: to provide an introduction to the traditional civilizations of Asia; to provide an understanding of cultural relativity and differing ways of viewing the world and organizing society so as to challenge ethnocentrism and education based on a single culture background; and to encourage analytical thinking and intellectual growth. All that is required is an open mind and a willingness to learn about other cultures. You are reminded of the wisdom of Master Kung (Confucius): "Learning without thought is labor lost; thought without learning is intellectual death."

Format: The format of the course is lecture and discussion. Two sessions a week I will lecture for 40-45 minutes and leave 10-15 minutes for questions and discussion. One session a week (usually Friday) a film or slide and music presentation will be scheduled. Students are expected to obtain a preliminary background to the topic by keeping up with the assigned readings. There are three paperback texts, all available at the campus bookstore and on reserve:

Conrad Schirokauer, A Brief History of Chinese and Japanese Civilizations (Harcourt Brace)

Paul Welty, The Asians: Their Evolving Heritage, 6th ed. (Harper & Row)

Donald Swearer, Southeast Asia (Dushkin)

We will read about one-half of Schirokauer and most of Welty during this semester. Schirokauer will also be used as a text in History 251.

There is also a recommended paperback anthology of Asian literature (fiction, poetry, philosophy, etc.), which is available on reserve:

Lynn Nelson and Patrick Peebles, eds., Classics of Eastern Thought (Harcourt   Brace)

The required texts are coded for reading in the weekly schedule as CS, W and DS. The recommended anthology is coded as N and marked with an asterisk (*) to indicate that the reading is strongly encouraged but not required for examination or discussion purposes.

We will also tentatively have ten film or slide presentations throughout the semester. The films are listed in the schedule. Lectures will be illustrated with overhead projections prepared by the instructor to clarify terms and increase understanding. In addition, some tapes of traditional Asian music will be played. You are expected to quickly familiarize yourself with the geography of Asia, including countries, major rivers, and leading cities. The maps in the texts provide a limited introduction to this subject but you may also wish to consult an atlas or obtain a good map (such as National

<u>Geographic</u>) of Asia. There will be a brief map quiz covering basic knowledge (present countries, major rivers, and cities) at the end of the third week.

<u>Tentative Class Schedule</u>:

Barring unforseen difficulties we will adhere closely to the tentative class schedule listed below.

Session	Date	Topic (Reading Assignment)
1	Sep. 4	Explanation of Syllabus
2	Sep. 6	Introductory Remarks (W: vii-ix, 1-6; CS: vi-xiii)
3	Sep. 9	Geography of Asia (W: 7-12, 21-32, 39-47)
4	Sep. 11	Birth of Chinese Civilization (CS: 3-26; *N: 15-29, 50-80)
5	Sep. 13	Age of Chinese Philosophers (CS: 27-49)
6	Sep. 16	Rise of Imperial China (CS 50-100)
7	Sep. 18	"Golden Age" of China I (CS: 101-129, 184-213)
8	Sep. 20	MAP QUIZ (10 minutes); <u>Slides</u>: "Chinese Mosaic"
9	Sep. 23	"Golden Age" of China II
10	Sep. 25	Late Imperial China I (CS: 214-260)
11	Sep. 27	<u>Film</u>: "Old Treasures From New China"
12	Sep. 30	Lake Imperial China II (CS: 328-353)
13	Oct. 2	Traditional Chinese Philosophy, Religion and Science (W: 78-85, 159-195; *N: 207-217, 324-340)
14	Oct. 4	<u>Film</u>: "Heart of the Dragon; Understanding"
15	Oct. 7	Traditional Chinese Society and Government (W: 196-224, 233-236, 238-240; *N: 91-111, 123-125, 299-308)
16	Oct. 9	Traditional Chinese Economy and Foreign Relations
17	Oct. 11	<u>Film</u>: "The Rise of the Dragon"
18	Oct. 14	Traditional Chinese Literature and Arts (*N: 149-172, 232-255, 341-357, 376-396)
19	Oct. 16	Traditional Korean History and Culture (W: 258-259; *N: 218-223)
20	Oct. 18	<u>Mid-Term Examination</u> (Sessions 2-19)

21	Oct. 21	Introduction to Japanese Civilization (CS: 130-154; W: 263-266)
22	Oct. 23	Rise of Japanese Civilization (CS: 155-183; W: 305-308)
23	Oct. 25	Slides: "Japanese History and Culture"
24	Oct. 28	Japan in the Feudal Era (CS: 261-310, 354-383; W: 266-268, 308-313)
25	Oct. 30	Traditional Japanese Religion, Arts and Culture (W: 269-281; *N: 174-206, 280-293, 358-375)
26	Nov. 1	Film: "Asian Insight: Japan"
27	Nov. 4	Traditional Japanese Society and Government (W: 282-289, 294-299; *N: 256-269)
28	Nov. 6	Rise of Indian Civilization I (W: 58-64, 117-121; *N: 7-15)
29	Nov. 8	Slides: "An Indian Panorama"
30	Nov. 11	Rise of Indian Civilization II (W: 65-85, 121-125; *N: 81-90)
31	Nov. 13	"Golden Age" of India (W: 125-126; *N: 30-49)
32	Nov. 15	Film: "Long Search: In the Footprints of the Buddha"
33	Nov. 18	India Under Islamic Domination (W: 126-127, 131-134, 139-152; *N: 293-298, 309-323)
34	Nov. 20	Traditional Indian Society and Culture (W: 86-116; *N: 127-149, 224-231)
35	Nov. 22	Rise of Southeast Asian Civilization I (W: 323-329; DS: 2-23)
36	Nov. 25	Rise of Southeast Asian Civilization II (DS: 23-29)
37	Nov. 27	Film: "Three Worlds of Bali" Due: Research Papers & Book Reviews

THANKSGIVING VACATION (Nov. 28 - Dec. 1)

38	Dec. 2	Island Southeast Asian Society and Culture (W: 330-331, 336-344; DS: 29-41)
39	Dec. 4	Mainland Southeast Asian Society and Culture (W: 332-336, 347-350, 356-357; DS: 53-91; *N: 425-441)
40	Dec. 6	Slides: "A Southeast Asian Mosaic" Due: Journals

41   Dec. 9   Traditional Asian Civilization in Perspective

42   Dec. 11   <u>Final Examination</u> (Sessions 21-41)

<u>Parting Thoughts</u>:

"After passing the Examination" by Meng Chiao (751-814), Chinese Poet:
   "The wretchedness of my former years I have no need to brag:
   Today's gaiety has freed my mind to wander without bounds.
   Lighthearted in the spring breeze, my horse's hoofs run fast;
   In a single day I have seen all the flowers of Ch'ang-an."

"The Seasons" by Sanpu (1647-1732), Japanese Poet:
   Cherry-bloom, cuckoo, moon,/snow--and already/the year is through!"

SYLLABUS: History 251   Professor Craig Lockard
Spring 1992   MWF 1:25-2:20, RH 342

MODERN ASIAN CIVILIZATIONS

Food for Thought

"The rise of the communists to power is no isolated event.
Certainly it is not merely the works of a group of
revolutionary extremists. Its roots reach far back into the
structure of the old society, the abuses of government, the
inequalities and miseries suffered by the people, and a
widespread demand for change"--Professor Ping-Chia Kuo

"Decades of change ... have destroyed China's inherited order
and created an unprecedented new one; yet those who see China
as broken loose from her old moorings and adrift on the flood
of revolution are using an inapt metaphor. One can better say
that the old structure has collapsed, its foundations washed
out, new plans were imported, and rebuilding is underway, but
the site is recognizably the same, the sense of identity
remains ..."--John K. Fairbank

"The modern history of Japan is in essence a record of the
clash and fusion of two cultures, the development of an
Asiatic civilization under the impact of western habits and
thought, the response of a crumbling feudal system based upon
agriculture to the demands of industrial society"--George B.
Samson

"A Westerner visiting India is immediately struck by the sharp
contrasts he sees. Aside from the contrast between wealth and
poverty, perhaps the most startling is that resulting from the
close juxtaposition of elements belonging to different
centuries and originating even in different continents.
Ancient customs, behavior patterns, and techniques exist side
by side with modern machines and ways of living that bear the
clear imprint of the West... But the incongruities of India
are not only those which lie on the surface to be seen; nor
are they as trivial as a bullock-drawn lawnmower. They extend
deep into the fabric of Indian society, affect every aspect of
Indian life, and constitute the pivotal problem of modern
India"--Beatrice Pitney Lamb

"In order to read the destiny of a people, it is necessary to
open the book of its past."--Jose Rizal (Philippine national
hero)

Introduction

This course serves as an introduction to Asian history and
civilization from about 1800 to the present, a period that can be
labeled as the modern era. The first semester (History 250)
discusses the traditional period (from prehistoric times up to

about 1800). Because of the pressure of time we will restrict
much of our attention to China and Japan, but South and Southeast
Asia will receive some analysis. Seven weeks are devoted to
developments since 1940. The course must cover nearly 200 years
of history of several major culture areas in a very brief time;
because of this problem we cannot delve as deeply into any one
subject area as many of us would like. Furthermore, we must move
through the material rather quickly; it is therefore important to
keep up with the readings and lectures. The course will be
concerned with such issues as the breakdown of traditional
Chinese civilization, Japanese modernization, Western imperialist
pressures on China, European colonization of South and Southeast
Asia, the evolution of anti-Western nationalism and revolutionary
movements, the building of the modern Japanese technocratic
society, the rise and development of Chinese communism, the
Korean and Vietnam wars, and the societies of Southern Asia since
independence. While political history will be stressed, some
attention will be paid to social, economic, cultural and
intellectual developments.

Some of the material we will discuss is controversial; I have
opinions on many of the interpretations and will try to make my
biases clear. You need not accept them, indeed are invited to
take issue with my views and will not be penalized for doing so.
This course was designed with several purposes: to provide an
introduction to recent and current developments in Asia; to
promote an understanding of cultural relativity and differing
ways of viewing the world and organizing society so as to
challenge ethnocentrism and education based on a single culture
background; and to encourage analytical thinking and intellectual
growth. All that is required is an open mind and an eagerness to
learn about other cultures. You are reminded of the wisdom of
master Kung (Confucius): "Learning without thought is labor
lost; thought without learning is intellectual death."

Format

The format of the course is lecture and discussion. Normally in
the Monday and Wednesday sessions I will lecture for 40-45
minutes and leave 10-15 minutes at the end for questions and
discussion. There will also be some time for discussion on some
of the Friday sessions, when a film or slide presentation will
generally be scheduled. Students are expected to obtain a
preliminary background to the lecture topic by keeping up with
the assigned readings. There are two major texts and one
supplementary text, all available in paperback at the campus
bookstore and on reserve.

Conrad Schirokauer, Modern China and Japan: A Brief History
    (Harcourt Brace)
Steven Warshaw, India Emerges (Diablo)
Milton Osborne, Southeast Asia: Illustrated Introductory
    History (Allen & Unwin)

There is also a recommended paperback anthology of Asian literature, available on reserve:

> Lynn Nelson and Patrick Peebles, eds., <u>Classics of Eastern Thought</u> (Harcourt Brace)

The required texts are coded for reading in the weekly schedule as S, W, and O. The recommended anthology is coded as N and marked with an asterisk (*) to indicate that the reading is suggested but not required for examination or discussion purposes. I have also ordered an inexpensive wall map of Asia (Hammond) for optional purchase. You are expected to familiarize yourself as soon as possible with a map of Asia, noting the countries, capital cities, main rivers, mountain ranges and islands of East, South and Southeast Asia. You will continually need this information throughout the course, indeed throughout life. There will be a brief map quiz covering basic knowledge. To give some "feel" for Asian civilization I will normally play taped examples of modern Asian music during slide presentations and before class. We will also tentatively have 12 films or other multimedia presentations throughout the semester, normally but not always scheduled for the Friday session. The films are listed in the schedule.

<u>Tentative Class Schedule</u>

The tentative schedule for discussion of the major subject areas is as follows:

Session	Date	Topic (Reading Assignment)
1	Feb. 10	Explanation of syllabus
2	Feb. 12	Introductory remarks
3	Feb. 14	Geography of Asia (S: 3-6; *N: 401-407)

ASIA FROM 1800 TO WORLD WAR II

4	Feb. 17	Nineteenth Century China I (S: 6-26, 61-64, 71-77; *N: 408-414, 442-449)
5	Feb. 19	Nineteenth Century China II (S: 81-108, 147-164)
6	Feb. 21	Slides: "A Chinese Mosaic"
7	Feb. 24	The Fall of Imperial China (S: 167-178; N: 449-457)
8	Feb. 25	Republican China I (S: 178-190)
9	Feb. 28	Slides: "China in 1906" Map quiz (10 minutes)

10	Mar. 2	Republican China II (S: 219-222, 224-231; *N: 483-496, 505-525)
11	Mar. 4	Nineteenth Century Japan I (S: 29-58, 64-71, 105-114; *N: 468-483)
12	Mar. 6	<u>Slides</u>: "Images of China and America"
13	Mar. 9	Nineteenth Century Japan II (S: 114-145)
14	Mar. 11	Early Twentieth Century Japan (S: 193-217; *N: 496-505)
15	Mar. 13	<u>Slides</u>: "Modern Japan"
16	Mar. 16	Colonial Southeast Asia I (O: 1-81; *N: 425-441)
17	Mar. 18	Colonial Southeast Asia II (O: 82-136)
18	Mar. 20	<u>Slides</u>: "Southeast Asia"
19	Mar. 23	Colonial India I (W: 1-76; *N: 415-424)
20	Mar. 25	Colonial India II (W: 76-103; *N: 458-468)
21	Mar. 27	<u>Film</u>: "Triumph of the West: Ironies of Empire"
22	Mar. 30	<u>Midterm Examination</u> (Sessions 2-21)

ASIA FROM WORLD WAR II TO PRESENT

23	Apr. 1	Japan in World War II (S: 219-224, 232-233, 237-241)
24	Apr. 3	<u>Film</u>: "Japan: Interdependent Nation"

SPRING VACATION (APRIL 4-12)

25	Apr. 13	New Japan I (S: 251-256, 267-287)
26	Apr. 15	New Japan II (*N: 544-587)
27	Apr. 17	<u>Film</u>: "The Japanese"
28	Apr. 20	China in War and Revolution (S: 231-237, 245-251; *N: 530-544)
29	Apr. 22	Peoples Republic of China I (S: 289-302)
30	Apr. 24	<u>Film</u>: "Shanghai; New China"

31	Apr. 27	Peoples Republic of China II (S: 302-312, 314)
32	Apr. 29	Peoples Republic of China III
33	May 1	Slides: "Heart of the Dragon: Living"
34	May 4	Peoples Republic of China IV
35	May 6	Southeast Asia Since Independence (O: 137-241)
36	May 8	Film: "Asian Insight: Malaysia"
37	May 11	War and Revolution in Indochina (S: 261-265; *N: 525-530)
38	May 13	Korea and Taiwan (S: 256-261, 312-314; *N: 587-602)
39	May 15	Slides: "The Village of My Ann"
40	May 18	South Asia Since Independence I (W: 104-172)
41	May 20	South Asia Since Independence II (W: 173-201; *N: 602-618) Due: Projects
42	May 22	Asia's Modern History
	May 27	Final Examination (Sessions 23-42): 1:30-2:30 p.m.

Department of History   C. M. Wilson
Northern Illinois University   Zulauf 613 - 753-6824
History 141: Asian Civilization Since 1500   Office Hours: 1-2 p.m. MTW
Spring Semester, 1992

Required Reading

All of the required books are available at the reserve desk in the library.
The following titles are also available in the bookstore.

Fairbank, The Great Chinese Revolution, 1800-1985.
Reischauer, The Japanese Today.
Tapp, Sovereignty And Rebellion: The White Hmong Of Northern Thailand.
Wolpert, A New History Of India.

Please handle all library and reserve materials with care. DO NOT DAMAGE
LIBRARY MATERIALS! DO NOT WRITE IN LIBRARY MATERIALS! The library does not
have the funds to replace damaged items. Please Xerox copies of anything you
want for your own use.

Grades   You have five grade units available.
                    1.   First midterm examination.
                    2.   Second midterm examination.
                    3.   Third midterm examination.
                    4.&5. Final examination (two hours for two units).

                You are urged to complete all five grade units.

                THERE WILL NOT BE ANY MAKE UP EXAMINATIONS!

The final grade for the course will be the average of the four highest grades
you receive from completing the five units.

Other comments

Please make every effort to stay ahead in your reading. You will get more out
of the course and you will do better on your examinations if you come to class
prepared.

All students are expected to do their own work on all assignments.

January 13   Introduction: The Geography of Asia.

Part I.   **The Hmong: A Tribal Society in Southeast Asia and the United States**

Tapp, <u>Sovereignty And Rebelion: The White Hmong Of Northern Thailand</u>.

Johnson, Ed., <u>The Flood: How Hmong Names Began: Six Hmong Folk Tales: The Woodcutter, His Rooster, And His Wife</u>. (Hmong children's books).

Bui Bao Thach, <u>Fun Alphabet</u> (A Vietnamese children's book).

January 15   Tapp, Chs. 1-3.

January 21   Tapp, Chs. 4-5.

January 27   Tapp, Chs. 6-8.

January 29   Tapp, Chs. 9-Epilogue.

February 3   Map Quiz.
                    Hmong and Vietnamese children's books.

February 5   **FIRST MIDTERM EXAMINATION.** Two essay questions.

Part II.   **India: Colonialism and Independence**.

Wolpert, <u>A New History Of India</u>.

February 10   Europe and the Mughal. Wolpert, Chs. 10-12.

February 12   Under Company Rule. Wolpert, Chs. 13-15.

February 17   The India Office. Wolpert, Chs. 16-18.

February 19   Indian Nationalism. Wolpert, Chs. 19-21.

February 24   Nehru and Independent India. Wolpert, Chs. 22-23.

February 26   Modern India. Wolpert, Chs. 24-26.

March 2   **SECOND MIDTERM EXAMINATION.** Two essay questions.

31

Part III.   China: From Imperial Rule To Republic To Communism.

Fairbank, The Great Chinese Revolution 1800-1985.

Peng, Chinese Radicals. A language text for Chinese children. The term radical refers to the basic elements in Chinese ideographs.

March 4 & 16   Late Imperial China.   Fairbank, Chs. 1-7.

March 18   Transformation of the Late Imperial Order. Fairbank, Chs. 8-9.

March 23-25   The First Chinese Republic. Fairbank, Chs. 10-14.

March 30-April 1   The Chinese People's Republic. Fairbank, Chs. 15-19.

April 6   THIRD MIDTERM EXAMINATION. Two essay questions.

Part IV.   Japan: From Isolation To Economic Superpower.

April 8   Background. Reischauer, Chs. 1-6.

April 13   Modern History. Reischauer, Chs. 7-11.

April 15 & 20   Society. Reischauer, Chs. 12-20.

April 22.   Government and Politics. Reischauer, Chs. 21-29.

April 27   Business. Reischauer, Chs. 30-34.

April 29   Japan and the World. Reischauer, Chs. 35-39. Review.

May 8   Friday, 1-2:50 p.m. FINAL EXAMINATION.
                    Part I.   Comprehensive/Comparative question.
                    Part II. Two essay questions.

32

University of Kansas
History 118: China and Japan, an Introductory History
Professor Daniel H. Bays. Spring 1989
3004 Wescoe, 864-3569
Home 749-2811 (never after 9 PM, please)

This course is intended to offer a brief introduction to the histories
of China and Japan, the two major countries of East Asia. I have chosen
a thematic approach to the subject, combined with a chronological
approach as well. I hope that by a combination of lectures, readings, and
visual materials, each student will gain at least a fundamental
understanding of some of the characteristics of East Asian history and
civilization. These are very different from our own, and the histories of
China and Japan are also strikingly different from each other.

Please purchase all four of the books listed below. Reading
assignments are noted for each week. Please have them done by the
early part of that week. Assignments vary widely in length, so be advised of
the wisdom of reading ahead on heavy assignments.

Tests/Assignments/Grades. There will be one mid-term exam worth 100 points
(March 10); two 4-5 page essays based on the Statler and Snow books,
respectively, 100 points each (due March 29 and May 5); the final exam,
worth 125 points; and eight 10-point quizzes or short movie reviews. This
totals 505 points. There may also be opportunity to earn up to 5 or 10
points by reporting on lectures or events. Grading will be on the basis
of 450 the lowest A, 400 the lowest B, 350 the lowest C, 300 the lowest D.
Schedule of short assignments:

1/27, class quiz	3/31 and 4/3, movie assignment,
2/3, movie assignment, turn in 2/6	turn in 4/5
2/17, class quiz	4/14, class quiz
2/24, class quiz	4/21, class quiz
3/24, class quiz	

Specific guidelines will be provided for the Statler and Snow essays, also
for the two movie reviews. On April 28 and May 3, two of the movies we
will see are extra long, and class will start at 8:00.

Please note: Any student who has a disability that prevents the fullest
expression of abilities should contact me as soon as possible to discuss
class requirements.

Texts

John King Fairbank, The United States and China, Fourth Edition, enlarged.
Kenneth Pyle, The Making of Modern Japan.
Edgar Snow, Red Star Over China.
Oliver Statler, Japanese Inn.

Of these four books, the Fairbank and Pyle texts are to provide, together
with class lectures, the basic chronological and thematic context of the
course. The Statler and Snow books, one a fictional account of real people
and the other a major piece of historical journalism, are to be the basis
of evaluative essays.

Dates		Topics	Readings
January 20	1.	Introduction	Fairbank ch. 1-2,
January 23-27	2.	Geography/topography, Livelihood and material life	Statler ch. 1
January 30-Feb. 3	3.	Society and Social Structure	Fairbank ch. 3
February 6-10	4.	Political Power and Political Organization	Fairbank ch. 5 Statler ch. 2
February 13-17	5.	Early Contacts with the Outside World	Fairbank pp. 81-91, 100-105, 143-163
February 20-24	6.	The Ch'ing (Manchu) System; Unification of Japan and the Tokugawa System	Fairbank, pp. 91-100 Statler ch. 3-5 Pyle ch. 1-2
February 27-Mar. 3	7.	Change within the Ch'ing and Tokugawa structures, 17th-19th centuries	Fairbank pp. 163-189 Statler ch. 6-10 Pyle ch. 3-4
March 6-10 SPRING BREAK	8.	Meiji Restoration of 1868; China to the 1870s (MIDTERM the 10th)	Pyle ch. 5 Fairbank pp. 190-195
March 20-24	9.	Late 19th-early 20th centuries	Fairbank ch. 8 Pyle ch. 6-8 Statler ch. 11-12
March 27-31	10.	The 1910's (STATLER ESSAY DUE 29th)	Fairbank pp. 220-230 Pyle ch. 9
April 3-7	11.	The 1920s	Fairbank, rest of ch. 9 Pyle ch. 10 Start Snow book.
April 10-14	12.	The 1930s	Fairbank, ch. 10, 12, and pp. 276-284 Pyle, ch. 11 Statler, ch. 13
April 17-21	13.	World War II in the Pacific	Fairbank finish ch. 11, also ch. 13 Pyle ch. 12 Statler ch. 14
April 24-28 also May 1-5	14.	1950s to the Present LAST CLASS May 5: Snow ESSAY DUE, also final exam study questions distributed	Pyle ch. 13 Statler ch. 15
May 9, T		9-12, FINAL EXAM	

34

Fall Term, 1989

Mr. Clifford
Munroe 304 (ext. 5320)
Home: 462-2909

History 235

The Modern History of East Asia,
1700-1912

The following books are available for purchase:

Fairbank, J.K., and Teng, S.Y., *China's Response to the West*
Fay, Peter, *The Opium War*
Feuerwerker, A., *Rebellion in Nineteenth Century China*
Hane, Mikiso, *Modern Japan: a Historical Survey*
Spence, Jonathan, *The Death of Woman Wang*
Spence, Jonathan, *To Change China*
Wakeman, Frederick, *The Fall of Imperial China*

The following books will be available on reserve:

de Bary, Chan, Watson, *Sources of Chinese Tradition*
Fairbank, J., Reischauer, E., Craig, A., *East Asia: Tradition and Transformation*
Fairbank, J., ed. *The Missionary Enterprise in China and America*
Jansen, Marius, *Changing Japanese Attitudes towards Modernization*
Morris, Ivan, *The Nobility of Failure*
Sansom, George, *The Western World and Japan*
Tsunoda, de Bary, Keene, *Sources of Japanese Tradition*
Ward, Robert, *Political Development in Modern Japan*
Wright, Mary, *China in Revolution: The First Phase*

The purpose of the course (and of its spring term continuation) is to introduce the modern history of one of the most important regions of the world today. Whether or not the twenty-first century will be the Asian century, as some say, no responsible citizen can afford to be ignorant of that part of the world. Nor is it sufficient simply to examine *contemporary* society; an understanding of the tradition, of the historical roots of that society is essential for anything more than a superficial acquaintance with Asia's development and future prospects.

This course deals only with East Asia: China, Japan, and --tangentially -- Korea. It is a region which despite its different forms of government and society today, has a common cultural heritage that marks it off from Southeast or South Asia. We open in the seventeenth and eighteenth centuries, the last flowering of the traditional world, and follow the very different histories of China and Japan to the early twentieth century, to the revolution that overthrew the two thousand year old Chinese empire and brought Japan onto the stage as a world power. There are no prerequisites. Those who have taken courses on traditional China or Japan will naturally profit from their knowledge, but History 235 and 236 are both designed for beginners. If you find yourself confused, or not understanding what is happening, please do not hesitate to come to see me, in or out of office hours.

The course, like virtually all other courses at the college, has an even more important purpose: the development of an ability to think, read, write, and speak thoughtfully. You are expected to do the reading *prior* to discussion, and to do it in a way that will enable you to raise critical questions rather than simply to absorb information like a sponge. The books are chosen to introduce you not only to East Asian history, but also to some of the kinds of historical writing that are now appearing in English on modern Japan and China. Wakeman and Hane will give you a generally chronological treatment of the histories of the two countries, although both try to strike a balance between the kind of text-bookishness that concentrates on the 'facts' and the kind of scholarship that concentrates on the major social, economic and cultural trends of the period. Through the translations of the original sources, you should gain some sense of the kinds of debates and controversies that have taken place among Japanese and Chinese statesmen, intellectuals, and reformers, as they were first forced to make the difficult and painful choices posed by the 19th century challenges to their traditional societies.

The course will meet three times a week, and generally there will be lectures on Monday and Wednesday and a discussion on Friday. Sometimes, however, the pattern will change in order to permit a different treatment of the material; the exceptions, as known at press time, are noted below, and others may be announced in class. There will be a mid-term examination, a paper, and a final examination.

WEEK OF 11 SEPTEMBER: Traditional China under the Ch'ing Dynasty

Read: Wakeman, *Decline of Imperial China*, 1-69; Fairbank, Reischauer and Craig, *East Asia*, 211-43, 435-48; Spence, *Woman Wang*, 1-32.

The readings this week will act as a general introduction to the Manchu dynasty during imperial China's last days of glory in the 18th century. Spence's book is an essay in local history, reconstructing through contemporary sources the life and attitudes of a small town in the late 17th century.

WEEK OF 18 SEPTEMBER: State, Society and the Dynastic Cycle

Read: Spence, *Woman Wang*, 33-139; Wakeman, 85-106; Fay, *Opium War*, 3-64.

Lectures and readings this week will examine the structures and values of Chinese society, and the first signs of weakness in the Ch'ing order which were evident in the White Lotus rising at the end of the 18th century.

WEEK OF 25 SEPTEMBER: Trade, Diplomacy, and the Opium War

Read: Wakeman, 111-42, 156-59; Fairbank and Teng, *China's Response to the West*, 17-46; Fay, 67-210.

The course this week will examine the ways in which China's traditional diplomatic institutions and approaches to foreign policy proved unable to deal with the expansionist forces of a west undergoing an industrial revolution.

WEEK OF 2 OCTOBER: The T'ai-p'ing Rising

Read: Wakeman, 143-56; Feuerwerker, *Rebellion in Nineteenth Century China* (complete); de Bary, *Sources of Chinese Tradition*, 680-704; Spence, *To Change China*, 57-92.

The T'ai-p'ing rising has always had a particular interest for westerners because of its Christian influences. More important in Chinese history is the way the rebellion and the social forces growing out of its suppression of would weaken the polity of the Chinese state until well into the twentieth century.

WEEK OF 9 OCTOBER: The First Stage of Chinese Modernization

NOTE: *There will be three lectures this week, and a discussion on Monday, 17 Oct., prior to the mid-term examination*

Read: Wakeman, 163-95; Fairbank and Teng, 47-97; Spence, Change, 93-128.

China's internal and external problems in mid-century did much to show the need for change. The reading examines some of the reasons for the successes and failures of the restoration of Ch'ing society after the rebellion and the Self-Strengthening Movement that followed it.

WEEK OF 16 OCTOBER: * MID-TERM EXAMINATION *
                     TOKUGAWA JAPAN

There will be a discussion on Monday, 16 October, and the mid-Term Examination will be held on Wednesday the 18th. On Friday 20 October, we will begin a discussion of the history of Japan in the 18th and 19th centuries.

WEEK OF 23 OCTOBER: * MID-TERM BREAK *
                     TOKUGAWA JAPAN

There will be no class on 23 October.

Read: Hane, *Modern Japan*, 1-64; Reischauer, Fairbank and Craig, *East Asia*, 392-434; Sansom, *Western World and Japan*, 223-43; Morris, *Nobility of Failure*, 180-216.

Much of the reading will serve as an introduction to the Tokugawa shogunate, its accomplishments, and also its failures to contain the changes that were brought by 250 years of peace and economic development. Morris' chapter on Oshio Heihachiro examines one response to these changes -- a kind of response that Morris believes mirrors an important facet of the Japanese character.

WEEK OF 30 OCTOBER: THE MEIJI RESTORATION

> Read: Tsunoda, *Sources of Japanese Tradition*, 552-578, 591-637; Hane, 65-109; Sansom, 243-274.

The readings in Tsunoda include translations of writings by a number of men who were the leaders in the intellectual ferment of the late Tokugawa and in the movement to overthrow the shogunate and to put a modern government in its place.

WEEK OF 6 NOVEMBER: MODERNIZATION UNDER THE MEIJI GOVERNMENT

> Read: Hane, 110-51; Sansom, 378-410, 420-67; Tsunoda, 638-700; Morris, 217-75.

The reading describes the beginnings of Japan's modernization, which contrasts strongly with the contemporary Self-Strengthening movement in post-T'ai-p'ing China. The break of Saigo Takamori, one of the heroes of the Restoration, and the reasons for it, are set forth by Morris. Sansom describes some of the earliest efforts at cultural and political westernization.

WEEK OF 13 NOVEMBER: Imperialism in East Asia.

> NOTE: *There will be three lectures this week, and a discussion on Monday 21 November*

> Read: Hane, 152-70; Fairbank and Teng, 97-131; M. Jansen, "Modernization and Foreign Policy," in Ward, *Political Development*, 149-188; R. Hackett, "The Meiji Leaders and Modernization: the Case of Yamagata Aritomo," in Jansen, *Changing Japanese Attitudes*, 243-273; Tsunoda, *Sources*, 700-713.

The readings examine China's response -- both reformist and reactionary -- to the imperialist upsurge of the late 19th century, and Japan's coming of age as a great power in the imperial world.

WEEK OF 20 NOVEMBER: IMPERIALISM

There will be a discussion on Monday, 21 November on last week's reading.

WEEK OF 27 NOVEMBER: Missionaries, Reform and Reaction in China

> Read: *China's Response*, 133-93; J. Cohen, "Littoral and Hinterland," and S.C. Miller, "Ends and Means," in Fairbank, *The Missionary Enterprise*; Spence, *To Change China*, 129-60; Wakeman, 199-221.

An examination of some of the effects of the Christian missions in China, which some have seen as beneficent and reformist, and others as an expression of arrogant cultural imperialism.

WEEK OF 4 DECEMBER: East Asia enters the Twentieth Century

Read: Hane, 171-191; Hackett, "Political Modernization and the Meiji *Genro*," in R.Ward, *Political Development*, 65-98; Wakeman, 225-55; Fairbank and Teng, 195-211; M. Wright, *China in Revolution*, 1-62.

An examination of the new currents of the 20th century in Asia, and their impact on the revolution of 1911 that overthrew the Chinese empire and proclaimed a new republic.

UNIVERSITY OF MICHIGAN
HISTORY/ASIAN STUDIES 122   THE MODERN TRANSFORMATION OF EAST ASIA   WINTER, 1991
                             MWF, 11-12, Angell C
Prof. Rhoads Murphey and guest lecturers. Regular office hours MWF 1:30-3:30 and by
appointment, but if you want to see me or the TA's, arrange a time after class.

This is an introduction to the modern evolution of China and Japan since about 1800,
with attention also to Vietnam and Korea as integral parts of East Asia. We begin with
the late traditional scene and then trace the interaction of each country with the West,
but with major attention to the indigenous factors which have been equally or more
important in shaping the societies of today. The course provides a basic part of any
educated person's acquaintance with the world, of which East Asia is by far the largest
unit. But since it deals with more than a quarter of the world (the U.S. is about **four**
per cent) and over a period about as long as the whole of U.S. history, it can be only
the most general survey. Students are thus encouraged to continue their study of
East Asia in upper level courses, through reading, and through time spent in the area.

Most of the required reading is in two textbooks, a short novel, a collection of stories,
and a short biographical account: J.K. Fairbank, THE UNITED STATES AND CHINA(4th. edit.);
Richard Storry, A HISTORY OF MODERN JAPAN (1982 edit.); Graham Greebe, THE QUIET AMER-
ICAN; Lu Hsun (Lu Xun), STORIES; and Ida Pruitt, ed., DAUGHTER OF HAN. Shorter bits
from other books, some fiction, and some articles are included in a COURSE PACK,
available at DOLLAR BILL COPY on Church St., which is an integral part of the reading
assignments, as is attendance at the sections as well as at the three lectures a week.
There will be one midterm and one final, mainly of the essay type, but no paper, so as
to give you time for careful reading. Total assigned reading is modest, and you will be
expected to master it, and not to skimp on the fiction, which is enjoyable as well as a
great way to learn. Two map exercises will be handed out in class. In the assignments
below, CP= COURSE PACK. You will find it helpful if not essential to do each reading
assignment by the dates indicated.

Wed. Jan. 9 Course mechanics; introduction to East Asia.

Fri. Jan. 11 East Asia: Physical Setting
              Readings: Fairbank, US and China, 1-8,11-14,17-27,32-39,45-52, 71-79.
Mon. Jan. 14 East Asia: Cultural Components
              Readings: as above
Wed. Jan. 16 High Ch'ing: Imperial Splendor
              Readings: US and China, 91-126, 134-39.
Fri. Jan. 18 The West Enters the Chinese Stage
              Readings: US and China, 143-75.
Mon. Jan. 21 Foreign Privilege: Semi-Colonialism
              Readings: Pruitt, Daughter of Han , Prologue and Part I, pp. 1-73.
Wed. Jan. 23 The Ch'ing in Decline   FIRST MAP ASSIGNMENT DUE
              Readings: US and China, 176-95.
Fri. Jan. 25 Rebellion, Reform, Legitimacy, and Identity
              Readings: US and China, 196-219; Lu Hsun,"Ku Hsiang"(My Old Home).
Mon. Jan. 28 The Emergence of Chinese Nationalism
              Readings: US and China, 220-43.
Wed. Jan. 30 The Revolution That Failed: 1911-1927
              Readings:Lu Hsun(Xun),"Preface to a Call to Arms," and "Kung I-chi;
                       Lucien Bianco, "The Intellectual Origins of Revolution", (CP)
Fri. Feb. 1   Film, "China in Revolution", Part I
              Readings: Lu Hsun, "Medicine", and "The True Story of Ah Q".
Mon. Feb. 4   The KMT Era, 1927-49
              Readings: US and China, 244-75.
Wed. Feb. 6   The Rise of the CCP, and the Anti-Japanese War
              Readings: US and China, 275-304.
Fri. Feb. 8   Film: "China in Revolution,"Part II
              Readings: Lu Hsun, "In the Wine Shop".
Mon. Feb. 11 The Peoples' Republic: First Phase, 1949-66
              Readings: US and China, 358-416.

Wed. Feb. 13   China in Frenzy: The Cultural Revolution
　　　　　　　Readings: US and China, 417-49; Chen Jo-hsi, "The Execution of
　　　　　　　　　　　Mayor Yin" (CP).

Fri. Feb. 15   China Since Mao: Overview and Appraisal
　　　　　　　Readings: US and China, 450-92.

Mon. Feb. 18   Modern China Through Literature   Prof. I-tze Feuerwerker
　　　　　　　Readings: Lu Hsun, "The New Year's Sacrifice"; Zhao Shuli, "Meng
　　　　　　　Xiangying Stands Up"; Lu Xinhua, "The Wounded"; Gao Xiaosheng,
　　　　　　　Li Shunda Builds a House". (CP)

Wed. Feb. 20   Film: From "Heart of the Dragon" -- "Eating"
　　　　　　　Readings: From R. Murphey, The Fading of the Maoist Vision, 116-39,144-53.
　　　　　　　　　　　　　　　　　　　　　　　　　　　　　　　　(CP)

Fri. Feb. 22   Slides of China
　　　　　　　Readings: Give yourself a break!

SO-CALLED SPRING VACATION

Mon. March 4   Women in Modern China   Guest Lecturer
　　　　　　　Readings: recover from vacation

Wed. Mar. 6   Contemporary Chinese Society: Rural Sector   Prof. Martin Whyte
　　　　　　　Readings: Pruitt, Daughter of Han , Part II, pp. 74-141.

Fri. Mar. 8   Contemporary Chinese Society: Urban Sector   Prof. Martin Whyte
　　　　　　　Readings: Daughter of Han, pp. 142-249.

Mon. Mar. 11   Vietnam: Two Millennia of Nationalism
　　　　　　　Readings: From Fairbank et al., East Asia, 602-09, 870-883. (CP)

Wed. Mar. 13   Vietnam: Endless War
　　　　　　　Readings: Frances Fitzgerald, Fire in the Lake, pp. 185-235. (CP)

Fri. Mar. 15   Film on Vietnam : "Sad Song of Yellow Skin" (bad title, great film)
　　　　　　　Readings: Graham Greene, The Quiet American , entire (it's short, and good

Mon. Mar. 18   The Ordeal of Korea, 1860-1950
　　　　　　　Readings: From Fairbank et al., East Asia, pp. 609-18, 883-94. (CP)

Wed. Mar. 20   War and Conflict in Korea, 1950-1990
　　　　　　　Readings: Fairbank, US and China, 336-53; R. Simmons, "The Korean Civil
　　　　　　　War", 143-171 in Baldwin, Without Parallel ; M. Lee, "How North Korea
　　　　　　　Sees Itself", pp. 118-41 in Journey in North Korea. (CP)

Fri. Mar. 22   Taiwan, 1600-1990
　　　　　　　Readings: Fairbank, US and China, 353-57; Fairbank et al., East Asia,
　　　　　　　　　　　pp. 937-38. (CP)

Mon. Mar. 25   Hong Kong, 1840-1997. Discussion and review.
　　　　　　　HAND OUT MID-TERM EXAM, DUE BACK MON. APRIL 1 (All Fools' Day!)

Wed. Mar. 27   The Origins of Modern Japan: Late Togugawa
                Readings: Storry, pp. 13-21, 45-93; Kuwabara Takeo, "The Meiji
                Revolution", (CP)

Fri. Mar. 29   Meiji Japan
                Readings: Storry, pp. 94-133.   SECOND MAP ASSIGNMENT DUE

Mon. April 1   The New Japanese Imperialism
                Readings: Storry, pp. 134-56; Peter Duus, "The Takeoff Point.." (CP)

Wed. April 3   Japanese Militarism, and "The Failure of Freedom"
                Readings: Storry, pp. 157-96; H. Conroy, "Japan's War in China.." (CP)

Fri. April 5   The Road to Pearl Harbor
                Readings: Storry, 196-213; Kato Shuichi,"Taisho Democracy" (CP)

Mon. April 8   The Pacific War; Film: Hiroshima-Nagasaki
                Readings: Storry, 214-37; S. Ienaga, The Pacific War, pp.3-54,181-202.(CP)

Wed. April 10   The American Occupation   Prof. John Campbell
                Readings: Storry, pp. 238-287.

Fri. April 12   Film: "Full Moon Lunch" (A Tokyo family)
                Readings: Hugh Patrick, "The Economic Miracle",   (CP)

Mon. April 15   The Japanese Political Scene   Prof. John Campbell
                Readings: van Wolferen, "The Japan Problem", from Foreign Affairs. (CP)

Wed. April 17   Japanese Women   Prof. Hitomi Tonomura
                Readings: From E.O. Reischauer, The Japanese, pp. 127-37, 146-66, 204-212.
                                                                      (CP)

Fri. April 19   Japanese Society and its Minorities
                Readings: From Reischauer, The Japanese, pp. 401-21; R. Dore,
                          Shinohata, pp. 266-81 and 312-18.   (CP)

Mon. April 22   Industrialization and Environmental Crisis in Japan
                Readings: From T.P. Rohlen, Japan's High Schools, pp. 77-110, 271-326.
                                                                      (CP)
Wed. April 24   The United States and East Asia: Story of a Troubled Relationship
                Readings: Fairbank, US and China, pp. 307-357.

                HAND OUT OF FINAL EXAM IN CLASS APRIL 24

HISTORY 315: EAST ASIA IN THE MODERN WORLD

Spring 1992

Taught by: Donald N. Clark, Professor of History, Trinity University

Office: Room 220-H, Chapman Graduate Center

Hours: By appointment. Sign up in the History Department Office or call the office at 736-7621.

Course description (from the catalogue): Modernization of China and Japan since 1800; Chinese and Japanese responses to the West and integration into the modern international system. The rise of America as a Pacific power and interactions among the peoples of East Asia and the United States through the Vietnam War.

Textbooks:

Cumings, Bruce. The Two Koreas. New York: Foreign Policy Association, 1991.

*Schirokauer, Conrad. Modern China and Japan: a Brief History New York: Harcourt Brace Jovanovich, 1982.
*Students may also use the second half of the textbook from East Asia to 1800 (History 316), by the same author.

Warren, John C. America's Intervention in Vietnam: an Anthology. White Plains, NY: Longman, 1987.

Strongly recommended: Turabian, Kate L. A Manual for Writers of Term Papers, Theses, and Dissertations. Any edition.

Course requirements and due dates:

Participation and quizzes	10%
Term paper consultation . . . (Feb. 25-27)	--
Term paper topic statement . . (March 3)	--
Hour Exam . . . . (March 5	20%
Term paper bibliographic essay (March 24)	15%
Term paper progress report . . (April 7)	--
Term Paper . . . . (due April 14)	25%
Final exam	30%

Policies: I expect you to attend. An absence is an absence. Work is late after the beginning of class on the due date. I give no extensions or makeups. All papers must be typed/printed.

Quizzes and exams. Quizzes will test whether you are getting basic facts. They can be in any format--objective or essay. Exams will be combinations of objective and essay questions.

Video exercises: Three videos are scheduled during the term. For each one you will be given an exercise sheet when you arrive in class. Each of these is a quiz, in effect, and will be collected at the end of the class. These are not Trinity-owned videos and they will not be re-shown for makeups.

Term paper requirement:

1. <u>Consultation</u> to work out topic possibilities. Sign up for an appointment in the last week of February.

2. <u>Decide on a topic</u> and write it up: what it is, what you intend to investigate, and how you intend to start. **(Due March 3)**

3. <u>Bibliographic essay</u>. A paper (about 5 pp.) in which you report on the sources you have found: reference works, indexes and abstracts, documents, primary sources, secondary sources, periodicals, and others. This is a formal paper, due March 24.

4. <u>Progress report</u>. This is a brief statement due April 7 telling how your project is going. If there are problems, state them here. If you need help, ask for it here. Otherwise simply reassure me that the project is well in hand.

5. <u>Final draft</u>. A paper in the range of 10 pp. due April 14. It should be organized into sections with headings which identify major elements, and it should have a conclusion in which you state the point of the paper clearly.

A word about mechanics. Students who are shaky on the elements of style invariably lose credit for failure to spell, proofread, paginate, print with a dark ribbon, or any one of dozens of basic things. Nothing I say seems to make much difference, but I continue to recommend serious attention to a style manual and have suggested a good one under the section on textbooks, above.

History 315: East Asia in the Modern World

The Course at a Glance

Readings: CS is **Modern China and Japan**; BC is **The Two Koreas**; and JW is **America's Intervention in Vietnam**

Unit I. Introduction: Traditional East Asia

January 14	China Under the Manchus	CS 1 & 3
January 16	Video: "Power in the Pacific: Japan First" [in-class work]	
January 22	Discussion of video and lecture on Tokugawa Japan	CS 2
January 24	Japan: The Traditional Basis for modernization	
January 28	China: the intrusion of the West	CS 4
January 30	Commodore Perry and the Opening of Japan	CS 5

Unit II. Imperialism and Revolution in East Asia

February 4	The Emergence of Modern Japan, 1874-1894	CS 6
February 6	Self-strengthening in China	CS 7
February 11	The End of the Old Order in East Asia	CS 8
February 13	The Rise of Chinese Nationalism	CS 8
February 18	Japan's Rise to World Power	CS 9
February 20	Nationalist China & Imperialist Japan	CS 10
February 25	The Rise of Chinese Communism **Term paper consultations**	
February 27	World War Two in the Pacific	CS 10
March 3	The American Occupation of Japan	CS 11
	Term paper topic statement due on March 3	
March 5	**Hour Exam**	

Unit III. The United States as an East Asian Power

March 17	Japan: the Postwar Pattern	CS 12
March 19	China: the Postwar Pattern	CS 13
March 24	Korea from Kingdom to Colony to Cold War Republics	
	Bibliographic essay due on March 24	
March 26	Americans in the Korean Civil War	BC
March 31	Video: "The Minidragons--South Korea" [in-class exercise]	
April 2	Video: "Power in the Pacific: Dreams of China" [in-class exc.]	
April 7	America's Colonial Adventure in the Philippines	
	Term paper progress report due April 7	
April 9	The Vietnamese, French, & Americans in Vietnam	JW 1-2
April 14	Americans in the Vietnamese Civil War	JW 3-4
	Term paper final draft due April 14	
April 16	Effects of the War in The U.S. and Vietnam	JW 5-6
April 21	Americans and the Opening to China	CS 13
April 23	Americans and the Japanese Superstate	CS 12
April 28	East Asia: Problems and Prospects	

April 29-May 1	**Reading Days**
May 1	**Final Exam for the 8:30 section** at 8:30 a.m.
May 4	**Final Exam for the 9:55 section** at 8:30 a.m.

EMPIRE STATE COLLEGE

Professor A.Tom Grunfeld   Monday/Wednesday
Spring 1991   9:55AM-11:10AM

HISTORY OF MODERN EAST ASIA

This course is designed to introduce students to the historical
development of China and Japan. While the course will touch on
the traditional aspects of these societies, the focus will be on
modern history and contemporary events (19th and 20th
centuries).

Given the vast history of these two cultures, this course can
only briefly touch on some of the more important events in order
to give students enough information to permit some basic
understanding.

It is hoped that this brief introduction to these societies will
allow for a better understanding of current events as depicted in
the mass media and, perhaps, be a spur to future interest in East
Asia.

Required Readings:

Conrad Schirokauer, Modern China & Japan. A Brief History (HBJ)
Ronald Dore,Shinohata. A Portrait of a Japanese Village
(Pantheon)
Yuan-tsung Chen,The Dragon's Village(Penguin)
Pa China, Family (Chuang & Tsui)
Gao Yuan, Born Red (Stanford UP)
Junichiro Tanizaki, Some Prefer Nettles (Perigree Books)

Suggested Readings:

John Dower, War Without Mercy (Pantheon)
Chen Jo-hsi,The Execution of Mayor Yin and Other Stories From the
Great Proletarian Cultural Revolution(Indiana University Press)
Tadashi Fukutake,The Japanese Social Structure: Its Evolution in
the Modern Century(Tokyo University Press)
Kay Ann Johnson,Women, The Family and Peasant Revolution in China
(Chicago University Press)
Liang Heng,Son of the Revolution (Vintage Books)
Ezra Vogel,Japan as Number One (Harvard University Press)

All these books are on reserve at the library.

Course requirements: Class attendance and participation, and 3
in-class examinations (mid-term, semi-final and final).

46

CLASS SCHEDULE

February 3   Housekeeping, questions answered, general
     discussion of course outline, etc. Why study East
   Asia?

February 8   Film, "Misunderstanding China"

February 10   Chinese traditional society
          Readings: Schirokauer, chapter 1

February 15   Holiday; no class

February 17   The West discovers China
          Readings: Schirokauer, chapters 3-4

February 22   Japanese traditional society
          Readings: Schirokauer, chapter 2
                    Dore, chapters 1-3

February 24   The West discovers Japan
          Readings: Schirokauer, chapter 5

February 29   Meiji Restoration
          Readings: Schirokauer, chapter 6

March 2   Party rule and the beginning of militarism in
          Japan
          Readings: Schirokauer, chapter 9

March 7   The end of dynastic rule in China
          Readings: Schirokauer, chapters 7, 8

March 9   China up to the Japanese War
          Readings: Schirokauer, chapters 8, 10

March 14   Japan on the road towards war and destruction
          Readings: Schirokauer, chapter 10,
                    Dore,
                    Dower, War Without Mercy

March 16   Guest speaker on Chinese literature

March 21   China in the throes of social change
          Readings: Pa Chin

March 23   Mid-term examination

SPRING BREAK

April 4   East Asia after World War II: part 1
          Readings: Schirokauer, chapter 11
                    Dore

April 6   East Asia after World War II: part 2
          Readings: Schirokauer, chapter 11
                    Dore

April 11   Japan today and U.S. policy towards Japan
          Readings: Schirokauer, chapter 12
                    Dore

April 13   The People's Republic of China: part 1
          Readings: Schirokauer, chapter 13
                    Chen

April 18   Guest speaker on Japanese literature

April 20   Japan in the throes of social change
          Readings: Tanizaki

April 25   The People's Republic of China: part 2
          Readings: Chen

April 27   Women in China and Japan

May 2   Film: "Small Happiness"

May 4   The Great Proletarian Cultural Revolution
          Readings: Gao

May 9   Current situation in East Asia

May 11   Asians in the United States
               Wrap-up and questions

May 16   Semi-final examination

May 20   Final examination

Spring Term, 1990

HISTORY 236

The Modern History of East Asia
Since 1912

The following books are available for purchase:

Dietrich, C. *People's China: a Brief History*
Hane, Mikiso, *Modern Japan: an Historical Survey*
Hane, Mikiso, *Peasants, Rebels and Outcastes*
Johnson, Chalmers, *Peasant Nationalism*
Reischauer, E., *The Japanese Today*
Sheridan, J.E., *China in Disintegration*
Spence, J., *The Gate of Heavenly Peace*

The following works are on reserve:

de Bary, Chan, Watson, *Sources of Chinese Tradition*
Clifford, N. "The Western Powers and the Shanghai Question..."
Cohen, P., "The Post-Mao Reforms in Historical Perspective"
Duus, P., *Party Rivalry and Political Change in Taisho Japan*
Havens, Thomas, *The Valley of Darkness*
Hsu, I., *The Rise of Modern China*, 3rd edition
Lu Hsün (Lu Xun), various stories
Morley, J., *Dilemmas of Growth in Prewar Japan*
Shillony, B., *Revolt in Japan*
Tsunoda, de Bary, Keene, *Sources of Japanese Tradition*
Ward, R., *Political Development in Modern Japan*
Young, E., "Politics in the Aftermath of Revolution: the Era of Yuan Shih-k'ai..."

Course Requirements: Usually there will be two lectures and one discussion section each week, though unfortunately disruptions in my timetable in early March will mean some rescheduling. Attendance and active participation at discussion sections is *required* and will count in the final reckoning. Each week half the class will write a brief paper of one to one and a half pages each, so that there will be six brief papers for everybody. There will be one longer paper, an hour examination and a self-scheduled final examination.

Important Dates:

24 March: Mid-term examination.
20 April: Longer paper due. Information follows.

INTRODUCTION TO THE READINGS

The books in this course are designed to complement the lectures, and to introduce you to some of the kinds of scholarship now appearing on modern Japan and China. Hane's *Japan* is a solid and up to date chronological history which will allow you to keep your bearings, and Reischauer's *The Japanese Today* is an excellent introduction to present-day Japan, its problems and prospects. The author is not only one of the leading scholars in the field, but also a former ambassador to that country. Keep your eyes also on the elections for the Lower House scheduled for 18 February.

Sheridan's *China in Disintegration* is a good combination of analysis and chronological history, and will serve as a general text (though it says little about foreign affairs). The mordant criticisms of Lu Hsün (Lu Xun), probably China's greatest fiction writer of the 20th century, will give you a Chinese view of the society of his day. Chalmers Johnson's book, first published in 1962, remains a center of controversy for its thesis about the reasons for the communist victory in China.

For good or ill, Mao is one of the greatest men of the twentieth century, and the question of how he should be evaluated has concerned scholars and propagandists both inside and outside China, particularly as his own country drifts further away from his teachings. Craig Dietrich's *People's China* gives a dispassionate view of the Maoist period and some of the developments since. These last are put in their historical context by Paul Cohen in the last reading. Jonathan Spence's work on the travail of the Chinese intellectuals during the long revolution of the twentieth century gives a view of the rapid changes in thought and action which the events of the last fifty years have made necessary.

It is not enough simply to read the books and to absorb the information they contain so that you can repeat it in discussions, papers, and examinations. You must read with a questioning mind, and try to integrate what you find week by week with the larger world not only of this course, or of other history courses, but with all that you are studying. To encourage the right sort of reading, every other week you must turn in a brief paper of one or one and a half pages, setting forth the main questions that emerge from the readings. Remember that the worth of a historian is often measured not so much by the questions answered as by the questions raised. Remember also that learning is a *communal*, not an individual, effort; hence the requirement for attendance at and active participation in discussion sections.

- - - - - - - - - - - - - - - - - -

Week of:

12 February: *East Asia at the Turn of the Century*

East Asia in the first decade of the twentieth century, a world which saw a weak but revolutionary China, and a Japan which was joining the ranks of the great powers.

Sheridan, *China in Disintegration*, pp. 5-56; Spence, *The Gate of Heavenly Peace*, 94-153; Young, "Politics in the Aftermath of Revolution," (*Cambridge History of China*, XII, pt. 1, pp. 208-255.

19 February: *Japan and the First World War*

Japan after the death of the Meiji Emperor, and the impact of the first World War on the balance of power in East Asia. Duus's book says something about the hopes and shortcomings of modern Japanese politics.

Hane, *Modern Japan*, 192-219; Duus, *Party Rivalry and Political Change*, pp. 1-106. (Hane, *Peasants, Rebels and Outcastes*, 29-101 left off syllabus by mistake).

N.B: *NO SECTION MEETING THIS WEEK BECAUSE OF WINTER CARNIVAL.*

26 February: *May Fourth and the Revolution of the Twenties*

The growth of intellectual and political radicalism, the alliance between Nationalists and Communists, and the "unification" of China under Chiang Kai-shek in 1928. Lu Hsün's short stories are representative of the work of the most influential writer of the period.

Spence, 154-244; Sheridan, 57-182; Lu Hsün (Lu Xun): "Preface to 'The Outcry';" "The New Year's Sacrifice;" "Diary of a Madman;" "Medicine;" "Kung I-chi;" Clifford, "The Western Powers and the Shanghai Question..."

5 March: *The Nanking Decade; Japanese Politics in the Twenties*

Japan's experiments with party and parliamentary government and the attempt by Chiang Kai-shek to modernize his country in the years before the outbreak of war with Japan in 1937.

Sheridan, 207-44; Spence, 245-302; Hane, 220-243; Hane, *Outcastes*, 103-36, 173-204

12 March: *The Manchurian Incident and Japanese Ultranationalism*

The impact of the Great Depression and the final breakdown of the post-war Asian order, marked by the Japanese seizure of Manchuria, and the rise of an ultranationalist movement in the 1930s.

Hane, 245-71; Shillony, *Revolt in Japan*, 56-80, 110-97, Tsunoda, *Sources*, 759-98 (252-91 ppbk).

19 March: *The China Incident and Pearl Harbor*

The second Sino-Japanese war, which broke out in the summer of 1937, led into the second world war, and with the attack on Pearl Harbor, made America a participant.

* * 24 March: *MID-TERM EXAMINATION* * *

Hane, 273-308; Iriye, "The Failure of Military Expansionism," and Crowley, "Intellectuals as Visionaries of the New Asian Order," in Morley, *Dilemmas of Growth*, 107-38, 319-73.

- -

24 March to 1 April: *SPRING VACATION*

- -

2 April: *Chinese Communism and the Rise of Mao Tse-tung*

Sheridan, 245-69; Chalmers Johnson, *Peasant Nationalism*, pp. 1-155; *Sources of Chinese Tradition*, 858-883 (196-221 ppbk.); Spence, 303-326.

** There will be NO MEETING on Wednesday, 4 April, and there will be a lecture on Friday, 6 April.**

9 April: *The Pacific War and the Occupation of Japan*

Japan's disastrous defeat in 1945 led directly to the American occupation, and perhaps the most extraordinary experiment in "guided democracy" the world has yet seen.

Hane, 310-339; Havens, *Valley of Darkness*, 33-52, 114-205; Ward, "Reflections on the Allied Occupation," in Ward, *Political Development in Modern Japan*, 477-535.

16 April: *Japan since the Allied Occupation*

We will look at some of the facets of Japan's "economic miracle" in the years since the American occupation, and at her rise to a leading position in the world.

Hane, 341-403; Reischauer, *The Japanese*, 127-66; 268-326, 340-79.

23 April: *The Chinese Civil War and the Founding of the P.R.C.*

The shortcomings of Nationalist China during the war carried over into the years after Japan's defeat; and the United States, though emerging as a leading Pacific power, was unable to do anything about the communist victory.

Sheridan, 269-94; Dietrich, *People's China*, 10-49; Spence, 327-52; de Bary, *Sources*, 883-94, 910-33 (221-32, 248-71 ppbk).

30 April: *Maoism and the Chinese Road to Socialism*

The Great Leap Forward and the Cultural Revolution represented a new approach to China's problems. We will examine their effects on the country's development, and the reasons for Mao's apparent attack on the Party he had helped to shape.

Dietrich, 50-204; de Bary, *Sources*, 933-46 (217-41 ppbk).

7 May: *The Legacy of Chairman Mao and the rise of Teng Hsiao-p'ing*

Since Mao died in 1976, and Teng Hsiao-p'ing returned to power in 1978, China has undergone changes that some observers suggest are even more radical than those of the Maoists. What have their effects been on China today? The reading also takes a brief look at Taiwan in recent times.

Hsu, *Rise of Modern China*, 759-771, 888-889; Dietrich, 204-298; Spence, 386-417; Cohen, "The Post-Mao Reforms in Historical Perspective," *Journal of Asian Studies* (Aug. 1988), pp. 518-540.

Asian Studies 320 (6)
HISTORY OF CHINESE CIVILIZATION
FALL TERM SCHEDULE

Instructor: René Goldman, University of British Columbia 1991–92

Office: Asian Centre 212　　　　　　　　　　　　**Winter Session**
Telephone: 822–5132
822–3881 (leave messages)

Office Hours: T.B.A.

This course is designed to provide the student with an overview of Chinese history before modern times: it retraces the growth of Chinese civilization from its pre-historical genesis until about the 18th century. The unfamiliarity of Chinese culture to most students, as well as the length and complexity of Chinese history, make it necessary to lay much greater stress on the formative centuries, than on the centuries of late Imperial China (from the 14th to the 18th century). The latter are extensively covered in Asian Studies 321. Please feel free to ask questions in class and to visit me to discuss anything that you wish after class, during office hours, or by appointment. Documentary films on Chinese history will be shown in class. Welcome! Bienvenue! Huan-ying!

REQUIRED READING: Franz Michael. *China Through the Ages*

STRONGLY RECOMMENDED: W.Th. DeBary, ed. *Sources of Chinese Tradition*, Vol. 1.

SUPPLEMENTARY TEXTBOOKS (optional reading):

Ray Huang. *China: A Macro-History*
Jacques Gernet. *A History of Chinese Civilization*
Conrad Schirokauer. *Brief History of Chinese and Japanese Civilization*

Recommended readings will be placed on loan in the Sedgewick Library. They are also available in the Main Library and/or the Asian Studies Reading Room. You are however urged to buy as many as you can afford.

FALL 1991 ASSIGNMENTS

Short Essay. Sources: DeBary textbook—*Sources of Chinese Tradition*, pp. 15-148.

1. Confucianism teaches about man's obligations to his family and to the state: is there a connection between those two kinds of obligations? Explain the Taoist attitude to these matters. State your own opinion or preferences. Compare the convictions held by the legalists in regard to man and the state with those of the Confucians and the Taoists. Explain the nature of the Confucian-legalist synthesis embodied in the Han state.

   Due: 15 October　　Length: 5 to 8 typed pages.

2. A short book report (instructions on separate sheet: read carefullly).

   Due: 19 November

GRADING SCHEME:

ASSIGNMENTS	PERCENTAGE	DEADLINE
1. Map of China	3	10 September
2. Short Essay	15	15 October
3. Book Report	12	19 November
4. Examination	20	December
5. Term Paper	25	5 March
6. Examination	20	April
7. Class Participation	5	

N.B.　The required readings are designated by the symbol (R): Please read them preferably ahead of, not after the lectures under which they are listed.

COMPREHENSIVE BOOKS ON CHINESE HISTORY, including other textbooks:

(* = recommended)
(** = strongly recommended)
(R = required)

** *The Cambridge History of China.*
Arthur Cotterell and David Morgan. *China's Civilization: A Survey of Its History, Arts & Technology.*
Jacques Gernet. *China and the Christian Impact: A Conflict of Cultures.*
* J. Fairbank and E.O. Reischauer. *China: Tradition and Transformation.*
* Ch'ien Mu. *Traditional Government in Imperial China: A Critical Analysis.*
* Wolfgang Bauer. *China and the Search for Happiness.*
* Richard J. Smith. *China's Cultural Heritage. The Ch'ing Dynasty, 1644-1912* (Westview 1983).
** Patricia Ebrey. *Chinese Civilization and Society* (collection of translated documents).
Raymond Dawson. *Imperial China.*
Raymond Dawson, edit. *The Legacy of China.*
* Raymond Dawson. *The Chinese Experience.*
Dun J. Li. *The Essence of Chinese Civilization.*
Dun J. Li. *The Civilization of China.*
** Henri Maspero. *China in Antiquity (La Chine Antique).*
* H.G. Creel. *The Origins of Statecraft in China.*
Carrington Goodrich. *A Short History of the Chinese People.*
Witold Rodzinski. *A History of China.*
Joseph Levenson and Franz Schurmann. *China: An Interpretive History from the Beginnings to the Fall of Han.*
* John Messkill. *The Pattern of Chinese History.*
* Eienne Balazs. *Chinese Civilization and Bureaucracy.*
Derk Bodde. *Essays on Chinese Civilization.*
Mark Elvin. *The Pattern of the Chinese Past.*
* Joseph Needham. *Science and Civilization in China.*
Joseph Needham. *Within the Four Seas: The Dialogue of East and West.*
Rudolf P. Hommel. *China at Work* (on China's material culture).
* Ch'u Tung-tsu. *Law and Society in Traditional China.*
James Liu & Tu Wei-ming. *Traditional China* (Spectrum).
Arthur F. Wright. *Studies in Chinese Thought* (Phoenix ppb. 1967).
John K. Fairbank (ed.). *Chinese Thought and Institutions,* 1957.
David S. Nivison and A.F. Wright (eds.). *Confuciansim in Action,* 1959.
Arthur F. Wright (ed.). *The Confucian Persuasion,* 1960.
· Sun E-Tu and J. De Francis (trans.). *Chinese Social History,* 1956.
Yang Lien-sheng. *Studies in Chinese Institutional History.*
Owen Lattimore. *The Inner Asian Frontiers of China* (on historical interactions between Chinese and neighbouring barbarians).
Chou Ching-sheng. *An Economic History of China.*
Recommended book on the importance of studying history:

> *Recommended book on the importance of studying history:*
> *Robert V. Daniels. Studying History: How and Why.*

IMPORTANT: Please keep this course schedule handy and consult it regularly, so as to know what is going on, and what is expected of you at all times.

LECTURE THEMES

N.B. All required readings are marked with an (R): other readings listed under the lecture themes are recommended.

SUGGESTED STUDY PRACTICE: Summarize in a few lines in your notebook the contents of the DeBary texts after each reading.

PART I: INTRODUCTION AND EARLY CHINA

SEPTEMBER

1) Reflections on the study of history, and on the study of Chinese history in particular. *Sources on Chinese History.*

> Readings: (R) Michael. *China Through the Ages*, to p. 10
> Huang, Preface and chpt. 1.

2) China in East Asia; the land and its people; Chinese and "National Minorities"; the cleavage between pastoral-nomadic economies and agricultural-sedentary economies in East Asia; the Chinese language and its dialects.

> Assignment: Map of China.

3) Film No. 1 in Chinese History Series: "The Beginnings."

>   a. The pre-history of China.
>   b. The beginnings of Chinese history: myths and known facts.
>   c. The Shang civilization (2nd millenium BCE).

> Readings: (R) Michael. *China Through the Ages*, pp. 11–26
> Ho Ping-ti. *The Cradle of the East.*
> David Keightley, ed. *The Origins of Chinese Civilization.*

4) The Zhou (Chou) conquest and the early Feudal period: Social and political structure, religion, culture.

> Readings: (R) Michael. *China Through the Ages*, to p. 43
> W.T. DeBary. *Sources of Chinese Tradition*, Vol. 1, pp. 1-14.
> C.S. Chang. *The Making of China*, up to p. 46.
> H. Maspero. *China in Antiquity.*
> K.C. Wu. *The Chinese Heritage.*

5) Eastern Zhou: the "Spring and Autumn Period" (77-468 BCE)

> Disintegration of the Zhou feudal system.

OCTOBER

6) Discussion of the main schools of the Classical Age of Chinese Thought.

> Readings: (R) Michael. *China Through the Ages*, pp. 44–55
> (R) DeBary, pp. 15-148.

> Short essay assigned.

7) The "Warring States Period": Progress and warfare; the transformation of Chinese Society (403-221 BCE).

> Readings: Hsu Cho-yun. *Ancient China in Transition.*
> (or read excerpt in Chang. *The Making of China*, pp. 62-71)

PART II. THE FIRST EMPIRE; QIN (CH'IN) AND HAN

8) The unification of China into one large empire: the short-lived dynasty of the First Emperor of Qin (Ch'in) (221-206 BCE).

> Readings: (R) Michael. *China Through the Ages*, pp. 56–57
> Arthur Cotterell. *The First Emperor of China* .

LECTURE THEMES; PART II (continued).

9) Beginnings of the Han Dynasty: the "Earlier," or "Western" Han Dynasty (202 BCE-9 CE); the Early Han emperors.

10) Early Han political thought and institutions.

11) The apogee of Early Han. Emperor Wu and the evolution of the Han philosophy of government: a Confucian-Legalist synthesis.

   Readings: DeBary, pp. 156-168, 184-190.
                Chang, pp. 87-115.
                Pirazzoli & Stertevens. *The Han Civilization of China.*
                Wang Zhongshu. *Han Civilization.*
                Hsu Cho-yun. *Han Agriculture.*

12) Early China and the "Barbarians." Zhang Qian's missions to Central Asia; the Xiongnu (Hsiung-nu) wars and imperial expansion.

   Readings: (R) Michael. *China Through the Ages,* pp. 56–89
                A.P. Hulsewe. *China in Central Asia: The Early Stage: 125 BC-AD 23*

13) Han China's Southward expansion.

14) The Han government.

15) Sima Qian (Ssu-ma Ch'ien), Ban Gu (Pan Ku) and the birth of Chinese historiography.

   Readings: DeBary, Chapt. 10.
                Burton Watson. *Courtier and Commoner in Ancient China.*
                Burton Watson. *Ssuma Ch'ien: Grand Historian of China.*
                Burton Watson. *Records of the Grand Historian.*
                H.Y. and Gladys Yang. *Records of the Historian.*

16) Han Economy and the aftermath of the reign of Emperor Wu.

   Class Presentation and Discussion:
                DeBary, Chapter 9
                Esson Gale. *Discourse on Salt and Iron: a debate on state control of commerce and industry in Ancient China.*
                Nancy Lee Swann. *Food and Money in Ancient China.*

17) The Wang Mang interlude (9-23 CE).

18) The restoration of the Han Dynasty: "Eastern" or "Latter Han" (25-220 CE).

   Readings: Hans Bielenstein, "The Restoration of the Han Dynasty," in vols. 31 to 39 of the *Bulletin of the MFEA,* Stockholm.

19) The evolution of Han society and Latter Han politics.

   Readings: Chang, pp. 116-139.
                Ch'u T'ung-tsu. *Han Social Structure.*
                Michael Loewe. *Crisis and Conflict in Han China.*
                Michael Loewe. *Chinese Ideas of Life and Death: Faith, Myth, and Reason in the Han Period* (1983).

20) The Decline and Fall of the Han Empire; Popular Taoism and the Yellow Turban Uprising.

21) Chinese culture in the Han period.

   Readings: *   Gernet, chpt. 8

22) The Age of the Three Kingdoms: Wei, Shu, and Wu.

ASIAN STUDIES 320
History of Chinese Civilization
Course Outline for the Second Term

JANUARY

Films from the Chinese history series: "The Great Cultural Mix" and "The Golden Age."

1) China fragmented: the North and South Dynasties: the "16 kingdoms of the Five Barbarians" in the North and the "Five Dynasties of the South."

2) The introduction of Buddhism and the "Indianization" of China; China's culture in the period of disunion.

   Readings: (R) Michael, chapter 8
   * DeBary, pp. 266-368.
   * Gernet, chapter 10
   Arthur Wright, Buddhism in Chinese History (or excerpt in Chang's Making of China pp. 159-170).

3) China's second unification - The Sui dynasty (581-618).

4) Fall of Sui and foundation of the Tang dynasty (618-907).
   Readings: (R) Michael, chapter 9
   Arthur Wright The Sui Dynasty
   Dennis Twitchett. The Cambridge History of China: Sui and Tang

5) Early Tang government: Emperor Tai Zong; Empress Wu Zetian

6) Tang society: economy, government, examination system, law

   Readings: Arthur Wright. Perspectives on the Tang
   J.C. Perry and B. Smith. Essays on Tang Society (Leiden, 1976).

7) Tang military expansion: the reconquest of Central Asia; the Korean Wars; Tibet.

8) The Golden Age of Tang: Emperor Xuan Zong (Hsuan Tsung).
   End of the Fubing militia system: emergence of professional armies and powerful regional commanders (jiedushi).

   Readings: *Edward Schafer, "The Glory of the Tang Empire" in C.S. Chang The Making of China, pp. 170-199

FEBRUARY

Films: "The Heavenly Khan" and "The Age of Maturity"

9) The Rebellion of An Lushan and its consequences.

   Reading: *E.G. Pulleyblank. The Background of the Rebellion of An Lu-shan (or excerpt in Chang, pp. 199-210).

10) Taxation reform. Late Tang economy.

11) Late Tang politics; the onslaught on Buddhism.
   Reading: *DeBary, pp. 369-389.
   *Gernet, chpt. 13.

12)   The Huang Cao (Huang Ts'ao) Rebellion; fall of Tang; Third Period of Disunity: "Five Dynasties and Ten   Countries."

      Reading: Wang Gungwu. The Structure of Power in North China During the Five
          Dynasties (or excerpt in Chang, pp. 211-229).

13)   The Sung Empire (960-1278) and its relations with its neighbors: the Qidan (Khitan) empire of Liao and the Tangut kingdom of Western Xia (Hsia).

14)   Sung government: liberal despotism; education and examinations: controversies over reforms. Ouyang Xiu and Fan Zhong yan (Ou-yang Hsiu and Fan Chung-yen).

      Reading: (R) Michael, chapter 10
          * DeBary, pp. 383-408.
          * Gernet, chpt. 14.

15)   The Reforms of Wang Anshi. Discussion.

      Readings: *John Meskill. Wang An-shih: Practical Reformer?
          *DeBary, pp. 409-435.
          *R.H. Williamson. Wang An-shih.
          James Liu. Reform in Sung China.

MARCH-APRIL

16)   Reform and Reaction. The Jurchen empire of Jin (Chin) and its conquest of North China.

17)   The Southern Sung Period (1127-1278).

18)   Economic and social transformations: agrarian and commercial revolutions; the scholar-official (shidafu) class.

      Readings: *Patricia Ebrey, Chinese Civilization and Society, 23-29.
          *Chang, pp. 287-297.
          *Liu and Golas. Change in Sung China: Innovation or Renovation?
          *Jacques Gernet. China at the Eve of the Mongol Invasion.

19)   "Sung Learning" or "Neo-Confucianism"; Sung culture.

      Readings: * Gernet, chpt. 15.
          * DeBary, pp. 455-525.
          Chang, pp. 266-287 (DeBary, "A Reappraisal of Neo-Confucianism")

20)   The Mongol Period - Khubilai Khan's Yuan Dynasty (1260-1341).

      Film: "China Under the Mongols".

      Readings: (R) Michael, chapter 11
          *Gernet, chpt. 17.
          John O. Langlois. China Under Mongol Rule (Princeton, 1981).
          Morris Rossabi. Khubilai Khan.

21)   The Ming Dynasty (1368-1644); apogee of imperial absolutism.

      Readings: (R) Michael, chapter 12
          * Hucker, ed. Chinese Government in Ming Times
          * Huang, China: A Macro-History, chapter 15

22) Ming society and economy; institutional decay.

   Reading: Ray Huang, 1589: A Year of No Significance

23) End of Ming; Manchu conquest; Contacts with the West in Late Ming - Early Qing (Ch'ing).

   Films: "The Restoration" and "The Manchu Rule"

24) Early Manchu rule: enlightened despotism?

   Readings: Michael, chapter 13
       *   Gernet, chpt. 23.

25) China at the eve of modern times.

   Readings: (R) Michael, chapter 14
           Mark Elvin, The Pattern of the Chinese Past
       *   Richard J. Smith, China's Cultural Heritage, The Ch'ing Dynasty.

HISTORY 5519
FRIDAY 1500-1700

NEO-CONFUCIANISM

Instructor:

    Edward L. Farmer, 772 Social Science
        Office hours: Tuesday 1430-1600
        Phone: 624-7301; Home: 379-7429

Purpose of the Course:

The purpose of this course is to explore some of the tendencies in
Chinese intellectual history which are denoted in English by the
term Neo-Confucianism. We will read and discuss both translations
of original texts and modern secondary literature. Selections will
be drawn from the ancient through the early modern periods with
emphasis on the Song and Ming periods.

Our goal will be to try to gain some understanding of the Chinese
intellectual tradition by examining how core concepts were
expressed and interpreted over time. The approach will be more
historical than purely philosophical. We will consider the
conditions under which texts were produced, transmitted, altered
and interpreted as well as the texts themselves.

Because this is a one quarter course it is not possible to cover
all areas of Neo-Confucianism. Instead, after spending several
sessions on background, we will focus on the role of Chu Hsi
(1130-1200) as the most influential thinker, and give secondary
consideration to the trends associated with Wang Yang-ming
(1472-1529).

Readings:

    Chan Wing-tsit. Sourcebook in Chinese Philosophy
    Taylor, Rodney. The Religious Dimensions of Confucianism
    Gardner, Daniel. Learning to Be a Sage: Selections from the
        Conversations of Master Chu, Arranged Topically
    Munro, Donald. Images of Human Nature: A Sung Portrait

The above titles are available in the Bookstore and should be
purchased. Additional readings will be placed on reserve in Wilson
Library, including:

    De Bary, Wm. Theodore, ed. Self and Society in Ming Thought
    De Bary. Neo-Confucian Orthodoxy and the Learning of Mind and
        Heart
    De Bary, ed., The Unfolding of Neo-Confucianism
    De Bary and John W. Chaffee, eds. Neo-Confucian Education:
        The Formative Stage
    Munro, Donald J., ed. Individualism and Holism: Studies in
        Confucian and Taoist Values
    Munro. Images of Human Nature: A Sung Portrait

Because the first of these two books are out of print they could
not be ordered in paperback editions for purchase in the
bookstore. Therefore it may be most convenient to borrow them from
the reserve window and xerox the specific selections assigned.

Requirements:

There are three requirements for successful completion of this
course. The percentage of the grade assigned for each is indicated
below in parentheses:

(1) Participation in class discussion (25%). This course is
intended to provide a forum for group discussion and debate in
which our understanding of the subject matter will be advanced
through collective inquiry. It might be helpful to bear in mind
that questions are more important than answers. All the knowledge
in the world is useless if one does not know what the issues are.
Curiosity, clear thinking and a nose for historical significance
are what will prove most useful in this course.

(2) Short presentations, both oral and written, of documents
and works of secondary literature (25%). Presentations of
documents, done individually or jointly, should introduce your
understanding of the documents and raise questions for group
discussion. Precis of secondary literature should be typed in a
single-spaced format not to exceed two pages and prepared in
sufficient numbers to be shared by the entire class. Precis should
give a complete citation of the work followed by a balanced and
objective summary of its contents.

(3) A course paper (50%). Papers should take up significant
questions about Neo-Confucianism from a historical perspective.
Precise topics should negotiated with the instructor. Papers
should be typed, double-spaced, in two copies, with a single staple
in the upper left corner. Aim for a length of 15 to 25 pages
depending on your subject matter and level of study. In matters of
form please follow Joseph Gibaldi and Walter S. Achtert, MLA
Handbook for Writers of Research Papers, third edition (New York:
The Modern Language Association of America, 1988). Chinese
characters should be restricted to a glossary at the back of the
paper. Papers are due by Tuesday, April 12.

Schedule:

Date/Week	Topic	Reading
Jan 4	1. Introduction	
Jan 11	2. Humanism and Confucius	Chan, 1, 2;

Optional:Donald J. Munro, "Introduction" in Individualism
and Holism, pp. 1-32.

Jan 18   3. Mencius & Hsun Tzu   Chan, 3, 6

    Tentative paper topics due: 1 page statement, some bibliography

Jan 25   4. Gt. Learning, Doct. of Mean   Chan, 4, 5

Feb 1   5. Early Neo-Confucianism   Chan, 27-30; Munro,
                                                  Images, 1,2

Feb 8   6. Ch'eng Brothers   Chan, 31, 32, 33;
                                                  Munro, Images, 3

Feb 15   7. Chu Hsi   Chan, 34; Gardner;
                                                  Munro, Images, 4

         Optional: "Introduction" in de Bary and Chaffee, eds,
         Neo-Confucian Education, pp. 1-15.

Feb 22   8. Orthodoxy   Munro, Images, 5;
                                                  De Bary, N-Confucian
             Draft Papers due   Orthodoxy ..., pp.
                                                  1-66, 147-85.

Mar 1   9. Wang Yang-ming   Chan, 35; de Bary,
             "Individualism and Humanitarianism in Late Ming
             thought," in de Bary, ed., Self and Society, 145-248.

Mar 8 10. Neo-Confucianism as a Religion   Taylor

             Optional: Munro, Images, 6

Mar 12 11. Tuesday, Papers Due (2 copies)

                        Additional Readings:

General Works:

Chan, Wing-tsit, trans and ed. A Sourcebook in Chinese Philosophy.
Chen, Kenneth. Buddhism in China.
_____. The Chinese Transformation of Buddhism.
De Bary, Wm. Theodore, Wing-tsit Chan, and Burton Watson, eds.
    Sources of the Chinese Tradition. 2 vols.
Fung Yu-lan. History of Chinese Philosophy, trans. Derk Bodde. 2
    vols.
Graham, A.C. Studies in Chinese Philosophy and Philosophical
    Literature.
Hsiao Kung-ch'uan. A History of Chinese Political Thought, trans.
    F. W. Mote.
Legge, James, trans. The Chinese Classics. 5 vols.
McNaughton, William, ed. The Confucian Vision.
Mote, Frederick W. Intellectual Foundations of China.
Munro, Donald. The Concept of Man in Early China.
Schwartz, Benjamin I. The World of Thought in Ancient China.

History 332

Modern Chinese History,
1700-1989

The following books are available for purchase:

Ch'en Jo-hsi, *The Execution of Mayor Yin*
Fairbank, J.K., and Teng, S.Y., *China's Response to the West*
Feuerwerker, A., *Rebellion in Nineteenth Century China*
Spence, Jonathan, *The Death of Woman Wang*
Spence, Jonathan, *The Search for Modern China*
Thomson, James, *While China Faced West*
Waley, Arthur, *The Opium War Through Chinese Eyes*

The following books and articles will be available on reserve:

Clifford, N., "The Western Powers and the Shanghai Question . . ."
Cohen, P., "The Post-Mao Reforms in Historical Perspective."
de Bary, Chan, and Watson, *Sources of Chinese Tradition*
Dorris, Carl, "Peasant Mobilization in North China and the Origins of Yenan
    Communism."
Fairbank, J., ed. *The Missionary Enterprise in China and   America*
Han Minzhu, ed., *Cries for Democracy*
Hu Kuo-tai, "The Struggle between the Kuomintang and the Chinese Communist Party
    during the War of Resistance."
Lu Xun, various stories
Schwartz, Benjamin, *Communism and China*
Wright, Mary, *China in Revolution: The First Phase*

The course is designed to give give an introduction to the history of China from the
Ch'ing (Qing) dynasty (1644-1912) to the present, and to understand something of the continuities as well as the changes that help to fashion Chinese society and the Chinese nation
today. There are several important reasons to include history as part of a liberal education,
and perhaps the best one is to enlarge, intellectually if not experientially, our knowledge of the
human condition. We occupy an infinitesimal point in space and time, and one way to
broaden ourselves is to try to understand and to take seriously the ways of life, the outlooks,
the values, and the institutions of people who are different from us chronologically, culturally,
and geographically. Moreover, the study of another great culture -- China's, in this case --
can help us better to understand and to define our own.

There are no prerequisites in this course. Those who have studied imperial China will
naturally profit from their knowledge, but History 332 is designed for beginners. If you find
yourself confused, or not understanding what is happening, please do not hesitate to come to
see me, in or out of office hours.

We open at the height of the Ch'ing dynasty, the last flowering of the traditional Chinese world order, and move from there through the long years of disintegration and the final collapse of the old empire. We will then spend most of the course examining the great revolution -- in both its communist and non-communist phases -- that has been one of the most significant episodes in the history of the twentieth century world. We will try to understand not only the events of the period, but also the ideas that have underlain the revolution, to see how they have come to fruition or been frustrated, and will close with a consideration of the ways in which the legacies of traditionalism and revolution have helped to shape today's China.

The course, like virtually all other courses at the college, has yet another purpose: the development of an ability to think, read, write, and speak thoughtfully. You are expected to do the reading *prior* to discussion, and to do it in a way that will enable you to raise critical questions rather than simply to absorb information like a sponge. It is not enough simply to read the books and to absorb the information they contain so that you can repeat it in discussions, papers, and examinations. I know what the books say, and am not interested in your repeating it to me; I am interested in what you think about what they say. To encourage the right sort of reading, every other week you must turn in a brief paper of one or one and a half pages, setting forth the main questions that emerge from the readings. Remember that the worth of a historian is often measured not so much by the questions answered as by the questions raised. Remember also that learning is a *communal*, not an individual, effort; hence the requirement for attendance at and active participation in discussion sections.

We are using Jonathan Spence's new book, *The Search for Modern China* in this course. I have some misgivings about choosing it, since its size threatens to dominate the other readings. However, it is so far the best and most recent book of its kind that it seems wrong not to choose it, and it is a book that you will no doubt like to keep. The other readings are designed to introduce you to some of the kinds of historical writing that are now appearing in English on modern China. Through the translations of the original sources, you should gain some sense of the kinds of debates and controversies that have taken place among Chinese statesmen, intellectuals, reformers, and revolutionaries, as they have been forced to make the difficult and painful choices posed by the challenges of the modern world to their society.

The course will meet three times a week, and generally there will be lectures on Monday and Wednesday and a discussion on Friday. Sometimes, however, the pattern will change in order to permit a different treatment of the material; the exceptions, as known at press time, are noted below, and others may be announced in class. There will be a mid-term examination, a paper, and a final examination.

WEEK OF 11 FEBRUARY: Traditional China under the Ch'ing Dynasty

Read: Spence, *The Search for Modern China*, pp. 49-116; Spence, *Woman Wang*, pp. 1-139.

The readings this week will act as a general introduction to the Manchu dynasty during imperial China's last days of glory in the 18th century. *Woman Wang* is an unconventional essay in local history, reconstructing through contemporary sources the life and attitudes of a small town in the late 17th century.

WEEK OF 18 FEBRUARY: China and the Outside World: the Establishment of the Treaty System.

Read: Spence, *Search*, 117-64; Arthur Waley, *The Opium War Through Chinese Eyes*, pp. 11-157; Fairbank and Teng, *China's Response to the West*, pp. 17-46.

The coming of the Opium War marked the start of the breakdown of China's traditional foreign policy, and the beginnings of her diplomatic subordination to the outside world.

N.B. No class 22 February (carnival)

WEEK OF 25 FEBRUARY: The Taiping Rebellion and the Beginnings of Modernization

Read: Spence, *Search*, 165-215; Albert Feuerwerker, *Rebellion in Nineteenth Century China*; Fairbank and Teng, *China's Response to the West*, pp. 55-59; de Bary, *Sources*, 680-704.

The T'ai-p'ing rising has always had a particular interest for westerners because of its Christian influences. More important in Chinese history is the way the rebellion and the social forces growing out of its suppression of would weaken the polity of the Chinese state until well into the twentieth century.

No class on 1 March; makeup to be scheduled

WEEK OF 4 MARCH: Modernization and Imperialism in Late Ch'ing China

Read: Spence, *Search*, 216-238; *China's Response*, 50-55, 61-79, 91-102, 108-116; Paul Cohen, "Littoral and Hinterland in Nineteenth Century China: the 'Christian' Reformers," in Fairbank, *The Missionary Enterprise*, pp. 197-225 (extra xerox copies).

China's internal disintegration, combined with the increasing pressure of the outside world, convinced some of China's leaders of the need for change, but left unanswered the question of what form that change should take. The reading examines some of the reasons for the successes and failures of Chinese modernization after the "restoration" of the Ch'ing government after the Taiping Rebellion.

WEEK OF 11 MARCH: Imperialism, the Open Door, and the Manchu Reform Movement China

Read: Spence, *Search*, 238-244; Mary Wright, *China in Revolution*, pp. 1-63; *China's Response*, 147-64, 175-87, 220-223; Adrian Bennett and K.C. Liu, "Christianity in the Chinese Idiom: Young J. Allen and . . ." in Fairbank, *Missionary Enterprise*, 159-196 (extra copies xeroxed).

China's defeat by Japan in 1895 showed how little had actually been accomplished in strengthening the country. The threat of foreign invasion led to a new and more radical approach to reform; but it also saw a return to a particular kind of tradition in the Boxer rising of 1900.

WEEK OF 18 MARCH: The Overthrow of the Ch'ing Dynasty and the Birth of the Chinese Republic

(this is also mid term week)
Read:Spence, *Search*, 245-99; review for mid-term.

The abdication of the last emperor and proclamation of the Chinese Republic in 1912 were attended with high hopes for a new and invigorated China. We will consider the question of what exactly changed as a result of the overthrow of the dynasty, and how far the events of 1911-1912 may be considered a revolution.

N.B. Mid term examination: 22 March.

23 March to 31 March: Spring Vacation

WEEK OF 1 APRIL: The May Fourth Movement and the Revolution of the Nineteen twenties.

Read: Spence, *Search*, pp. 300-360; Lu Hsün (Lu Xun): "Preface to 'The Outcry';" "The New Year's Sacrifice;" "Diary of a Madman;" "Medicine;" "Kung I-chi" (xerox); Clifford, "The Western Powers and the Shanghai Question..."

The failure of the 1911 revolution led Chinese intellectuals to a deeper analysis of their country's plight, and to the growth of a new intellectual and political radicalism, which saw a short-lived alliance between the Nationalists and the Communists. Lu Xun's short stories are representative of the work of the most influential writer of the period.

No class on 3 April; makeup to be scheduled

WEEK OF 8 APRIL. The Nationalists in Power: the Nanking Decade.

Read: Spence, *Search*, 361-434; James Thomson, *While China Faced West*, 1-42, 76-121, 151-74, 196-241.

For all its shortcomings, the Chinese Nationalist regime, under Chiang Kai-shek, represented yet another attempt to integrate Chinese as a modern nation. We will look at their successes and failures, and at the the coming of the great war that brought their hopes to an end.

WEEK OF 15 APRIL: The Rise and Triumph of Chinese Communism.

Read: Spence, *Search*, 437-513; de Bary, *Sources*, pp. 865-891; Hu Kuo-tai, "The Struggle between the Kuomintang and the Chinese Communist Party during the War of Resistance"; Carl Dorris, "Peasant Mobilization in North China and the Origins of Yenan Communism" (copies on reserve).

Despite the difficulties of applying Marxism to China, and for all the effectiveness of Nationalist suppression, within twenty two years of the great purge of 1927, the Chinese Communists had become the rulers of the country.

WEEK OF 22 APRIL: The Consolidation of the P.R.C. and the Emergence of Maoism.

Read: Spence, *Search*, 514-90; de Bary, *Sources*, 891-894; 925-941; Benjamin Schwartz, "Modernization and the Maoist Vision," in *Communism and China*, pp. 162-85 (extra copies on reserve).

The early successes of the P.R.C. in restoring order to a country in chaos were soon jeopardized by Mao Tse-tung's demand for a more rapid development. We will examine the strengths and weaknesses of Maoism during the first decade of the P.R.C.'s history.

WEEK OF 29 APRIL: The Great Proletarian Cultural Revolution.

Read: Spence, *Search*, 560-652; Ch'en Jo-hsi, stories from *The Execution of Mayor Yin*: "The Execution of Mayor Yin," 3-36; "The Big Fish,", 137-150; "Keng Erh in Peking," 151-207.

The Cultural Revolution reflects Maoism in its most extreme form, and though now considered by the Chinese themselves to have been a disaster, it has left a long lasting impact on the country.

WEEK OF 6 MAY: China under Deng Xiaoping.

Read: Spence, *Search*, 653-747; Han Minzhu, *Cries for Democracy*, pp. 83-111, 197-215, 342-66.

Since Mao's death in 1976, China's government has instituted a wide range of changes, particularly in the country's economic life. Social and political change, however, has been less clear, as the Peking massacre of June 4, 1989, shows.

Suzanne W. Barnett
Library 242, (756-) 3168
Office hours: as posted,
  or by appointment
Home: 752-8107

Spring 1992
TTh 2:00-3:30 p.m.
Library 211

University of Puget Sound
<u>History 346</u>
CHINA SINCE 1800: REFORM AND REVOLUTION

-Syllabus-

Note: History 346 counts toward the major-minor in History or in
Asian Studies and is the prerequisite for History 347. For major-
minor credit, Pass/Fail does not apply; only letter grades apply.

China in the nineteenth and twentieth centuries has experienced a
continuous process of reform and revolution, resulting in a new order
that differs from China's dynastic past. But how "new" is New China,
and at what price has it emerged? Our task in this course is no less
than the critical examination of the meaning of revolution in Chinese
history, with careful attention to evolutionary patterns of social,
political, economic, and conceptual change.

The theme of our inquiry is continuity and change, and we will pay
special attention to the triumphs and frustrations of China's
intellectuals and political leaders. Because such people have been most
visible among China's vast population, they have been the most closely
watched and judged. How did China's scholar-gentry elite respond to the
internal challenges of popular rebellion and radical re-interpretations
of the Confucian tradition? How did China's leaders hope to make
China's rural economy fit into an industrializing world? How could
traditional Chinese perceptions of the world order (focusing on the
Middle Kingdom) fit into the age of Western expansion and nationalism?
How did Marxist ideology find a place in Chinese thought and politics?
How has revolution involved and affected "ordinary people"?

This course proceeds topically and chronologically, from the late Ch'ing
(dynastic period 1644-1912) through the Republican Revolution of 1911,
the rise to power of the Kuomintang (Nationalist Party) in 1927, and the
rise to power of the Chinese Communist Party in 1949. The course should
equip each participant with an informed understanding of the historical
experience of the People's Republic of China (founded 1949; "China") and
the Republic of China (founded 1912, relocated on Taiwan in 1948-49).

Our study is both substantive and methodological. The course should
lead to a command of events, processes, and persons in Chinese history
from before the Opium War to the early 1990s; the course also should
lead to sharpened skills of analysis and explanation. The systematic
exploration of China's revolution has broad application, for cultural
adjustment is a universal phenomenon.

Books for purchase (also available on library reserve):
    Frederic Wakeman, Jr., The Fall of Imperial China.
    Jonathan D. Spence, The Death of Woman Wang.
    TENG Ssu-yu and John K. Fairbank, China's Response to the West: A
        Documentary Survey, 1839-1923.
    ONO Kazuko, Chinese Women in a Century of Revolution, 1850-1950.
    Michael Gasster, China's Struggle to Modernize, 2nd edn. (1983).
    Jonathan D. Spence, The Gate of Heavenly Peace: The Chinese and
        Their Revolution, 1895-1980.
    LU Hsun, Selected Stories of Lu Hsun.
    Ida Pruitt, A Daughter of Han: The Autobiography of a Chinese
        Working Woman.

    Note: Additional assigned readings include class handouts and some
           materials available on library reserve or otherwise in the library.

Be prepared. This course depends on your learning from the assigned
readings, which include documents and other primary sources, literary
materials, and secondary analytical works. You will want to read each
assignment for (1) topic as defined by the author, (2) author's point of
view (find the thesis), and (3) evidence and information employed by the
author to support the thesis. All assigned readings, including each
document in the Teng and Fairbank collection, Wakeman's well-written
account of the nineteenth century, and every story by Lu Hsun, involves
interpretation; and each of us engages in the process of historical
interpretation as we struggle to understand the readings and see how
they relate to each other. Come to class prepared to make specific
reference to assigned readings in dealing with issues under discussion.

Expectations and evaluation
    Class participation (being in class regularly, listening
    thoughtfully offering ideas, questioning), including discussion
    leadership. Discussion is always in order, and a record of it
    belongs in your class notes.

    Thoughtful reading: learn to do it efficiently (not line-by-line
    plodding) and effectively (remembering central themes, "need-to-know"
    facts, and how arguments proceed). Systematic notes make a difference.

    Intelligent assessment of audiovisual materials and points of
    discussion.

    Written work:
        Thursday Themes (10 of them, due every Thursday except Weeks 5,
            8, 12, 13, and 15)
        1 hour examination (20 February)
        1 position paper (due 24 March), preliminary abstract due 10
            March
        1 paper (due 21 April), preliminary abstract due 14 April.
        Final examination (Monday, 11 May, 11:00 a.m. - 1:00 p.m.)

Thursday Themes. On Thursday of each week except Weeks 5, 8, 12,

13, and 15, each student will submit a short essay of at least
one substantial paragraph. The topic will vary from writer to
writer. The task is as follows: First, pick a specific reading
(a chapter, a primary document, or a whole book) from readings
assigned on the syllabus for that particular week. Second,
provide an original, meaningful title for your essay. Third,
provide a full bibliographic reference in correct form. Fourth,
express in your own words the author's subject, theme, argument,
and evidence.

Advice: (1) Don't miss a week; keeping up with this assignment
will enable you to get more out of the course. (2) Type your
essay if you can (that's more professional), but remember that
handwritten form is acceptable for this assignment because it is
a "pre-writing" step and not for polished presentation.
(3) As you proceed through the semester, try your hand at
accomplishing the assignment, which is to focus on a single
reading, by showing mastery of a second reading used to "bounce
off" the one selected for the focus.

Grading: roughly 3/4 written work, 1/4 class. In general,
individual writing assignments count more as the course
proceeds, allowing students to build on previous efforts.
Papers and exams count more than Thursday Themes (though these
are essential to learning, are important to do routinely, and do
add up). The final exam, which will allow each student to
demonstrate individual command of the course material, should
constitute approximately 25% of the overall course grade.

As a matter of policy, there should be no extensions on papers,
no examinations at other than the scheduled times, and no
"Incomplete" grades. The "W" grade (for official withdrawal)
should apply only when the student has followed official
withdrawal procedures, by the stated deadline (17 February).
Note: the current Academic Handbook (available from the
Registrar's Office) defines University policies and procedures
that apply in this course.

INTRODUCTION

Week 1   Tiananmen as venue of change   21, 23 Jan

The "Gate of Heavenly Peace" (T'ien-an men; Tiananmen), located
conspicuously in China's long-time capital city (Peking, Beijing),
has symbolized both imperial and revolutionary authority. Recently,
Tiananmen became synonymous with the Chinese Democracy Movement of
1989 ("Beijing Spring") and the tragic put-down of public protest in
Tiananmen Square on 3-4 June 1989.

Our task this week is to begin to explore abstract concepts and
idealizations that bear on Tiananmen 1989 in the context of modern
China: "order," "revolution," "class," "democracy,"
"individualism."

Reading: Course syllabus, entire.
            Handouts (NOT available as subjects for the Thursday Theme):
                "Lan Ting-yuan's Casebook," from Patricia Buckley
                    Ebrey, ed., Chinese Civilization and Society (New
                    York, 1981), pp. 200-202
                MAO Tse-tung, "Analysis of the Classes in Chinese
                    Society" (March 1926).
                FANG Lizhi, "'Now No One Can Intimidate Anyone Else'"
                    and "In China, as Elsewhere, People are Born With
                    Rights," International Herald Tribune, 20 January
                    1987, p. 4; 21 January 1987, p. 8.
            ON RESERVE. One of the following (use for the Thursday theme):
                Andrew J. Nathan, "Paradoxes of Reform and Pressures
                    for Change," chapter 7 of his China's Crisis:
                    Dilemmas of Reform and Prospects for Democracy
                    (New York, 1990), pp. 116-126 plus notes.
                Andrew J. Nathan, "A Culture of Cruelty," New
                    Republic, 203, 5-6: 30, 32-35 (30 July and 6
                    August 1990).
                Lucian W. Pye, "The State and the Individual: An
                    Overview Interpretation," China Quarterly, 127:
                    443-466 (September 1991).

Thursday Theme #1 due.

I. LATE IMPERIAL CHINA

In this section of the course we confront the Chinese scene in the period including the Opium War (1839-1842) and the Taiping Rebellion (1850-1864). Our immediate task is to understand the fundamental equilibrium of the Ch'ing system and challenges to the system both from within (corruption, popular protest) and without (Western intruders).

OPTIONAL PRELIMINARY READING: ON RESERVE. John King Fairbank, The United States and China, 4th edn., chapters 1-5 (pp. 1-140). Key questions: Who governed traditional China, and how? Who were the "gentry," and what was their function? What was Confucianism, and how did it relate to wealth and power? What was the nature of the "Chinese world order"?

Week 2	Order	28, 30 Jan

Reading: Wakeman, pp. 1-102. Be sure you have a good grasp of Ch'ing society and polity.

Class: Peasants, gentry, and merchants in late traditional China; the Manchu conquest; the Ch'ing system.

Thursday Theme #2 due.

Week 3	"Elite culture" and "popular culture"	4, 6 Feb

Reading: Spence, Woman Wang, entire.
Ono, Prefaces, Introduction, and ch. 8 ("The Impact of the Marriage Law of 1950").

Class: The elite and the non-elite in late imperial China: scholar-officials, the gentry, and "the people," including women.

Thursday Theme #3 due.

Week 4	Disorder	11, 13 Feb

Reading: Wakeman, pp. 102-141.
Teng and Fairbank, pp. 1-46.
Gasster, Preface and pp. 1-21.

Class: Plunderers, politics, and profits; the West in China. Commissioner Lin Tse-hsu and the Opium War (why was it the "opium" war? what were the Ch'ing emperor's options?); treaty ports. What was new in China in the 1840s?

Thursday Theme #4 due.

Do you want to do some optional reading on the Opium War? if so, the following relevant books are in the library:

CHANG Hsin-pao, Commissioner Lin and the Opium War (on reserve).
Arthur Waley, The Opium War through Chinese Eyes (on reserve).
Arthur W. Hummel, Eminent Chinese of the Ch'ing Period, entry on "Lin Tse-hsu" (reference).
The Opium War (published by the Foreign Languages Press, Peking, 1976; in the stacks).

II. STRATEGIES FOR SURVIVAL

Here we concern ourselves with a critical period in modern Chinese history, the innovative mid-/late-nineteenth century, when both rebels and bureaucrats began, in their separate ways, to alter the Ch'ing system. Of special interest is the "self-strengthening" movement that was the late-Ch'ing official, Confucian, response to disorder. Figure out the meaning of "self-strengthening" and "restoration" in the reign of the T'ung-chih Emperor and the implications of reform. Was Confucianism into its "last stand"? Was "the state" in decline or, as some recently have argued, was it on the rise?

> HOUR EXAMINATION, Thursday, 20 February. Bring bluebooks. This in-class writing opportunity will presume comprehensive familiarity with everything in the course to date, including the Taipings.

Week 5   The Taipings and revolutionary stirrings   18, 20 Feb
Reading: Wakeman, pp. 141-162.
          Ono, ch. 1 ("Women Who Took to Battle Dress").
          ON RESERVE. Wm. Theodore deBary, ed., Sources of Chinese
              Tradition, vol. II, pp. 18-42 (chapter on the Taipings;
              page numbers in the one-vol. hardcover edn. differ.
          Teng and Fairbank, pp. 55-59.

          Optional: ON RESERVE. deBary, II, pp. 285-314 (chapter on
              traditional Chinese popular religion and secret societies;
              compare and contrast the Taipings).

Class: Who were the Taipings? Were they rebels or revolutionaries?
          Was Hung Hsiu-ch'uan a hero? -- a megalomaniac? What was
          there about the mid-century popular uprisings that made them
          more unsettling than both previous rebellions and barbarian
          intrusion?

Week 6	Reconstruction	25, 27 Feb

Reading: Wakeman, pp. 163-182.
Teng and Fairbank, pp. 46-55, 61-90.
ON RESERVE. Mary Clabaugh Wright, The Last Stand of Chinese Conservatism: The T'ung-Chih Restoration, 1862-1874, pp. 1-20, 43-67. What is Wright's point of view?

Class: Analysis -- 1860 as a turning point; from the Tientsin-Peking treaties to restoration; the consequences of reform. Conservative readjustment to cultural change, with special and specific reference to Mary Wright's classic book and documents in Teng and Fairbank. Did the 1860s change the nature of Chinese state and society?

Thursday Theme #5 due.

Plan ahead

DUE Tuesday, 24 March: position paper (polished abstract plus 5 doublespaced typewritten pages, submitted in duplicate). Topic: proposals for "self-strengthening." Original title, thesis-argument, Notes (end-notes are fine, but footnotes are also acceptable), Bibliography. PRELIMINARY ABSTRACT: 50-100 words expressing the central point and substantive thrust of your paper-in-progress due Tuesday, 10 March; type the abstract, copy it, and submit the copy.

Assume you are a recent "graduate" in the T'ung-chih era (1862-1874) who has passed exams qualifying you for official service. What do you recommend as China's policy in dealing with internal unrest and external pressure? Your task is a tough one, for you must protect the integrity of the empire and your class interests, but survival seems bound to require some concessions on both accounts.

Write your paper as a memorial (imagination is important here). "Men of talent" are in great demand in China at the moment, and your job prospects are good if you command a Confucian liberal education, have a sense of Confucian civic responsibility, and can write to make a point. Consider yourself appointed to the staff of either Tseng Kuo-fan or Li Hung-chang (choose one). His Excellency (Tseng or Li) has just asked several staff members each to prepare a 5-page position paper spelling out a "self-strengthening" policy (program and rationale). Clear thinking, range and responsible use of sources, sophistication of argument, and brilliance of style can result in the selection of your paper for circulation (and no doubt will win you a promotion).

Week 7   Innovation for self-strengthening   3, 5 Mar
Reading: Teng and Fairbank, pp. 91-131.
           Ono, ch. 2 ("Between Footbinding and Nationhood").

           Optional: ON RESERVE. Wright, _Last Stand_, pp. 125-147,
           196-221.

Class: Strategy sessions. There's thoughtful leadership in the
           Palace (Prince Kung), but the accommodation of foreign
           barbarians is deeply troubling (and some say it should not be
           allowed). Why do we need the telegraph, railroads, shipyards,
           and Western subjects in the curriculum? Should women be
           equal in status to men?

Thursday Theme #6 due.

DUE Tuesday, 10 March: preliminary abstract.

Week 8   International conflicts and the heightening of reform   10, 12 Mar
Reading: Wakeman, pp. 182-224.
           Teng and Fairbank, pp. 133-193.
           Ono, ch. 3 ("The Red Lanterns and the Boxer Rebellion").

Class: Imperialism in China, Chinese antiforeignism, missionary
           incidents, and increasing Western intrusion. Sino-French War,
           Sino-Japanese War, the "scramble for concessions," and the
           movement toward radical reform. What was the 1898 reform
           movement, and why was it so important? The Boxer Uprising
           (1900).

DUE Tuesday, 24 March: position paper (memorial) on "self-
strengthening" (please be in class on Tuesday even if your paper still
needs typing/ copying). You may turn in the paper in class (or after
class, but only if you were in class).

SPRING BREAK, 14-22 March (no classes)

                    III. EMERGENCE OF A NEW ORDER

    Restoration policies had bought time for the Ch'ing dynasty, but
    there were limits to conservative reform. In this section of the
    course we turn our attention to the dynasty's efforts to reform the
    empire after the Boxer fiasco and under the direction of the Empress
    Dowager Tz'u Hsi. But the overthrow of the Manchu Ch'ing rulers was
    on its way despite (because of?) reform.

                                76

<u>Week 9:</u>   <u>New visions, new directions</u>   24, 26 Mar
Reading: Wakeman, pp. 225-256.
           Teng and Fairbank, pp. 195-229. Read with care.

           Optional: ON RESERVE. Mary Clabaugh Wright, <u>China in</u>
              <u>Revolution: The First Phase, 1900-1913</u>, pp. 1-63
              ("Introduction: The Rising Tide of Change"). Good
              consolidation for exam.

Class: How can we get out of our current dilemma and still be true to
           our ancestors? The 1898 reform, dynastic reform, and,
           paradoxically, the end of the dynasty.

Thursday Theme #7 due.

<u>Week 10</u>   <u>From empire to republic</u>   31 Mar, 2 Apr
Reading: Spence, <u>Gate</u>, Preface and chapters 1-4 (pp. 17-153).
           Gasster, pp. 22-46.

           Ono, ch. 4 ("Women in the 1911 Revolution")

Class: On Tuesday, be prepared to talk about Spence's engaging book.
           About what and whom does Spence write? What is his central
           point? What is his argument? Note: The book will remind you
           where we have been and herald where we are going.

           The 1911 revolution: Sun Yat-sen, Yuan Shih-k'ai, and
           republican government; World War I and the changing
           international order in East Asia; warlords and Chinese
           nationalism.

Thursday Theme #8 due.

<u>Week 11</u>   <u>May Fourth and the New Culture Movement</u>   7, 9 Apr
Reading: Teng and Fairbank, pp. 231-276.
           LU Hsun (may be under CHOU Shu-jen in the library), entire.
              For focus and discussion, the following:
                 Introduction
                 "Preface to . . . 'Call to Arms'"
                 "A Madman's Diary"
                 "Kung I-chi"
                 "My Old Home"
                 "The True Story of Ah Q"
           Spence, <u>Gate</u>, chapters 5-7 (pp. 154-244).

           Optional: ON RESERVE. CHOW Tse-tsung, <u>The May Fourth</u>
              <u>Movement</u>.

Class: May Fourth (incident and movement) and the search for a
         Chinese cultural style in a world dominated by Western ideas,
         wealth, and power. The art of Lu Hsun and its revolutionary
         applications: "New Youth," "Save the children," "Chinese
         renaissance," "Mr. Science and Mr. Democracy."

         Why did Marxism seem so appealing in the 1920s? What was
         wrong with Confucianism? What political trends underlay May
         Fourth, and what separate trends (such as warlord politics and
         the labor movement) proceeded alongside? The Chinese
         Communist Party (CCP), the rise of the Kuomintang (KMT) -- or
         Guomindang, which of course upsets the acronym.

Thursday Theme #9 due.

Plan ahead
DUE Tuesday, 21 April: paper (polished abstract plus 8-10
doublespaced typewritten pages, submitted in duplicate). Topic:
What were the values, objectives, and achievements of the May
Fourth movement, whose values were they, and how revolutionary
was the movement? Sources must include Teng and Fairbank
documents, Spence's book, Lu Hsun's stories, and perhaps also
Ono's chapter 5 and Pruitt's book. Original title, thesis-
argument, Notes, Bibliography. PRELIMINARY ABSTRACT due
Tuesday, 14 April.

DUE Tuesday, 14 April: preliminary abstract.

Week 12   Confucian society under fire   14, 16 Apr
Reading: Pruitt, entire.
          Ono, ch. 5 ("The Shackles of the Family").

          Optional. ON RESERVE. Marjorie King, "Ida Pruitt: Heir and
             Critic of American Missionary Reform Efforts in China," pp.
             133-148 of Patricia Neils, ed., United States Attitudes and
             Policies Toward China (on reserve under Neils).

Class: Daughter of Han: Why have we ignored her for so long?

DUE Tuesday, 21 April: paper on May Fourth. Please be in class on
Tuesday even if your paper still needs typing/copying. You may turn in
the paper in class (or after class, but only if you were in class).

IV. REVOLUTIONARY ORDER

The Nationalists under Chiang Kai-shek came to power in 1927-28, but the
problems of governing China were legion. Invasion by the Japanese caused
an unprecedented crisis for the leadership, already besieged by
overwhelming economic problems and Communist revolutionary activity.

Week 13   Mobilizing a nation   21, 23 Apr

Reading: Spence, <u>Gate</u>, chapters 8-11 (pp. 245-352).
            Gasster, pp. 47-91.

            Optional: Ono, ch. 6 ("The Transformation of Rural Women").

Class: The Nanking decade, the second Sino-Japanese War, and World
            War II in the Pacific. Communists in the countryside, on the
            march, and during the war of resistance.

Week 14   The People's Republic   28, 30 Apr

Reading: Spence, <u>Gate</u>, chapters 12-13 (pp. 353-417).
            Gasster, pp. 92-129.
            Mao Tse-tung, "Persevere in Plain Living and Hard Struggle:
                Maintain Close Ties with the Masses" (March 1957).

Class: Civil war and the Communist victory in the late 1940s. Who
            benefited? Who "lost"? How did the revolutionaries institute
            order? Land to the peasants, communes, the struggle to
            industrialize, accommodating ideals and practical reality.

Thursday Theme #10 due.

Week 15   The new order in crisis, recovery, and change   5 May

Reading: Gasster, pp. 130-189.
            2 handout articles.

Class: Reflections on the Cultural Revolution and cultural tension
            and accommodation in modern Chinese history. China since
            Mao's death in 1976, overcoming the "Gang of Four," pursuing
            the "Four Modernizations"; and the waning leadership of Deng
            Xiaoping in the post-Tiananmen era.

READING PERIOD, Th-Sun, 7-10 May (no class).

> FINAL EXAMINATION: Monday, 11 May, 11:00-1:00.
> Bring bluebooks. The scheduled time of the exam is
> fixed; the place will be the regular classroom. The
> final exam will presume familiarity with the course
> work of the entire semester.

Asian Studies/History 275
Modern Chinese History
Kidder Smith, Bowdoin College
Fall 1990

The transformation of China from a traditional Confucian empire in 1840 to a communist state in the 1980s is among the most complex series of events in modern world history. This course addresses the interactions that constitute these changes.

Two themes will help us make sense of this history. First is the individual actor within society: people's relationships to themselves, their families, and the larger world, and the choices they make. The second theme is human suffering. What keeps people from getting what they need or want? What are the structural reasons for China's unhappy recent history? Why are these obstacles so hard to overcome? Which of them are especially Chinese, and which are more broadly shared with humankind?

The political history of modern China divides readily into three periods: the final seventy years of the Ch'ing/Qing dynasty (1839-1911), the forty years of Nationalist China (1911-1949), and the forty years of the People's Republic of China (1949 - ?). In each period we will follow the lives of three groups in particular. These are the peasantry, who still constitute 80% of the Chinese people; students and intellectuals; and rulers, who have been drawn from one or the other of the two preceeding groups. The changing nature and relationships of these groups can be used to represent the shifting complexities of modern China.

We will use a new textbook by the well-known historian Jonathan Spence. However much greater it is than its competitors, however, it is still a textbook. It is too long and too detailed. You will need to learn to read it quickly, and for the major ideas. In any case, most of our readings will be in accounts by Chinese of their own circum-stances. These include essays, novels, and autobiographies. These materials will provide access to the experiences of men and women living through and creating the history of modern China.

Once the semester is underway, we will break into discussion groups on Monday and rejoin for a full class session on Wednesday. In discussion sections we will engage in close readings of the assigned texts. We'll try to identify their central themes and make connections with other course readings. On Wednesday I will take these ideas further, bringing in material that is not covered in the readings or offering a framework within which to approach a particular historical problem. Throughout I will assume that you have already put together the chronology of modern China for yourselves, based on the assigned readings. You will usually be reading the textbook accounts of this material about a week before we get to it in discussions or lecture. All this puts a lot of responsibility on you. Since we are studying both history and literature, the readings will be unusually heavy.

There will be two mid-term exams (3 October and 31 October) and a take-home final. The final will be due on Saturday, 15 December at 2:00 (when the Registrar had scheduled the in-class exam to take place). The mid-terms will have both an in-class and a take-home portion. In addition we will have frequent short exercises, either assigned one-page papers or in-class quizzes. Some of these will be graded, some will be pass/fail. Whether graded or not, a missed exercise still counts as a zero. Attendance is required at all class meetings. More than two unexcused absences will result in a grade penalty. The final grade will be calculated as follows: two mid-terms 15% each; final exam 20%; short papers 20%; class participation 20%. (I know this only adds up to 90%.)

My office is at 38 College Street. Office hours are Monday and Wednesday 10:00 to 11:00; Thursday 9:15 to 10:00; and by appointment. My office phone is ext. 3524.

The following books should be available for purchase in the Bookstore:

> Jonathan Spence, *The Search for Modern China*
> Arthur Waley, *The Opium War Through Chinese Eyes*
> Ba Jin, *Family*
> Chen Yuan-tsung, *The Dragon's Village*
> Liang Heng, *Son of the Revolution*

In addition, I will distribute copies of a Sourcebook of readings. There will be no need to go to the Library for reserve readings.

ASSIGNMENTS
PART I: IMPERIAL CHINA
Monday, September 3
    Introduction

Wednesday, September 5
    Studying modern Chinese history
        Spence, *Modern China*, pp. 1-136

Monday, September 10
    The economic geography of China
        Make a free-hand sketch map of China.
        In Sourcebook, read Gentzler, *Changing China*, #1 and 4.

Wednesday, September 12
    Autocracy and the gentry
        Spence, *Modern China*, pp. 133-215

Monday, September 17
    Note: Discussion sections begin today.
        Read Waley, *The Opium War Through Chinese Eyes*,
    pp. 11-185.

Wednesday, September 19
    The Opium War (lecture)

Monday, September 24--discussion sections
    Reform in the middle and late Ch'ing/Qing
        Read Spence, pp 216-68
        In Sourcebook, read Patricia Ebrey, *Chinese Civilization
    and Society*, #56, 57 & 61.
        In Sourcebook, read Gentzler, *Changing China*, #22-28.

Wednesday, September 26
    The shifting paradigm

Monday, October 1
    Review session. Reading to be assigned

Wednesday, October 3
    First mid-term exam

PART TWO: THE REPUBLIC OF CHINA

Monday, October 8--discussion sections
        Read Spence, 269-333; and in Sourcebook, read:
        "K'ung I-chi," in *Selected Stories of Lu Hsun*
        "In the Tavern," in *Silent China, Selectd Writings of Lu Xun*
        Ebrey #67, "Hai-feng Peasant Association"
        Gentzler, selections #57-63

Wednesday, October 10--lecture
        The May Fourth Movements

Monday, October 15
   and
Wednesday, October 17
        Movie week--I will be in China this week. Documentary
footage of twentieth-century China will be shown during class time.
Additionally, you will be asked to view a Chinese feature film one
evening. Please read Spence, 334-434, *before* you see these movies.

FALL BREAK - October 19-24

Wednesday, October 24--lecture
        The new sources of power

Monday, October 29
        Read all of Ba Jin, *Family*

Wednesday, October 31
        Second mid-term exam

PART 3: THE PEOPLE'S REPUBLIC OF CHINA

Monday, November 5--NO separate discussion sections today--meet
together as if it were Wednesday. Frederic Wakeman, an important
historian of China, will be giving a talk in Daggett Lounge at 7:30
tonight. You are required to attend. He will also be visiting our class
today.
        Read all of Chen, *The Dragon's Village*

Wednesday, November 7
    Peasants and the CCP

Monday, November 12
    Read Spence, 504-617, and in your Sourcebook, from Ebrey's
Chinese Civilization and Society, read "A New Young Man Arrives in
the Organization Department."

Wednesday, November 14
    The pattern of PRC history

Monday, November 19
    Read all of Liang Heng and Judith Shapiro, *Son of the
Revolution*

THANKSGIVING VACATION - November 21-25

Note: Several films on China today will be shown in the evenings
during the last two weeks of class.   Schedule to be announced.

Monday, November 26
    Read in your Sourcebook:
        "A Foot of Mud and a Pile of Shit," from *Mao's People*
        "What is the Ideal Life of a Revolutionary Youth," from
        Chinese Sociology and Anthropology
        Gentzler, #110, "The Program for the Cultural Revolution"

Wednesday, November 28
    The Cultural Revolution

Monday, December 3
    Read, very quickly, Spence, pp. 619-747.   More slowly, read the
remaining pages in your Sourcebook.

Wednesday, December 5
    China in the 1980s

The take-home final exam, an essay ten pages long, will be due
Saturday, 15 December, at 2:00, the day that the final would
normally take place.

***See end of page 6 for book list

Mr. Duiker	**HISTORY 486** Pennsylvania State University
	TWENTIETH CENTURY CHINA

Course Outline

Part I.   The Decline of the Manchus, 1900-1911

1. The Disintegration of Confucian Society (Fairbank, Ch. 1-6: Meisner, Ch. 1)
    A. Introduction. The beginnings of political and cultural crisis in China.
    B. Some characteristics of traditional society.
    C. The external and internal decline of the Manchu dynasty.
    D. The cultural challenge of the West.

Questions for discussion:

1. What are the distinctive political and social characteristics of traditional Chinese civilization? How do they compare and contrast with the values and institutions of the modern West brought to China in the 19th century?

2. Was the decline of the Manchu dynasty in the nineteenth century caused more by internal or external factors? Why?

3. What were the major characteristics of Western imperialism in nineteenth century East Asia? What were its primary motivations, and what were the consequences?

2. First Chinese Revolution (Fairbank, Ch. 7-9; Schaller, 1)
    A. Patterns of Chinese response to the West.
    B. Birth of the revolutionary party.
    C. Period of Manchu reforms.
    D. The 1911 Revolution.

Questions for discussion:

1. Why was China so reluctant to abandon its Confucian heritage, despite the evident seriousness of the challenge from the West? Why, in other words, was China a "consummatory" civilization?

2. Why did the early stages of China's response to the West fail to stem the tide of defeat? Were they intrinsic reasons for this failure, or were there other causes?

3. Was the fall of the dynastic system inevitable, or do you feel that it might be ascribed to other factors? What other factors might explain its collapse? It is sometimes said that had the 1911 revolution not occurred, the dynasty might have been able to modernize gracefully. Do you agree?

4. Although the dynasty was overthrown, the revolution did not succeed. What were the primary causes of revolutionary weakness? Why, in other words, did the first revolutionary fail to achieve its goals?

5. What was the ideological basis for the revolutionary forces, and what social classes were enrolled under its banner? Can the 1911 revolution be considered a classic model of modern revolution? Why or why not?

Part II.   The Republican Period, 1911-1949

3. The New Culture Movement and May Four (Meisner, Ch. 2; Fairbank, Ch. 10-11)
   A. The New Culture Movement.
   B. May Four and the Rise of Nationalism.
   C. The May Fourth Movement in historical context.

Questions for discussion:

1. Why do historians distinguish between the New Culture and the May Fourth Movements? Discuss the two, and their relationship to each other.

2. The May Fourth period is often considered the high point in the popularity of liberal democratic ideals in China. What were the reasons for this popularity, and why did it fail to take hold in later years?

3. May Four is often considered the breeding ground of Chinese communism. Do you agree? Discuss.

4. Viewed in an historical context, the May Four period is an important stage in the Chinese revolution. Discuss.

4. The Birth of the Communist Party, 1921-1926 (Meisner, Ch. 3; Fairbank, Ch. 12)
   A. Marxism and China. Lenin and the Concept of the four-class alliance.
   B. The Early Growth of the CCP.
   C. The alliance with the KMT.

Questions for discussion:

1. Marxism attracted great interest among Chinese intellectuals during the early republic. Why do you think this was true? How would you compare Marxist-Leninst doctrine with traditional Confucian views of man, society, and the universe? Can Marxism be considered a form of neo-Confuciansim?

2. Martin Wilbur, in his article in Lewis, discusses the divergent social and geographical origins of the members of the Kuomintang and the CCP. What were these origins, and why were they different?

3. Maurice Meisner analyzes Li Ta-chao's distinctive approach to Marxism
    in terms of the issue of "being" versus "consciousness". What do these
    two terms mean, and how did they effect his views of Marxist doctrine?

5. The Northern Expedition and the Rise of Chiang Kai-shek, 1926-1927
    A. The Northern Expedition.
    B. The Disintegration of the KMT/CCP Alliance.
    C. The Development of Maoist Strategy.

Questions for discussion:

1. How would you evaluate the Northern Expedition in a revolutionary
    context? That is, was it a genuine revolution? What classes appeared
    to support the KMT and the CCP? Why was the CCP defeated in 1927?

2. Many historians are critical of the role of Moscow in the events of the
    mid-twenties in China. Why? Would you agree? How would you assess
    Soviet policy during this period?

3. By 1927, a split had begun to develop in the CCP over the nature of
    revolutionary strategy and how to apply Marsixm-Leninism to China.
    Discuss the nature of the split, and its consequences.

6. The Nanking Regime, 1928-1937 (Fairbank, Ch. 13)
    A. China at Quarter Century.
    B. The Legacy of Sun Yat-sen.
    C. The Character of the Nanking Regime.

Questions for discussion:

1. What are the essentials of Sun Yat-sen's political philosophy? How
    does Sunyatsenism differ from Western liberal democracy? How would you
    compare it with Marxism?

2. To what extent did Chiang Kai-shek apply Sun's Three People's
    Principles in the Nanking Republic? Was the attempt a success or a
    failure, all things considered? Why?

3. Some people have claimed that Chiang was a fascist. What is a fascist?
    Does the label seem appropriate in Chiang's case?

7. China in Foreign Relations, 1911-1945 (Fairbank, Ch. 14; Schaller, Ch. 2-4)
    A. The Great Powers and Manchuria.
    B. Japan's Quest for Hegemony in Asia.
    C. The Washington Treaty System.
    D. The Mukden Crisis.
    E. The Sian Mutiny and the Second United Front.
    F. Marco Polo Bridge and the Coming of War, 1937-1941.

Questions for discussion:

1. How did foreign relations affect the course of the Chinese revolution
    during the 1920s and 1930s? Did it serve to exacerbate political and
    social tensions or ease them? Why?

2. Chiang Kai-shek attempted to relieve China from the menace of imperialism. Did he succeed? How would you evaluate his policies?

3. During this period, American foreign policy was a factor in East Asian international policies. What were the principles behind the American effort? How would you assess its effectiveness?

8. World War and Civil War, 1945-1949 (Meisner, Ch. 4; Schaller, Ch. 5-6)
   A. The World War.
   B. Yalta and the Soviet Interest.
   C. Civil War and the American Dilemma. (Discussion of America's China Policy.)

Questions for discussion:

1. War is often a precipitant of revolution. Do you agree with this proposition in the Chinese case? Discuss.

2. One of the controversial arguments in American scholarship is over the reasons for the communist victory in 1949. Was it because of nationalism or social reforms? Or a sell-out by Washington? Or Chiang's own weakness? Discuss.

3. The China policy of the Truman administration has been heavily criticized--not only by the GOP but by scholars in later years. What are the essentials of this criticism? Do you agree? Why did Truman decide to abandon the effort to save Chiang?

Part III. The Communist Period, 1949-1975

9. The Early Years, 1949-1958 (Fairbank, Ch. 15; Meisner, Part II)
   A. New Democracy.
   B. Period of Consolidation.
   C. Land Reform.
   D. Collectivization.
   E. The Hundred Flowers.

Questions for discussion:

1. Mao Tse-tung described the Chinese road to socialism as New Democracy. What is New Democacy, and what are its distinctive Chinese components?

2. The essence of Chinese communism has been sometimes described as the "mass line". What is the mass line? Do you agree that the use of this tool was a major factor in the early successes of the Peking regime?

3. The major elements of Maotsetung Thought had begun to emerge by 1958. What is Maoism? What were its major components, and how does it differ from orthodox Marxism-Leninism?

4. In China, agriculture became the key to building socialism. Why was this? Did the decision inspire disagreements in the party?

10. The Great Leap and Its Aftermath, 1958-1965 (Fairbank, Ch. 16; Meisner, Part IV)
    A. Great Leap Forward.
    B. Socialist Education Movement, 1962-1965.

Questions for discussion:

1. What were the reasons behind the Great Leap Forward?

2. The Leap strained party unity and led to an increasing divergence between "two lines" in the leadership. What were these two lines, and what were the origins of their disagreement?

11. The Great Proletarian Cultural Revolution, 1966-1969 (Fairbank, Ch. 17; Meisner, Part V)
    A. The Events.
    B. The Meaning of the GPCR.
    C. The Stability of Fatigue.

Questions for discussion:

1. While the GPCR did not begin until the mid-1960s, its origins can be ascertained a full decade earlier. What are the origins of the Cultural Revolution?

2. What were Mao's motives for launching the GPCR? Some say it was simply a power play, while others maintain there were basic issues involved. Discuss.

3. The GPCR was, from one perspective, simply the latest stage of the Chinese revolution. Discuss.

12. The Post Mao Era, 1976-1982 (Fairbank, Ch. 18-19; Meisner, Part VI)
    A. The Death of Mao and the Victory of the Moderates.
    B. Building the New China.

Questions for discussion:

1. How would you explain the recent victory of the moderates in the political struggles in Peking? Were the inherent reaons for their triumph, or is it likely to be temporary?

2. Now that China appears to be moving in a new direction, what is likely to happen to Maotsetung Thought? What is its current status in China? Does it have a role to play in the future of the Chinese nation?

13. Foreign Affairs (Schaller 7-9)
    A. Lean to one side (1950-1957).
    B. China goes it alone (1957-1965).
    C. The Cultural Revolution and Foreign Policy.
    D. The New Balance of Power in Asia.

Questions for discussion:

1. Why did China decide to "lean to one side" in 1950? Is there evidence that Peking might have preferred to play a neutral role in world politics?

2. Many Americans viewed China's behavior in the early 1950s as "international outlawry." Others contended China's motives were defensive. Discuss these two points of view. What is your own view?

3. By the mid-1950s, China had begun to detach itself from the Soviet Union. What were the root causes of the momentous shift in her foreign policy? Was ideology the major factor, or were there other issues of equal importance?

4. During the late 1950s and early 1960s, Chinese foreign policy seemed to be more radical than Moscow's. Does this appear to be true? What were the reasons for Peking's behavior during this period?

5. The Sino-American rapproachement began in 1969. Why then? What were the major issues, and why were they not considered impediments to better relations?

6. In recent years, Chinese foreign policy has changed in major ways. What are the essential principles in Chinese foreign policy today? Do they appear to be consonant with Peking's national interests, or not?

7. Normalization of relations between Washington and Peking has raised a number of major questions about American national interests in East Asia. What are these interests, and how might they be affected by the election of Ronald Reagan?

8. The international politics of East Asia, has now been transformed from a bipolar Cold War struggle of ideologies into a quadripolar balance of Great Powers. How and why has this shift come about? What are its implications?

READING LIST

**** 1. John Fairbank – The Great Chinese Revolution, 1800-1985
     2. Joseph Esherick – Reform and Revolution in China
     3. Maurice Meisner – Mao's China and After
     4. Michael Schaller – The United States and China in the Twentieth Century

University of Wisconsin - Green Bay
Professor Craig Lockard
MWF 1:25-2:20, RH 346

Syllabus: SCD 875-333
Spring, 1991

SOCIAL CHANGE IN MODERN CHINA

Food For Thought:

"October 1, 1949, is a symbolically important date in Chinese and
world history....But a history of the People's Republic cannot begin
with that official holiday...The Chinese Revolution and the People's
Republic are the products of particular circumstances and experiences
inherited and transmitted from China's past...And those who prepared
and brought about that revolution were...The products of a specific
Chinese historical situation as well as makers of Chinese history" --
Maurice Meisner

"The rise of the communists to power is no isolated event. Certainly
it is not merely the work of a group of revolutionary extremists.
Its roots reach far back into the structure of the old society, the
abuses of government, the inequalities and miseries suffered by the
people, and a widespread demand for change" -- Kuo Ping-Chia

"In a profound way....ours has become, to a degree we do not yet
understand, the post-Chinese revolutionary era...The world is just
beginning to come to grips with its significance...Chinese Communist
prescriptions for social change...challenge widely held Western
notions. Is China's experience relevant for quite different
societies?" -- Michel Oksenberg

"A revolution is not a dinner party, or writing an essay, or painting
a picture, or doing embroidery; it cannot be so refined, so leisurely
and gentle, so temperate, kind, courteous, restrained or magnanimous.
A revolution is an insurrection, an act of violence by which one
class overthrows another" -- Mao Zedong

Introduction

This course surveys in an interdisciplinary fashion the development of
Chinese society in the nineteenth and twentieth centuries, with an emphasis
on the period since 1945. An introduction to social change in China
requires a consideration of many facets of human activity, a general
mapping of the terrain that includes economic, political, and cultural
developments. However, we will place the major stress on the rise,
evolution, and impact of Chinese communism, with particular attention to
changes in China since the communist victory of 1949. The course will be
divided into two segments: the first segment focuses on the background of
communist ascendance: geographic contexts, the nature of traditional
Chinese society and politics, the decline of Imperial China, the emergence
of nationalism, the trials and tribulations of Republican China, the
origins and development of Chinese communism. The second segment will

analyze developments in China since 1949, with particular concentration on the reconstruction of Chinese life under communist rule and the changing policies under Mao Zedong and Deng Xiaoping. This part of the course includes a more detailed examination of politics, economics, society, culture, and foreign relations in the People's Republic, as well as coverage of the Chinese societies in Taiwan, Hong Kong, and Southeast Asia.

Both SCD majors and students from other fields are welcome in the course, which assumes no previous knowledge of China and has no prerequisites (History 250-251 are helpful but not essential). Many facets of Chinese development are open to controversy in their evaluation and interpretation, which should be clear from the differing perspectives to be found in the readings, lectures and films. I have opinions on many of the subjects to be discussed and will try to make my biases clear throughout. Obviously you need not agree with my views; indeed you are invited to take issue with them and will not be penalized for doing so. The course is directed at several goals: to develop information and insights so as to make China and the Chinese more intelligible; to examine a society with very different values and attitudes from ours so as to generate cross-cultural understanding and broaden intellectual horizons; and to promote an increased ability to think and analyze. All that is required is an open mind and a willingness to learn about other peoples and cultures. You are reminded of the wisdom of Confucius: "learning without thought is labor lost; thought without learning is intellectual death."

Format

The format of the course is lecture, discussion and film viewing. Normally in each lecture session I will lecture for about 45 minutes, followed by questions and discussion. Students are expected to obtain a preliminary background to the topic by keeping up with the assigned readings. This course also makes extensive use of some of the many fine media materials available, especially documentary films. These films, as well as several slide presentations based on my various trips to China, are intended to add breadth and depth to the material covered in the lectures and texts, and to provide a more "intimate" and direct view of China. Many of the films are part of a British documentary series called "Heart of the Dragon," which was also shown on Public Television in this country. There are two main texts, three supplementary books, and one recommended book. All are available in paperback at the campus bookstore and on reserve in the library. The main texts include:

John K. Fairbank, The United States and China, 4th ed., enlarged (Harvard University)
Marc Blecher, China: Politics, Economics and Society (Pinter)

The supplementary texts to be used are:

David Goodman and Gerald Segal, eds., China at Forty: Midlife Crisis? (Oxford University)

Jonathan Spence, The Gate of Heavenly Peace: The Chinese and Their
    Revolution, 1895-1980 (Penguin)
Zhang Xinxin and Sang Ye, Chinese Lives: An Oral History of Contemporary
    China (Pantheon)

The recommended book (available on reserve) is:

Ed Hammond, To Embrace the Moon: An Illustrated Biography of Mao Zedong
    (Lancaster-Miller)

The required books are coded for reading as F,B,G,S and Z. The recommended
book is coded as *H. To give some "feel" for Chinese society some tapes of
Chinese music will be played at the beginning of class sessions and during
some slide presentations. Lectures will be illustrated with overhead
projections prepared by the instructor to clarify terms and increase
understanding. With or without the help of the recommended atlas you are
expected to quickly familiarize yourself with the geography of China,
including major cities, regions, provinces, rivers, and mountain ranges.
You will frequently need this information throughout the course. There
will be a brief map quiz on March 1.

Tentative Class Schedule:

Session	Date	Topic (Reading Assignment)
1	Feb. 11	Explanation of Syllabus
2	Feb. 13	Introductory Remarks (F:xiii-xvii)
		BACKGROUND TO MODERN ERA
3	Feb. 15	Geographical Contexts (F:1-8; B:xv-4)
4	Feb. 18	Traditional China I (F:140, 9-14, 80-105; B:5-13)
5	Feb. 20	Traditional China II (F:17-79, 106-151)
6	Feb. 22	Film: "Heart of the Dragon: Remembering"
		THE NINETEENTH CENTURY
7	Feb. 25	Challenges to Imperial System (F:151-175)
8	Feb. 27	Civilization in Crisis (F:176-205, 307-320; S:17-93)
9	Mar. 1	Slides: "China in 1906" MAP QUIZ (10 minutes)
		CHINA IN TRANSITION, 1900-1949
10	Mar. 4	From Imperial to Republican China (F:205-226, 320-324; S:94-153; *H:3-18) Due: Project Outline

11	Mar. 6	Warlord China (F:226-239, 276-279; S:154-244; *H:19-40)
12	Mar. 8	Slides: "A Chinese Mosaic"
13	Mar. 11	The Apex of Republican China (F:239-275, 279-289, 324-335; B:324-335; S:245-302; *H:41-56)
14	Mar. 13	China in War and Revolution (F:289-304, 336-353; B:23-41; S:303-352; Z:xiii, xv-xxvii, 29-48; *H:57-112)
15	Mar. 15	Slides: "Images of China and America"

OVERVIEW OF PEOPLE'S CHINA

16	Mar. 18	Socialist Construction (F:358-416; B:42-80; S:353-385; Z:3-25)
17	Mar. 20	Film: "Felix Greene's China"
18	Mar. 22	Film: "Heart of the Dragon: Living"
19	Mar. 25	Great Proletarian Cultural Revolution (F:417-442; B:80-90; S:386-417; *H:147-170)
20	Mar. 27	Summary Discussion
21	Mar. 29	Midterm Examination (Sessions 2-20)

SPRING VACATION (MARCH 30 - APRIL 7)

| 22 | Apr. 8 | Four Modernizations and Repression (F:442-449, 479-492; B:90-102; G:1-9; *H:171) |

ANALYZING CONTEMPORARY CHINESE SOCIETY

23	Apr. 10	Government and Politics (D:279-283; B:103-135; G:10-17, 42-65; Z:87-114, 183-199, 229-250, 267-284)
24	Apr. 12	Film: "Shanghai: New China"
25	Apr. 15	Film: "Heart of the Dragon: Believing"
26	Apr. 17	Economic Life (B:158-192; G:18-41; Z:117-180, 253-264, 301-324)
27	Apr. 19	Film: "Heart of the Dragon: Working"
28	Apr. 22	Film: "One Village in China: All Under Heaven"
29	Apr. 24	Social Structures and Relations (B:136-157; G:66-85; Z:51-84, 203-225, 287-298, 347-358)

30	Apr. 26	<u>Film</u>: "Heart of the Dragon: Marrying"
31	Apr. 29	<u>Film</u>: "One Village in China: A Small Happiness"
32	May 1	Cultural Life (B:193-202; Z:327-343)
33	May 3	<u>Film</u>: "Heart of the Dragon: Mediating"
34	May 6	<u>Film</u>: "Heart of the Dragon: Creating"
35	May 8	China and the World (F:450-462; B:202-209; G:86-139)
36	May 10	<u>Film</u>: "Heart of the Dragon: Trading"
37	May 13	<u>Slides</u>: "China Off the Beaten Track"
38	May 15	<u>Film</u>: "One Village in China: To Taste a Hundred Herbs"

OTHER CHINAS

39	May 17	Hong Kong and Taiwan (F:353-357; G:140-171)
40	May 20	Chinese in Southeast Asia <u>Due</u>: Projects
41	May 22	<u>Film</u>: "Asian Insight: Hong Kong and Singapore"
42	May 24	Summary Discussion (F:462-478)
	May 31	<u>Final Examination</u> (Sessions 16-42): 1-2 p.m.

History 409

Chinese Revolutions

The following books are available for purchase:

> Bianco, Lucien, *Origins of the Chinese Revolution*
> Chan, Anita, *Chen Village*
> Chen Yuan-tsung, *Dragon Village*
> Malraux, André, *Man's Fate*
> Mao Tse-tung, *The Chinese Revolution and the Chinese Communist Party*
> Marx, Karl, *The Communist Manifesto*
> Nathan, Andrew, *Chinese Democracy*
> Perry, Elizabeth, *Rebels and Revolutionaries in North China*
> Rankin, Mary, *Early Chinese Revolutionaries*
> Saich, Tony, ed., *The Chinese People's Movement*
> Selden, Mark, *The Yenan Way in Revolutionary China*
> Wilbur, C. Martin, *The Nationalist Revolution in China*
> Yue Daiyun and Carolyn Wakeman, *To the Storm*

Purpose of the Course:

The study of Chinese communism and of the People's Republic of China has undergone some startling changes in the western world, and more particularly in the United States, in the last several decades. Thirty-five years ago there was still a tendency to see Communist China as a member of a bloc dominated by Moscow; twenty years ago, there was a tendency -- on the left, at any rate -- to see an idealized version of China where the Maoists had conquered the age-old problems of disunity, social disintegration, and want. After Mao's death, a more balanced view emerged, soon to be replaced by the vision of a country which, in its opening to the outside world, and in its economic reforms, was taking the first steps towards liberalization and perhaps even democracy. That vision was destroyed by the events of June 4, 1989, and China now appears to many in the west simply as a large third world country facing overwhelming problems, under a government whose primary concern seems to be the maintenance of power while socialism has collapsed in eastern Europe and what used to be the Soviet Union.

Each of these views of China has colored the ways in which foreigners look at China, and try to understand her current situation. In reading studies of Chinese history, politics, economics, or culture, it is important to remember when and under what conditions the individual works were written. Those published some years ago may see the coming of communism as a revolutionary break with the past, yet also as a logical outgrowth of China's earlier history; more recent studies, however, may believe that communism has perpetuated certain "traditional" traits of China's socio-political culture rather than overcoming them.

There is more to the Chinese revolution than communism, however. In this course, we will look at the ways in which the Chinese revolution has developed in the twentieth century, and more particularly in the ways in which Marxism -- a nineteenth century western European political and social philosophy -- has become adapted to the world's largest country, and to a culture that owed little to nineteenth century western political ideas. We will be reading several different kinds of works: scholarly secondary studies, personal accounts, one of the more important theoretical works of Mao Tse-tung, even some fiction. The course will be as much concerned with raising questions as with answering them, and will be more concerned with the quality of argumentation than with the "correctness" of the answers.

Finally the course, as is appropriate for courses on this level, will be concerned with history in general: how it is written, how it is used, and how it is remembered. For history is more than simply a dispassionate chronicle of facts; faced with the facts, the historian must choose, must emphasize some while relegating others to the background (or even ignoring them), must arrange, to produce what is a work of art, an art whose aim is the translation of the world of the past into a language that makes sense to the present without betraying the men and women who made the world that is being studied.

Organization of the course:

We will meet once a week to discuss the reading. Since the course is a seminar, attendance at each meeting is presumed, and since a seminar is an exercise in communal learning, full participation in each meeting is assumed In addition, each student will, every other week, write a 750 word (three double spaced typewritten pages) scholarly review of the week's book, so that by the end of the term each will have done half of the books. Imagine that you are producing the piece for publication, and cover such topics as the following, among others:

What questions does the author raise?
How well are they answered?
Are there questions that should be raised and are not?
What are the main sources used?
How far do the author's political predilections influence the book's findings?

At the end of the course, you will have a choice of writing a ten page term paper on a topic of your choosing, or taking a final examination.

SCHEDULE

(Note that dates refer to Monday,
the first day of the week; the
class meets on Tuesday)

10 February: Organizational Meeting.

17 February: Marx, *Communist Manifesto*; Mao, *The Chinese Revolution and the Chinese Communist Party*; Bianco, *Origins of the Chinese Revolution*.

The course opens with a Marxist classic, and one of the Maoist applications of Marxism to Chinese history. Bianco's book provides an overview of the conditions that led up to the Communist victory of 1949.

24 February: Rankin, *Early Chinese Revolutionaries*.

Rankin explores a particular part of the world of the early revolutionaries seeking to bring the Ch'ing dynasty to an end in the first decade of this century.

2 March: Wilbur, *The Nationalist Revolution in China*.

The Chinese revolution of the 1920s was one of the first third world revolutions of a kind that has become familiar to us today. It was also a formative experience in the lives of the men that were to lead both the Communist and Nationalist parties for the next half-century.

9 March: Malraux, *Man's Fate*.

Malraux's book first appeared in 1934, and has been one of the classic accounts of the Chinese revolution, and more particularly of Shanghai, China's greatest city. A reading of it raises the question of how far a novel can be treated as a historical document?

16 March: Perry, *Rebels and Revolutionaries in North China*.

Elizabeth Perry examines what she calls the ecology of revolution in a particularly depressed and unstable part of China, south of the Yellow River plain. In it she looks at some of the differences that set the Communists off from earlier rebels.

23 March: SPRING BREAK

30 March: Selden, *The Yenan Way*.

Selden's book examines some of the ways in which the Chinese Communists Party was able to turn the war against Japan to its own benefit, and thus to come out of that war far stronger, while the Kuomintang was growing weaker.

6 April: Ch'en, *Dragon Village*.

Another novel, but this time by one of the participants in the first great drive for land reform shortly after the Communist victory in 1949.

13 April: Chan, *Chen Village*.

There have been several village studies made in China since the partial opening of the country to foreign researchers in the late 1970s. Chan's book examines the experiences of one particular small community through the vicissitudes of the Maoist years.

20 April: Yue, *To the Storm*.

Yue Daiyun, a professor of literature at Peking University, has written one of the best of an ever-growing number of memoirs of covering the difficult years from the Anti-Rightist campaign of 1957 through the Cultural Revolution.

27 April: Nathan, *Chinese Democracy.*

"Democracy" is a word that was used a great deal by Mao and continues to be used by Mao's successors. It has also been used more recently by the regime's opponents in the democratic movement of 1989 and since then. What does it mean in China? What is the relationship between the Chinese understanding of the word and ours? How far is democracy a universal value? and how far is it bound to a particular culture like our own?

4 May: Saich, *The Chinese People's Movement.*

The "China Spring" of 1989 saw the largest popular demonstrations in Chinese history, and seriously challenged the legitimacy of the regime. Three years later, the great study of this outbreak has yet to be written. For the moment, however, Saich's book provides a collection of essays on the movement that culminated in the Peking massacre of June 4th.

University of Washington
SISEA 241   JAPANESE CIVILIZATION   Autumn 1991

Class: M,T,W,F 11:30   Sections: Th
                Savery 249

Instructor:
                Susan B. Hanley   Teaching Assistant:
                Professor of Japanese   Walter Hatch
                Studies and History   Graduate student in
                                         Japan Regional Studies

Office Hrs: Thomson 429   Thomson
                T 1:30-3; W 8:30-10;
                F 10-11

Welcome to SISEA 241. The purpose of this course is to introduce
students to Japan through a multi-disciplinary approach based in
history. The course is one of two that serves as an introduction
to Japanese studies (and the Japan Regional Studies major) and
will provide a background to upper division courses on Japan.
SISEA 241 covers Japanese civilization through World War II, and
the new SISEA 242 will introduce students to contemporary Japan.
The focus of both courses is to help students understand modern
Japan.

No background is necessary or expected, but students are expected
to be able to read and write English well at the college level.
This course will help you to analyze writings in various
disciplines and to write short essays through practice in the
hour exams and quizzes.

Course Goals

The first goal is to give you a knowledge of Japanese culture and
civilization so that no matter what approach or discipline you
take in the future, you will have a wide, solid background and
therefore be able to understand Japanese values, principles,
traditional ways of doing things, constraints, and the like.
Since Americans share many common values and history with
European nations, it is not considered necessary to give students
a background in religion, principles of government, or social
values before studying European art or business, but this common
background cannot be taken for granted with regard to Asia.
Thus, we will study this quarter the most important elements of
Japan's civilization in the past as they affect contemporary
Japan.

The second goal is to prepare you for further work in Japan
Studies in the Jackson School and for upper-level work in the
social sciences. In addition to the textbook, there are
assignments in primary sources (translated from Japanese) and in
analytical research articles. These will be discussed in lecture
and sections. There will also be exercises in writing short

analyses and arguments in quizzes and exams, so you will have practice in writing essays and essay exams.

Course Requirements

Map quiz: Thursday, October 3, 10 minutes
Hour exam: Friday, November 1, 11:30-12:20
Final: Thursday, December 17, 2:30-4:30

There will be pop quizzes in section based on the discussion questions for the week.

Exams must be written in bluebooks so we can "blind grade." Two points will be deducted from any exam answer not written in a new bluebook.

Course Rules

The UW rules regarding absences, exams, incompletes, etc. will be followed. If you are having problems, please see the instructor or teaching assistant as soon as possible. If you are ill on the day of an exam, please either see your doctor or go to Hall Health and obtain a written excuse, but do not come to class or office hours when you are ill. Exams can be made up without penalty with a written excuse for illness, for death in the immediate family, or for religious observances.

Grading

Your exams and quizzes will be graded on a scale of 1-100 or with a letter grade. These are converted to the 4.0 system as follows:

4.0	95	A	3.0	85	B
3.9	94		2.9	84	
3.5	90	A- to B+	2.8	83	B-
3.4	89		2.0	75	C Lowest grade to be S
3.3	88	B+	0.7	62	Lowest decimal grade recorded by registrar

Videotapes

Four one-half hour videotapes on premodern Japanese history will be available for viewing in the Media Center of OUGL during the dates listed. Class time has been set aside for viewing them for those who cannot view at other times, but remember that the Media Center will not hold everyone at the same time. Viewing is optional but recommended. The tapes will provide visual reinforcement for material in the textbooks and are a good source for review.

"Early Japan" Parts I and II. Available October 1-25.
"The Feudal Experience" Parts I and II. Available October 15-November 1.

Reading Assignments

All reading assignments are required. Assignments should be
completed by your discussion section the week for which they are
assigned, but if you find you are having difficulty following the
lectures, try reading ahead.

One book is available for purchase at University Book Store:

    John W. Hall, From Prehistory to Modern Times

All of the other readings will be available at the Copy Center at
Suzzallo Library in a packet listed under SISEA 241.

Lectures and Reading Assignments

(Note: the lectures are subject to change, but the following
schedule of weekly topics and reading assignments will be
followed).

Week 1   EARLY JAPANESE SOCIETY

9/30   M   Introduction
10/1   T   Prehistory: Who are the Japanese People?
10/2   W   Protohistory: The Tomb Culture, Imported or Indigenous?
10/3   Th   Map Quiz and Discussion
10/4   F   Prehistoric Legacy: Religion and Society

ASSIGNMENT:

Edwin O. Reischauer, The Japanese Today, pp. 3-30.
John W. Hall, Japan from Prehistory to Modern Times, pp. 1-23.

Week 2   THE FORMATION OF THE JAPANESE STATE

10/7   M   The Formation of the Japanese State
10/8   T   Borrowing from the Chinese I
10/9   W   The Early Land System
10/10 Th   Discussion
10/11 F   Free for viewing "Early Japan," Parts I and II

ASSIGNMENT:

Hall, pp. 24-74.
Donald Keene, Anthology of Japanese Literature, Vol. 1, pp. 19-
   30, 40-48, 51-53.
Wm. T. deBary, ed., Sources of Japanese Tradition, Vol. I, pp.
   52-76.

Week 3   HEIAN JAPAN AND "THE TALE OF GENJI"

10/14 M   The Return to Japanese Ways: Heian Japan
10/15 T   The World of The Tale of Genji

10/16 W   Heian Women: Exploited Playthings or Economic Powers?
10/17 Th Discussion of <u>The Tale of Genji</u>
10/18 F   The Rise of the Samurai

ASSIGNMENT:

Ivan Morris, <u>The World of the Shining Prince</u>, pp. 103-167.
Murasaki, "Evening Faces," Chapter 4 from <u>Tale of Genji</u>
  (Seidensticker translation), pp. 57-83.
"Kagero Nikki" and "The Pillow Book," excerpts from Keene,
  <u>Anthology</u>, pp. 97-105, 137-144.

Week 4   THE SAMURAI RISE TO POWER: KAMAKURA BAKUFU

10/21 M   The Samurai Rise to Power
10/22 T   The Influence of the Samurai on Japanese Culture
10/23 W   Buddhism in Japan
10/24 Th Discussion
10/25 F   Free for viewing "The Feudal Experience", Parts I and
       II.

ASSIGNMENT:

Hall, pp. 75-102.
Keene, <u>Anthology</u>, pp. 179-191, 197-223.

Week 5   FEUDAL JAPAN

10/28 M   The Muromachi Bakufu: An Unstable Oligarchy
10/29 T   Muromachi Culture and Aesthetics: Formation of the
       Japanese Tradition
10/30 W   Japan's Feudal Experience: An Overview
10/31 Th Review for hour exam
11/1 F   HOUR EXAM

ASSIGNMENT:
Hall, pp. 102-159.
John W. Hall, "Foundations of the Modern Japanese Daimyo," in
  Hall and Jansen, eds., <u>Studies in the Institutional History of</u>
  <u>Early Modern Japan</u>, pp. 65-77.
Ito Teiji, "The Development of Shoin-Style Architecture," in
  Hall and Toyoda, eds., <u>Japan in the Muromachi Age</u>, pp. 227-239.

Week 6   THE TOKUGAWA BAKUFU

11/4 M   Unification and the Formation of the Tokugawa Bakufu
11/5 T   Tokugawa Policies and Their Effects
11/6 W   The Impact of Peace: Economic Growth
11/7 Th Discussion
11/8 F   The Japanese Village

ASSIGNMENT:

Hall, pp. 160-232.

Susan B. Hanley, "Economic Growth and Population Control in Preindustrial Japan," Research in Economic Anthropology, Vol. 5 (1983), pp. 185-221.

Week 7   TOKUGAWA CULTURAL AND SOCIAL CHANGE

11/11 M   HOLIDAY
11/12 T   Urbanization and Demographic Change
11/13 W   The Rise of a Commoner Culture
11/14 Th   Film and discussion on Japanese Theater (249 Savery)
11/15 F   Transformation of the Samurai

ASSIGNMENT:

R.P. Dore, Education in Tokugawa Japan, pp. 291-326.
Kozo Yamamura, "The Houseman and the Daimyo Retainer," from A Study of Samurai Income and Entrepreneurship, pp. 119-133.
Susan B. Hanley, "Urban Sanitation in Preindustrial Japan," Journal of Interdisciplinary History, XVIII,1 (1987), pp. 1-26.
Saikaku, selections from Keene anthology, pp. 340-353, 357-362.

Week 8   MEIJI RESTORATION

11/18 M   Unrest and Change: The Bakufu Failure to Cope
11/19 T   The Meiji Restoration
11/20 W   Changing Goals and the National Identity
11/21 Th   Discussion
11/22 F   Politics, the Emperor, and Religion in Meiji Japan

ASSIGNMENT:

Hall, pp. 233-307.
Marius B. Jansen, "Tokugawa and Modern Japan," in Hall and Jansen, pp. 317-330.

Week 9   MODERN JAPAN

11/25 M   Japan's Industrialization
11/26 T   Social Change I
11/27 W   Social Change II
11/28 Th   HOLIDAY
11/29 F   HOLIDAY

ASSIGNMENT:

Sydney Crawcour, "The Tokugawa Period and Japan's Preparation for Modern Economic Growth, Journal of Japanese Studies, Vol. 1, No. 1 (1974), pp. 113-125.
Susan B. Hanley, "The Material Culture: Stability in Transition," in Jansen and Rozman, eds., Japan in Transition, pp. 447-469.
"Woman (Status of)", Entry in Basil Hall Chamberlain, Things Japanese (1904), pp. 500-509.
Fukuzawa Yukichi on Japanese Women, pp. 37-50.

Baroness Shidzue Ishimoto, Facing Two Ways (orig. pub. 1930s), pp. 101-141.
Nagatsuka Takashi, The Soil (trans. by A. Waswo) (written in 1910), pp. viii-27, 203.

Week 10   JAPAN ENTERS THE TWENTIETH CENTURY

12/2 M   Life Styles: The Village
12/3 T   Life Styles: The City
12/4 W   Domestic Problems and Military Solutions
12/5 Th   Discussion of Social Change
12/6 F   Film "Collision with Japan" and Discussion

ASSIGNMENT:

Hall, pp. 308-357.
John F. Embree, "The Life-History of the Individual," from Suye Mura, pp. 18-38.
Robert J. Smith, "Japanese Village Women: Suye Mura 1935-1936," Journal of Japanese Studies, Vol. 7, No. 2 (1981), pp. 259-284.
Japanese Ministry of Education, "The Unique National Polity," in Ivan Morris, ed., Japan 1931-1945, pp. 46-52.

Week 11   JAPAN IN MID-CENTURY

12/9 M   World War II and its Legacy
12/10 T   Postwar Japan
12/11 W   Overview of Course and Review for Exam

ASSIGNMENT:

Hall, pp. 349-357.

EMPIRE STATE COLLEGE
HISTORY DEPARTMENT

HISTORY OF JAPAN   PROF. A. TOM GRUNFELD
                    FALL 1991

This course is designed to introduce students to the essence of
Japanese culture and to give them an understanding of modern
Japanese history. By examining the historical development of its
society, economy and politics, we will study the process by which
Japan emerged from a feudal state to its present status as an
economic superpower. Foreign intervention and the influence of
foreign cultures will also be an important topic.

Class participation is strongly encouraged. It will be expected
that students will collect material on Japan from newspapers and
periodicals and discuss them in class, particularly in the last
quarter of the class when the discussions will be about
contemporary issues. Requirements include class attendance,
readings (all the readings are on reserve in the library), and 2
in-class examinations.

Reading List:

Mikiso Hane, Modern Japan. A Historical Survey (Westview)
Gail Lee Bernstein, Haruko's World. A Japanese Farm Woman and Her
Community (Stanford U. P.)
Junichiro Tanazaki, Some Prefer Nettles (Perigee Books)
Frederik Schodt, Manga! Manga! The World of Japanese Comics
(Kodansha)
Akio Morita & Shintaro Ishihara, "The Japan That Can Say 'No'"
[on reserve]
Heritage Foundation, "A Japan That Can Say 'Yes'" [on reserve]

Recommended Supplemental Reading:

E. Patricia Tsurumi, The Other Japan. Postwar Realities

Class Requirements

1. Class attendance and participation.

2. Mid-term and final examinations

CLASS SCHEDULE

September 4, 9:   Early Japan: geography, culture and history
                    Readings: Hane, chapter 1

September 11:   Film, "The Japanese Version"

September 16:   Tokugawa Japan
                    Readings: Hane, chapter 2-4

September 18, 23:   The arrival of the Westerners and the
                    Japanese response.

September 25, 30, October 2: Meiji Restoration
                    Readings: Hane, chapter 5-8
                              Schodt, pages 28-67

October 7:   Japan as a Colonial Power
                    Readings: Hane, chapter 9

October 9, 14:   Taisho Japan
                    Readings: Hane, chapter 10-11

October 16:   Film "The Threat From Japan"

October 21:   Taisho Japan/Review for Mid-term
                    Readings: Tanazaki, entire novel

October 23:   Midterm

October 28, 30:   Japan's Road to War
                    Readings: Hane, chapter 12-13
                              Schodt, pages 68-87

November 4:   Film "Hirohito: Behind the Myth"

November 6:   War and Defeat
                    Readings: Hane, chapter 14
                              Tsurumi, chapter "The Cloud Remains"

November 11, 13:   American Occupation
                    Readings: Hane, chapter 15
                              Bernstein, Part I and II
                              Tsurumi, pages 14-35

November 18:   Film "Japan: the Sword and the Chrysanthemum"

November 20:   Women in Japan
                    Readings: Bernstein, Part III & "Bessho Revisited"
                              Schodt, pages 88-105
                              Tsurumi, pages 5-13

November 25, 27:   Japan's Recovery: the 1950s-1970s
               Readings: Schodt, pages 106-158

December 2, 4, 9:   Japan Bashing and the Future
               Readings: Morita and Ishihara
                         The Heritage Foundation

December 11:   The Current Situation
               Readings: Hane, chapter 16
                         Tsurumi, chapter "The Economic Miracle
                                           in Perspective"

December 16:   Final examination

108

University of Tennessee at Chattanooga

History 365   **Traditional** **Japan:** **History** **and** **Culture**   <u>Spring 1991</u>
Section 001 Brock 401   TT 10:50-12:05

Richard Rice   755-5303
Office Hours in Guerry Hall (Honors Program):
M 9:00-4:00; T 8:00-10:00,1:00-3:00; W 9:00-4:00; TH 8:00-10:00,1:00-3:00

Readings:

Earhart, Byron <u>Japanese</u> <u>Religion:</u> <u>Unity</u> <u>and</u> <u>Diversity</u>
Keene, Donald <u>Anthology</u> <u>of</u> <u>Japanese</u> <u>Literature</u>
Stanley-Baker, <u>Japanese</u> <u>Art</u>
Totman, Conrad <u>Japan</u> <u>Before</u> <u>Perry</u>
Additional readings may be put on reserve in the library

<u>Date</u>	<u>Topic</u>	<u>Reading</u>
Jan 3 (TH)	Introduction and Geography	
Jan 8 (T)	Prehistory and Myths	Totman, 1 Stanley-Baker, 1-2 Keene, pp.54-58
Jan 10 (TH)	Shinto and Buddhism	Earhart, 1-5 Keene, pp.33-53 Stanley-Baker, 3
Jan 15 (T)	Taika Reforms Discussion One: Taoism	Totman, pp.18-26 Earhart, 6-8
Jan 17 (TH)	Asuka and Nara Japan; Shoen	Totman, pp.26-41
Jan 22 (T)	Heian Society and Religion. Discussion Two: Buddhism	Earhart, 9-10
Jan 24 (TH)	Heian Culture	Totman, 42-63 Stanley-Baker, 4
Jan 29 (T)	Heian Literature Discussion Three: Heian Literature	Keene. pp.67-105; 137-144
Jan 31 (TH)	Exam I	
Feb 5 (T)	Rise of the Taira	Totman, 63-69
Feb 7 (TH)	Kamakura Japan: The Samurai State	Totman, 70-84 Stanley-Baker, 105-116

Feb 12 (T)	Medieval Culture	Totman, 85-106 Earhart, 11
Feb 14 (TH)	Ashikaga Japan: High Feudalism	Totman, 80-84
Feb 19 (T)	Literature and Society; Zen Culture	Totman, 106-132 Stanley-Baker, 115-137
Feb 21 (TH)	Discussion Four: Medieval Literature	Keene, pp.179-228; 231-241; 258-293; 301-304
Feb 26 (T)	Discussion Five: Zen	Reserve reading or handout
Feb 28 (TH)	Nobunaga, Hideyoshi and Ieyasu	

--- Spring Break ---

Mar 12 (T)	Rise and Fall of Christianity	Earhart, 12-13
Mar 14 (TH)	Azuchi-Momoyama Culture	Stanley-Baker, 138-158
Mar 19 (T)	Ran	
Mar 21 (TH)	Ran	
Mar 26 (T)	Exam II	
Mar 28 (TH)	The Warrior-Merchant State	Totman, pp.133-164
April 2 (T)	Tokugawa Society and Religion	Earhart, 14
April 4 (TH)	Tokugawa Economy	Totman, 188-199
April 9 (T)	Discussion Six: Tokugawa Literature	Totman, 164-188 Keene, pp.335-409; 415-435
April 11(TH)	Video on Traditional Japan	
April 16(T)	Tokugawa Art	Stanley-Baker, 159-190
April 18(TH)	Late Tokugawa Reforms	

April 23(T) Perry and the Bakumatsu   Totman, 199-232
         Papers Due

April 25(TH) Meiji Restoration and Modernization   Earhart, 15
                                                          Stanley-Baker, 7

April 29 (M) Final Exam (11:00-1:00)

Exams: There will be three exams, each covering about one-third of the
material. They will consist of two essay questions which will be handed
out in advance. You will be asked to write on one of them, to be designated on the day of the exam. In addition, a list of identification questions will be included, from which you will pick four.

Japanese Names: These will be kept at a minimum consistent with a sound
understanding of traditional Japan. Be sure to ask for definition whenever
a term is used in class or text that you do not understand: other students
will benefit from your initiative.

Discussions: Good discussion sessions do not just happen. To assist the
class in preparation, and also to help me assess your engagement with the
materials to be discussed, I will hand out discussion worksheets to use
when you are reading and also to use for note-taking during the discussions. Group discussion does not seek to convince others, but to deal with
unsolved matters and help members find meaning. The most important issues
are ones with no clear answer; that is why they are interesting. Using our
worksheets, we will work on communications skills and recognition of both
positive and negative roles in discussion. You will be asked to complete
six worksheets, and your lowest score will be dropped in assessing your
discussion contribution.

Paper: One typed ten-page paper (give or take a paragraph or two) is
required on a subject in the course: consult with me on your choice. The
final draft is due April 23. We will set up individual conferences to discuss your topic, research plan and note-taking, and organization.

Grades:
Exam I	100	
Exam II	100	
Final	150	
Discussion	100	(Top five scores)
Paper	150	(Due April 23)
Total:	600	(540 and above is an A; 480 and above a B and so on)

Make-up Policy: In fairness to all students, no make-up will be allowed
unless strong and documented evidence suggests circumstances truly beyond
your control. No make-up will be allowed unless I am notified before the
exam that a problem exists. You can leave a message or send an emissary
to notify me of your inability to take the exam on the date assigned. All
make-ups will be administered on April 29, at 9:00-10:00.

History 3853

(History of Japanese Civilization to 1800)

Fall, 1990

Schedule of Lectures and Discussions

OFFICE: Sidney D. Brown, University of Oklahoma
         Dale Hall Tower 423,
         Wed., 1:30 p.m.; Fri., 11:30 a.m.; and by appointment
         Telephone: 325-6572, or 325-6002

REQUIRED BOOKS:

Sir George Sansom, Japan: a Short Cultural History. Stanford
     University Press, 1962.
Ivan Morris, The Pillow Book of Sei Shonagon. Penguin, 1971.
Helen Craig McCullough, The Tale of the Heike. Stanford
     University Press, 1990.
Donald Keene, tr., Essays in Idleness: the Tsurezuregusa of
     Kenko. Columbia University Press, 1967.
Donald Keene, tr., Four Plays of Chikamatsu. Columbia
     University Press, 1961.
Thomas C. Smith, The Agrarian Origins of Modern Japan.
     Stanford University Press, 1959.

FIRST WEEK
August 27   Introduction
August 29   Prehistoric Japan: the Horse-Riders
     Sansom, Chapter I
     Recommended: Gari Ledyard, "Galloping along with the
     Horse-Riders: Looking for the Founders of Japan,"
     Journal of Japanese Studies, I (Spring, 1975), 217-254.
     Walter Edwards, "Event and Process in the Founding of
     Japan: the Horserider Theory in Archaeological
     Perspective," Journal of Japanese Studies, IX (Summer,
     1983), 265-296.
     J. Edward Kidder, jr., "The Archaeology of the Early
     Horse-Riders in Japan," The Transactions of the
     Asiatic Society of Japan, Third Series, XX (1985), 89-
     124.
August 31   Prehistoric Japan: the Ainu
     Sansom, II
     Recommended: H. Inez Hilger, Together with the Ainu.
     1971.

SECOND WEEK
September 5   Formation of the Yamato State
     Sansom, II
     Recommended: John Young, The Location of Yamatai.
     1958.
September 7   Shinto: the Native Faith   SLIDE LECTURE
     Sansom, III

Recommended: Daniel C. Holtom, <u>The National Faith of Japan: a Study of Modern Shinto</u>. 1938.

THIRD WEEK
September 10 Historical Geography of Japan
     Map assignment due.
     Recommended: Edwin O. Reischauer, <u>The Japanese Today: Change and Continuity</u>. 1988.
September 12 Prince Shotoku (574-622) and the Chinese Enlightenment
     Sansom, IV
     Recommended: Sir George Sansom, <u>History of Japan to 1333</u>. 1958.
September 14 The Taika Reforms of 645
     Sansom, V
     Recommended: Richard J. Miller, <u>Japan's First Bureaucracy</u>. 1958.

FOURTH WEEK
September 17 Nara Society and Culture
     Sansom, VI-VII
     Recommended: Donald J. Philippi, tr., <u>Kojiki</u>. 1969.
September 19 Heian Politics and Society (794-1068)
     Sansom, VIII-IX
     Recommended: Ivan Morris, <u>The World of the Shining Prince</u>. 1964.
September 21 CLASS DISCUSSION: The Worldview of a Japanese Court Lady
     Ivan Morris, tr., <u>The Pillow-Book of Lady Sei Shonagon</u>. 1967.
     Discussion questions to be distributed.
     Prepare for ten-minute written quiz over book.

FIFTH WEEK
September 24 Golden Age of Japanese Literature
     Sansom, X-XI
     Recommended: Lady Murasaki, <u>The Tale of Genji</u>, Edward Seidensticker, tr., 2 vols., 1975.
September 26 Cloister Court: Government by Retired Emperors, 1068-1185
     Sansom, XII-XIII
     Recommended: G. Cameron Hurst III, <u>Insei: the Government of the Cloister Court</u>. 1976.
September 28 FIRST HOUR EXAMINATION

SIXTH WEEK
October 1   The Samurai and the Origins of Feudalism
     Sansom, XIV
     Recommended: S.R.Turnbull, <u>The Samurai: a Military History</u>. 1977.
October 3   Minamoto Yoritomo (1144-1199) and the Kamakura Shogunate
     Sansom, XV

Recommended: Jeffrey P. Mass, Warrior Government in Early Medieval Japan. 1974.
October 5   Medieval Military Romances
     Recommended: Ivan Morris, The Nobility of Failure (1975), Chapters on Minamoto no Yoshitsune and Kusunoki Masashige.

SEVENTH WEEK
October 8   CLASS DISCUSSION: The Warrior Tradition in Literature.
     Helen Craig McCullough, tr., The Tale of the Heike. 1988. Prepare essay on this Japanese epic tale in accordance with instructions.
October 10   Japanese Buddhism: the Popular Faith Sects
     Sansom, XVI
     Recommended: Alfred Bloom, Shinran: the Gospel of Pure Grace. 1965.
October 12   Japan's First Musical Tradition: Gagaku
     VIDEO: "Gagaku: the Court Music of Japan," Dr. Eugene Enrico, producer, 1989.

EIGHTH WEEK
October 15   Japanese Buddhism: Nichiren and the Lotus Sect
     Recommended: Ryusaku Tsunoda, Sources of Japanese Tradition, XI (The Sun and the Lotus).
October 17   The Mongol Invasions, 1274, 1281
     Recommended: Kyotsu Hori, "The Economic and Political Effect of the Mongol Wars," in Hall and Mass, Medieval Japan (1974), VIII.
October 19   Imperial Restoration in Medieval Japan, 1333
     Recommended: H. Paul Varley, Imperial Restoation in Medieval Japan. 1970.

NINTH WEEK
October 22   CLASS DISCUSSION: The Counterculture in Medieval Japan
     Donald Keene, tr., Essays in Idleness: the Tsurezuregusa of Kenko. 1967. Discussion questions to be distributed; prepare for quiz.
October 24   Ashikaga Takauji (1305-1358) and the Muromachi Shogunate
     Sansom, XVII
     Recommended: John Whitney Hall, ed., Japan in the Muromachi Age. 1977.
October 26   Zen and Muromachi Culture
     Sansom, XVIII
     Hee-jin Kim, Dogen: Mystical Realist. 1975.

TENTH WEEK
October 29   Zen Painting: Sesshu (1420-1506)   SLIDE LECTURE
     Recommended: T. Akiyama, The History of Japanese Painting. 1960.

October 31   Sino-Japanese Relations under the Ashikaga
        Shogunate
        Kwan-wai So, Japanese Piracy in Ming China. 1978.
November 2   SECOND HOUR EXAMINATION

ELEVENTH WEEK
November 5   Sengoku Jidai: Age of the Country at War
        Sansom, XIX
        Recommended: H. Paul Varley, The Onin War: History of
        its Origins. 1967.
November 7   The Portuguese Century in Japan
        Recommended: Michael Cooper, They Came to Japan.
        1965.
November 9   Oda Nobunaga (1534-1582) and the Reunification
        of Japan
        Sansom, XX
        Recommended: C.R.Boxer, The Christian Century in
        Japan. 1950.

TWELFTH WEEK
November 12   Toyotomi Hideyoshi (1536-1598) and the Invasion
        of Korea
        Recommended: Mary Elizabeth Berry, Hideyoshi. 1983.
November 14   Tokugawa Ieyasu (1542-1616) and the Bakuhan
        System
        Sansom, XXI
        Recommended: Conrad Totman, Politics in the Tokugawa
        Bakufu. 1967.
November 16   Tokugawa Castles and Castletowns   SLIDE LECTURE
        Recommended: John Whitney Hall, "The Castle Town and
        Japan's Modern Urbanization," Far Eastern Quarterly,
        XV (November, 1955), 37-56.

THIRTEENTH WEEK
November 19   Alternate Residence System for Daimyo: Sankin
        Kotai
        Sansom, 463-470.
        Recommended: T.G.Tsukahira, Feudal Control in Tokugawa
        Japan. 1966.

FOURTEENTH WEEK
November 26   The Rise of the Merchant Class: Chonin
        Sansom, XXII
        Recommended: Charles Sheldon, The Rise of the Merchant
        Class. 1958.
November 28   CLASS DISCUSSION: Rural Tokugawa Japan--
        Stagnation or Development?
        Thomas C. Smith, The Agrarian Origins of Modern Japan.
        1959. Questions to be distributed; quiz.
November 30   Traditional Agriculture and the Peasantry
        Recommended: C.J.Dunn, Everyday Life in Traditional
        Japan. 1969.

FIFTEENTH WEEK

December 3   Tokugawa Political Crises
        Recommended: John Whitney Hall, <u>Tanuma Okitsugu</u>.
        1955.
December 5   Genroku Culture and the Woodblock Print: <u>Ukiyoe</u>
        SLIDE LECTURE
        Recommended: James Michener, <u>The Floating World</u>.
        1953.
December 7   CLASS DISCUSSION: Classics of the Bunraku
        Theatre--Domestic Tragedies and Historical Epics
        Was Chikamatsu a Japanese Shakespeare?
        Donald Keene, tr., <u>Four Plays of Chikamatsu</u>. 1961.
        VIDEO: BUNRAKU MUSIC, Dr. Eugene Enrico, producer
SIXTEENTH WEEK
December 10   Education in Tokugawa Japan
        Sansom, XXIII
        Recommended: Ronald P. Dore, <u>Education in Tokugawa
        Japan</u>. 1964.
December 12   The Dutch Learning in Tokugawa Japan
        Recommended: Grant K. Goodman, <u>Japan: the Dutch
        Experience</u>. 1986.

FINAL EXAMINATION   Thursday, December 20, 1990   8-10 a.m.

History/Asian Studies 278--The Foundations of Tokugawa Japan
Spring 1989
Kidder Smith , Bowdoin College

In 1600 Tokugawa Ieyasu achieved dominance over all
Japan, ending a century of civil war. His descendants ruled
Japan as Shoguns for the next 250 years, a period remarkable
for its peace and prosperity. This course examines the
foundations of Tokugawa Japan and what grew upon them in the
first century of Tokugawa rule. We will begin with mid-
sixteenth-century warfare, discuss the institutional and
economic basis of the Shogunate, and continue through to the
early 1700s, with the unanticipated (and somewhat frowned
upon) flourishing of an urban culture.

The course has three parts. In the first we will
concentrate on the rulers and their ways of ruling,
especially the transformation of samurai from professional
warriors into professional bureaucrats. In the second we
will read more by and about the sophisticated townspeople--
their stories, plays and haiku poetry. We'll conclude with
an examination of Zen, which touches on both haiku and the
samurai ethic.

Once the semester is underway, I will generally lecture
on Tuesday, and we will break for section meetings on
Thursday. Reading assignments should be completed by the
class meeting under which they are listed. There will be a
mid-term exam (Tuesday, 7 February), a short paper of five
pages (due Thursday, 16 March), and a final paper of ten
pages, due the day that the final exam is scheduled to
occur. There will be no final exam. In addition we will
have frequent short exercizes, either assigned one-page
papers or in-class quizzes. Some of these will be informal
and ungraded, some will be graded. Whether graded or not, a
missed exercize still counts as a zero. I'll ignore one or
possibly two such zeros, but if you get three it will lower
your grade a full degree, e.g. from HH to H, or from P to F.
An excused absence is of course acceptable; in such case
there is no need to make up the exercize. The final grade
will be calculated as follows: mid-term exam and short
paper, 15% each; final paper, 20%; quizzes and one-page
papers, 20%; class participation, 20%. (I know that only
adds up to 90%.)

My office is in the new Asian Studies/Religion building
at 38 College Street, next to Kappa Sig. Office hours are
Monday 11:00 to 12:00, Wednesday 10:00 to 11:00, and Friday
9:00 to 10:00, and by appointment. My office phone is
-3524.

The following books should be available for purchase in
the Bookstore:
Basho, The Narrow Road to the Deep North
Donald Keene, tr., Chushingura
Noel Perrin, Giving Up the Gun
Thomas Smith, Agrarian Origins of Modern Japan
John Stevens, The Sword of No Sword
Suzuki, Zen Mind, Beginner's Mind
Wetering, The Empty Mirror

As well, a Sourcebook of readings will be handed out in
class.

ASSIGNMENTS
PART 1: SAMURAI AND FARMERS

Thursday, 19 January
Introduction

Tuesday, 24 January
Japan before the Tokugawa
    Readings:
        1. From the Sourcebook: Edwin Reischauer, Japan,
        Story of a Nation, pp. 74-105. Read this with some care.
        2. Sourcebook: Tsunoda and deBary, Sources of Japanese
        Tradition, Volume I, 302-334.
        2. Reischauer and Fairbank, East Asia, Tradition and
        Transformation, 392-418. (On reserve.)

Thursday, 26 January
Tokugawa Japan (1)
    Readings:
        George Sansom, Japan, A Short Cultural History, 404-497.
        (On reserve--read with greater speed, but not hastily,
        to catch the development of these first 100 years.)

Tuesday, 31 January
Tokugawa Japan (2)
    Readings:
        1. Sourcebook: Michael Cooper, They Came to Japan, 3-7,
        53-65, 151-159.
        2. Reischauer and Fairbank, East Asia, Tradition and
        Transformation, 418-434. (on reserve)
        3. Sourcebook: Peter Duus, Feudalism in Japan, 81-104.

Thursday, 2 February
Christianity in Japan
    Readings:
        1. From the Sourcebook: Peter Duus, The Rise of Modern
        Japan, "Traditional Attitudes," 9-24
        2. Sourcebook: David John Lu, Sources of Japanese History,
        Vol I, 199-204

Tuesday, 7 February
        Mid-term exam

Thursday, 9 February
Conferences
    Readings:
        Noel Perrin, Giving Up the Gun (all)

Tuesday, 14 February
"Farm Song"

Thursday, 16 February
Conferences
    Readings:
        1. Sourcebook: David John Lu, Sources of Japanese History,
        204-210
        2. Thomas Smith, The Agrarian Origins of Modern Japan (all)

Tuesday, 21 February
The samurai, revisited.
    Readings:
        1. Hagakure, 1-80 (on reserve)
        2. Musui's Story, 43-65 & 119-146 (in your Sourcebook)

Thursday, 23 February
NO CONFERENCES TODAY
"Seppuku/Harakiri"
        Note: This is a two-hour feature film, and it will extend
        past the end of class time. If possible, please try to stay
        for the end--there's a great fight scene as your reward.

Tuesday, 28 February
Japanese Social Structure
    Readings:
        Ruth Benedict, The Chrysanthemum & The Sword, 98-144
        (on reserve)

Thursday, 2 March
Conferences

PART 2: MERCHANTS AND ARTISANS

Tuesday, 7 March
Genroku style

Thursday, 9 March
Conferences
    Readings:
        Keene, tr., Chushingura (all)

Tuesday, 14 March
The commercial revolution
     Readings:
          1. David John Lu, Sources of Japanese History, 210-215
          (Sourcebook)
          2. Saikaku, The Life of an Amorous Woman, 55-99, 211-232
          (on reserve)

Thursday, 16 March
Conferences
Papers due today

PART 3:   ZEN BUDDHISM
Tuesday, 4 April   NOTE: This class meets in Kresge!!
What is Zen?
     Reading:
          Wetering, The Empty Mirror, all

Thursday, 6 April
Conferences

Tuesday, 11 April
Zen and Japanese Culture
     Readings:
          Suzuki, Zen Mind, Beginner's Mind (all)

Thursday, 13 April
Conferences

Tuesday, 18 April
Basho and Haiku
     Readings:
          Basho, The Narrow Road to the Deep North, especially
          pages 97-143

Thursday, 20 April
Conferences

Tuesday, 25 April
Warriorship
     Readings:
          John Stevens, The Sword of No Sword (all)

Thursday, 27 April
Conferences

Tuesday, 2 May
The Tokugawa in review

Thursday, 4 May
NO CONFERENCES-regular class meeting

AGE OF THE SAMURAI
History 162, Spring, 1990
Jim Huffman, Professor
Wittenberg University

JAPANESE SOCIETY always has defied easy explanation. It resembles the cultures of mainland Asia yet refuses to follow many Asian stereotypes. Several of its governmental systems have followed those of Europe but others remain worlds apart. No era presents these baffling contradictions more graphically than that of the samurai in Japan's Middle Ages. The brash, ruling warriors seem almost like coarse, violent cowboys in some tellings; yet they also wear delicate makeup and enjoy the gentle art of serving tea. The institutional structures are as feudal as those of medieval Europe; yet the ruling class is more bookish and less chivalrous. Who are these medieval Japanese?

We may never fully comprehend the seeming paradoxes, but neither will we ever understand contemporary Japan if we do not begin with the samurai. And we will make a start at that effort this term. Specifically, we will attempt to:

1. Learn the broad factual patterns of Japanese history from 1100 to 1868.

2. Understand the nature of samurai life and culture.

3. Gain an appreciation of the positive value of cultural differences.

4. Sharpen our skills: analysis, writing, communication.

5. Enjoy ourselves!

The Instructor The course is taught by Jim Huffman, whose office is 122 Leamer. His office hours are:

Monday	9:00 to 12:00	4:00 to 5:00
Tuesday	10:15 to 11:45	
Wednesday	11:00 to 12:00	4:00 to 5:00
Thursday	by appointment	
Friday	12:00 to 1:00	

Feel free to stop in or call about matters of any kind. His phone numbers are 327-7846 (office) and 399-9728 (home). It would be appreciated if calls were made before 9:00 p.m.

Requirements. During the next ten weeks, you will be expected to complete the following.

1. Attendance and discussion, both of which are essential if we are to develop a sense of community in the class. Each unexcused absence, beyond two misses of any kind, will result in a three-point deduction.

2. Two tests.

3. Four "term" quizzes.

4. All readings, by the assigned dates.

5. Participation in a group project. Each group will present an assigned topic to the entire class. The presentation will be graded on: a) quality and organization of information, b) cohesiveness and c) liveliness and success in stimulating interest. Grades will assigned to both the entire project and the individual components, with the relative

121

balance determined by the nature of the project.

Topics of presentations will be:

  Life of Yoshitsune (Morris, 5)

  Life of Kusunoki (Morris, 6)

  Bushido and Revenge (Statler, 10)

  Debate on Religion (Endo, entire book)

  Life of the Tokugawa Underside (Statler, 5, 9, 12; Morris, 7, 8)

  Tokugawa Merchant Life (Statler, 1-3, 8)

  Arts and Pleasure in Tokugawa (Statler, 7, 11)

  Life of Saigo (Morris, 9)

Types of possible presentations include (but are not limited to) plays/skits, slide and/or tape presentations, individual reports (the least preferred), videotape presentations, bazaars, "day in the life" skits, etc. Be as creative as you can be!

6. Four one-page papers on the topics of four group presentations. You may choose the presentations, but you must include at least one paper on each of the three books.

Grading. Grading normally be on a basis of 90-100, A; 80-89, B; 70-79, C; 60-69, D; under 60, F (though adjustments may be made on the basis of overall class performance). Points also may be added or substracted in the "credit" areas for exceptional performances.

    Attendance-discussion. . . . . credit

    One-page papers . . . . 40 (10 each)

    Midterm 100

    Final 100

    Quizzes. . . . . 40 (10 each)

    Group Project. 120

    NOTES. 1. Students should be aware of the Wittenberg policy on academic honesty; violations (including cheating and plagiarism) will result in severe penalties.

    2. Deadlines are absolute. Late work will be assessed a five-percent penalty the first day and an additional percent each day thereafter. No papers will be accepted after the final exam.

    3. No makeup tests or quizzes will be given; if the student has an excused absence, her/his term grade simply will be based on the remainder of the course work.

Required Readings. Students will be expected to read the following.

  Endo Shusaku. The Samurai. Aventura, 1984.

  Morris, Ivan. The Nobility of Failure. New American Library, 1975.

Sansom, George. *Japan, A Short Cultural History*. Stanford, 1952.

Statler, Oliver. *Japanese Inc*. Hawaii, 1982.

Tentative Class Schedule.

Week 1. Before the Warriors (to 1100)

3-26

M.	Introduction	Sansom, 178-87, 260-73
W.	Classical Japan	Morris, 1-3
F.	Warriors in the Provinces	Morris, 4; choose proj.

Week 2. Emergence of the Warriors (1100-1185)

4-2

M.	Taira Victory	Sansom, XIV
M.	3:45, East Asia Colloquium	
W.	"World of Heike," AV I	
Th.	History Colloquium, 3:30	
F.	no class	

Week 3. Kamakura: Rough and Ready Warriors (1185-1333)

4-9

M.	Establishing the Bakufu	Sansom, XV, XVI; quiz
W.	Group: Yoshitsune	Morris, 5
F.	The Minamoto Years	

Week 4. Ashikaga: The Elegant Warriors (1333-1477)

4-16

M.	Minamoto Culture	Sansom, XVII, XVIII
W.	Triumph of the Ashikaga	Morris, 6
F.	Group: Kusunoki	

Week 5. Feudal Years (1477-1560)

4-23

M.	A Feudal Era	Sansom, XIX; quiz
M.	7:15, review (109 Synod)	
W.	Midterm test	
Th.	3:30, History Colloquium	
F.	Zen and the Arts	Morris, 7

Week 6. Reunification (1560-1600)

4-30

M.	Feudal Literature	Sansom, XX
W.	6:00, "Seven Samurai," AV II	(3 1/2 hours!)
F.	Reunification	Statler, 1-8

Week 7.   The Tokugawa Take Control (1600-1640)

5-7

M.	Establishing a System	Sansom, XXI
W.	Group: Bushido and Revenge	quiz
F.	Group: Debate on religion	Endo (all)

Week 8.   The Tokugawa in Power (1650-1868)

5-14

M.	Group: Tokugawa Underside	Morris, 8
M.	3:45, EA Colloquium	
W.	The Tokugawa Administrative Style	
F.	Group: Tokugawa Merchants	Statler, 9-13

Week 9.   Life Under the Tokugawa (1650-1868)

5-21

M.	Group: Tokugawa Arts, Pleasure	Sansom, XXII, XXIII
W.	Daily Life in Tokugawa	
F.	Group: Saigo Takamori	Morris, 9

Week 10.   The Modern Residue (1868-1990)

5-28

M.	7:15, "Rickshaw Man," AV II	Morris, 10
W.	The Samurai Legacy	
F.	Review	quiz

AGE OF THE SAMURAI: SOME HELPFUL BOOKS

Ackroyd, Joyce, trans. Told Round a Brushwood Fire, the Autobiography of Arai Hakuseki. Princeton, 1979.

Anesaki Masaharu. History of Japanese Religion. Tuttle, 1963.

Arnesen, Peter. The Medieval Japanese Daimyo. Yale, 1979.

Basho. The Narrow Road to the Deep North and Other Travel Sketches. Penguin, 1966.

Bellah, Robert. Tokugawa Religion—Values of Preindustrial Japan. Free Press, 1957.

Berry, Mary Elizabeth. Hideyoshi. Harvard, 1982.

Blecher, Richard. The Needle Watcher—The Will Adams Story. Tuttle, 1973.

Bolitho, Harold. Treasures Among Men—The Fudai Daimyo in Tokugawa Japan. Yale, 1974.

Borgen, Robert. Sugawara no Michizane and the Early Heian Court. Harvard, 1986.

Borton, Hugh. Peasant Uprisings in Japan of the Tokugawa Period. Paragon Reprint, 1968.

Boxer, C.R. The Christian Century in Japan. California, 1967.

Clavell, James. Shogun. Dell, 1975.

Cooper, Michael. They Came to Japan—An Anthology of European Reports on Japan, 1543-1640. California, 1965.

_____, ed. This Island of Japon—Joao Rodrigues' Account of 16th-Century Japan. Kodansha, 1973.

Dore, Ronald. Education in Tokugawa Japan. California, 1965.

Dunn, C.J. Everyday Life in Traditional Japan. Putnam, 1969.

Duus, Peter. Feudalism in Japan. Random House, 1969.

Earhart, Byron H. Japanese Religion—Unity and Diversity. Dickenson, 1974.

Elison, George. Deus Destroyed. The Image of Christianity in Early Modern Japan. Harvard, 1973.

_____ and Bardwell Smith, eds. Warlords, Artists and Commoners—Japan in the Sixteenth Century. Hawaii, 1981.

Endo Shusaku. Silence. Tuttle, 1969.

_____. The Samurai. Harper and Row, 1982.

Frederic, Louis. Daily Life in Japan in the Time of the Samurai. Tuttle, 1972.

Grossberg, Kenneth. Japan's Renaissance—The Politics of the Muromachi Bakufu. Harvard, 1981.

Hall, John W. Government and Local Power in Japan, 500-1700. Princeton, 1966.

_____. Japan from Prehistory to Modern Times. Delta, 1971.

_____ and Marius Jansen, eds. Studies in the Institutional History of Early Modern Japan. Princeton, 1968.

Hall, John W., Nagahara Keiji and Kozo Yamamura, eds. Japan Before Tokugawa. Political Consolidation and Economic Growth, 1500-1650. Princeton, 1981.

Hauser, William. Economic Institutional Change in Tokugawa Japan. Cambridge, 1974.

Hane, Mikiso. Japan—A Historical Survey. Scribners, 1972.

Henderson, Harold. An Introduction to Haiku. Doubleday, 1958.

Hibbett, Howard. The Floating World in Japanese Fiction. Grove, 1960.

Hurst, G. Cameron. Insei: Abdicated Sovereigns in the Politics of Late Heian Japan, 1086-1185. Columbia, 1976.

Ihara Saikaku. Tales of Japanese Justice. Hawaii, 1980.

_____. Tales of Samurai Honor. Sophia, 1981.

Ikku Jippensha. Shank's Mare. Tuttle, 1960.

Jansen, Marius. Japan and Its World. Princeton, 1981.

Kato Shuichi. A History of Japanese Literature, The First Thousand Years. Kodansha, 1979.

Keene, Donald. Anthology of Japanese Literature, From the Earliest Era to the Mid-Nineteenth Century. Grove, 1960.

125

_____. Chushingura (The Treasury of Loyal Retainers). Columbia, 1971.

_____. Japanese Literature. An Introduction for Western Readers. Grove, 1955.

_____. The Japanese Discovery of Europe. Kegan Paul, 1952.

_____. World Within Walls—Japanese Literature of the Premodern Era, 1600–1867. Holt, Rinehart and Winston, 1976.

Lach, Donald. Japan in the Eyes of Europe—the Sixteenth Century. Chicago, 1965.

Maruyama Masao. Studies in the Intellectual History of Tokugawa Japan. University of Tokyo, 1975.

Mass, Jeffrey. Warrior Government in Early Medieval Japan—A Study of the Kamakura Bakufu, Shugo and Jito. Yale, 1974.

_____ and William B. Hauser, eds. The Bakufu in Japanese History. Stanford, 1985.

Matsumoto Shigeru. Motoori Norinaga, 1730–1801. Harvard, 1970.

Morris, Ivan. The Nobility of Failure. Holt, Rinehart and Winston, 1975.

Musashi Miyamoto. A Book of Five Rings. Overlook Press, 1982.

Najita Tetsuo. Japan. University of Chicago, 1974.

Nitobe Inazo. Bushido, the Warrior Code. Ohara, 1969.

Okakura Kakuzo. The Book of Tea. Tuttle, 1956.

Ooms, Herman. Tokugawa Ideology: Early Constructs, 1570–1680. Princeton, 1985.

Perrin, Noel. Giving Up the Gun, Japan's Reversion to the Sword, 1543–1879. Godline, 1979.

Plummer, Katherine. The Shogun's Reluctant Ambassadors—Sea Drifters. Lotus, 1984.

Reischauer, Edwin. Japan, the Story of a Nation. Knopf, 1974.

Rodd, Laurel. Nichiren—Selected Writings. Hawaii, 1980.

Sadler, A. L. The Maker of Modern Japan—Life of Tokugawa Ieyasu. Tuttle, 1978.

_____, trans. Ten Foot Square Hut and Tales of Heike. Tuttle, 1972.

Sansom, George. Japan—A Short Cultural History. Stanford, 1952.

_____. A History of Japan. (3 vols.) Stanford, 1963.

Saunders, E. Dale. Buddhism in Japan. Tuttle, 1964.

Sheldon, Charles. The Rise of the Merchant Class in Tokugawa Japan, 1600–1868, an Introductory Survey. Association for Asian Studies, 1958.

Shinoda Minoru. The Founding of the Kamakura Shogunate. Columbia, 1960.

Smith, Bardwell, ed. Unsui—A Diary of Zen Monastic Life. Hawaii, 1973.

Smith, Henry. Learning from Shogun. California—Asian Studies, 1980.

Statler, Oliver. Japanese Inn. Hawaii, 1982.

Storry, Richard. The Way of the Samurai. Orbis, London, 1978.

Sugimoto Masayoshi and David L. Swain, eds. Science and Culture in Traditional Japan, A.D. 600–1854, MIT, 1978.

Suzuki Daisetz. Zen and Japanese Culture. Princeton, 1970.

Totman, Conrad. Politics in the Tokugawa Bakufu. Harvard, 1967.

_____. Japan Before Perry. California, 1981.

Tsunoda Ryusaku, et al., eds. Sources of Japanese Tradition. (2 vols.) Columbia, 1958.

Turnbull, S. R. The Samurai—A Military History. MacMillan, 1977.

Van Zandt, Howard F. Pioneer American Merchants in Japan. Lotus, 1980.

Varley, H. Paul. Japanese Culture—A Short History. Praeger, 1973.

_____. The Onin War. Columbia, 1967.

_____. The Samurai. Weidenfeld and Nicolson, 1970.

Webb, Herschel. Japanese Imperial Institution in the Tokugawa Period. Columbia, 1968.

Yamamoto Tsunetomo. Hagakure—the Book of the Samurai. Kodansha, 1979.

Yoshida Kenko. Essays in Idleness. Columbia.

Yoshikawa Eiji. The Heike Story. Tuttle, 1972.

History 385   Modern Japan

TT 1:40-2:55   Brock 403
Richard Rice   Phone: 755-5303   Office Hours: M 9-12; W 9-3
                                      Honors Program, Guerry Hall
     University of Tennessee at Chattanooga
Course Description:

A survey of modern Japan since the Tokugawa period. Historical readings will
be supplemented by modern literature. Major topics will be traditional
society, the Meiji Restoration and modernization, economic development, militarism and empire, World War II, the Occupation, postwar growth and social
change, Japanese society and culture, Japan's role in the world. Special
attention will be paid to Japanese history where it has influenced the rise of
nationalism in other parts of Asia.

Readings:

Tasker, The Japanese
Gordon, The Evolution of Labor Relations in Japan
Frost, For Richer, For Poorer
Kornicki (with Spry-Leverton), Japan

Schedule: Readings

                    Traditional Japan

Aug 28 Introduction and Geography   Tasker, Prologue &
                                                Epilogue, 1

     30 Aristocratic and Warrior Japan   Tasker, 2; Kornicki,
                                                pp.59-63

Sept 4 Tokugawa Unification: Kornicki, 1
        The Samurai-Merchant Balance

     6 The Rural and Urban Economy of Tokugawa Japan   Kornicki, 2

    11 Chonin Culture and Literature of the
        Floating World

                    Meiji Japan

    13 The Meiji Restoration: Gordon, Intro & 1
        Political and Cultural Change

    18 Economic Development and Imperialism: Gordon, 2
        Japan as Role Model

    20 Video: Japan Enters the Modern World

    25 Emerging Japan in the early Twentieth Century   Gordon, 3

    27 Exam I: Transformation of Traditional Japan

                         128

Japan in the Early Twentieth Century

Oct 2 Taisho Culture

      4 Emergence of the Labor Movement   Gordon, 4

      9 Japan and the World Economic Crisis   Gordon, 5

   11 The 1930s: Militarism, Mobilization,   Gordon, 6
          and the China War

   16 Video: Road to the Pacific War   Kornicki, pp.68-85

   18 The Pacific War: Gordon, 7
          A Strategic and Economic Analysis

   23 Japanese Society in Wartime   Gordon, 8

   25 Video: Hellfire, and discussion of the nuclear age.

   30 The Occupation and Transwar Analysis

Nov 1 Exam II: Modernization and Militarism

Postwar Japan

    6 Postwar Economic Growth: Flexible Rigidity   Tasker, 3; Gordon 9

    8 Society, Education and Gender in Modern Japan   Tasker, 4; Frost, 4

   13 The Political System and Citizen Politics   Tasker, 6-7; Frost 6

   15 Video: Japan Reaches for the 20th Century   Frost, 2; Kornicki 5

   20 Leadership and Business in Japan   Tasker,8; Gordon 10
                                              Frost, 5
   27 Contemporary Culture and Literature   Tasker 5, Kornicki 6

   29 Technology, Trade, and Business Practices   Tasker 9, Frost 3;
                                             Kornicki, 4

Dec 4 The Nichi-bei Economy   Tasker, 10; Frost 1

    6 The Future of U.S.-Japan Relations   Frost,7 & Conclusion
                                             Kornicki, 7

13 Exam III: Postwar Japan (2:00-4:00)

Method of Evaluation:

Exam I	Transformation of Japan	100
Exam II	Modernization and Militarism	100
Exam III	Postwar Japan	100
5-6 Page Topical Paper		100
Total		400

HISTORY OF MODERN JAPAN SINCE 1800

Significant Dates:
Feb.14, First Hour Examination
Mar.27 Second Hour Examination
Apr.10 Term Paper
May.4   Final Examination

REQUIRED BOOKS:

Mikiso Hane, Modern Japan: A Historical Survey. Westview
    Press, 1936
Soskei Natsume, Kokoro, trans. by Edwin B. McClellan.
    Regnery: Gateway, 1957
Peter B. Wiley, Yankees in the Land of The Gods. Penguin,
    1991
Yasunari Kawabata, Snow Country, trans. by Edward B.
    Seidensticker. Putnam: Perigree. 1981
Gail Bernstein, ed., Recreating Japanese Women, 1600-1945
    University of California Press. 1991
Chalmers Johnson, MITI and the Japanese Miracle. Stanford
    University Press. 1982

SCHEDULE OF LECTURES AND DISCUSSION:

FIRST WEEK

January 13   Introduction: The Fiftieth Anniversary of Pearl
             Harbor
        15   The Rise of Imperial Loyalism
             Hane. Introduction: Ch.3 (The Late Tokugawa
             Period)
             Recommended (for those who wish to read more
             deeply): Marius B. Jansen, The Nineteenth
             Century: Cambridge History of Japan, Vol.V. 1989
        17   The End of Seclusion
             Hane, Ch.4 (The Fall of the Tokugawa Bakufu)
             Recommended: Conrad Totman, The Collapse of the
             Tokugawa Bakufu, 1862-1868. 1980

SECOND WEEK
        20   The Coming of the Meiji Restoration

Hane, 5 (The Meiji Restoration: the New
Order)
Recommended: E. Herbert Norman, Japan's Emergence
as a Modern State. 1940.
22 The Abolition of Feudalism, 1868-1871
Recommended: William G. Beasley, The Meiji
Restoration. 1972.
24 Dissolution of the Samurai Class
Recommended: August H. Mounsey, The Satsuma
Rebellion. 1879.

THIRD WEEK
January 27 The Iwakura Embassy in America and Europe,
1871-1873
Hane, 6 (The Continuing Meiji Revolution:
Political Developments)
Recommended: IROKAWA Daikichi, The Culture of the
Meiji Period, ed. by Marius B. Jansen. 1985.
29 Meiji Economic Modernization
Hane, 7 (The Continuing Meiji Revolution:
Cultural, Economic, and Social Developments)
Recommended: Carol Gluck, Japan's Modern Myths.
1985.
31 CLASS DISCUSSION: The Individual and
Modernization in Literature. NATSUME Soseki,
Kokoro, tr. by Edwin B. McClellan. 1957. QUIZ.
Questions to be distributed later.

FOURTH WEEK
February 3 The Meiji Constitution of 1889
Hane, 8 (Political Developments in Later Meiji)
Recommended: George Akita, The Foundations of
Constitutional Government in Modern Japan. 1967.
5 The Genro and the Political Parties, 1890-1901
Recommended: R.H.P.Mason, Japan's First General
Election, 1890. 1969.
7 Labor and the Social Movement
Recommended: Mikiso Hane, Reflections on the Way
to the Gallows: Voices of Japanese Rebel Women.
1982.

FIFTH WEEK
February 10 The Europeanization of Japanese Painting in
the Meiji Era SLIDE LECTURE
Recommended: Shuji Takashina. Thomas Rimer,
Gerald D. Bolas, Paris in Japan: the Japanese
Encounter with European Painting. 1987.
12 Meiji Military Modernization and the Russo-
Japanese War
Hane, 9 (The Conclusion of the Meiji Era)
Recommended: Roger Hackett, Yamagata Aritomo and
the Rise of Modern Japan. 1971.
14 FIRST HOUR EXAMINATION

131

SIXTH WEEK
February 17 ʾThe Annexation of Korea, 1910
        Recommended: **Hilary Conroy**, The Japanese Seizure
of Korea. 1960.
        19 Transitional Politics, 1901-1918
        Hane, 10 (The Era of Parliamentary Ascendancy, I)
        Recommended: **Tetsuo Najita, Hara Kei and the**
Politics of Compromise. 1967.
        21 CLASS DISCUSSION: **The** Opening of Japan and
Problems of the Treaty-System
        Read Peter B. Wiley, Yankees in the Land of the
Gods. 1991. **Prepare for 10-minute quiz; questions**
for discussion to be distributed.

SEVENTH WEEK
February 24 Taisho Democracy, 1918-1932
        Hane, 11 (Era of Parliamentary Ascendancy, II)
        Recommended: **Peter Duus**, Party Rivalry and
Political Change in Taisho Japan. 1968.
        26 Ascendancy of the Zaibatsu, 1920s
        Recommended: **John G. Roberts**, Mitsui: Three
Centuries of Japanese Business. 1989 edition.
        28 Toward the Agrarian Crisis, 1930
        Recommended: **Penelope Francks**, Technology and
the Agricultural Development in Prewar Japan.
1984.

EIGHTH WEEK
March 2   Showa Militarism, 1932-1937
        Hane, 12 (The Ascendancy of Militarism)
        Recommended: **Ben-Ami Shillony**, Revolt in Japan.
1973.
        4   Emperor Orthodoxy and Japanese Education
        Recommended: **Helen Hardacre**, Shinto and the State
1868-1988. 1989.
        6   Western Music in Prewar Japan: the Example of
Jazz
        Recommended: **William P. Malm**, "The Modern Music
of Meiji Japan," in D. Shiveley, ed., Tradition and
Modernization in Japanese Culture (1971), 257-304.

NINTH WEEK
March 16 The China Quagmire, 1931-1945
        Hane, 13 (The Road to War)
        Recommended: **Oka Yoshitake**, Konoe Fumimaro.
1983.
        18 The Modern Japanese Novel
        Recommended: **Donald Keene**, Dawn to the West:
Japanese Literature in the Modern Era, Fiction.
1984.
        Tanizaki Junichiro. The Makioka Sisters, tr. by
Edward Seidensticker. 1957.
        20 CLASS DISCUSSION: Cultural Traditionalism in
the Age of Showa Militarism

Read Kawabata Yasunari, <u>Snow Country</u>, tr. by
Edward Seidensticker. [1935-7], 1955. Prepare for
10-minute quiz; discussion questions to be
distributed.

TENTH WEEK
March 23 Pearl Harbor and the Pacific War, 1941-1945
          Hane, 14 (War and Defeat)
          Recommended: Gordon Prange, <u>At Dawn We Slept</u>.
          1983.
       25 War on the Home Front, 1941-5
          Recommended: Ienaga Saburo, <u>The Pacific War</u>.
          1979.
       27 SECOND HOUR EXAMINATION

ELEVENTH WEEK
March 30 The Tokyo War Crimes Trials, 1946-1948
          VIDEO: Excerpts from <u>The Tokyo Court</u>. Kodansha,
          1983.
          Recommended: Richard Minear, <u>Victor's Justice</u>.
          1971.
April 1 Yoshida Shigeru and the American Occupation,
         1945-1952
          Hane, 15 (The Postwar Years: Reform and
          Reconstruction)
          Recommended: Kazuo Kawai, <u>Japan's American
          Interlude</u>. 1960.
       3 CLASS DISCUSSION: The Status of Women in Modern
          Japan
          Read assigned articles in Gail Bernstein, ed.,
          <u>Recreating Japanese Women, 1600-1945</u>. 1991. Ten-
          minute quiz; discussion questions to be
          distributed.

TWELFTH WEEK
April 6 Land Reform in Postwar Japan
          Recommended: Ronald P. Dore, <u>Land Reform in Japan</u>.
          1959.
       8 Liberal-Democratic Party and Conservative
          Ascendancy, 1945-1960
          Recommended: Nathaniel B. Thayer, <u>How the
          Conservatives Rules Japan</u>. 1969.
      10 Progressive Intellectuals and the Socialist
          Opposition
          Recommended: Chalmers Johnson, <u>Conspiracy at
          Matsukawa</u>. 1971.
          TERM PAPER DUE: Ten-page essay in approved form;
          see separate instructions.

THIRTEENTH WEEK
April 13 Japanese-American Security Treaty, 1952-1992
          Recommended: George Packard, <u>Protest in Tokyo</u>.
          1964.
       15 Economic Miracle in the New Japan

Hane, 16 (Developments since 1970)
Recommended: Ezra T. Vogel, Japan as Number One.
1979.
17 CLASS DISCUSSION: Industrial Policy as a Source
of Japan's Economic Miracle
Read Chalmers Johnson, MITI and the Japanese
Miracle. 1982. Ten-minute quiz, discussion
questions to be distributed.

FOURTEENTH WEEK
April 20 Literature in the New Japan: Mishima Yukio
Reconsidered
Recommended: Mishima Yukio, The Temple of the
Golden Pavilion. 1968.
22 Environmental Movement in Recent Japan
Recommended: Frank K. Upham, Law and Social Change
in Postwar Japan. 1987.
24 Bureaucracy in Modern Japan
Recommended: Robert Spaulding, Imperial Japan's
Higher Civil Service Examinations. 1967.

FIFTEENTH WEEK
April 27. Contemporary Politics: Miyazawa Kiichi as Prime
Minister, 1991-   , His Policies
Recommended: Sato Seizaburo, Postwar Politician:
The Life of   Former Prime Minister, Ohira Masayishi.1990
29 The Coronation of the Heisei Emperor, 1991
Recommended: Edward Behr, Hirohito: Behind the
Myth. 1989.

May 4, 8:00-10:00 a.m. FINAL EXAMINATION

INFORMATION ABOUT THE COURSE:

1. Grades are assigned on the following basis: First Hour
Examination, 20%; Second Hour Examination, 20%;
Final Examination, 40%; Quizzes over Extra Books,
10%; Term Paper, 10%.
2. Bluebooks are needed for the examinations, so be sure
to bring them to class on the assigned days.
3. Numerical grades are assigned on the university scale:
90-100, A; 80-89, B; 70-79, C; 60-69, D; 0-59, F.
4. Class attendance is expected. If you cannot attend on
a regular basis, you should enroll in another
course.
5. All makeup examinations (for those who miss for
unavoidable reasons) will be given at 1:30 p.m., on
Friday, May 1, in Room 408, Dale Hall Tower. The
quizzes in connection with Class Discussions cannot
be made up.
6. Please feel free to come by my office during my office
hours, or at other arranged times.

HIS 344: MODERN JAPAN

Spring 1991   M. Barnhart
                                                        SUNY at StonyBrook

Nature of the course

This course traces the evolution of Japan from its emergence from Tokugawa feudalism to a modern, centralized and imperial state, that state's destruction and reconstitution at the hands of the Americans, and its subsequent economic "miracle."

The course will focus primarily on political and diplomatic events, since these were central to Japan's modern history and are closest to the instructor's interests. But it will trace the changing status of farm and country in Japan, the stunted development of organized labor, and the organization and function of Japan's system of education.

Course work

Assignments from the text of the course, Modern Japan, by Mikiso Hane, average forty pages per week. As well, there will be five discussion meetings in class roughly every other week. Each of these discussions will focus on a particular supplemental book as indicated in the course schedule below. Readings from these books, which are required, generally run to 200 pages each. The average reading load per week for the course therefore comes to about 130 pages.

In addition, each student must write three essays during the term. Each essay must not be longer than five pages. Each should be typed and in any event must be double spaced and written on only one side of each sheet of paper. Papers not meeting these criteria will be returned ungraded. Each essay will be written on a supplemental book. Questions on each book will be handed out in advance by the instructor. A student should write the essay to answer only one of those questions. Each student may select any three supplemental books to write essays on, except that at least one of the three must be handed in before the midterm examination. Essays are due--in class-- before discussion begins on the chosen supplemental book. No late essays will be accepted without a valid excuse cleared in advance of the due time by the instructor.

Evaluation

The three written essays together count for one half of your course grade. Accordingly, each essay itself counts as one-sixth of your overall grade. I evaluate written work in terms of three questions: How cogent, compelling, and consistent is the argument of the paper? How well have you employed evidence drawn from the reading to support your argument, and how extensively? And, how clear and correct is the prose of the essay?

The remaining half of your grade is determined by your performance on the midterm (one-sixth of your total grade) and final (one-third of your total grade) examinations. These two principally will be made up of questions requiring essay-type answers, although both may have other sorts of questions as well. In the event your final grade is "borderline," consideration will be given to the quality and degree of your participation in class discussion.

135.

Make-ups, Incompletes, Other Course Rules

It is possible to make-up a late essay only by having secured the instructor's permission in advance of the due time for that essay. An examination may be made-up only by giving the instructor appropriate and timely evidence of your inability to attend the exam at the proper time.

Incompletes will be given only in the very rarest of cases. They are not automatically given to students failing to submit the required course work. They must be requested by the student --in writing--no later than the commencement of the final exam, and preferably much before that time. They must be accompanied by an excuse the instructor finds valid and acceptable.

Please read the attached statement on plagiarism. Note that the first offense of plagiarism, even if unintentional, will result in a failing grade for the course. More severe penalties are possible as well.

At the instructor's discretion, any student failing to submit on time any component of the course's requirements may be given a grade of "F".

Office Hours

Hours will be announced at the first class sessions. They will also be posted on my office door, room N-321 in the (Ward Melville) Social & Behavioral Sciences Building. My office phone is 632-7508.

Course Schedule and Assignments:

I. THE RESTORATION (weeks 1-2)

    Text: Mikiso Hane, Modern Japan: A Historical Survey, chs. 3-4.
    Lectures:
        1. The Origins of the Meiji Restoration
        2. The Meiji Crisis
        3. Establishing the Meiji State
        DISCUSSION: Nakae Chōmin, A Discourse by Three Drunkards on
                    Government.

III. CONSOLIDATION & EXPANSION (weeks 3-4)

    Text: Hane, chs. 5-8.
    Lectures:
        1. First Paths to Empire
        2. The Agrarian Base
        3. Foundations of Industry & Labor
        4. The Best Education for the Best Men
        5. The Bureaucrats

IV. BECOMING AN EMPIRE (week 5)

Text: Hane, chs. 9-10.
Lectures:
1. First Adventures
2. War against Russia
3. First Crisis with America
4. The Taishō Crisis

V. BECOMING A DEMOCRACY (week 6)

Text: Hane, chs. 11-12.
Lectures:
1. The Concept of Taisho
2. Crushing Free Labor
3. The Eclipse of the Parties
4. The Rise of the Militarists
DISCUSSION: Michael Barnhart, <u>Japan Prepares for Total War</u>.

VI. THE VALLEY OF DARKNESS (weeks 7-8)

Text: Hane, chs. 13-14.
Lectures:
1. The Quest for Autonomy
2. The Fateful Decisions
3. "Victory Disease"
5. The Great Defeats
6. "Hell on Earth"
DISCUSSION: Thomas Havens, <u>Valley of Darkness</u>.

VII. FROM THE ASHES (weeks 9-10)

Text: Hane, ch. 15.
Lectures:
1. The New (Institutional) Arena
2. The American Interlude
3. Occupation: Politics & Society
4. The Peace Treaty: Limits on Sovereignty
5. A Hard New Life
DISCUSSION: Junichi Saga, <u>Memories of Silk and Straw</u> (Kodansha)
or Gail Bernstein, <u>Haruko's World: A Japanese Farm Woman and
Her Community</u> (Stanford, 1983).

VIII. THE MIRACLE & ITS CONSEQUENCES (weeks 11-12)

Text: Hane, ch. 16
Lectures:
1. MITI comes into its Own
2. Suburbs and Salarymen
3. The Conservative Equation
4. Nixon's Great Quake
5. The Conquest of the West
6. The Politics of Sclerosis
DISCUSSION: Mishima Yukio, <u>After the Banquet</u>.

Japan, say some, is an intoxicant. One who tastes a little of its culture often must taste more__and more. Others call it an enigma. The more they know about Japanese society, the less they really understand. Japan seems so simple yet so complex, so beautiful yet so ugly, so dynamic yet so traditional. And in trying to solve the enigma, they too become intoxicated.

This all may sound a bit too abstract to explain what will happen to most of us as we study Japan this term. But ten weeks of contact with the history ought, at the least, to whet our appetites, perhaps occasionally even to inebriate us a bit. We will attempt, in the time together, to survey the major political, cultural, economic, military and diplomatic events that have brought Japan from sheltered feudalism to international preeminence--all in just over a century. And we will spend more than a little time looking at the people who experienced and shaped those events.

THE INSTRUCTOR. The course is taught by Jim Huffman. When on campus, he resides at 122 Leamer and his office hours are:

Mon.   9:15 to 10:15

Tue.   9:15 to 10:15

Wed.   9:15 to 11:45

Fri.   9:15 to 12:45

Other times, by appointment

His phone numbers are 327-7846 (office) and 399-9728 (home). Please feel free to talk with him or call about matters of any kind--before 9:00 p.m.

CLASS GOALS. The goals of the course are to:

1. Learn the major "facts" and trends of Japan's modern history.

2. Face the question of interpretation in history.

3. Learn to think critically and express ideas clearly.

4. Enjoy the study of history.

REQUIREMENTS. The following are required.

1. Attendance and discussion. Unexcused absences, over two absences of any kind, will result in three points deduction per day.

2. A midterm and a final.

3. One map quiz and three term-identification quizzes.

4. Four current events sketches. For each, you are to list (briefly) the two or three most important news items about Japan you have read in the previous two weeks. The source of each item also should be included.

5. Participation in a discussion/debate. You will be assigned a topic, based on your indication of preferences, as well as an individual whose ideas you should represent. Your material should come from careful reading of the class's assigned works. It is strongly urged that each discussion/debate group plan its session carefully to assure a lively and complete approach to the issues. Groups also are urged to come in costume.

6. A five-page analysis of the differing coverage by the Japan Times and the New York Times of a specific historic event. You are to devote about three pages to a comparison/contrast of the two papers' coverage, then give at least two pages to what you learned from this study about the use of newspapers in understanding the past. To be considered for an A, the paper must inculcate outside research. Possible events include:

Hibiya riots (9-5-05)	Pearl Harbor (12-7-41)
Meiji's death (7-30-12)	Any WW II campaign
Rice riots (August, 1918)	Atom bomb (8-6, 9-45)
Tokyo earthquake (9-1-23)	Surrender (8-15-45)
Universal suffrage law (3-2-25)	New const. (5-3-47)
Manchurian Incident (9-18-31)	War trials (Nov., 1948)
2-26 Incident (2-26-36)	May Day riots (5-1-52)
London Naval Conf. (4-21-30)	Sec. Tr. crisis (5, 60)
	Yasuda battle (1, 69)

7. A five- to seven-page paper on "Japanese Women before World War II." Focusing on assigned readings, the paper should compare/contrast rural and urban women at that time. You should take a single theme (eg., economic roles, sexual attitudes, political philosophies and activities, family relationships, etc.), discuss similarities and differences between city and peasant women in this area, then analyze the reasons for, and meanings of, the differences. Outside research is strongly encouraged.

GRADING. Grades will be assigned according to the following scale.

```
Attendance-discussion. . . . . . . . . . . . . . . . . . . . . . . . . . . . . . . . . . . . . . . credit
Current events. . . . . . . . . . . . . . . . . . . . . . . . . . . . . . . . . . . . . . . . . . . . . . credit
Midterm . . . . . . . . . . . . . . . . . . . . . . . . . . . . . . . . . . . . . . . . . . . . . . . . . . 100
Final . . . . . . . . . . . . . . . . . . . . . . . . . . . . . . . . . . . . . . . . . . . . . . . . . . . . . 100
Quizzes. . . . . . . . . . . . . . . . . . . . . . . . . . . . . . . . . . . . . . . . . . . 40 (10 each)
Debate . . . . . . . . . . . . . . . . . . . . . . . . . . . . . . . . . . . . . . . . . . . . . . . . . . . . 40
Newspaper essay . . . . . . . . . . . . . . . . . . . . . . . . . . . . . . . . . . . . . . . . . . . . . 50
"Japanese women" . . . . . . . . . . . . . . . . . . . . . . . . . . . . . . . . . . . . . . . . . . . 70
```

1. Absences over two will result in an automatic deduction of three points per absence.

2. Deadlines are absolute. If a paper is a day late, its score will be reduced by five percent; each subsequent day will result in an additional one percent off. Papers will not be accepted after the final exam.

3. Dishonesty, including cheating and plagiarism, will be treated severely, according to the Wittenberg academic honesty policy.

4. There will be no makeups for tests or quizzes. In case of excused absences, that test's score simply will not be averaged into the final grade total.

5. Major papers are to be typed, in proper style, on white paper. Current events discussions may be handwritten (neatly).

REQUIRED READINGS. The following books are required.

Hane, Mikiso. Modern Japan: Historical Survey. Westview, 1986.

Hane, Mikiso. Reflections on the Way to the Gallows. Pantheon, 1988.

Ishimoto Shidzue. Facing Two Ways. Stanford, 1963

Smith, Robert, ed. The Women of Suye Mura. Chicago, 1982.

Pacific War Research Society. Japan's Longest Day. Kodansha, 1968.

SCHEDULE. The following schedule is tentative. Lecture topics are sure to be shifted and changed! Due dates, however, are solid, unless a change is announced.

WEEK ONE, Sept. 10.   TRADITIONAL JAPAN. (MJ, 1-64)

M.	Introduction	
W.	Modern Japan: Key Themes	
F.	Japan in 1850	map quiz; deb. topic

WEEK TWO, Sept. 17.   THE ORDER CHANGES. (MJ, 65-109)

M.	3:45. Colloquium: Carol Gluck	
M.	7:30. Special session: Carol Gluck	c.e.
W.	Attacks on the Old Order	
F.	Restoration and a New Regime	

WEEK THREE, Sept. 24.   A MODERNIZING REGIME. (MJ, 110-151)

M.	Creating New Structures	Smith
W.	The "People" and A Constitution	
F.	no class	

WEEK FOUR, Oct. 1.   THE SYSTEM MATURES. (MJ, 152-191)

M.	Movie: "Full Moon Lunch"	c.e.
M.	8:00, Japan-U.S. Symposium	
W.	Private Modernization	quiz
F.	No class; paper due	nwsp essay

WEEK FIVE, Oct. 8.   JAPAN TURNS OUTWARD.

M.	Costs of Modernization	
T.	3:45, Colloquium: David Keightley	
W.	Nationalism and Japan's First Wars	
F.	Review Session	quiz

WEEK SIX, Oct. 15.   AN EMERGING PUBLIC. (MJ, 192-244)

M.	Midterm Test	
W.	Moving Toward Democracy	c.e.
F.	Pluralism and a New Mood	Hane: G

WEEK SEVEN, Oct. 22.   AN IMPERIALISTIC TURN. (MJ, 245-309)

M.	Official Responses and 3 Crises	
M.	7:15, Movie: "Sandakan #8"	
W.	Debates: What's Wrong with the Government? What Are Socialist Men Like?	
F.	Deb: Proper Role of Japanese Women; How Should We Rear our Childen?	Ishimoto

WEEK EIGHT, Oct. 29.   THE PACIFIC WAR. (MJ, 310-340)

M.	The Dark Thirties	Paper due
W.	War in East Asia	
F.	Occupation and a New System	

WEEK NINE, Nov. 5.   WAR'S AFTERMATH. (MJ, 341-374)

M.	Deb: Should Japan Surrender (8-1-45)? Should the Bomb have been Dropped?	PWRS
W.	Japan Reasserts Itself	
F.	Guest: Charles Cook	

WEEK TEN, Nov. 12.   THE SUPERPOWER. (MJ, 375-404)

M.	Films, AV Theater I	c.e.
W.	To the Front of the World	quiz
F.	Review Discussion (optional)	

WEEK ELEVEN, Nov. 20.

W.	8:30, Final Exam

History H675
COLLOQUIUM IN EAST ASIAN HISTORY

Topic:

Conflicting Interpretations in Japanese History

G. M. Wilson, University of Indiana   M 3:35-5:30 p.m.
Spring 1991   Library E851

Interpretation is the true staple of historical writing; it is the one
thing sure to inhere in every historian's work. Since authorial views
differ and conflict, it follows that any history we read must rely on
interpretation just as much as it does on the record of historical facts.

So it is that whenever we read history, we are reading interpretation.
It is embedded in the story being told; it emanates from the source
materials being used. No matter how important "the facts" are, we dare not
approach the events that occurred in history without taking cognizance of
the mediating effect produced by the language and style of writing and by
the mode of presentation used by the historian who is finally the one
telling us about the past. In this course, therefore, we shall examine key
interpretive issues--chiefly conflicts--in Japanese history since 1600.

There are no exams or term papers in H675. The purpose of the course
is to help graduate students prepare for written and oral prelims in East
Asian history. To achieve this purpose, broad reading in secondary sources
and systematic discussion in class are indispensable. At Indiana we call
such a course a "colloquium." Generic labels in use elsewhere include
"conference course" (Harvard), "problems course" (Chicago), and "studies
course" (Michigan). Note that you are to buy five paperbacks; they are
marked with an asterisk (*). The other readings are on reserve in the UGL
under the rubric "Wilson H675."

Reviews in professional journals written by peers of the authors whom
you will read are valuable tools for decoding the interpretations expressed
in these books and articles. Students will also be responsible for
preparing four or five reviews of their own in the form of two-page double-
spaced introductions to the assigned readings; copies of these
introductions will be distributed to all members of the class on the dates
when the readings are to be discussed. Soon after the semester starts we
shall work out a schedule of assignments.

OFFICE HOURS: WR 2:30-3:30 in Memorial Hall West 201 (855-3765).

Weekly Topics and Readings

Monday:
January 7   INTRODUCTION

January 14   HISTORIOGRAPHY AND HISTORICAL INTERPRETATION (1)

R. G. Collingwood, *The Idea of History*, pp. 1-10, 113-133, 231-302.
Hayden White, *Tropics of Discourse*, chs. 1-3.
W. J. T. Mitchell, ed., *On Narrative*, arts. by Paul Ricoeur, Hayden
     White.
James Clifford & George E. Marcus, eds., *Writing Culture: The Poetics
     and Politics of Ethnography*, arts. by Vincent Crapanzano, George
     E. Marcus (on contemporary problems), Stephen A. Tyler, Paul
     Rabinow.

January 21   HISTORIOGRAPHY AND HISTORICAL INTERPRETATION (2)

Dominick LaCapra & Steven L. Kaplan, eds., *Modern European
     Intellectual History: Reappraisals and New Perspectives*, arts.
     by Roger Chartier, Dominick LaCapra, Martin Jay, Keith Baker.
John E. Toews, "Intellectual History after the Linguistic Turn: The
     Autonomy of Meaning and the Irreducibility of Experience,"
     American Historical Review 92: 879-907 (1987).
Roland Barthes, "Historical Discourse," in *Introduction to
     Structuralism*, ed. Michael Lane.

January 28   MODERNIZATION THEORY AND HISTORIOGRAPHY

Thomas S. Kuhn, *The Structure of Scientific Revolutions*, 2d ed., chs.
     1, 5, 9-10, 13, Postscript.
Cyril E. Black, *The Dynamics of Modernization*, chs. 1-2.
Marius B. Jansen, *Changing Japanese Attitudes Toward Modernization*,
     art. by John W. Hall.
*Robert Bellah, *Tokugawa Religion: The Cultural Roots of Modern
     Japan*, intro. & chs. 1-2 & 6-7.

February 4   BAKUFU AND DAIMYO

Conrad D. Totman, *Politics in the Tokugawa Bakufu*, intro. & chs. 8-10.
_____, *The Collapse of the Tokugawa Bakufu*, intro., chs. 6-7, 12-
     13, recap.
Harold Bolitho, *Treasures Among Men: The Fudai Daimyo in Tokugawa
     Japan*, intro. & chs. 5-6.
Kate Wildman Nakai, *Shogunal Politics: Arai Hakuseki and the Premises
     of Tokugawa Rule*, preface, chs. 1, 12, concl.
Review of Nakai by Harry Harootunian, *Journal of Japanese Studies* 16:
     156-160 (1990).

February 11   TOKUGAWA INSTITUTIONAL HISTORY

*John W. Hall & Marius B. Jansen, *Studies in the Institutional History of Early Modern Japan*, arts. by John W. Hall (daimyo, castle— town), Sydney Crawcour, Donald H. Shively, Thomas C. Smith (village, land tax), Harumi Befu, Ronald Dore.
Ronald P. Toby, *State and Diplomacy in Early Modern Japan*, chs. 1 & 6.

February 18   TOKUGAWA INTELLECTUAL HISTORY (1)

Maruyama Masao, *Studies in the Intellectual History of Tokugawa Japan*, intro. & pp. 189-273.
Harry Harootunian, *Toward Restoration*, preface, chs. 3-4, epilogue.
Tetsuo Najita & Irwin Scheiner, eds., *Japanese Thought in the Tokugawa Period*, arts. by Tetsuo Najita, Harry Harootunian.
*Tetsuo Najita, *Visions of Virtue in Tokugawa Japan*, prologue, chs. 2 & 6, epilogue.
Review of Najita-Scheiner by Harold Bolitho in *Monumenta Nipponica* 35: 89-98 (1980); plus Harootunian-Bolitho exchange of correspondence, ibid., pp. 368-374.
Review of Najita by Richard Rubinger, *MN* 43: 483-486 (1988).
Review of Najita by Richard Minear, *Harvard Journal of Asiatic Studies* 49: 259-266 (1989).

February 25   TOKUGAWA INTELLETUAL HISTORY (2)

Herman Ooms, *Tokugawa Ideology*, chs. 1, 3, 5, 8.
Peter Nosco, *Remembering Paradise: Nativism and Nostalgia in Eighteenth-Century Japan*, chs. 1-2 & 8.
H. D. Harootunian, *Things Seen and Unseen: Discourse and Ideology in Tokugawa Nativism*, prologue, ch. 1, epilogue.
Bob Tadashi Wakabayashi, *Anti-Foreignism and Western Learning in Early-Modern Japan: The New Theses of 1825*, prologue & ch. 4.
Review of Ooms by Sam Yamashita, *MN* 42: 495-498 (1987).
Review of Harootunian by Kate Nakai, *MN* 44: 224-228 (1989).
Review of Wakabayashi by Harry Harootunian, *JJS* 14: 159-169 (1988).

March 4   MEIJI RESTORATION HISTORIOGRAPHY (1)

E. Herbert Norman, *Japan's Emergence as a Modern State*, chs. 2-3, in *Origins of the Modern Japanese State*, ed. John W. Dower.
Albert M. Craig, *Choshu in the Meiji Restoration*, intro., chs. 1-3, 8.
Thomas M. Huber, *The Revolutionary Origins of Modern Japan*, chs. 1-2 & 9.
George Akita, "An Examination of E. H. Norman's Scholarship," *JJS* 3: 375-419.
Review of Thomas Huber by Craig in *JJS* 9: 139-149 (1983); plus Huber's reply, ibid., pp. 449-460.
Harold Bolitho, "Idealization and Restoration," *Harvard Journal of Asiatic Studies* 45: 667-684 (1985).

March 11   (Spring break)

March 18   MEIJI RESTORATION HISTORIOGRAPHY (2)

Tetsuo Najita & J. Victor Koschmann, eds., *Conflict in Modern Japanese History*, arts. by Tetsuo Najita, Stephen Vlastos, George M. Wilson.

M. William Steele, "Edo in 1868: The View from Below," *MN* 45: 127-155 (1990).

Harry Harootunian, "Late Tokugawa Culture and Thought," in *The Nineteenth Century, The Cambridge History of Japan* 5: 168-258 (1989).

F. G. Notehelfer, "Meiji in the Rear-View Mirror: Top Down vs. Bottom Up History," *MN* 45: 207-228 (1990).

Review of Najita-Koschmann by Nishida Yoshiaki in *JJS* 11: 200-206 (1985).

March 25   MEIJI POLITICAL AND ECONOMIC HISTORY

George Akita, *Foundations of Constitutional Government in Modern Japan*, intro., chs. 3 & 6, epilogue.

Roger W. Bowen, *Rebellion and Democracy in Meiji Japan*, intro., chs. 1, 5.

Irokawa Kaikichi, *The Culture of the Meiji Period*, intro., chs. 1, 8.

William W. Lockwood, ed., *The State and Economic Enterprise in Japan*, arts. by Ohkawa & Rosovsky, James Nakamura.

Henry Rosovsky, "Rumbles in the Rice Fields," *Journal of Asian Studies* 27: 347-360 (1967-68).

April 1   THE ROAD TO WAR?

Maruyama Masao, *Thought and Behaviour in Modern Japanese Politics*, chs. 2-4.

George M. Wilson, "A New Look at the Problem of 'Japanese Fascism,'" in *Reappraisals of Fascism*, ed. Henry A. Turner.

James B. Crowley, *Japan's Quest for Autonomy*, prologue, ch. 5, epilogue.

*Carol Gluck, *Japan's Modern Myths*, chs. 1, 4, 8-9.

Atsuko Hirai, "The State and Ideology in Meiji Japan" (review article on Gluck), *JAS* 46: 89-103 (1987).

April 8   INTERPRETING CONFLICT IN JAPANESE HISTORY

William W. Kelly, *Deference and Defiance in Nineteenth-Century Japan*, chs. 1-2, 5, 10-11.

Akira Iriye, *The Chinese and the Japanese*, arts. by Harry Harootunian, Lloyd Eastman, Hashikawa Bunzo.

George M. Wilson, "Plots and Motives in Japan's Meiji Restoration," *Comparative Studies in Society and History* 25: 407-427 (1983).

_____, "*Ee ja nai ka* on the Eve of the Meiji Restoration in Japan," *Semiotica* 70: 301-319 (1988).

April 15 & 22   NEW DEPARTURES IN 20TH-CENTURY JAPANESE HISTORY

Here are some significant new works in history and the social sciences
dealing with recent Japan. Discussions in class will center on the
Miyoshi-Harootunian postmodernism book and David Pollack's review of it.

Sheldon Garon, "Toward a History of Twentieth-Century Japan," *MN*, 45
    (1990), 339-352.
Joshua Fogel, *Politics and Sinology: The Case of Naito Konan*, chs. 4,
    6.
Sheldon Garon, *The State and Labor in Modern Japan*, intro., chs. 1-2,
    epilogue.
Andrew Gordon, *Labor and Imperial Democracy in Japan*, intro., concl.
Michael Lewis, *Rioters and Citizens: Mass Protest in Imperial Japan*,
    intro., ch. 1
Miriam Silverberg, *Changing Song: The Marxist Manifestos of Nakano
    Shigeharu*, intro., chs. 1, 3.
William D. Wray, ed., *Managing Industrial Enterprise: Cases from
    Japan's Prewar Experience*, arts. by Barbara Molony & Michael
    Cusumano.
*Mas ao Miyoshi & H. D. Harootunian, eds., *Postmodernism and Japan*,
    arts. by Tetsuo Najita, Marilyn Ivy, H. D. Harootunian, J. Victor
    Koschmann, Karatani Jokin, Akira Asada.
David Pollack, "Modernism Minceur, or Is Japan Postmodern?" *MN* 44: 75-
    97 (1989).

THE UNIVERSITY OF ARIZONA

ORIENTAL STUDIES/HISTORY 474C
HISTORY OF MODERN JAPAN

INSTRUCTIONS FOR COMPARATIVE BOOK REVIEW

Gail Bernstein

The purpose of this assignment is to demonstrate that history-writing involves the historian's interpretation of facts. Historians often disagree over their interpretation of a given subject. They may even disagree over what are the facts or which facts are important. As a critical, sceptical reader of history, you should always be aware of the subjective nature of the historian's craft.

In this assignment, you are requested to wend your way through one of a number of complicated subjects within the general field of Japan's modern history. After reading several works on any one subject, try to reach some kind of judgment about which interpretation, or combination of interpretations, is most valid. You need not confine your choice of topic to those listed below. However, please consult with me before beginning any topic which is not on this list.

In evaluating and comparing these differing interpretations, consider the following points:

1. First, establish the main argument or thesis or point of view of each author. In what ways do they differ?

2. Then consider reasons for the difference. You may want to take into account:

    - the year in which the publication first appeared
    - the background of the author (journalist? academic? military personnel? State Department?)
    - evidence used (Japanese materials? English-language materials only? Interviews? Impressions? Statistics?)
    - Do conclusions follow logically from the sources used?

3. Pay close attention to dates of publication. Historians study change over time, and to evaluate a writer's work, you must try to see him or her as part of his or her times. What were the major forces impinging on the author? An individual is part of society but also is part of a generation. Your particular society and your particular generation influence your entire life. For example, was it a time of scarcity or prosperity? Was there a wartime draft? Did the writer experience war or revolution? Did his parents? Did the writer go abroad or only read about foreign lands?

    An individual's life and views are also affected by the family's social class standing, and by education, sex role, and numerous other factors. These are especially important when comparing autobiographies.

4. Do not automatically assume that somebody who was present when a certain event occurred is more or less biased than the scholar who studies the event years later. You can say that different points of view or perspectives are involved.

147

WP:A2

HISTORICAL INTERPRETATION
TOPICS

I.   On the causes of the Pacific War

   A. Compare Feis, Herbert, The Road to Pearl Harbor, with
               Butow, Robert, Tojo and the Coming of the War, OR
               Schroeder, Paul, The Axis Alliance and Japanese-American Relations
                  with The Memoirs of Cordell Hull

   B. Compare any of the above-listed authors with

               Togo Shigenori, The Cause of Japan
               Shigemitsu Mamoru, Japan and Her Destiny
               Kase Toshikazu, Journey to the Missouri
               Ienaga Saburo, Pacific War, World War II, and the Japanese,
                  1931-1945
            See also Ike, Nobutake, Japan's Decision for War
               Crowley, James, Japan's Quest for Autonomy

II. On Pearl Harbor

     Baker, L. Roosevelt and Pearl Harbor (1970)
     Borg, D., and Okamoto, S., Pearl Harbor As History (1973)
     Beard, Charles, President Roosevelt and the Coming of the War
     Lord, Walter, Day of Infamy
     Churchill, Winston, Gathering Storm
     Kimmel, Husb., Admiral Kimmel's Story
     Farago, Ladislas, The Broken Seal
     Theobold, Robert, The Final Secret of Pearl Harbor
     Tonshill, Charles, Back Door to War
     Walter, Pearl Harbor, Roosevelt and the War
     Wohlstetter, Roberta, Pearl Harbor: Warning and Decision

III. On the American Occupation of Japan

     Textor, Robert B., Failure in Japan (1951)
     Willoughby, Charles A., and Chamberlain, John, MacArthur, 1941-1951: Victory
        in the Pacific
     Kawai, Kazuo, Japan's American Interlude

IV. Popular American Images of Japan

     Read several popular novels about Japan and compare these with Lafcadio
     Hearn's depiction of Japan in Kokoro (1896), Japan, an Interpretation (1904),
     or Glimpses of Unfamiliar Japan (1894).

     Examples of popular novels include James Michener, Sayonara (1953); Robert
     Payne, The Barbarian and the Geisha (1958); William Clavelle, Shogun (1975).

     Are there common themes linking these novels with Hearn's early interpre-
     tations of Japan? For example, how are Japanese women depicted? Which
     aspects of Japanese culture are emphasized?

WP:A2

V.   Zen Buddhism: Salvation or Sham?

     Compare Alan Watts, Psychotherapy, East, West OR
             Erich Fromm, Zen Buddhism and Psychoanalysis WITH
             Arthur Koestler, The Lotus and the Robot

VI.   Village Studies

     Compare the pre-World War II village of Suye described in John Embree, Suye Mura
     with post-World War II village of Kurusu, studied by Robert Smith. What changes
     occurred in the intervening years?

     Compare John Embree's Suye Mura with Ella Wiswell's The Women of Suye Mura. Or
     Compare Ella Wiswell's The Women of Suye Mura with Gail Bernstein's Haruko's
     World, a Japanese Farm Woman and Her Community.

VII. Views of Japan

     Compare Arthur Koestler's Lotus and the Robot WITH
             Nikos Kazantzakis, China, Japan
                   OR
             Richard Halloran, Japan: Images and Realities
                   OR
             Ichiro Kawasaki, Japan Unmasked

     Compare Ezra Vogel's Japan as Number One with Frank Gibney's Japan, the Fragile
     Superpower

VIII. Compare autobiographies of Meiji Samurai:

     Male: The Autobiography of Fukuzawa Yukichi   or compare either one of these
     Female: The Daughter of a Samurai   with Clara Whitney, Clara's
                                                          Diary, an American Girl in Meiji
IX.   Was the A-Bomb necessary?   Japan

     Baker, Leonard, The Atomic Bomb
     Butow, Japan's Decision to Surrender
     Freed, The Decision to Drop the Bomb   Hanson Baldwin, The Atomic Bomb (1968)
     Admiral Wm. Leahy, I Was There (1950)   Robert Batchelder, The Atomic Bomb (1968)
     Samuel E. Morison, The Atomic Bomb   Toshikazu Kase, Journey to the
     Gar Alperowitz, The Atomic Bomb (1968)   Missouri (1950)
                                                 Pacific War Research Society, The Day Man
                                                    Lost: Hiroshima, 6 August 1945

X.   Was the Pacific War a "Conspiracy" on the part of the Japanese Emperor?

     Bergamini, David, Japan's Imperial Conspiracy
     Mosley, Leonard, Hirohito, Emperor of Japan
     Crowley, James, Japan's Quest for Autonomy
         Hane, Mikiso, Emperor Hirohito and His Chief Aide-de-Camp: The Honjo Diary,
         1933-1936 (Read Part II)

Crowley, James, Review of Bergamini's Japan's Imperial Conspiracy, in New York
    Times Book Review Section, August 24, 1971
Coffy, Thomas, Imperial Tragedy

XI.   Bakumatsu Japan and the Americans

Compare Robert Payne's "Barbarian and the Geisha" WITH
        Townsend Harris' Journal and Statler's Shimoda Story or WITH
        Henry Heusken, Japan Journal 1855-61 (written by Harris' interpreter)

XII.   History textbooks

Compare Beasley's interpretation of modern Japanese history
(The Modern History of Japan) with William Neumann
(America Encounters Japan)

Compare Reischauer's presentation of modern Japanese history (Japan, Story of
a Nation) with Livingston (Imperial Japan reader) or Mikiso Hane, Peasants,
Rebels, and Outcastes

XIII. Marriages

Compare Fumiko Enchi's novel, The Waiting Years (set in the Meiji period) with
Junichiro Tanizaki's novel, Some Prefer Nettles (set in the period before the
Pacific War). Or compare either one with Anyoshi, Sawako, The River Ki, which
spans the modern period.

XIV.   The Tokyo War Crimes Trials
       Arnold C. Brackman, The Other Nuremberg
       Richard Minear, Victors' Justice
       Junji Kinoshita, Between God and Man: A Judgment on War Crimes
       Philip R. Piccigallo, The Japanese on Trial: Allied War Crimes Operations in the
          East, 1945-1951 (1979).
       Saburo Shiroyama, War Criminal, the Life and Death of Hirota Kōki
       Kazuko Tsurumi, Social Change and the Individual, chapters III and IV

Compare one of the above with one of the following studies of German war
criminals:

Albert Speer, Spandau, the Secret Diaries of Albert Speer (in Special Collections)
Matthias Schmidt, Albert Speer, the End of a Myth

XV.
       . Japan's Decision to Surrender

Robert Butow, Japan's Decision to Surrender
        Kase, Journey to the Missouri

XVI. Firsthand Accounts of the Pacific War

William Manchester,Goodbye Darkness (1979)   (marines in the South Pacific)
Kazuo Sakamaki, I Attacked Pearl Harbor (1949)
Richard Minear, tr. , The Yamato(about life on a Japanese submarine)
Ray C. Hunt and Bernard Norling, Behind Japanese Lines, An American Guerrilla in
   the Philippines (a first-person account, written by an airforce sergeant)

Paul R. Schratz, Submarine Commander, a Story of World War II and Korea
Frank E. Walton, Once They Were Eagles, the Men of the Black Sheep (Pilots in the
   South Pacific)

XVII Conflicting Views of Japanese Women

Takie Sugiyama Lebra, Japanese Women, Constraints and Fulfillment
Jane Condon, One Step Behind

OR

Alice Beard, Japanese Girls and Women (turn -of-the-century observations of
Japanese women by an American woman living and traveling in Japan)

Enchi, Fumiko, The Waiting Years (a novel set in the Meiji period--when
Alice Beard was in Japan--and written by a contemporary Japanese writer)

XVIII Two Views of Japan

G.C. Allen, Japan: The Hungry Ghost (1938)
Frank Gibney, Japan: The Fragile Superpower (1985:second revised edition.
Originally published in 1975)

XVIX Japanese Education

Ezra Vogel, Japan as Number One, ch. 7: "Basic Education: Quality and
Equality" OR Japanese Education Today (U.S. Department of Education
report)

and
Thomas Rohlen, The Japanese High School

or
Merry White, The Japanese Educational Challenge

XX On the Internment of Japanese Americans During World War II

Richard Drinnon, Keeper of Concentration Camps: Dillon S. Myer and
American Racism

and
Jeanne Wakatsuki Houston, Farewell to Manzanar (1973)

or
Michi Weglyn, Years of Infamy: The Untold Story of America's
Concentration Camps (1976)

XXI Two Views of Japanese FArm Women

Ella Wiswell and Robert Smith, Women of Suye Mura
Gail Lee Bernstein, Haruko's World

XXII Two Meiji Educators

The Autobiography of Fukuzawa Yukichi
F.G. Notehelfer, American Samurai: Captain L.L. Janese and Japan (1985)

OR
Edward R. Beauchamp, An AMerican Teacher in Early Meiji Japan(1976)

XXIII The Russo-Japanese War of 1904-5

   Aleksei Kuropatkin, The Russian Army and the Japanese War (1909)
   Ian Nish, The Origins of the Russo-Japanese War (1985)
   J.N. Westwood,Russia Against Japan: A New Look at the Russo - Japanese War

XXIV   Novels that Depict the End of an Era

   Natsume Soseki, Kokoro (1914: at the end of the Meiji period)
   Dazai Osamu, The Setting Sun(1947: immediately afterthe end of the Pacific
      War)   (The surnames are Soseki and Dazai respectively)

XXV   The Allied Occupation of Japan (see also Item Number Three above)

   John Curtis Perry, Beneath the Eagle's Wings: Americans in Occupied Japan (1980
   Theodore Cohen, Remaking Japan: The American Occupation as New Deal, edited
      by Herbert Passin (1987)

   John Toland, Occupation (1987): Note: This is a historical novel--fiction
      set in Japan at the time of the Occupation.

   D. Clayton James, The Years of MacArthur, volume 3: Triumph and Disaster,
      1945И64

   Michael Schaller, Douglas MacArthur

XXVI   More Images of Japan

   Lafcadio Hearn, Kokoro (1896)   This is a description of Japan written by
                                          an American who lived in Japan for many year:

   James Michener, Sayonara (1953)   This is a novel .

   James Clavelle, Shogun (1976)   This is a historical novel.

XXVII Documentary films on Japanese society andhistory also contain points of
   view which shape their material andinterpret itin various ways. You may
   choose to compare a film or video cassette presentationof a given topic with
   either another film or a book on the same subject. See, for example,
   "The Bomb" and compare it with one of the recommended readings. Or see
   "The Nation Family" (51 minutes, 1983) with "We Are Driven" (1984).
   Or see "Japan, Inc.: Lessons for North America "(1981) and "Faces of Japan:
   A Small Businessman " (video-cassette).

XXVIII Generals and Admirals

   D. Clayton James, The Years of MacArthur, Vol. 3: Triumph and Disaster, 1945-6·
   Michael Schaller, Douglas MacArthur
   Hiroyuki Agawa, The Reluctant Admiral: Yamamoto and the Imperial Navy

University of Tennessee at Chattanooga

SEMESTER AT SEA   FALL 1989

HISTORY 196   JAPANESE BUSINESS/ECONOMIC HISTORY   -RICHARD RICE

Course Description:
This course will trace the economic and business history of Japan to
show how the Japanese managed their way to prosperity. About half the
course will analyze important factors of modern Japanese management.
Many comparisons will be made with American practices and also European
to avoid a we-they dichotomy.

Course Objectives:
The objective of the course is to prepare students as future employees,
clients, and competitors with Japanese multi-national firms. Through
understanding of Japanese business and economics, we will gain a greater
understanding of the economic interdependence of the world and the role
Japan plays. While there are lessons here for America and Europe, there
are also cautions. The course is designed for those interested in
international business, but is not too technical for the liberal arts
student. Frequent reference will be made to Paul Kennedy's analysis of
Japan in his The Rise and Fall of the Great Powers.

Texts:
Allen. G.C. A Short Economic History of Modern Japan. St. Martin's
Press, 1981 or later edition. ISBN 0-312-71771-7. "A" in the schedule.

Abegglen, James and Stalk, George. Kaisha: The Japanese Corporation.
Basic Books, 1985. ISBN 0-465-03711-9.

Thurow, Lester (ed.). The Management Challenge: Japanese Views. The
MIT Press, 1985. ISBN 0-262-20053-8. "T" in the schedule.

Library Reserve (Five copies of each):
Thomas Smith, "The Growth of the Market"

Bryon Marshall, "The Meiji Business Elite and the Way of the Warrior"

Daniel Okimoto and Gary Saxonhouse, "Technology and the Future of the
                                     Economy"
"A Survey of the Yen Block," Economist (July 1989)

"A Survey of Japanese Finance," Economist (December 1988)

Class Schedule (Subject to change):

1. "Japan Reaches for the Twenty-First Century" and discussion.
   A II-6; T11
2. The Traditional Economy: Roots of Modern Success
   A1; Smith (Library Reserve)
3. Origins of Modern Business: Meiji Modernization
   A2-3
4. Meiji Entrepreneurs; Early Labor Practices
   A4-5; Marshall (Library Reserve)

153

5. War and Modernization: The Imperial Era and World War I—
   A6-7
6. Rise of Economic Nationalism and Government Planning
   A8-9
7. The Zaibatsu and Economic Mobilization: Business and Military in
   Conflict
   A9-11
8. Reports on company visits
9. The American Occupation Policies and Economic Recovery; Transwar
   Trends
   A II-1
10. Rise of the Postwar Corporation and the Economic "Miracle"
    A II-2; Abegglen 1
11. Midterm Exam
12. Education and Management Training
    T1; Abegglen 2
13. Corporate Structure: Management, Labor, Capital
    A II-4; T2&4; Abegglen 3-4
14. Industrial Relations in Historical Perspective
    T3
15. Production Planning and Control
    T6; Abegglen 5
16. Accounting and Finance: A Non-Technical Overview
    A II-3; Abegglen 6; A Survey of Japanese Finance (Library Reserve)
17. The Government Policy Debate: MITI
    A II-5; T9-10
18. Technology Management
    Abegglen 6; Okimoto & Saxonhouse (Library Reserve)
19. Japan in the World Market
    T7; Abegglen 7-9; A Survey of the Yen Block (Library Reserve)
20. Foreign Firms in Japan
    Abegglen 10-11
    Paper Due
21. Japanese Direct Investment Overseas: Promises and Problems
    Video: Japanese in Rutherford County, Tennessee
22. Final Examination

Method of Evaluation:		Points
In-country reports	13%	50
Mid-Term Examination	25%	100
Final Examination	37%	150
5-6 Page Topical Paper	25%	100

In addition, there will be in-class writing to monitor comprehension and
focus attention on the course material. These will not count as part of
the grade, but will help you prepare for the exam and test your own
progress. Attendance is mandatory in all courses; failure to observe
this requirement will be reflected in the grade.

Wittenberg University

History 400
JAPAN AND THE UNITED STATES—TURBULENT CENTURY
Autumn, 1991
Jim Huffman, Instructor

American students of Japan love to swap stories of cultural confrontation and challenge: the hostess who says yes when she means no, the calculating, ambitious prime minister who practices Zen meditation daily, the clerk who breaks down with giggles when she hears a foreigner say, "excuse me," in Japanese. And Japanese visitors to the United States boast similar (albeit reverse) collections of tales. No two nations in history have been closer politically than Japan and the United States; yet few have been more diverse culturally——or more competitive.

Culture seldom comes up directly in discussions of historical events or international relationships. Wars break out; treaties are signed; disasters occur; trade mushrooms or declines; analysts describe the "soaring tensions." And we go to great analytical lengths to account for all of them, constructing economic charts, looking at topography and geography, studying ideologies and political systems, scrutinizing leadership, educational systems and technological developments.

But what about CULTURE? Does it have an impact? Are the cooler, more abstract factors the only determinants of relationships? Or does the way people view reality, the way they interact, the way they express their sensitivities—in short, their culture—help to determine the nature of evolving relationships?

It is too important a question to be ignored; and the point of this class is to study it: to examine the historical relationships of these two, dynamic Pacific powers—in the light of culture. Put more concretely, our course goals will be:

1. To develop an understanding of key cultural characteristics of Japanese and American societies.

2. To analyze the impact of these cultural characteristics on several crucial binational episodes and developments—and to consider the broader question of what impact culture has on institutions.

3. To refine our communication skills: critical thinking, oral expression and writing.

4. To experience the joy and exhilaration of learning and thinking.

The Teacher. The study will be led by Jim Huffman, whose office is in Leamer 122. His office hours are:

Monday	9:15 to 11:15
Tuesday	9:15 to 10:30
Wednesday	9:15 to 11:15
Thursday	by appointment
Friday	9:15 to 12:00

Feel free to make appointments or call at other times (preferably, before 9:00 p.m.). His numbers are 327-7846 (office) and 399-9728 (home).

<u>Requirements</u>. To facilitate the learning experience, each person will be expected to meet the following requirements.

1. Attend regularly; 3 points will be deducted for each unexcused absence above one.

2. Participate actively in discussions. This is important both for the development of a sense of community and for the exchange of ideas. To not share orally is to deprive the rest of the class of what you have to offer, and EVERYONE has things to offer. It also is important to develop confidence in one's discussion skills. (40 points)

3. Lead a 40-minute discussion, in concert with another person. Attention should be paid to both content <u>and the stimulation of lively exchange</u>. Topics/sessions will be assigned during the first week. (30 points)

4. Read, understand and evaluate the following books. (Unannounced quizzes may occasionally be given over readings, to encourage keeping up-to-date.)

> Chie Nakane. <u>Japanese Society</u>. California, 1970.
>
> A biography of a Meiji-era figure.
>
> John Dower. <u>War Without Mercy</u>. Pantheon, 1986.
>
> John Okada. <u>No-No Boy</u>. Hawaii, 1975.
>
> Charles Neu. <u>The Troubled Encounter</u>. Krieger, 1975.

You also will be expected to read the following xeroxed essays and chapters:

> Robert N. Bellah, et al. "The Pursuit of Happiness."
>
> Daniel Okimoto. "The Intolerance of Success."
>
> Fox Butterfield. "Why They Excel."
>
> Benjamin Duke. "Lessons for the United States from Japan."
>
> George Packard. "The Coming U.S.-Japan Crisis."
>
> Karel G. van Wolferen. "The Japan Problem."
>
> Reischauer Center, <u>The United States and Japan in 1989</u>: "Security."
>
> James Fallows. "Is Japan the Enemy?"

5. Present (orally) the ideas of a book on a significant personality of the Meiji era. You are to indicate your top three choices by Friday of the first week. The presentation should be divided between summary (one-third) and discussion of the book's <u>ideas</u> (two-thirds). (50 points)

6. Write two, 7-page papers on the topics presented in the Class Schedule below. Each paper should explain and critique a major point made by one of the assigned authors, using others readings, class materials and your own ideas to support the critique. (150 points total)

7. Write a 10-page, culminating essay on the impact of culture on one aspect of the U.S.-Japan relationship. You should choose a sharply focused, contemporary issue (eg., rice imports, role of the Security Treaty, debate over textbooks, debate over the "coming war," fiftieth anniversary of Pearl Harbor), then show, through both class readings and outside research, the historical/cultural context that gives that issue its particular form today. (100 points) You also will summarize your findings in class. (10 points)

<u>Class Schedule</u>. The class normally will meet on Mondays, Wednesdays and Fridays and will focus, most often, on discussion of assigned readings.

WEEKS 1-2 (Sept. 9 to 20).   <u>Two Cultures</u>

M.	Introduction	
W.	The Idea of National Culture	Choose biog, disc
F.	no class	
M.	Japanese Cultural Traits	Nakane
W.	American Cultural Traits	Bellah
F.	Disc: Differences/Similarities	

WEEKS 3-4 (Sept. 23 to Oct. 4).   <u>Westerners in Japan</u>, NEU, 1-65

M.	Meiji Japan: Domestic Transformation (L)	
W.	Meiji Japan: Overseas Expansion (L)	
F.	Presentations	
M.	Presentations	
W.	Presentations	
F.	Disc: Culture and the Meiji Experience	PAPER: Culture and Meiji experience

WEEKS 5-7 (Oct. 7 to 25).   <u>At War With Each Other</u>, NEU, 66-196

M.	Taisho: A Shifting Relationship (L)	
W.	Early Showa: Estrangement	
F.	American Views of Japan (D)	Dower, 1-200
M.	Japanese Views of America (D)	Dower, 203-290
W.	Was It A Race War? (D)	Dower, 293-317
F.	The Japanese in America (L)	
M.	Understanding Ichiro: His Views, Reactions and Problems (D)	Okada
F.	Evaluating Nisei Successes (D)	Okimoto, Butterfield PAPER: Racism

WEEKS 8-10 (Oc 28 to Nov. 15).   <u>The Growing Rivalry</u>, NEU, 197-227

M.	A Unique Relationship (L)	
W.	Military Matters (D)	Reischauer Center
F.	Economic Competition (D)	Packard, V. Wolferen
M.	Educational Differences (D)	Duke
W.	Paper presentations	PAPER due

Sidney D. Brown   History 3863
University of Oklahoma, Norman   Spring, 1992

                        HISTORY OF KOREA

Required books:

Ki-baik Lee, A New History of Korea. 1988
Clark W. Sorenson, Over the Mountains are Mountains: Korean
     Peasant Households and their Adaptations to Rapid
     Industrialization. 1988
Bruce Cumings, The Origins of the Korean War. 1981
Robert A. Scalapino, ed., North Korea in a Regional and
     Global Context. 1986

Schedule of Lectures and Discussions:

FIRST WEEK
January 13   Korea in World History
         15   Korea in Prehistory
             Lee, A New History of Korea, chapter 1 (The
             Communal Societies of Prehistoric Times)
             Recommended: Jeong-hak Kim, The Prehistory of
             Korea. 1979
         17   Geographic Foundations of Korean History
             Recommended: Shannon McCune, Korea's Heritage: A
             Regional and Social Geography. 1956

SECOND WEEK
January 20   Korea's Beginnings in Mythology: the Confederated
             Kingdoms of Old Choson
             Lee, 2 (Wall-Town States and Confederated
             Kingdoms)
             Recommended: Andrew Nahm, Korea - Tradition and
             Transformation: A History of the Korean People.
             1988. (This study parallels the text-book, but
             has greater emphasis on the recent period. The
             author is a Korean who was educated in the United
             States and has lived here most of his life.)
         22   Aristocratic Societies of the Three Kingdoms
             Lee, 3 (Aristocratic Societies under Monarchical
             Rule)
             Recommended: K. H. J. Gardiner, The Early
             History of Korea: To the Introduction of Buddhism
             1969.

24 The Rise of Silla and National Unification
        Lee, 4 (The Fashioning of an Authoritarian
Monarchy)
        Recommended: Takashi Hatada, A History of
Korea, tr. by Warren W. Smith, Jr., and Benjamin
Hazard. 1969. (This provides a history of Korea
from the Japanese point-of-view, a sound history
with a different focus.)

THIRD WEEK
January 27 Kyongju in the Culture and Society of Unified
        Silla
        Lee, 5 (The Age of Powerful Gentry Families)
Recommended: Cornelius Osgood, The Koreans and
their Culture. 1951.
    29 The Transformation of the Early Koryo Period
        Lee, 6 (The Hereditary Aristocratic Order of
Koryo)
Recommended: Richard Rutt, James Scarth Gale's
History of the Korean People. 1975. Structured
sequence of vignettes on highlights of Korean
historical and cultural experience.
    31 The Decline and Fall of the Koryo Dynasty
        Lee, 7 (Rule by the Military)
        Recommended: Edward W. Wagner has assisted
in preparing a scholarly, but simpler account of
Korean history in John K. Fairbank, Edwin O.
Reischauer, and Albert M. Craig, East Asia:
Tradition and Transformation (Houghton, Mifflin,
1989), Chapter 11 (Early Korea), 12 (Yi Dynasty
Korea), pp. 690-618 (Korea's Response to the
Outside World), pp. 907-924 (Korea, from Colony to
Divided Nation, pp. 907-924). You might wish to
read this for greater clarity of the main trends.

FOURTH WEEK
February 3 The Mongols in Korea
        Lee, 8 (The Emergence of the Literati)
Recommended: William E. Henthorn, Korea: the
Mongol Invasions. 1963.
    5 CLASS DISCUSSION: Changing Traditional
Society in a Mountain Village
        Read Clark Sorenson, Over the Mountains are
Mountains. 1988. Prepare for ten-minute quiz;
discussion questions to be distributed.
    7 Establishment of the Yi Dynasty, 1392
        Recommended: Edward W. Wagner, The Literati
Purges: Political Conflict in Early Yi Korea.
1974.

FIFTH WEEK
February 10 Characteristics of the Yangban Aristocracy
        Lee, 9 (The Creation of a Yangban Society)

Recommended: John Meskill, Ch'oe Pu's Diary: a
Record of Drifting Across the Sea. 1965.
  12 FIRST HOUR EXAMINATION
  14 Traditional Korean Painting: SLIDE LECTURE
Recommended: Choi Sunu. 5000 Years of Korean Art.
1979.

SIXTH WEEK
February 17 Main Currents in Traditional Korean
  Literature
  Recommended: Peter H. Lee, tr. Anthology of Korean
  Literature from Early Times to tdhe Nineteenth
  Century. 1981.
   19 The Japanese Invasion of Korea, 1592-1598
  Recommended: Park Yune-hee, Admiral Yi Sun-shin
  and his Turtleboat Armada. 1975.
   21 Chinese Pattern Perfected under Neo-
  Confucianism
    Lee, 10 (The Rise of the Neo-Confucian
  Literati)
  Recommended: Younghill Kang, The Grass Roof.
  1975. This Charming autobiography of one of the
  last persons trained in the Confucian tradition in
  late Yi Korea provides a graphic picture of what
  was expected of the student.

SEVENTH WEEK
February 24 Yi Korea: Farmers and Merchants
  Lee, 11 (The Emergence of Landed Farmers and
  Wholesale Merchants)
  Recommended: Vicent S. R. Brandt, A Korean
  Village: between Farm and Sea. 1971.
   26 Challenges to the Yangban Status System
    Lee, 12 (Instability in the Yangban Status
  System and the Outbreak of Popular Uprisings)
  Recommended: William Shaw, Legal Norms in a
  Confucian State. 1981.
   28 Sirhak: Practical Learning in Yi Korea
  Recommended: Hugh H.W Kang, ed., The Traditional
  Culture and Society of Korea: Thought and
  Institutions. 1975. One of the three studies
  deals with Sirhak.

EIGHTH WEEK
March 2 Foreign Challenge: the Arrival of Catholicism
  Recommended: Donald L. Baker, "Jesuit Science
  through Korean Eyes," Journal of Korean Studies
  (1982-1983), 207-239.
   4 CLASS DISCUSSION: The Origins of the Korean War
   Read Bruce Cumings, The Origins of the Korean
  War: Liberation and the Emergence of Separate
  Regimes, 1945-1947. 1981. Prepare essay in
  accordance with instructions. Discussion questions
  to be distributed.

6 Conservative Reform and Isolation in Late Yi
Korea: the Taewon'gun's Policies
Recommended: Choe Ching Young, *The Rule of the
Taewon'gun, 1864-1873.* 1972.

NINTH WEEK
March 16 Revolutionary Uprising: the Tonghak Peasant
Army
Lee, 13 (Growth of the Forces of Enlightenment)
Recommended: Benjamin B. Weems, *Reform, Rebellion,
and the Heave ly Way.* 1964.
18 Opening of the Hermit Kingdom
Recommended: C. I. Eugene Kim and Han-kyo Kim,
Korea and the Politics of Imperialism, 1876-1910.
1967.
Jongsuk Chay, *Diplomacy of Assymetry: Korean-
American Relations to 1910.* 1990.
20 Korea under Japanese Domination, and the
Abortive Reforms of Inoue Kaoru, 1894-1895
Recommended: Fred Harvey Harrington, *God, Mammon,
and the Japanese: Horace N. Allen.* 1944.

TENTH WEEK
March 23 So Chae-p'il and the Independence Club
Lee, 14 (Nationalist Stirrings and Imperialist
Aggression)
Recommended: Yur-bok Lee and Wayne Patterson, *One
Hundred Years of Korean-American Relations.* 1986.
25 SECOND HOUR EXAMINATION
27 Japan's Annexation of Korea, 1910
Recommended: F. Hilary Conroy, *The Japanese
Seizure of Korea, 1868-1910.* 1960.

ELEVENTH WEEK
March 30 The March First Movement, 1919
Recommended: Chong-sik Lee, *The Politics of Korean
Nationalism.* 1965.
April 1 The Colonial Experience, 1921-1930
Lee, 15 (Development of the Nationalist
Movement)
Recommended: Andrew C. Nahm, ed., *Korea under
Japanese Colonial Rule.* 1973.
3 The Colonial Experience, 1930-1942
Recommended: E. I. Eugene Kim, ed., *Korea's
Response to Japan: the Colonial Period.* 1975.
Dennis L. McNamara, *The Colonial Origins of Korean
Enterprise, 1919-1945.* 1990.

TWELFTH WEEK
April 6 Korea in the Diplomacy of World War II
Recommended: Gregory Henderson, *Korea: the
Politics of the Vortex.* 1968.
8 Allied Occupation of Korea, 1945-1950
Lee, 16 (The Beginnings of Democracy)

          Recommended: E. Grant Meade, American Military
          Government in Korea. 1951.
      10 Korea's Civil War, 1950-1953
          Recommended: Max Hastings, The Korean War. 1987.
          Harold J. Noble, Embassy at War. 1975.

THIRTEENTH WEEK
April 13 Syngman Rhee and South Korea, 1948-1960
          Recommended: Robert T. Oliver, Syngman Rhee: the
          Man behind the Myth. 1954.
      15 Chung Hee Park and South Korea, 1961-1979
          TERM PAPER: on Images of Korea through the Eyes of
          Foreign Travellers. Instructions to be
          distributed. Ten pages or more.
          Recommended: John Kie-chiang Oh, Korea: Democracy
          on Trial. 1968.
      17 Kim Il-sung and North Korea
          Recommended: Robert A. Scalapino and Chong-sik
          Lee, Communism in Korea. 2 vols., 1972.

FOURTEENTH WEEK
April 20 Economic Prosperity in South Korea
          Recommended: T. W. Kang, Is Korea the Next Japan?
          Understanding the Structure, Strategy, and Tactics
          of America's Next Competitor. 1989.
      22 CLASS DISCUSSION: The Enigma of North Korea's
          Foreign Policy
          Read: Robert A. Scalapino and Hongkoo Lee, North
          Korea in a Regional and Global Context. 1986.
          Prepare for ten-minute quiz; discussion questions
          to be distributed.
      24 Trends in Recent Korean Literature
          Recommended: Peter H. Lee, ed., Flowers of Fire:
          Twentieth-Century Korean Stories. 1974.

FIFTEENTH WEEK
April 27 South Korea: Military Rule and Political
          Dissidence, 1979-1992
          Recommended: Donald N. Clark, ed., the Kwangju
          Risings: Shadows over the Regime in South Korea.
          1988.
      29 Prospects for the Reunification of Korea. 1992

FINAL EXAMINATION
May 5 1:30-3:30 p.m.

Information about the Course:
1. Examinations are of the essay type, so please bring
   bluebooks.
2. Numerical grades will conform to the university grading
   scale: 91-100, A; 81-90, B; 71-80, C; 61-70, D; 0-
   59,F.
3. The final grade will be computed on this basis: first
   hour examination, 20%; second hour examination,

204; final examination, 40%; term paper and reading
    quizzes, 20%.
4. Regular class attendance is expected.
5. You are encouraged to visit me during my office hours
    to talk about the course, or your interests in
    Korea generally.
6. Your term essay should be done carefully in good
    literary style, and in accordance with standard
    style.

The University of Kansas

Department of History

MODERN KOREA

Instructor: Dr. Wayne Patterson
Visiting Associate Professor of History

Course Number: History 593/EALC 593   Line Number 35086

Year: Spring Semester 1992

Course Hours/Credits: Three (3)

Course Description:
An examination of Korea's history, culture, society, politics and foreign relations during the nineteenth and twentieth centuries. Topics include traditional Yi Dynasty Korea and its decline (1392-1910), the coming of the West, Japanese imperialism and big power rivalry, domestic factionalism, the colonial period and the resultant independence movement, including the role of overseas Koreans (1910-45), the American occupation, division into hostile regimes, the Korean War, and current issues facing both north and south Korea (1945-present).

Instructor's Office Telephone: 864-4809

History Department Telephone: 864-3569

Class Times: Tuesday and Thursday, 8:00-9:20 a.m.

Classroom: Fraser Hall, Room Four

Instructor's Office: Wescoe 2004

Office Hours: Tuesday and Thursday 9:30 - 11:00 and by appointment
Note: There will be additional office hours during those weeks in which there is an examination or a paper due and these will be announced during the preceding week in class.

Books Required for Purchase:

Andrew C. Nahm. *Korea: Tradition and Transformation - A History of the Korean People*. Elizabeth, New Jersey: Hollym, 1988

Yur-Bok Lee and Wayne Patterson, editors. *One Hundred Years of Korean-American Relations, 1882-1982*. University, Alabama: University of Alabama Press, 1986

Wayne Patterson. *The Korean Frontier in America: Immigration to Hawaii, 1896-1910*. Honolulu: University of Hawaii Press, 1988

Packet of supplementary readings at Kinko's Copies, 622 West Twelfth Street.

Readings:

In addition to the readings from the materials listed above, students may from time to time be assigned readings from other sources. These will be placed on reserve at the library and added to the weekly reading assignments. Students should also familiarize themselves with the library holdings on Korea. The assigned readings should be considered the minimum required reading. Students are urged to read further if their time and interest allow them. Each week's assignment will consist of required reading and optional reading. For additonal reading, students are urged to consult Han-Kyo Kim, editor, *Studies on Korea: A Scholar's Guide*. Honolulu: University of Hawaii Press, 1980.

Papers:

There will be two papers, each of which will be from four to five typewritten pages in length. Late papers are marked down at the rate of one half grade per class session. Papers are graded with equal attention to writing competence and content. Each paper is worth 20% of the final grade. The first paper is due on Thursday, February 27. The second paper is due on Thursday, March 19. The papers will be worth 40% of the final grade. Note: Graduate students enrolled in this course will be assigned further work to be announced.

Examinations:

There will be three unit examinations. Examinations are non-cumulative and subjective (essay) in nature. They are read without reference to the name on the front cover. Each examination is worth 20% of the final grade for a total of 60%. Examinations will be scheduled at regular intervals of four to five weeks. The first examination is scheduled for Thursday, February 20. The second examination is scheduled for Tuesday, March 31. The final examination will be held on Wednesday, May 6 at nine in the morning.

Attendance:

Attendance will be taken at each class session to allow the instructor to become familiar with students in the class. It is also a vehicle to identify those students who are regular attenders since they will be given the benefit of the doubt in borderline cases at the time of the assignment of final grades.

Attendance at Examinations:

No absences are permitted without a note from a dean or a health professional. This will also be in effect for the paper due dates.

Evaluation:
First Examination: 20%
First Paper: 20%
Second Examination: 20%
Second Paper: 20%
Final Examination: 20%
TOTAL: 100%

Academic Integrity: The University has instituted a set of policies designed
to encourage academic integrity. It is the intention of the
instructor to abide by these policies. Please consult the student
handbook for further information.

Disclaimer:
Nothing in this syllabus will prevent the instructor from deviating in
terms of required assignments, scheduling, or the like if he deems it
appropriate. In such cases, adequate notice of any changes will be
given. It is the responsiblity of the student to be aware of any such
changes.

COURSE SCHEDULE:

January 13   Introduction

Class will not meet on Tuesday, January 14

Required Reading:

Nahm, Chapter One, Pages 17-22

Recommended Reading:

Nahm, Chapters Two and Three, Pages 23-93

January 20   Confucianism and Yi Korea to 1863

Required Reading:

Nahm, Chapter Four, Pages 94-143
Michael C. Kalton, "Korean Ideas and Values," Pages 1-21

Recommended Reading:

Key P. Yang and Gregory Henderson, "An Outline History of Korean
Confucianism," Journal of Asian Studies, XVI (1958), Pages 259-76 (Part Two)
Edward W. Wagner, "The Ladder of Success in Yi Dynasty Korea,"
Occasional Papers on Korea, No. 1 (1974).
Martina Deuchler, "Neo-Confucianism: The Impulse for Social Action in
Early Yi Korea," Journal of Korean Studies, Volume Two (1980), Pages 71-112
Michael C. Kalton, "Chong Ta-san's Philosophy of Man: A Radical
Critique of the Neo-Confucian World View," Journal of Korean Studies, Volume
Three (1981), Pages 3-38.

Donald N. Clark, "Choson's Founding Fathers: A Study of Merit Subjects in the Early Yi Dynasty," Korean Studies, Volume Six (1982), Pages 17-40.

January 27   The Taewongun and the Opening of Korea, 1864-1876

        Required Reading:

        Key-Hiuk Kim, The Last Phase of the East Asian World Order (1980) Chapter One, Pages 1-38.

        Recommended Reading:

        Hilary Conroy and Wayne Patterson, "Recent Studies of Korea," Pacific Affairs (Fall, 1972).
        Hae-jong Chun, "Sino-Korean Tributary Relations in the Ch'ing Period," in John King Fairbank, ed. The Chinese World Order, Pages 90-111.
        Takashi Hatada, A History of Korea, Chapter Five, Pages 61-89.
        James B. Palais, Politics and Policy in Traditional Korea (1975) Pages 1-22, 176-201, 237-51 and 272-86.
        Martina Deuchler, Confucian Gentlemen and Barbarian Envoys, (1977) Pages 11-50.
        Ching Young Choe, The Rule of the Taewongun, 1864-1873: Restoration in Yi Korea (1972).
        Yong-Ho Ch'oe, "Sino-Korean Relations, 1866-1876" Asea yon'gu 9:1 (March 1966).
        Frederick Drake, Empire of the Seas: A Biography of Rear Admiral Robert Wilson Shufeldt, USN (1985), Chapters 12-15 and Conclusion, Pages 233-353.
        Albert A. Altman, "Korea's First Newspaper: The Japanese Chosen Shinpo," Journal of Asian Studies, Vol 43, No. 4 (August 1984), Pages 685-96
        Conroy, The Japanese Seizure of Korea, 1868-1910: A Study of Realism and Idealism in International Relations, Pages 17-168.

February 3   Reform Versus Reaction, 1877-1893

        Required Reading:

        Nahm, Chapter Five, Pages 144-84
        Yur-Bok Lee and Wayne Patterson, One Hundred Years of Korean-American Relations, 1882-1982, (1986) Chapters One and Two, Pages 1-45.

        Recommended Reading:

        Robert Swartout, Jr., Mandarins, Gunboats and Power Politics (1980) Conclusion, Pages 147-52.
        Harold Cook, Korea's 1884 Incident, (1972) Epilogue, Pages 219-25.
        Yur-Bok Lee, West Goes East: Paul Georg Von Mollendorff and Great Power Imperialism in Late Yi Korea (1988).
        In Kwan Hwang, The Korean Reform Movement of the 1880s (1978).
        Yong-ho Ch'oe, "The Kapsin Coup of 1884: A Reassessment," Korean Studies, Volume Six (1982), Pages 105-24.

In Kwan Hwang, "A Translation and Critical Review of Yu Kil-Chun's On Neutrality," Korean Studies, Volume Nine (1985), Pages 1-13.

George Alexander Lensen, Balance of Intrigue: International Rivalry in Korea and Manchuria, 1884-1899, (1982) Volume One.

Robert Swartout, Jr., An American Adviser in Late Yi Korea: The Letters of Owen Nickerson Denny (1984).

Young Ick Lew, "Yuan Shih-k'ai's Residency and the Korean Enlightenment Movement," Journal of Korean Studies, Volume Five (1984), Pages 63-107.

Fred Harvey Harrington, God, Mammon and the Japanese: Horace N. Allen and American-Korean Relations, 1884-1905, (1944).

James B. Palais, "Political Participation in Traditional Korea, 1876-1910," Journal of Korean Studies, Volume One (1979).

February 10   The Sino-Japanese War and Its Aftermath, 1894-1903

Required Reading:

Nahm, Chapter Six, Pages 185-219

Lee and Patterson, Chapter Three, Pages 46-67.

Mikhail Nikolaevich Pak and Wayne Patterson, "Russian Policy Toward Korea Before and During the Sino-Japanese War of 1894-95" Journal of Korean Studies, Volume Five (1984), Pages 109-19.

Recommended Reading:

Vipan Chandra, "The Independence Club and Korea's First Proposal for a Natinal Legislative Assembly," Occasional Papers on Korea, 4 (1975), Pages 19-35.

Benjamin Weems, Reforms, Rebellion and the Heavenly Way, (1964) Pages 1-48.

Young-Ick Lew, "The Reform Efforts and Ideas of Pak Yong-hyo, 1894-95," Korean Studies, Volume One (1977), Pages 21-61.

George Alexander Lensen, Balance of Intrigue, Volume Two.

Wayne Patterson, "The First Attempt to Obtain Korean Laborers for Hawaii, 1896-97," in Hyung-chan Kim, ed. The Korean Diaspora: Historical and Sociological Studies of Korean Immigration and Assimilation in North America (1977).

William F. Sands, Undiplomatic Memories: The Far East, 1896-1904 (1975).

Kenneth Quinones, "The Impact of the Kabo Reforms upon Political Role Allocation in Late Yi Korea, 1884-1902," Occasional Papers on Korea, University of Washington, 1978.

Susan Shin, "The Tonghak Movement," Korean Studies Forum, 5 (Winter-Spring, 1978-79), Pages 1-76.

February 17   First Unit Examination

No Required Reading

Examination will be held on Thursday, February 20

168

February 24   The Japanese Seizure of Korea, 1904-1910

First Paper Due on Thursday, February 27

Turn in an essay of approximately four to five pages based on your
reading of any forty (40) consecutive pages of the diary of Yun Ch'i-ho during
the years 1890 through 1903, Volumes Two through Six. The citation is: Yun
Ch'i-ho Ilgi, Ed. Kuksa p'yonch'an wiwonhoe (Seoul: T'amgudang, 1973-76).
(On Reserve at the Library). There will be extended office hours during this
week to assist students with their paper.

Required Reading:

C. I. Eugene Kim and Han-Kyo Kim, Korea and the Politics of
Imperialism. 1876-1910, Chapters 8, 12, 13, and Conclusion. Pages 121-35 and
196-223.

Recommended Reading:

Hilary Conroy, Chapter Seven, Pages 325-82.
Donald N. Clark, "Yun Ch'i-ho (1864-1945): Portrait of a Korean
Intellectual in an Era of Transition," Occasional Papers on Korea, University
of Washington, 1977, Pages 36-65.
Ian Nish, The Origins of the Russo-Japanese War (1985).
Vipan Chandra, "An Outline Study of the Ilchin-hoe (Advancement
Society) of Korea," Occasional Papers on Korea 2 (1974), Pages 43-72.
James B. Palais, "Political Participation in Traditional Korea, 1876-
1910," Journal of Korean Studies 1 (1979), Pages 73-122.
Karl Moskowitz, "The Creation of the Oriental Development Company:
Japanese Illusions Meet Korean Reality," Occasional Papers on Korea 2 (1974),
Pages 73-122.

March 2   The March First Movement, 1911-1925

Required Reading:

Nahm, Chapter Seven, Pages 223-60.
Lee and Patterson, Chapter Four, Pages 68-85.
Hyung-chan Kim and Wayne Patterson, eds. The Koreans in America.
1882-1974 (1974) Pages 99-104.
Wayne Patterson, "Upward Social Mobility of the Koreans in Hawaii,"
Korean Studies, Volume Three (1979), Pages 81-92.

Recommended Reading:

George DeVos and Changsoo Lee, The Koreans in Japan: Ethnic Conflict
and Accomodation (1982) Chapters One and Two, Pages 3-57.
Shannon McCune, The Mansei Movement. March 1. 1919 (1976) Pages 3-39.
Younghill Kang, The Grass Roof (1931) Chapter 21, Pages 328-44.
Frank P. Baldwin, "Participatory Anti-Imperialism: The 1919
Independence Movement" Journal of Korean Studies, Vol. One (1979), Pages 123-
62.
Andrew C. Nahm, ed. Korea Under Japanese Colonial Rule (1973).
Peter Hyun, Manseil: The Making of a Korean-American (1986).

Henry Chung, The Case of Korea (1921).
Pearl Buck, The Living Reed (1963).
C. I. Eugene Kim and D. Mortimore, Korea's Response to Japan: The Colonial Period (1975).

March 9   Spring Vacation

          Class will not meet

          No Reading Assignment

March 16   The Colonial Experience, 1926-42

          Second paper due on Thursday, March 19

          Write a paper of approximately four to five pages on one of the following aspects of The Korean Frontier in America: Immigration to Hawaii, 1896-1910: 1) American policy toward Korea, 2) the nature of the Korean government, 3) Japanese policy toward Korea, 4) the role of Koreans in the Hawaiian economy, 5) Korean government view of the United States, 6) the role of Horace Allen. Note: One of these items will appear as a question on the second unit examination.

          Required Reading:

          Nahm, Chapter Eight, Pages 261-325.
          Chong-Sik Lee, The Politics of Korean Nationalism (1965), Chapter Fourteen, and Conclusion, Pages 257-79.
          Han-Kyo Kim, "The Japanese Colonial Administration in Korea: An Overview" Pages 41-51.

          Recommended Reading:

          David Brudnoy, "Japan's Experiment in Korea," Monumenta Nipponica, 25 (1970), Pages 155-95.
          Michael Robinson, Cultural Nationalism in Colonial Korea, 1920-25 (1988).
          Edward Baker, "The Role of Legal Reforms," David McCann, et. al., eds. tudies of Korea in Transition.
          Andrew Grajdanzev, Modern Korea (1944) Pages 72-122 and 148-84.
          Michael Robinson, "National Identity and the Thought of Sin Ch'aeho: Sadaejuui and Chuch'e in History and Politics," Journal of Korean Studies, Volume Five (1984), Pages 121-42.
          Michael Robinson, "Ideological Schism in the Korean Nationalist Movement, 1920-30: Cultural Nationalism and the Radical Critique," Journal of Korean Studies 4 (1982-83), Pages 241-68.
          Mirok Li, The Yalu Flows: A Korean Childhood (1956).
          Yunshik Chang, "Colonization as Planned Change: The Korean Case" Modern Asian Studies, Vol. 5 (1971), Pages 160-82.
          Ronald Toby, "Education in Korea under the Japanese: Attitudes and Manifestations," Occasional Papers on Korea 1 (1974), Pages 55-64.
          Dae-Sook Suh, The Korean Communist Movement, 1918-1948 (1967).
          Chong-Sik Lee, Pages 1-236.

Gregory Henderson, Korea: The Politics of the Vortex (1968), Chapter Four, Pages 72-112 (On Reserve).
　　　Richard Kim, Lost Names: Scenes from a Korean Boyhood (1970).

March 23　　　　　Liberation and Occupation, 1943-49

　　　Required Reading:

　　　Nahm, Chapter Nine, Pages 329-65.
　　　Lee and Patterson, Chapter Five, Pages 86-107.
　　　Wayne Patterson, "The Divided East Asian Nations: A Comparative Approach to Partition in China, Korea and Vietnam," Asian Forum, Volume Ten, Number One (Spring/Summer 1979), Pages 61-66.
　　　Bruce Cumings, The Origins of the Korean War: Liberation and the Emergence of Separate Regimes, 1945-1947 (1981) Chapter Twelve, Pages 428-44.

　　　Recommended Reading:

　　　Noble, Embassy at War (1975).
　　　Glenn D. Paige, The Korean Decision.
　　　John Merrill, "The Cheju-Do Rebellion," Journal of Korean Studies, Volume Two (1980).
　　　Soon Sung Cho, Korea in World Politics, 1940-50, Pages 1-285.
　　　Bruce Cumings, ed. Child of Conflict: The Korean-American Relationship, 1943-53 (1983).
　　　Richard Kim, The Martyred (1964).
　　　Michael C. Sandusky, America's Parallel (1983).
　　　James Irving Matray, The Reluctant Crusade: American Foreign Policy in Korea, 1941-50 (1985).
　　　Masao Okonogi, "The Shifting Strategic Value of Korea, 1942-50," Korean Studies Volume Three (1979), Pages 49-80.
　　　Gregory Henderson, Korea: The Politics of the Vortex Chapter Five, Pages 113-47.

March 30　　　　　Second Unit Examination

　　　No Required Reading

　　　Examination will be held on Tuesday, March 31

　　　Class will not meet and there will be no office hours on Thursday, April 2 (Instructor Attending the Annual Meeting of the Association for Asian Studies (AAS) in Washington, DC).

April 6　　　　　The Korean War and the Syngman Rhee Regime, 1950-1960

　　　Required Reading:

　　　Nahm, Chapter Eleven, Pages 421-39
　　　Lee and Patterson, Chapter Six, Pages 108-126

Recommended Reading:

Bruce Cumings, The Origins of the Korean War, Volume Two: The Roaring of the Cataract (1990).
Richard Kim, The Marytred.
John Kie-Chang Oh, Democracy on Trial (1968).
Chapter Three, Pages 51-71
Wayne Patterson, "The Partition of Korea: Cold War Casuality," in Thomas E. Hachey, ed. The Problem of Partition: Peril to World Peace (1977).
Allen, Korea's Syngman Rhee.
Robert T. Oliver, Syngman Rhee: The-Man Behind the Myth.
Quee-Young Kim, The Fall of Syngman Rhee (1983).
Tae-Hwan Kwak, Wayne Patterson and Edward Olsen, eds. The Two Koreas in World Politics (1983).
James B. Palais, "'Democracy' in South Korea, 1948-72," in Frank Baldwin, ed. Without Parallel, Pages 318-31.
Sung-joo Han, The Failure of Democracy in South Korea.
Gregory Henderson, Korea: The Politics of the Vortex Chapters Ten and Twelve, Pages 273-311 and 334-60.

April 13   The Park Chung-hee Regime, 1961-79

Required Reading:

Nahm, Chapter Eleven, Pages 439-464.
Wayne Patterson, "Public Criticism Versus Private Diplomacy in the Carter Human Rights Policy Toward Korea," (1984) Pges 1-27.
Wayne Patterson, "The State Department, the KCIA, and the Korean Community in the United States, 1971-1976" (1980) Pages 1-22.

Recommended Reading:

Se-Jin Kim, The Politics of Military Revolution in Korea, Pages 18-35 and 125-76.
Bae Ho Hahn, "Policy Toward Japan," in Youngnok Koo and Sung Joo Han, editors, The Foreign Policy of the Repubic of Korea (1985) Pages 167-97.
James B. Palais, "'Democracy'...Pages 331-52.
Cole and Lyman, Korean Development: The Interplay of Politics and Economics, Pages 78-97
Joungwon Alexander Kim, Divided Korea: The Politics of Development.
Robert Boettcher, Gifts of Deceit.
Parvez Hasan, et. al., eds. Korea: Policy Issues for Long-Term Development (1979).
Vincent Brandt, A Korean Village Between Farm and Sea.
DeVos and Lee, Koreans in Japan: Ethnic Conflict and Accomodation (1981) Chapters 10 and 12, Pages 225-51 and 304-33.
Setsure Tsurushima, "The Effects of the Cultural Revolution on the Korean Minority in Yenpien," Korean Studies, Volume Three (1979), Pages 93-124.
Hyung-Chan Kim, ed. The Korean Diaspora (1977)
Bong-Youn Choy, Koreans in America (1979) Pages 217-334.
DeVos and Lee, Pages 133-224, 252-303 and 334-83.
Amerasia Journal Various Issues.

Won Moo Hurh and Kwang Chung Kim, <u>Korean Immigrants in America: A</u>
<u>Structural Analysis of Ethnic Confinement and Adhesive Adaptation</u> (1980).
        Ilsoo Kim, <u>New Urban Immigrants</u> (1982).

April 20   North Korea, 1980-1992

        Required Reading:

        Nahm, Chapter Ten, Pages 366-420.
        Bruce Cumings, "Report on a Visit to North Korea" (1981) Pages 1-25.
        <u>Asian Survey</u> January, 1992 article on North Korea in 1991 (to be
placed on reserve when it becomes available).

        Recommended Reading:

        Changsoo Lee, "Social Policy and Development in North Korea," in
Robert A. Scalapino and Youngnok Koo, editors, <u>North Korea Today: Strategic</u>
<u>and Domestic Issues</u> (1983), Pages 114-32.
        Sung-Joo Han, "North Korea's Security Policy and Military Strategy,"
in Scalapino and Koo, Pages 144-63.
        Joseph S. Chung, "Economic Planning in North Korea," in Scalapino and
Koo, Pages 164-88.
        Chong-Sik Lee, "Land Reform, Collectivisation and the Peasants in
North Korea" Scalapino, ed. <u>North Korea Today</u> Pages 65-81.
        Joseph Sang-Hoon Chung, <u>The North Korean Economy: Structure and</u>
<u>Development</u>.
        Robert Scalapino and Chong-Sik Lee, <u>Communism in Korea</u>, Volume One,
Pages 1-232 and 313-381; Volume Two, Pages 687-918.
        Dae-Sook Suh, "Communist Party Leadership," in Suh and Lee, editors.
<u>Political Leadership in Korea</u> (1976).
        <u>Asian Survey</u> Various issues.
        Dae-Sook Sun, <u>Kim Il Sung: The North Korean Leader</u> (1988).
        Ilpyong J. Kim, <u>Communist Politics in North Korea</u>.
        Byung-chul Koh, <u>The Foreign Policy of North Korea</u>.
        Young Whan Kihl, <u>Politics and Policies in Divided Korea: Regimes in</u>
<u>Contest</u> (1984).
        <u>Pyongyang Times</u>.

April 27   South Korea, 1980-1992

        Required Reading:

        Nahm, Chapter Eleven and Twelve, Pages 464-515.
        Donald S. MacDonald, "American Imperialism: Myth or Reality?" (1986)
Pages 1-28.
        <u>Asian Survey</u> January, 1992 article on South Korea in 1991 (to be
placed on reserve when it becomes available).

        Recommended Reading:

        Hak-Joon Kim, "Prospects for Korean Unification in the Changing East
Asian International Politics," in Tae-Hwan Kwak, Wayne Patterson, and Edward
Olsen, eds. <u>The Two Koreas in World Politics</u> (1983) Chapter Seventeen, Pages
383-400.

<u>Far</u> <u>Eastern</u> <u>Economic</u> <u>Review</u> <u>Yearbook</u> (1981) Pages 171-73.
Byung Chul Koh, "Unification Policy and North-South Relations" in
Scalapino and Koo, Pages 264-308.

May 4   Final Examination Week

               Final Examination will be held on Wednesday, May 6 at nine in the
               morning

May 11   Summer Vacation Begins

Spring 1991
History 341
Foundations of Southeast Asian History
Mondays, Wednesdays, Fridays, 1:20-2:30 p.m., Old Main 301

Concordia College
Bruce Cruikshank   Office: 327 Old Main (History)   Telephones: 299-3523 (office) and
                                                                          236-7756 (home)
Office hours: Monday, Wednesday. Friday: 4:00 p.m.-5:00 p.m.;
              Tuesdays and Thursdays, 4:30-5:00 p.m.; and, of course, you should always
              feel free to just stop by 327 Old Main and chat.

Required texts (available at the Cobber Bookstore):

   G. Coedès.
        The Making of Southeast Asia. Tr. H. M. Wright.
        Berkeley: University of California Press, 1966 (1st pub. 1962). 268pp.

   Kenneth R. Hall.
        Maritime Trade and State Development in Early Southeast Asia.
        Honolulu: University of Hawaii. 1985. 368pp.

   Robert Heine-Geldern.
        Conceptions of State and Kingship in Southeast Asia.
        Ithaca, New York: Southeast Asia Program (Data Paper, no. 18), Department of
        Far Eastern Studies, Cornell University, April 1956. 17pp.

   Anthony Reid, ed.
        Slavery, Bondage and Dependency in Southeast Asia.
        New York: St. Martin's Press, 1983. 382pp.

Other Required Materials (available at the Reserve Desk, Carl B. Ylvisaker Library, unless
                            otherwise noted)
   Please see Appendix One at the end of the Syllabus

   History 341 is a course designed to look at institutional aspects of ancient or pre-1800
Asian civilizations. Ordinarily we work with China and Japan. This semester we have the
opportunity to examine pre-1800 Southeast Asia.

   The keys to a successful learning experience in this course (not necessarily in order of
importance) are:

              reading as scheduled,
              class attendance,
              interpretive, comprehensive, and intensive discussion in your written work, and
              active and full participation in debate and discussion in class.

Most of these "keys" and the themes come directly or indirectly from the <u>Agenda for Concordia's Academic Life: A Curriculum Plan for Concordia College</u>, most notably with our emphases here at Concordia on love of learning, a commitment to excellence, self-discipline, growth in thinking and problem-solving skills, independent thinking. breadth of knowledge, exposure to the rigor and precision found in historical studies, and exposure to and testing of our religious and ethical values and practices. I have tried to design a broad approach emphasizing themes using a multiplicity of approaches and academic disciplines to help show how the interaction of many "branches" of knowledge with particular perspectives and values make history the exciting field of knowledge that it is. Even more specifically, I have tried to design a course that speaks to the Across-the-Curriculum Requirements of

> Verbal Competence,
> Ethnic Studies,
> Global Studies, and
> Women's Studies.

In constructing this course I have had of necessity to require a substantial amount of reading. This might seem burdensome to some of you. It will be a manageable load for all of you <u>if</u> you keep up with the syllabus <u>and</u> if you focus on the following six of the major themes of this course, namely

> (1) political forms;
> (2) economic and technological constraints and advantages;
> (3) religious-ideological systems.

These three themes interrelate and often seem to circle endlessly. For instance, political structures are founded on economic and technological bases and often are in turn justified and supported in terms of ideological constructs; and political conflicts often are based on ideological conflicts regarding distribution of power and resources, which are often exacerbated when there are economic crises; and so forth.

(4) Gender--that is, at least as I see the term at this time. the social meaning, roles, <u>and</u> expectations assigned to perceptions of sexual difference among humans;

(5) Race--that is, at least as I see the term at this time, the social meaning, roles, <u>and</u> expectations assigned to perceptions of divisions among our <u>one</u> human race based usually on skin color or the common or racist assumptions that social behaviors are genetically determined for whole groups as defined by skin color or other external markings; and

(6) Class--that is, again as I see the term at this time, the divisions in a society due to economic levels of wealth along with the associated patterns of roles, expectations, and restrictions assigned to ones "class".

With a focus on these themes you can read <u>selectively</u>. These, of course, are very general themese. More particular attention will be given to the following:

(7) <u>Patterns of State Formation and Organization</u>, and

(8) <u>Forms of Slavery</u> in many of these Southeast Asian
cultures and polities.

Given the nature of the papers (see below). you can further identify the useful data for analysis and comparison. Discussions and peer presentations--usually with new material and, thus, supplementary to the assigned reading--will further allow you to glean what you will need to know in order to learn and perform well in the course.

These themes are not exhaustive of the materials you will study. Nor are they meant to exclude pursuit of other themes you may want to study during this period of your educational growth. Such "tangents" are legitimate and may be introduced in discussion and even (in special cases) individual projects.

Requirements for participation in the course:

I expect regular <u>attendance</u> and active participation in discussion. Since your grade substantially depends on

        (1) written work, done in a timely fashion;
        (2) active participation in class discussion and presentations; and
        (3) careful and regular reading of the class assignments,

it follows that absences will hurt your performance and your class standing. It also seems self-evident (in order to be fair to all members of the class) that scheduled presentations and papers should be performed as scheduled; non-medical or other excuses should (if possible) be arranged ahead of time and will be granted or not granted at my discretion. I follow the regulation concerning class attendance set forth in <u>The Record</u>, namely (p. 19) that "You are expected to attend all classes" and would call to your attention that "A student delinquent in class attendance also must expect that grades will be seriously affected." I tend to reduce your "A" grade for attendance 1/5-1/3 grade for each <u>unexcused</u> absence.

Class <u>discussions</u> of the assigned readings and peer presentations are the centerpiece of this course. It will work only if you are prepared to participate and prepare for such participation by doing the assigned reading and reflection.

In addition, you will be expected to make <u>class presentations</u>. This is an experiement that I am trying in our class—the goals are both to more actively involve you in the course as well as to speak directly to the Verbal Competence Across-the-Curriculum requirement mentioned earlier. In oral presentation I will be looking for

        clear presentation of objectives;
        good organization and preparation;
        communication of dates, names, etc., through use of chalkboard,
            overhead projector, or other audio-visual aids;
        accurate and comprehensive materials used; and
        confidence, poise, eye contact, clear and sufficiently loud voice.

In terms of formal written work, you will be responsible for presenting four papers. In all of your written work I expect evidence, logic, and organization. Structurally I expect essays characterized by the following:

        a) a clear statement of intent and focus (what you intend to demonstrate),
        that shows you understand the question or topic of the paper and indicates
        how you plan to answer or respond to it;

        b) an orderly organization with logical arguments and facts progressing
        steadily through your essay to the conclusion;

        c) separate points and subordinate arguments developed in coherent
        paragraphs with natural and effective transitions from paragraph to
        paragraph;

d) evidence and logical argument supporting claims and generalizations;

e) a strong conclusion reflecting your previous argument and indicating how you answered the essay question; and, where relevant,

f) a use and understanding of the historical mainstays of who, when, where, what, how, and why.

Papers One, Two, and Three are review essays, roughly patterned on the usual form for a book review. For your convenience, I include a quotation in Appendix Two (below) from a book by Jacques Barzun and Henry F. Graff describing good book reviews. From this quotation and my own emphases in our course, you can anticipate having your formal writing evaluated on the bases of

> I.   Essay Form;
> II. Completeness of Summary of work(s) reviewed;
> III. Completeness and Accuracy of Summary of Author's Point of View;
> IV. Use of Other Course Materials for Comparisons and Criticisms;
> V.   Use of Discussion and Peer Presentation materials for
>   Comparisons and Criticisms;
> VI. General Plausibility and Weight of Your Evaluation.

We now have, consequently, the following components of the course (I of course reserve the right to modify the percentages of sequence or content of the course as necessary as we proceed through the semester):

Presentations, Attendance, and Class Preparations	counting 15% of your course grade
Paper One/Coedès	20%
Paper Two/Hall	25%
Paper Three/Reid	25%
Paper Four/Separate Paper Critique	15%

"The students and faculty of Concordia College are committed to the expectations and procedures set forth in the Joint Statement on Academic Responsibility."

Schedule of Topics and Readings:
N.B.: Please have the reading done before the class time of the day listed

Monday, 7 January 1991: Introduction to the Course and Each Other

Wednesday, 9 January:
   Coedès, pp. v-xi and 1-33 (Part I): PLEASE IDENTIFY ASSUMPTIONS, EMPHASES,
                                        AND THEMES BEFORE CLASS
 Film--North Dakota State Film Library
      3. Buddhism: Footprint of the Buddha India 52min. Color. $18.50 (1978)

<u>Friday, 11 January</u>:
David Joel Steinberg, ed., <u>In Search of Southeast Asia: A Modern History</u> (Honolulu:
    University of Hawaii Press, 1987. Revised Edition.
    PLEASE IDENTIFY ASSUMPTIONS, EMPHASES, AND THEMES BEFORE CLASS

W. R. Geddes, "The Countryside and the Jungle." IN Robert O. Tilman, ed.
    <u>Man, State, and Society in Contemporary Southeast Asia</u> (New York:
    Praeger Publishers, 1969), pp. 88-97.

    Film--North Dakota State Film Library
            Bali: Isle of Temples. 27 min. Color. $13.00 (1977)

<u>Monday, 14 January</u>:
    Coedes, pp. 37-70 (Part II). PLEASE IDENTIFY WHAT, HOW, WHO, WHEN, WHY, WHERE OF
                                SINIFICATION AND INDIANIZATION IN SOUTHEAST
                                ASIA; PLEASE ALSO COMPARE AND CONTRAST THE TWO SETS.
        Bruce might ask to see your notes showing that you have done this before class.

<u>Wednesday, 16 January</u>:
    Coedes, pp. 73-117 (Part III). PLEASE IDENTIFY AND OUTLINE HIS SOURCES OF INFORMATION.
                                AS WELL AS THE WHAT, WHEN, WHERE, HOW, WHY, AND
                                WHO OF THESE SPECIFIC "three great civilizations".
        Bruce might ask to see your notes showing that you have done this before class.

<u>Friday, 18 January</u>:
    Coedes, pp. 121-134 (Part IV). PLEASE NOTE THE WHAT, WHEN, WHERE, WHY, HOW, AND WHO
                                WERE AFFECTED BY THE CRISIS OF THE 13TH CENTURY.
        Bruce might ask to see your notes showing that you have done this before class.

<u>Monday, 21 January</u>:
    Coedès, pp. 137-230 (Part V). PLEASE IDENTIFY AND OUTLINE HIS SOURCES,
                                AS WELL AS THE WHAT, WHEN, WHERE, AND
                                WHO OF THESE 5 STATES.
        Bruce might ask to see your notes showing that you have done this before class.

<u>Wednesday, 23 January</u>:
    Continuation and Review

<u>Friday, 25 January</u>:
    Continuation and Review

<u>Monday, 28 January</u>: NO CLASS/PAPER ONE, Coedès book review. with focus on themes
                                developed in class.
    Please include with your essay reference to and use where appropriate of
Lawrence Palmer Briggs, "The Hinduized States of Southeast Asia: A Review," IN <u>Enduring</u>
    <u>Scholarship Selected From the Far Eastern Quarterly-The Journal of Asian Studies</u>
    <u>1941-1971: Volume 3: South and Southeast Asia</u>, ed. by John A. Harrison (Tucson: The
    University of Arizona Press. 1972), pp. 179-196 (first published in the <u>Far Eastern</u>
    <u>Quarterly</u>, 7:4 (August 1948).

<u>Wednesday, 30 January</u>: NO CLASS/PAPER ONE, Coedès book review, with focus on themes
                                developed in class.
        Please include with your essay reference to and use where appropriate of
Lawrence Palmer Briggs, "The Hinduized States of Southeast Asia: A Review." IN <u>Enduring</u>
        <u>Scholarship Selected From the Far Eastern Quarterly-The Journal of Asian Studies</u>
        <u>1941-1971: Volume 3: South and Southeast Asia</u>, ed. by John A. Harrison (Tucson: The
        University of Arizona Press, 1972), pp. 179-196 (first published in the <u>Far Eastern</u>
        <u>Quarterly</u>, 7:4 (August 1948).

<u>Friday, 1 February</u>:
        Heine-Geldern, all. PLEASE IDENTIFY ASSUMPTIONS, EMPHASES, AND THEMES; PLEASE
                             COMPARE AND CONTRAST THEM TO COEDES APPROACH

<u>Monday, 4 February</u>:
        STUDENT-LED CLASS PRESENTATION BASED ON PREVIOUS COURSE WORK AND, FROM THE
            BOOK BY HALL, CHAPTER 1

        PEER PRESENTATIONS OF
Bennet Bronson, "Exchange at the Upstream and Downstream Ends: Notes toward a Functional Model
        of the Coastal State in Southeast Asia," IN Karl L. Hutterer, ed., <u>Economic Exchange and</u>
        <u>Social Interaction in Southeast Asia: Perspectives from Prehistory, History, and</u>
        <u>Ethnography</u> (Ann Arbor: Center for South and Southeast Asian Studies (Michigan Papers on
        South and Southeast Asia, no. 13), The University of Michigan, 1977), pp. 39-52.

                                        AND

Karl L. Hutterer, "Prehistoric Trade and the Evolution of Philippine Societies: A
        Reconsideration," IN Karl L. Hutterer, ed., <u>Economic Exchange and Social Interaction in</u>
        <u>Southeast Asia: Perspectives from Prehistory, History, and Ethnography</u> (Ann Arbor: Center
        for South and Southeast Asian Studies (Michigan Papers on South and Southeast Asia, no.
        13), The University of Michigan, 1977), pp. 177-196.

<u>Wednesday, 6 February</u>:
        STUDENT-LED CLASS PRESENTATION BASED ON PREVIOUS COURSE WORK AND, FROM THE
            BOOK BY HALL, CHAPTER 2

        PEER PRESENTATION OF
Kenneth R. Hall and John K. Whitmore, "Southeast Asian Trade and the Isthmian Struggle,
        1000-1200 A.D.," IN Kenneth R. Hall and John K. Whitmore. eds., <u>Explorations in Early</u>
        <u>Southeast Asian History: The Origins of Southeast Asian Statecraft</u> (Ann Arbor: Center for
        South and Southeast Asian Studies (Michigan papers on South and Southeast Asia, no. 11),
        The University of Michigan, 1976), pp. 303-340.

<u>Friday, 8 February</u>:
        STUDENT-LED CLASS PRESENTATION BASED ON PREVIOUS COURSE WORK AND, FROM THE
            BOOK BY HALL, CHAPTER 3

        PEER PRESENTATION OF TWO ESSAYS,
Keith Taylor, "The Rise of Dai Viet and the Establishment of Thang-Long," IN Kenneth R. Hall
        and John K. Whitmore, eds., <u>Explorations in Early Southeast Asian History: The Origins of</u>
        <u>Southeast Asian Statecraft</u> (Ann Arbor: Center for South and Southeast Asian Studies

(Michigan papers on South and Southeast Asia, no. 11), The University of Michigan, 1976), pp. 149-191.   AND

John K. Whitmore, "Note: The Vietnamese Confucian Scholar's View of His Country's Early History," IN Kenneth R. Hall and John K. Whitmore, eds., Explorations in Early Southeast Asian History: The Origins of Southeast Asian Statecraft (Ann Arbor: Center for South and Southeast Asian Studies (Michigan papers on South and Southeast Asia, no. 11), The University of Michigan, 1976), pp. 193-203.

Monday, 11 February:
     STUDENT-LED CLASS PRESENTATION BASED ON PREVIOUS COURSE WORK AND, FROM THE
          BOOK BY HALL, CHAPTER 4

     PEER PRESENTATION OF
Lorraine Gesick, "The Rise and Fall of King Taksin: A Drama of Buddhist Kingship,"
     IN Lorraine Gesick, ed., Centers, Symbols, and Hierarchies: Essays on the Classical
     States of Southeast Asia (New Haven, Conn.: Yale University Southeast Asia Studies
     (Monograph Series, no. 26), 1983), pp. 87-105.

Wednesday, 13 February:
     STUDENT-LED CLASS PRESENTATION BASED ON PREVIOUS COURSE WORK AND, FROM THE
          BOOK BY HALL, CHAPTER 5

     PEER PRESENTATION OF
Anthony Day, "The Drama of Bangun Tapa's Exile in Ambon, The Poetry of Kingship in Surakarta,
     1830-58," IN Lorraine Gesick, ed., Centers, Symbols, and Hierarchies: Essays on the
     Classical States of Southeast Asia (New Haven, Conn.: Yale University Southeast Asia
     Studies (Monograph Series, no. 26), 1983), pp. 125-193.

Friday, 15 February:
     STUDENT-LED CLASS PRESENTATION BASED ON PREVIOUS COURSE WORK AND, FROM THE
          BOOK BY HALL, CHAPTER 6

     PEER PRESENTATION OF
Nidhi Aeusrivongse, "Devaraja Cult and Khmer Kingship at Angkor," IN Kenneth R. Hall and John
     K. Whitmore, eds., Explorations in Early Southeast Asian History: The Origins of Southeast
     Asian Statecraft (Ann Arbor: Center for South and Southeast Asian Studies (Michigan papers
     on South and Southeast Asia, no. 11), The University of Michigan, 1976), pp. 107-148.

Monday, 18 February:
     STUDENT-LED CLASS PRESENTATION BASED ON PREVIOUS COURSE WORK AND, FROM THE
          BOOK BY HALL, CHAPTER 7

     PEER PRESENTATION OF
David P. Chandler, "Going Through the Motions: Ritual Aspects of the Reign of King Duang of
     Cambodia (1848-1860)," IN Lorraine Gesick, ed., Centers, Symbols, and Hierarchies: Essays
     on the Classical States of Southeast Asia (New Haven, Conn.: Yale University Southeast
     Asia Studies (Monograph Series, no. 26), 1983), pp. 106-124.

Wednesday, 20 February:
     STUDENT-LED CLASS PRESENTATION BASED ON PREVIOUS COURSE WORK AND, FROM THE
          BOOK BY HALL, CHAPTER 8

     TWO PEER PRESENTATIONS OF
Michael Aung-Thwin, "Divinity, Spirit, and Human: Conceptions of Classical Burmese Kingship,"
     IN Lorraine Gesick, ed., Centers, Symbols, and Hierarchies: Essays on the Classical
     States of Southeast Asia (New Haven, Conn.: Yale University Southeast Asia Studies
     (Monograph Series, no. 26), 1983), pp. 45-86.

                                   AND

Michael Aung Thwin, " Kingship, the <u>Sangha</u>, and Society in Pagan," IN Kenneth R. Hall and John
     K. Whitmore, eds., Explorations in Early Southeast Asian History: The Origins of Southeast
     Asian Statecraft (Ann Arbor: Center for South and Southeast Asian Studies (Michigan papers
     on South and Southeast Asia, no. 11), The University of Michigan, 1976), pp. 205-256.

Friday, 22 February:
     STUDENT-LED CLASS PRESENTATION BASED ON PREVIOUS COURSE WORK AND, FROM THE
          BOOK BY HALL, CHAPTER 9

     PEER PRESENTATION OF
Jan Wisseman Christie, "Raja and Rama: The Classical State in Early Java,"
     IN Lorraine Gesick, ed., Centers, Symbols, and Hierarchies: Essays on the Classical
     States of Southeast Asia (New Haven, Conn.: Yale University Southeast Asia Studies
     (Monograph Series, no. 26), 1983), pp. 9-44.

                      MIDSEMESTER BREAK, 23 FEBRUARY-3 MARCH 1991

Monday, 4 March: NO CLASS/PAPER TWO, HALL, Book Review with focus on themes developed in class

Wednesday, 6 March: NO CLASS/PAPER TWO, HALL, Book Review with focus on themes developed in
                                        class

Friday, 8 March:
     Begin Reid book--required for today are the Preface and Chapter One (pp. xv-xvi and 1-43)

Monday, 11 March:
     STUDENT-LED CLASS PRESENTATION BASED ON PREVIOUS COURSE WORK AND, FROM THE
          BOOK BY REID, CHAPTER 2

Wednesday, 13 March:
     STUDENT-LED CLASS PRESENTATION BASED ON PREVIOUS COURSE WORK AND, FROM THE
          BOOK BY REID, CHAPTER 3

                                    182

<u>Friday, 15 March</u>:
     STUDENT-LED CLASS PRESENTATION BASED ON PREVIOUS COURSE WORK AND, FROM THE
        BOOK BY REID, CHAPTER 4

<u>Monday, 18 March</u>:
     STUDENT-LED CLASS PRESENTATION BASED ON PREVIOUS COURSE WORK AND, FROM THE
        BOOK BY REID, CHAPTER 5

     PEER PRESENTATION OF
Andrew Turton, "Thai Institutions of Slavery," IN James L. Watson, ed.,
    <u>Asian and African Systems of Slavery</u> (Berkeley: University of California
    Press, 1980), pp. 251-292.

<u>Wednesday, 20 March</u>:
     STUDENT-LED CLASS PRESENTATION BASED ON PREVIOUS COURSE WORK AND, FROM THE
        BOOK BY REID, CHAPTER 6

<u>Friday, 22 March</u>:
     STUDENT-LED CLASS PRESENTATION BASED ON PREVIOUS COURSE WORK AND, FROM THE
        BOOK BY REID, CHAPTER 7

<u>Monday, 25 March</u>:
     STUDENT-LED CLASS PRESENTATION BASED ON PREVIOUS COURSE WORK AND, FROM THE
        BOOK BY REID, CHAPTER 8

<u>Wednesday, 27 March</u>:
     STUDENT-LED CLASS PRESENTATION BASED ON PREVIOUS COURSE WORK AND, FROM THE
        BOOK BY REID, CHAPTER 9

EASTER BREAK, 28 MARCH-1 APRIL 1991

<u>Wednesday, 3 April</u>:
     STUDENT-LED CLASS PRESENTATION BASED ON PREVIOUS COURSE WORK AND, FROM THE
        BOOK BY REID, CHAPTER 10

<u>Friday, 5 April</u>:
     STUDENT-LED CLASS PRESENTATION BASED ON PREVIOUS COURSE WORK AND, FROM THE
        BOOK BY REID, CHAPTER 11

<u>Monday, 8 April</u>:
     STUDENT-LED CLASS PRESENTATION BASED ON PREVIOUS COURSE WORK AND, FROM THE
        BOOK BY REID, CHAPTER 12

STUDENT-LED CLASS PRESENTATION BASED ON PREVIOUS COURSE WORK AND. FROM THE
BOOK BY REID. CHAPTER 13

Friday, 12 April:
STUDENT-LED CLASS PRESENTATION BASED ON PREVIOUS COURSE WORK AND. FROM THE
BOOK BY REID, CHAPTER 14

Monday, 15 April:
STUDENT-LED CLASS PRESENTATION BASED ON PREVIOUS COURSE WORK AND, FROM THE
BOOK BY REID. CHAPTER 15

PEER PRESENTATION OF
H. S. Morris, "Slaves, Aristocrats and Export of Sago in Sarawak," IN James L. Watson, ed..
Asian and African Systems of Slavery (Berkeley: University of California
Press, 1980), pp. 293-308.

Wednesday, 17 April: NO CLASS/PAPER III, REID, book review with focus on themes
developed in class

Friday, 19 April: NO CLASS/PAPER III, REID, book review with focus on themes
developed in class

Monday, 22 April:
PEER OR GROUP PRESENTATIONS OF EACH OF THE FOLLOWING ARTICLES OR SET OF ARTICLES:

Harry J. Benda, "The Structure of Southeast Asian History: Some Preliminary Observations."
IN Robert O. Tilman, ed. Man, State, and Society in Contemporary Southeast Asia (New
York: Praeger Publishers, 1969), pp. 23-33 [part of the essay, only, required].
AND
John Bastin and Harry J. Benda. A History of Modern Southeast Asia: Colonialism, Nationalism,
and Decolonization (Englewood Cliffs, N.J.: Prentice-Hall, Inc., 1968), "Introduction",
pp. 1-14.

Donald K. Emmerson, ""Southeast Asia": What's in a Name?" Journal of Southeast Asian
Studies (15:1 (March 1984), pp. 1-21; and """Southeast Asia": What's in a Name", Another
Point of View," by Wilhelm G. Solheim II, in Journal of Southeast Asian Studies, 16:1
(March 1985), pp. 141-147.

Masao Nishimura. "Long Distance Trade and the Development of Complex Societies in the
Prehistory of the Central Philippines--The Cebu Archaeological Project: Basic Concept and
First Results." Philippine Quarterly of Culture & Society, 16 (June 1988), pp. 107-157.

    PEER OR GROUP PRESENTATIONS OF EACH OF THE FOLLOWING ARTICLES OR SET OF ARTICLES, CONT.:

Harry J. Benda, "The Structure of Southeast Asian History: Some Preliminary Observations."
    IN Robert O. Tilman, ed. Man, State, and Society in Contemporary Southeast Asia (New
    York: Praeger Publishers, 1969), pp. 23-33 [part of the essay, only, required].
                AND
John Bastin and Harry J. Benda. A History of Modern Southeast Asia: Colonialism, Nationalism,
    and Decolonization (Englewood Cliffs, N.J.: Prentice-Hall, Inc., 1968), "Introduction".
    pp. 1-14.

Donald K. Emmerson, ""Southeast Asia": What's in a Name?" Journal of Southeast Asian
    Studies (15:1 (March 1984), pp. 1-21; and """Southeast Asia": What's in a Name", Another
    Point of View," by Wilhelm G. Solheim II, in Journal of Southeast Asian Studies, 16:1
    (March 1985), pp. 141-147.

Masao Nishimura, "Long Distance Trade and the Development of Complex Societies in the
    Prehistory of the Central Philippines--The Cebu Archaeological Project: Basic Concept and
    First Results." Philippine Quarterly of Culture & Society, 16 (June 1988), pp. 107-157.

Friday, 26 April:
    PEER OR GROUP PRESENTATIONS OF EACH OF THE FOLLOWING ARTICLES OR SET OF ARTICLES, CONT.:

Harry J. Benda, "The Structure of Southeast Asian History: Some Preliminary Observations."
    IN Robert O. Tilman, ed. Man, State, and Society in Contemporary Southeast Asia (New
    York: Praeger Publishers, 1969), pp. 23-33 [part of the essay, only, required].
                AND
John Bastin and Harry J. Benda. A History of Modern Southeast Asia: Colonialism, Nationalism,
    and Decolonization (Englewood Cliffs, N.J.: Prentice-Hall, Inc., 1968), "Introduction",
    pp. 1-14.

Donald K. Emmerson, ""Southeast Asia": What's in a Name?" Journal of Southeast Asian
    Studies (15:1 (March 1984), pp. 1-21; and """Southeast Asia": What's in a Name", Another
    Point of View," by Wilhelm G. Solheim II, in Journal of Southeast Asian Studies, 16:1
    (March 1985), pp. 141-147.

Masao Nishimura, "Long Distance Trade and the Development of Complex Societies in the
    Prehistory of the Central Philippines--The Cebu Archaeological Project: Basic Concept and
    First Results." Philippine Quarterly of Culture & Society, 16 (June 1988), pp. 107-157.

Monday, 29 April: NO CLASS/PAPER IV. Critique of one of the above articles
    or set of articles, based on coursework to date. The choice or choices will be made by
    Bruce on Friday, 26 April, based on presentations and controversy suggested thereby.
    (It would seem to pay each group or individual presenter to try make that
    presentation the most provocative and promising of the ones made Wednesday or Friday)

Tuesday, 30 April: Study Day

Final Examinations, 1-3 May 1991

<u>Other Required Materials</u> (available at the Reserve Desk, Carl B. Ylvisaker Library, unless otherwise noted)

Nidhi Aeusrivongse, "<u>Devaraja</u> Cult and Khmer Kingship at Angkor," IN Kenneth R. Hall and John K. Whitmore, eds., <u>Explorations in Early Southeast Asian History: The Origins of Southeast Asian Statecraft</u> (Ann Arbor: Center for South and Southeast Asian Studies (Michigan papers on South and Southeast Asia, no. 11), The University of Michigan, 1976), pp. 107-148.

Michael Aung-Thwin, "Divinity, Spirit, and Human: Conceptions of Classical Burmese Kingship," IN Lorraine Gesick, ed., Centers, Symbols, and Hierarchies: Essays on the Classical <u>States of Southeast Asia</u> (New Haven, Conn.: Yale University Southeast Asia Studies (Monograph Series, no. 26), 1983), pp. 45-86.

Michael Aung Thwin," Kingship, the <u>Sangha</u>, and Society in Pagan," IN Kenneth R. Hall and John K. Whitmore, eds., <u>Explorations in Early Southeast Asian History: The Origins of Southeast Asian Statecraft</u> (Ann Arbor: Center for South and Southeast Asian Studies (Michigan papers on South and Southeast Asia, no. 11), The University of Michigan, 1976), pp. 205-256.

John Bastin and Harry J. Benda. <u>A History of Modern Southeast Asia: Colonialism, Nationalism, and Decolonization</u> (Englewood Cliffs, N.J.: Prentice-Hall, Inc., 1968), "Introduction", pp. 1-14.

Harry J. Benda, "The Structure of Southeast Asian History: Some Preliminary Observations." IN Robert O. Tilman, ed. <u>Man, State, and Society in Contemporary Southeast Asia</u> (New York: Praeger Publishers, 1969), pp. 23-33 [<u>part</u> of the essay, only, required].

Lawrence Palmer Briggs, "The Hinduized States of Southeast Asia: A Review," IN <u>Enduring Scholarship Selected From the Far Eastern Quarterly-The Journal of Asian Studies 1941-1971: Volume 3: South and Southeast Asia</u>, ed. by John A. Harrison (Tucson: The University of Arizona Press, 1972), pp. 179-196 (first published in the <u>Far Eastern Quarterly</u>, 7:4 (August 1948).

Bennet Bronson, "Exchange at the Upstream and Downstream Ends: Notes toward a Functional Model of the Coastal State in Southeast Asia," IN Karl L. Hutterer, ed., <u>Economic Exchange and Social Interaction in Southeast Asia: Perspectives from Prehistory, History, and Ethnography</u> (Ann Arbor: Center for South and Southeast Asian Studies (Michigan Papers on South and Southeast Asia, no. 13), The University of Michigan, 1977), pp. 39-52.

David P. Chandler, "Going Through the Motions: Ritual Aspects of the Reign of King Duang of Cambodia (1848-1860)," IN Lorraine Gesick, ed., Centers, Symbols, and Hierarchies: Essays <u>on the Classical States of Southeast Asia</u> (New Haven, Conn.: Yale University Southeast Asia Studies (Monograph Series, no. 26), 1983), pp. 106-124.

Jan Wisseman Christie, "Raja and Rama: The Classical State in Early Java," IN Lorraine Gesick, ed., Centers, Symbols, and Hierarchies: Essays on the Classical <u>States of Southeast Asia</u> (New Haven, Conn.: Yale University Southeast Asia Studies (Monograph Series, no. 26), 1983), pp. 9-44.

Anthony Day, "The Drama of Bangun Tapa's Exile in Ambon, The Poetry of Kingship in Surakarta, 1830-58," IN Lorraine Gesick, ed., Centers, Symbols, and Hierarchies: Essays on the <u>Classical States of Southeast Asia</u> (New Haven, Conn.: Yale University Southeast Asia Studies (Monograph Series, no. 26), 1983), pp. 125-193.

Donald K. Emmerson. ""Southeast Asia": What's in a Name?" <u>Journal of Southeast Asian Studies</u> (15:1 (March 1984). pp. 1-21; <u>and</u> """Southeast Asia": What's in a Name", Another Point of View." by Wilhelm G. Solheim II, in <u>Journal of Southeast Asian Studies,</u> 16:1 (March 1985), pp. 141-147.

W. R. Geddes, "The Countryside and the Jungle." IN Robert O. Tilman. ed. <u>Man, State, and Society in Contemporary Southeast Asia</u> (New York: Praeger Publishers, 1969), pp. 88-97.

Lorraine Gesick. "The Rise and Fall of King Taksin: A Drama of Buddhist Kingship." IN Lorraine Gesick, ed., Centers, Symbols, and Hierarchies: Essays on the Classical <u>States of Southeast Asia</u> (New Haven, Conn.: Yale University Southeast Asia Studies (Monograph Series, no. 26), 1983), pp. 87-105.

Kenneth R. Hall and John K. Whitmore, "Southeast Asian Trade and the Isthmian Struggle, 1000-1200 A.D.," IN Kenneth R. Hall and John K. Whitmore, eds., <u>Explorations in Early Southeast Asian History: The Origins of Southeast Asian Statecraft</u> (Ann Arbor: Center for South and Southeast Asian Studies (Michigan papers on South and Southeast Asia, no. 11), The University of Michigan. 1976), pp. 303-340.

Karl L. Hutterer, "Prehistoric Trade and the Evolution of Philippine Societies: A Reconsideration," IN Karl L. Hutterer, ed., <u>Economic Exchange and Social Interaction in Southeast Asia: Perspectives from Prehistory, History, and Ethnography</u> (Ann Arbor: Center for South and Southeast Asian Studies (Michigan Papers on South and Southeast Asia, no. 13), The University of Michigan, 1977), pp. 177-196.

H. S. Morris. "Slaves, Aristocrats and Export of Sago in Sarawak," IN James L. Watson, ed., <u>Asian and African Systems of Slavery</u> (Berkeley: University of California Press, 1980), pp. 293-308.

Masao Nishimura, "Long Distance Trade and the Development of Complex Societies in the Prehistory of the Central Philippines--The Cebu Archaeological Project: Basic Concept and First Results." <u>Philippine Quarterly of Culture & Society,</u> 16 (June 1988), pp. 107-157.

Wilhelm G. Solheim, II. SEE under Donald K. Emmerson.

David Joel Steinberg, ed., <u>In Search of Southeast Asia: A Modern History</u> (Honolulu: University of Hawaii Press, 1987. Revised Edition.

Keith Taylor, "The Rise of Dai Viet and the Establishment of Thang-Long," IN Kenneth R. Hall and John K. Whitmore, eds., <u>Explorations in Early Southeast Asian History: The Origins of Southeast Asian Statecraft</u> (Ann Arbor: Center for South and Southeast Asian Studies (Michigan papers on South and Southeast Asia, no. 11), The University of Michigan, 1976), pp. 149-191.

Andrew Turton, "Thai Institutions of Slavery," IN James L. Watson, ed., <u>Asian and African Systems of Slavery</u> (Berkeley: University of California Press, 1980), pp. 251-292.

John K. Whitmore, "Note: The Vietnamese Confucian Scholar's View of His Country's Early History," IN Kenneth R. Hall and John K. Whitmore, eds., <u>Explorations in Early Southeast Asian History: The Origins of Southeast Asian Statecraft</u> (Ann Arbor: Center for South and Southeast Asian Studies (Michigan papers on South and Southeast Asia, no. 11), The University of Michigan, 1976), pp. 193-203.

History 3893

(History of Southeast Asia)

Spring, 1990

Sidney D. Brown,   University of Oklahoma
Professor of History,
Dale Hall Tower 423,
Office Hours: Wednesday, 1:30 p.m.; Friday, 10:30 a.m.; and
      by appointment
Telephone: 325-6572 (Office); 325-6002 (History)

REQUIRED BOOKS:
David Joel Steinberg, In Search of Southeast Asia: a Modern
      History. 1987 edition.
Samuel L. Popkin, The Rational Peasant: the Political Economy
      of Rural Society in Vietnam. 1979.
Multatuli, Max Havelaar, or the Coffee Auctions of the Dutch
      Trading Company. 1982.
Raden Adjeng Kartini, Letters of a Javanese Princess. 1964.
David Howard Bain, Sitting in Darkness: Americans in the
      Philippines. 1987.
J.D.Legge, Sukarno: a Political Biography. 1972.
Bernard B. Fall, Hell in a Very Small Place: the Siege of
      Dienbienphu. 1966.

SCHEDULE OF LECTURES AND DISCUSSIONS:

FIRST WEEK
January 15   Introduction
January 17   Historical Geography of Southeast Asia: Unity and
      Diversity
                  Steinberg, In Search of Southeast Asia,
                  Introduction, Chapters 1 (The Peasant World), 2
                  (Non-State Peoples)
January 19   Indianization of Southeast Asia
                  Steinberg, 3(Authority and Village Society),
                  6(Traders and Markets)
                  Recommended: G. Coedes, The Indianized States
                  of Southeast Asia. 1968

SECOND WEEK
January 22   Buddhist Kings: Pagan Burma
                  Steinberg, 5(Religious Life and Leadership),
                  7(The Buddhist Kings)
                  Recommended: Htin Aung, A History of Burma.
                  1967.
January 24   God-Kings in Angkor: the Khmer Empire
                  Steinberg, 4(Provincial Powers)
                  Recommended: Bernard Groslier, The Arts and
                  Civilization of Angkor. 1957.
                  SLIDE LECTURE
January 26   Confucian Empire in Vietnam
                  Steinberg, 8(The Vietnamese Emperors)

Recommended: John K. Whitmore, <u>Vietnam, Ho Quy Ly, and the Ming 1371-1421</u>. 1985.

THIRD WEEK
January 29   The Malay Sultans
                       Steinberg, 9(The Malay Sultans)
                       Recommended: K.G.Tregonning, <u>A History of Modern Malaya</u>. 1964.
January 31   European Imperialism in Southeast Asia: the
             Portuguese and the Dutch
                       Steinberg, 10(The Javanese KIngs)
                       Henry Hart, <u>The Sea Road to the Indies</u>. 1950.
February 2   Spanish Governors in the Philippines
                       Steinberg, 11(The Spanish Governors)
                       Recommended: John L. Phelan, <u>Hispanization of the Philippines</u>. 1959.

FOURTH WEEK
February 5   Dutch Culture System in Java
                       Steinberg, 18(Java, 1757-1875)
                       Recommended: J.S.Furnivall, <u>The Netherlands Indies: a Study of Plural Economy</u>. 1944.
February 7   CLASS DISCUSSION: Dutch Imperialism in Literature
                       Multatuli, <u>Max Havelaar, or the Coffee Auctions of the Dutch Trading Company</u>. 1859.
                       Questions to be distributed; prepare for quiz.
February 9   Nationalist Movement in Indonesia
                       Steinberg, 20 (The Making of New States), 27
                       (Indonesia)
                       Recommended: George Kahin, <u>Nationalism and Revolution in Indonesia</u>. 1952.

FIFTH WEEK
February 12 The Maintenance of Independence in Siam
                       Steinberg, 13 (Siam, 1767-1868)
                       Recommended: David Wyatt, <u>A History of Thailand</u>. 1984.
February 14 FIRST HOUR EXAMINATION
February 16 Siam's Early Modernization: Kings Mongkut and
             Chulalongkorn
                       Steinberg, 21 (Bureaucratic and Economic Frameworks)
                       Recommended: A.B.Moffatt, <u>King Mongkut of Siam</u>. 1961.

SIXTH WEEK
February 19 Democratic Revolution of 1932 in Siam
                       Steinberg, 27 (Siam)
                       Recommended: Kenneth P. Landon, <u>Siam in Transition</u>. 1939.
February 21 CLASS DISCUSSION: Worldview of a Feminist
             Patriot in Java
                       Raden Adjeng Kartini, <u>Letters of a Javanese Princess</u>. 1964.
                       Questions to be distributed; prepare for quiz.
February 23 Raffles and the Founding of Singapore, 1819
                       Steinberg, 16 (The Malay Peninsula to 1874)

Recommended: C.E.Wurzberg, <u>Raffles of the Eastern Isles</u>. 1954.

SEVENTH WEEK
February 26   Formation of Straits Settlements, 1874
              Steinberg, 17 (The Archipelago, 1750-1870)
              Recommended: C. Northcote Parkinson, <u>British Intervention in Malay</u>. 1960.
February 28   British Malaya
              Steinberg, 23 (Preludes), 30 (Malaya)
              Recommended: William R. Roff, <u>The Origins of Malayan Nationalism</u>. 1967.
March 2   British Conquest of Burma
              Steinberg, 12 (Burma, 1752-1878)
              Recommended: Oliver B. Pollack, <u>Empires in Collision: Anglo-Burmese Relations in the Mid-Nineteenth Century</u>. 1979.

EIGHTH WEEK
March 5   Nationalist Movement in Burma
          Steinberg, 24 (Channels of Change), 26 (Burma)
          Recommended: Maurice Collis, <u>Trials in Burma</u>. 1938.
March 7   Jose Rizal and the Early Nationalist Movement in the
     Philippines
          Steinberg, 19 (The Philippines, 1762-1872)
          Recommended: Jose Rizal, <u>The Lost Eden</u>, tr. by Leon Ma. Guerrero. 1961.
March 9   CLASS DISCUSSION: American Imperialism in the
     Philippines--its Origins
          David Howard Bain, <u>Sitting in Darkness</u>. 1987.
          Questions to be distributed; prepare for quiz.

NINTH WEEK
March 19   American Rule in the Philippines, 1898-1941
           Steinberg, 25 (The Philippines)
           Recommended: Peter W. Stanley, <u>A Nation in the Making: The Philippines and the United States, 1899-1921</u>. 1974.
March 21   French Conquest of Vietnam
           Steinberg, 15 (Vietnam)
           Recommended: Joseph Buttinger, <u>Vietnam: The Smaller Dragon</u>. 1958.
March 23   Ho Chi Minh and Vietnamese Nationalism
           Steinberg, 28 (Vietnam)
           Recommended: Jean LaCouture, <u>Ho Chi Minh, a Political Biography</u>. 1968.

TENTH WEEK
March 26   Kingdom of Cambodia as French Protectorate
           Steinberg, 14 (Cambodia, 1779-1863); 31 (Laos and Cambodia)
           Recommended: David P. Chandler, <u>A History of Cambodia</u>. 1983.
March 28   SECOND HOUR EXAMINATION
March 30   Japan's Conquest of Southeast Asia, 1941-1945

Steinberg, 32 (War, Independence, and Political
Transition)
Recommended: Alfred W. McCoy, ed., Southeast
Asia under Japanese Occupation. 1980.

ELEVENTH WEEK
April 2   Sukarno and Indonesian Independence
           Steinberg, 38 (Indonesia)
           Recommended: Soetan Sjharir, Out of Exile.
           1948
April 4...CLASS DISCUSSION: Sukarno--Statesman or Charlatan?
           J.D.Legge, Sukarno: a Political Biography.
           1972.
           Questions to be distributed; prepare for quiz.
April 6   Coup and Countercoup in Indonesia, 1965
           Guest Lecture, Dr. Stephen Sloan, Professor of
           Political Science, University of Oklahoma
           Recommended: Stephen Sloan, Political Violence
           in Indonesia. 1970.

TWELFTH WEEK
April 9   Suharto and Military Rule in Indonesia, 1990
           Steinberg, 38 (The Republic of Indonesia)
           Recommended: Harold Crouch, The Army and
           Politics in Indonesia. 1978.
April 11   French Withdrawal from Vietnam
           Steinberg, 33 (Vietnam)
           Recommended: Frances Fitzgerald, The Fire in
           the Lake. 1975.
April 13   United States Intervention in Vietnam, 1954-1975
           Recommended: Stanley Karnow, Vietnam: a
           History. 1983.

THIRTEENTH WEEK
April 16   Democratic Republic of Vietnam: its Problems, 1975-
           1990
           Recommended: William J. Duiker, Vietnam since
           the Fall of Saigon. 1985.
April 18   CLASS DISCUSSION: Social Change in Vietnamese
           Peasant Society--an Evaluation
           Samuel I. Popkin, The Rational Peasant. 1979.
           Ten-page essay in accordance with instructions.
April 20   Cambodia: from Norodom Sihanouk to Hun Sen
           Steinberg, 34 (Cambodia and Laos)
           Recommended: Sydney H. Schamberg, The Life and
           Death of Dith Pran. 1985.

FOURTEENTH WEEK
April 23   Postwar Thailand: Army and Büreaucracy
           Steinberg, 35 (The Kingdom of Thailand)
           Recommended: Fred W. Riggs, Thailand: the
           Modernization of a Bureaucratic Polity. 1966.
April 25   Ne Win and Military Socialism in Burma
           36 (The Union of Burma)
           Recommended: Frank N. Trager, Burma: from
           Kingdom to Republic. 1966.

April 27   Crisis in the Philippines: Corazan Aquino's Rise to
           Power, 1986
                    Steinberg, 39 (The Republic of the Philippines)
                    Recommended: Lewis M. Simons, Worth Dying For.
                    1987.

FIFTEENTH WEEK
April 30   CLASS DISCUSSION: Why the French Withdrew from
           Vietnam
                    Bernard B. Fall, Dienbienphu: Hell in a Very
                    Small Place. 1967.
                    Questions to be distributed; prepare for quiz.
May 2.....Malaysia and Singapore: Politics in Multiracial
           Societies
                    Steinberg, 39 (Malaysia, Singapore, and
                    Brunei), 40 (Transformation of Southeast Asia)
                    Recommended: Willard A. Hanna, The Formation
                    of Malaysia: New Factor in World Politics.
                    1964.

MAKEUP EXAMINATIONS: Friday, May 4, 1:30-2:30 p.m., 408 Dale
           Hall Tower.   Make arrangements in advance.

FINAL EXAMINATION: Wednesday, May 9, 8-10 a.m.

INSTRUCTIONS:
1. Class attendance is expected; roll will be taken.
2. Makeup examinations will be given to those who miss the
      regular examinations unavoidably--at the end of the
      semester. Make arrangements with the professor.
3. Attendance at class discussion is required; and its is a
      factor in your grade, as is the quiz.
4. You are welcome to discuss matters relating to Southeast
      Asian history with me during office hours, or at other
      times.   Make special appointments if you have conflicts
      with my office hours.
5. The class grade breaks down as follows: First Hour
      Examination, 20%; Second Hour Examination, 20%; Final
      Examination, 40%; Additional Books and Essay, 20%.
6. Bring bluebooks to examinations which are primarily of the
      essay type.
7. Numerical grades are assigned as follows: A,90-100; B,80-
      89; C,70-79; D,60-69; F,0-59.

EARLY HISTORY OF SOUTHEAST ASIA

TEXT: Sar Desai, D.R., Southeast Asia - Past and Present, Boulder, Colorado,
       Westview Press, 1989 (Second Edition).

For General Reference:

BOOKS: Cowan, C.D. and O.W. Wolters, (Eds.) Southeast Asian History and
        Historiography, Essays Presented to D.G.E. Hall, Ithaca, 1976.

        Fisher, C.A., South-East Asia: A Social, Economic and Political
        Geography, New York, 1964.

        Gesick, Lorraine, (Ed.), Centers, Symbols, and Hierarchies:
        Essays on the Classical States of Southern Asia, New Haven, 1983.

        Hall, D.G.E., History of Southeast Asia, London, 1968.

        _____, (ed.), Historians of Southeast Asia, London, 1961.

        Hall, Kenneth R., (Ed.) Maritime Trade and State Development in
        Early Southeast Asia, Honolulu, 1985.

        Hall, Kenneth R. and John K. Whitmore (Eds.), Explorations in
        Early Southeast Asian History: The Origins of Southeast Asian
        Statecraft, Ann Arbor, 1976.

        Hutterer, Karl L. (Ed.), Economic Exchange and Soviet Interaction
        In Southeast Asia: Perspectives from Prehistory, History and
        Ethnography, Ann Arbor, 1977.

        Reid, Anthony and L. Castles, (Eds.), Pre-colonial State Systems
        in Southeast Asia, Kuala Lumpur, 1975.

        Reid, Anthony and David Marr, (Eds.), Perceptions of the Past in
        Southeast Asia, Singapore, 1979.

        Smith R.B. and W. Watson, (Eds.), Early Southeast Asia: Essays
        in Archaeology, History and Historical Geography, London, 1979.

        Wolters, O.W., History, Culture and Religion in Southeast Asian
        Perspectives, Singapore, 1982.

ATLAS: Hall, D.G.E., Atlas of Southeast Asia, Amsterdam, 1964.

BIBLIOGRAPHY: Hay, Stephen and Case, Margaret, Southeast Asian History,
               A Bibliographic Guide, New York, 1962.
               Tregonning, K.G., Southeast Asia: A Critical Bibliography,
               Tucson, Arizona, 1969.

Introduction: Mainland Southeast Asia Up to 1200
                 Sar Desai, Chapters 1 and 2

Recommended: Bayard, D.T., "The Roots of Indochinese Civilization: Recent
                     Developments in the Pre-History of Southeast Asia,"
                     Pacific Affairs, LIII (1980), pp. 89-114.
                 Briggs, Lawrence P., The Ancient Khmer Empire, Philadelphia,
                     1951.
                 Chatterjee, B.R., Indian Cultural Influence in Cambodia,
                     Calcutta, 1928.
                 Coedes, Georges, The Indianized States of Southeast Asia,
                     Honolulu, 1968.
                 Conze, Edward, Buddhism: Its Essence and Development, Chicago,
                     1959.
                 Coomaraswamy, A.K., History of Indian and Indonesian Art,
                     New York, 1965.
                 Ghosh, Manmohan, A History of Cambodia, Saigon, 1960.
                 Groslier, B.P., Angkor, London, 1957 or The Art of Indochina,
                     New York, 1962.
                 Hall, Kenneth R. and John K. Whitmore, Eds., Explorations in
                     Early Southeast Asian History: The Origins of Southeast
                     Asian Statecraft, Ann Arbor, 1976.
                 Herz, Martin, A Short History of Cambodia, N.Y., 1958.
                 Heine-Geldern, Robert D., The Conceptions of State and Kingship
                     in Southeast Asia, Ithaca, N.Y., 1956.
                 Kulke, Hermann, The Devaraja Cult, Ithaca, 1978.
                 Le May, Reginald, The Culture of Southeast Asia, New Delhi,
                     1962, Chapters V-VI.
                 Mabbett, I.W., "The Indianization of Southeast Asia:
                     Reflections on the Prehistoric Sources," Journal of Southeast
                     Asian Studies, VIII, 2 (September 1977), pp. 143-161.
                 Mabbett, I.W., "Devaraja," Journal of Southeast Asian History,
                     X, September, 1969), pp. 202-23.
                 Majumdar, R.C., Hindu Colonies, Calcutta, 1963, pp. 1-112.
                     _____, Kambuja-Desa, Madras, 1944.
                 Mus, Paul, India Seen From the East: Indian and Indigenous Cults
                     in Champa, trans. I.W. Mabbett and D.P. Chandler, Clayton,
                     Victoria, 1975.
                 Quaritch-Wales, H.G., The Making of Greater India, London, 1961.
                 Ray, Niharranjan, Theravada Buddhism in Burma, Calcutta, 1946.
                 Smith, R.B. and W. Watson, Eds., Early Southeast Asia: Essays
                     in Archaeology, History and Historical Geography, London, 1979.
                 Taylor, Keith W., The Birth of Vietnam, Berkeley, 1983.
                 Van Liere, W.J., "Traditional Water Management in the Lower
                     Mekong Basin," World Archaeology, II, 3(1980), pp. 265-280.

Insular Southeast Asia Before Islamization,
Sar Desai, Chapter 3

Recommended: Coedes, Georges, The Indianized States of Southeast Asia,
Honolulu, 1968.
Coomaraswamy, A.K., History of Indian and Indonesian Art,
New York, 1965.
Gomez, Louis and Hiram Woodward, Jr., (Eds.), Barabudur:
History and Significance of a Buddhist Monument, Berkeley,
1981.
Hall, Kenneth, Maritime Trade and State Development in Early
Southeast Asia, Honolulu, 1985.
Legge, J.D., Indonesia, Englewood Cliffs, 1964.
Le May, Reginald, The Culture of Southeast Asia, New Delhi,
1962, Chapters V-VI.
Majumdar, R.C., Hindu Colonies, Calcutta, 1963, pp. 1-112.
Spencer, George W., The Politics of Expansion: The Chola
Conquest of Sri Lanka and Sri Vijaya, Madras, 1983.
Van der Meer, N.C. Van Setten, Sawah Cultivation in Ancient
Java: Aspects of Development during the Indo-Javanese Period,
5th to 15th Century, Canberra, 1979.
Van Naerssen, F.H. and R.C. de Iongh, The Economic and
Administrative History of Early Indonesia, Leiden, 1977.
Wake, C.H., "Malacca's Early Kings and the Reception of Islam,"
Journal of Southeast Asian History, V, 2 (September, 1964),
pp. 104-128.
Wales, H.G. Quaritch, "The Extent of Sri Vijaya's Influence
Abroad," Journal of Malaya Branch Royal Asiatic Society, 51, 1
(1978), pp. 5-12.
Wheatley, Paul, The Golden Chersonese, Kuala Lumpur, 1961, parts
III, VI.
Wolters, O.W., Early Indonesian Commerce: A Case Study of the
Origins of Srivijaya, Ithaca, New York, 1967.

WEEKS VI and VII

Mainland Southeast Asia - 13th to 15th Century
Southeast Asia on the Eve of Portuguese Advent,
Arrival and Spread of Islam
Sar Desai, chapter 4

Alatas, Syed H. "On the Need for an Historical Study of
Islamization," Journal of Southeast Asian History, IV, 1
(March, 1963) pp. 62-74.
Fatimi, S.Q., Islam Comes to Malaysia, Singapore, 1963.
Ghosh, Manmohan, A History of Cambodia, Saigon, 1960.
Herz, Martin, A Short History of Cambodia, New York, 1958.
Hill, A.H., "The Coming of Islam to North Sumatra," Journal
of Southeast Asian History, IV, 1 (March, 1963), pp. 6-19.
Johns, A.H., "Malay Sufism," Journal of the Malayan Branch of
the Royal Asiatic Society, XXX, Part 2 (August, 1957).

Le May, Reginald, The Culture of Southeast Asia, New Delhi,
1962, Chapters IX-XII.
Marr, David G. and A.C. Milner, Eds. Southeast-Asia in the
Ninth to Fourteenth Centuries, Singapore, 1986.
Shrieke, B., Indonesian Sociological Studies, II, Ruler and
Realm in Early Java, The Hague, 1957, pp. 230-267.
Tambiah, Stanley J., World Conqueror and World Renouncer:
A Study of Buddhism and Polity in Thailand, Cambridge, 1976.
Van Leur, J.C., Indonesian Trade and Society, The Hague, 1955.
Wells, Kenneth E., Thai Buddhism, Its Rites and Activities
Bangkok, 1960.
Wheatley, Paul, The Golden Chersonese, Kuala Lumpur, 1961,
Chapter VII.
Wood, W.A.R., History of Siam, Bangkok, 1933.
Woodside, Alexander, "Early Ming Expansionism, 1406-1427;
China's Abortive Conquest of Vietnam," Papers on China, Vol.
XVII, Cambridge, MA., East Asia Research Center, December,
1965.

WEEKS VIII, IX, X
    (a)   European Powers in Southeast Asia - The Early Phase
           Sar Desai, Chapter 5

Recommended: Boxer, C.R., The Dutch Seaborne Empire, 1600-1800, London, 1965.
           Corpuz, Onofre, The Philippines, Englewood Cliffs, 1965.
           Lach, Donald, Asia in the Making of Europe, Volume I, Chicago,
           1965.
           Meilink-Roelofsz, M.A.P., Asian Trade and European Influence,
           The Hague, 1962.
           Phelan, J.L., The Hispanization of the Philippines, Madison,
           1959.
           Smith, George V., The Dutch in Seventeenth Century Thailand,
           De Kalb, Ill., 1977.
           Van Leur, J.C., Indonesian Trade & Society, The Hague, 1955.

    (b)   Mainland Southeast Asia - 16th to 18th Century
           Sar Desai, Chapter 6

Recommended: Buttinger, Joseph, The Smaller Dragon, New York, 1968.
           Hall, D.G.E., Burma London, 1960.
           Harvey, G.E., History of Burma, London, 1925 (Second Edition
1967).
           Htin, Aung, U., A History of Burma, New York, 1967.
           Wenk, Laus, The Restoration of Thailand Under Rama I, Tucson,
           1968.
           Wood, A.R., History of Siam, Bangkok, 1933.
           Woodside, Alexander, Vietnamese and the Chinese Model,
           Cambridge, 1970.

Department of History   C. M. Wilson
Northern Illinois University   Zulauf 613
History 342: Southeast Asia to c. 1800   Phone 753-6824
Spring Semester, 1991   M + W 1-2 P.M.

Textbooks. All of the necessary books and articles are available at the
reserve desk in Founders Library. Please check the list in the black notebook
under History. Xerox copies of articles will be on file at the reserve desk.
The following titles are also available in the bookstore:

> Buck. Choice of either the Mahabharata or the Ramayana.
> Hall. Maritime Trade and State Development in Early Southeast
>   Asia.
> Higham. The Archaeology of Mainland Southeast Asia.
> Reid. Southeast Asia in the Age of Commerce, 1450-1680. Vol.1.

Please handle all library and reserve materials with care. PLEASE DO NOT
DAMAGE LIBRARY MATERIALS! PLEASE DO NOT WRITE IN OR UNDERLINE LIBRARY
MATERIALS! Remember that other students need to use these materials. The
library does not have the funds to replace damaged items. Please xerox copies
of anything that you want for your own use.

Examinations. There will be two midterm examinations and a final. All
examinations will consist of essay questions. A choice of essays is always
offered. NO MAKE UP EXAMINATIONS WILL BE GIVEN.

The map work and paper are required.

Grades. There are five grade units for the course, the two midterm
examinations, the paper, and the two sections of the final. The average of
the four highest grades will be your course grade. The map quiz will be an
"add on". You will be graded on how good your work is. 90-95 is A; 80-89 is
B; 70-79 is C; 60-69 is D; 50-59 is F. "No show" is 40.

Note. All students are expected to do their own work. This is especially
important on examinations and papers.

Please make every effort to stay ahead in your reading. You will get more out
of the course and will do better on your examinations if you come to class
prepared.

Part I. Origins of Civilization in Southeast Asia.

January 14.   Introduction, Geography, Ethnic Groups.

January 16 & 23.   Prehistory: From Communities of Hunter-Gatherers to
                     Chiefdoms.

                     Higham. Archaeology. Chs. 1-4.
                     Holt. Art in Indonesia. Part I, Ch. 1.

January 28 & 30.   "Indianization": Statecraft and Religion.

197

Higham. <u>Archaeology</u>. Ch. 5, pp. 239-279.
Hall. <u>Maritime Trade</u>. Chs. 1, 2, & 3.
Basham. <u>The Wonder that was India</u>. Hinduism, pp. 297-323;
Buddhism, pp. 256-287

Browse through either the <u>Mahabharata</u> or the <u>Ramayana</u>, and
read a chapter or two so that you begin to develop a sense
of what Indian epic poetry is like.

Part II. The Classical States of Southeast Asia.

February 4 & 6   Srivijaya and the Sailendras.

Hall. <u>Maritime Trade</u>. Chs. 4 & 5.
Holt. <u>Art in Indonesia</u>. Part I. Ch. 2

February 11 & 13. Angkor & Champa.

Higham. <u>Archaeology</u>, Ch. 5, pp. 297-363.
Hall. <u>Maritime Trade</u>. Chs. 6 & 7.
Groslier. <u>The Art of Indochina</u>. Chs. 3-10.

February 18.   FIRST MIDTERM EXAMINATION & MAP QUIZ.
There will be a choice of two essay questions.

February 20 & 25. Pagan, Burma.

Aung-Thwin. <u>Pagan: Origins of Modern Burma</u>. Chs. 2, 3, 4,
7 & 9.
Griswold, "Burma" in <u>The Art of Burma, Tibet & Korea</u>
pp. 13 - 60.

February 27.   Sukhothai & Lanna Thai.

Wyatt. <u>Thailand: A Short History</u>. Chs. 3 & 4.

Video. Sukhothai.

Part III. Change in the Patterns of Historical Development in Southeast Asia

March 4 & 6   New Systems of Trade. The Introduction of Islam.

Hall. <u>Maritime Trade</u>. Chs. 8 & 9.
Holt. <u>Art in Indonesia</u>. Part I. Ch. 3
Morgan. <u>Islam: The Straight Path</u>. Chs. 1 & 10.
You should have finished reading either the <u>Mahabharata</u> or
the <u>Ramayana</u> by now and blocked out your paper topic.

March 18.   The Arrival of the Europeans and Their Initial Impact.

Sar Desai. "The Portuguese Administration in Malacca,
1511-1641," <u>Journal of Southeast Asian History, Vol. 10,
No. 3 (December 1969) pp. 501-512.

Part IV. Chinese Cultural Influence in Southeast Asia: Vietnam.

March 20, 25, 27. Vietnam: Chinese Rule, Independence and Expansion South.
Higham. Archaeology. Ch. 5, pp. 287-296.
Buttinger. The Smaller Dragon. Chs. 1-4.
Cotter, "Towards a Social History of the Vietnamese South-
ward Movement", JSEAH, Vol. IX, no. 1 (1968): 90-98

April 1.   SECOND MIDTERM EXAMINATION.
Choice of two essay questions.

Part V. Spain in Southeast Asia.

April 3, 8, 10,   The Philippines: Spain, Catholicism and Islam.
  & 15.
Phelan. The Hispanization of the Philippines. All. Gowing
& McAmis. The Muslim Filipinos. Essays by Majul, "The
Muslims in the Philippines: An Historical Perspective," pp.
1-12; and Mednick, "Some Problems of Moro History and Political Organization," pp. 13-26.

Part VI. The Culture of Southeast Asia in the 15th & 17th Centuries.

April 17, 22,   Life in Southeast Asia.
  24 & 29.
Reid. Southeast Asia in the Age of Commerce. All.

April 22.   Your paper is due on this date. (Penalty date April 24).

May 1.   REVIEW.

May 9.   FINAL EXAMINATION. 1-2:50 P.M.
Part I. One essay (one hour). General Comparative.
Part II. Two short essays.

SOUTHEAST ASIA TO 1750:

THE CREATIVE SYNTHESIS

William H. Frederick
Ohio University

MWTTh 2-3
Bentley 306

Purpose:

The first installment of a three-part survey of Southeast Asian history, this course attempts to introduce the highlights of the region's past before the rise of Western imperialism and modernizing indigenous states. Few people realize how important Southeast Asia was on the stage of world history in early times -- it was, for example, one of the first centers of agriculture and metallurgy, developed at a very early date a highly sophisticated maritime technology and trade, and reached great heights of religious and artistic achievement -- and the primary goal of this course is to put the region in proper perspective in light of these developments. The nature and meaning of Southeast Asians' contributions to civilization --their own as well as that of the world at large -- are the focus of the reading and lectures. In the process, much about the connection between Southeast Asia's far past and the region's more recent history can also be clarified.

The approach is one favoring the examination of social and cultural change, and encouraging wherever possible cross-regional comparison. While the standard "kings and wars" perspective is not entirely ignored, the emphasis is on achieving a fuller and more realistic view of the societies of Southeast Asia in their "traditional" state. In addition, considerable effort is taken to outline and discuss the problems and debates associated with chronology, interpretation, and types of evidence in this complex but rewarding field of non-Western history.

Texts:

The works listed below are assigned -- many of them, of course, only in part -- as the basic reading for the course. Items marked with an asterisk (*) are available for purchase at the College Book Store. All titles are on reserve in the Reserve Book Room, 3rd floor, Alden Library, under the course number. If you have any problems locating materials, please report them immediately. Competition for reserve materials may be heavy, especially near examination times; it will be advantageous to purchase the texts which are available, get reading done as early as possible in the assignment period, and be courteous and thoughtful of the needs of classmates when borrowing the other items. Since the purchased texts are few in number, you may feel it worth your while to photocopy many of the reading materials on reserve.

Bellwood, P. S. Man's Conquest of the Pacific. London: Oxford University Press, 1979.
Bellwood, P. S. Prehistory of the Indo-Malaysian Archipelago. Sydney and Orlando: Academic Press, 1985,
Benda, H. J., and J. A. Larkin. The World of Southeast Asia. New York: Harper and Row, 1967.

Bosch, F. D. K. Selected Studies in Indonesian Archaeology. The Hague: M. Nijhoff, 1961.

Brandon, J. On Thrones of Gold. Cambridge: Harvard University Press, 1970.

Briggs, L. P. The Ancient Khmer Empire. Philadelphia: American Philosophical Society, 1951.

van Buitenen, J. A. B. (trans.) Tales of Ancient India. Chicago: University of Chicago Press, 1959.

Coedès, G. The Indianized States of Southeast Asia. Honolulu: University Press of Hawaii, 1968.

Coedès, G. The Making of Southeast Asia. London: Routledge and Kegan Paul, 1966.

Hall, D. G. E. A History of Southeast Asia. 4th edition. New York: St. Martin's Press, 1981.

*Hall, K. R. Maritime Trade and State Development in Early Southeast Asia. Honolulu: University of Hawaii Press, 1985.

Hall, K. R., and J. K. Whitmore (eds.). Explorations in Early Southeast Asian History: The Origins of Southeast Asian
     Statecraft. Ann Arbor: University of Michigan Center for South and Southeast Asian Studies, 1976.

*Higham, Charles. The Archaeology of Mainland Southeast Asia. Cambridge: Cambridge University Press, 1989.

Lach, D. F. Southeast Asia in the Eyes of Europe. Chicago: Phoenix Books, 1968.

Marr, David G. and A. C. Milner, eds. Southeast Asia in the 9th to 14th Centuries. Singapore: ISEAS, 1986.

Rawson, P. S. The Art of Southeast Asia. New York: Praeger, 1967.

*Reid, Anthony J. S. Southeast Asia in the Age of Commerce, 1450-1680; The Lands Below the Winds. New Haven: Yale
     University Press, 1988.

Skinner, C. (ed. and trans.) Sja'ir Perang Mengkassar. s'-Gravenhage: M. Nijhoff, 1963.

Skinner, G. W. and A. Thomas Kirsch (eds.). Change and Persistence in Thai Society. Ithaca: Cornell University Press,
     1975.

Smith, R. B., and W. Watson (eds.). Early South East Asia. New York and Kuala Lumpur: Oxford University Press, 1979.

Solheim, W. G. "An Earlier Agricultural Revolution," Scientific American 226, 4 (1972), pp. 34-41.

Solheim, W. G. "The 'New Look' of Southeast Asian Pre-History," Journal of the Siam Society 60, part 1 (January, 1972),
     pp. 1-20.

Valmiki (W. Buck, trans.). Ramayana. New York: Mentor, 1978).

White, J. Ban Chiang: Discovery of a Lost Bronze Age. Philadelphia: University of Pennsylvania Press, 1982.

Wyatt, D. K., and A. Woodside (eds.). Moral Order and the Question of Change: Essays on Southeast Asian Thought. New
     Haven: Yale University Southeast Asia Studies, 1982.

Outline and assignments:

NOTE: All students are required to complete the portions listed under "ALL" in each section;
the materials tagged "GRADUATE" are required for graduates (they won't irreparably damage
curious undergraduates, however). A portion of the two examinations will test specifically for
material covered in these readings, and a general knowledge of them is assumed in the essay
portions of the examinations (see the appropriate section of this syllabus for more information). Please keep in mind,
also, that instructor will check from time to time the names on the blue readers' slips in reserve books, in order to get
some idea whether the assignments are being completed.

● *Monday, September 10*

     Introduction to the course.

● *Tuesday, September 11* (1 class)

I. INTRODUCTION: SOME PROBLEMS IN THE STUDY OF EARLY SOUTHEAST ASIAN HISTORY.

ALL: Higham, Ch. 1; D G E Hall, Ch. 1; Coedès, Indianized, Intro and start Ch. 1.
GRADUATE: Coedès, "Some Problems"; Hall, "Recent Tendencies"; Hutterer, "Old Wine"; Wyatt and Woodside, pp. 78-103; Smith and Watson, Introduction.

● *Wednesday, September 12 - Wednesday, September 19* (5 classes)

II. SOUTHEAST ASIA BEFORE INDIANIZATION.

ALL: Higham, Chs. 2-4; Coedès, Indianized, finish Ch. 1; K. R. Hall, Chs. 1 and 2; Coedès, Making, I; Solheim, "New Look," and "Earlier"; White, Ban Chiang; Hall and Whitmore, pp. 25-60.
GRADUATE: Gorman; Smith and Watson, 3-14, 15-32, 98-124, 215-222, 242-252; Solheim, "Reflections"; Bayard, "Roots"; Piggot, 277-300; Loofs-Wissowa; Bellwood titles, browse.

● *Thursday, September 20 - Thursday, September 27* (5 classes)

III. INDIANIZATION AND THE EARLY PRINCIPALITIES, TO 700.

ALL: Higham, Ch. 5; K. R. Hall, Chs. 3 and 4; Coedès, Indianized, Chs. 2-5; D G E Hall, Ch 2; Bosch, pp. 1-22; Marr and Milner, Ch. 1; van Buitenen, pp. 74-95; Rawson, Ch. 1; Valmiki, Introduction and browse remainder.
GRADUATE: Coedès, Making, II; Smith and Watson, pp. 273-280, 288-303, 406-426, 427-443, 444-456; Wheatley, pp. 37-45; Mabbett, "Indianised," both, entire.

● *Monday, October 1 - Tuesday October 9* (6 classes)

IV. THE RISE OF EMPIRES AND STATES, 700 TO 1000.

ALL: Higham, Ch. 6; K. R. Hall, Chs. 6 and 7; Coedès, Indianized, Chs. 6-8; D G E Hall, Chs. 3-6; Rawson, Chs. 2, 4, 7; Hall and Whitmore, pp. 61-106, 149-204; Marr and Milner, Chs. 3-5.
GRADUATE: Coedès, Making, III; Coedès, Indianized, Chs. 6-8; Briggs, Khmer Empire, browse; Boisselier, browse; Wolters, Commerce, Chs. 1 and 14; Wolters, "Jayavarman II"; Bronson and Wisseman; Gesick, pp. 9-44.

● *Wednesday, October 10*

Mid-term Examination

● *Thursday, October 11 - Wednesday, October 24* (4 classes)

V. THE APOGEE AND FALL OF THE GREAT ANCIENT CIVILIZATIONS, 1000 TO 1400.

ALL: Higham, Ch. 6; K. R. Hall, Chs. 8 and 9; Coedès, Indianized, Chs. 9-12; Benda and Larkin, pp. 33-37; D G E Hall, Chs. 7-12; Hall and Whitmore, pp. 107-148, 205-256; Marr and Milner, Chs. 6-8, 20.

GRADUATE: Coedès, Making, IV; Kulke, entire; Bennett, pp. 3-56; Briggs, "Syncretism"; Ricklefs; Moron; Groslier, browse; Giteau, browse.

● *Thursday, October 25 - Wednesday, November 14* (12 classes)

VI. THE CLASSICAL ERA, 1400-1750.

ALL: Reid, entire; Benda and Larkin, pp. 10-27, 37-71, 77-101; Cowan and Wolters, pp. 227-245; Skinner and Kirsch. pp. 29-92; Skinner, Sja'ir, Introduction and browse; Brandon, pp. 1-10, 82-110.
GRADUATE: Coedès, Chs, 13, 14 and Conclusion; Coedès Making, V; Drewes; Cowan and Wolters, pp. 107-122; van Leur, pp. 269-289; Meilink-Roelofsz, Introduction and pp. 1-59; Willetts; Reid; Manguin; Sears; Lach, entire; D G E Hall, Chs 13-27.

● *Tuesday, November 20, 8:00 AM*

Final examination

Map assignment:

It is always a good idea to know where things are, and equally helpful to know where they were. As part of the final examination, you will be asked to fill in, on a blank map of Southeast Asia, a selection of ten or so items from the following list. You will be provided with practice maps during the quarter; a good source of information is the Atlas of Southeast Asia, introduction by D. G. E Hall (London: MacMillan, 1964); you might also try R. Ulack and G. Pauer, Atlas of Southeast Asia (New York: MacMillan, 1988), but this more recent work is rather short on history and is rather simplistic as well. Both volumes are held behind the desk in the Southeast Asia Collection, 1st floor of Alden Library. The Coedès, Hall, Smith & Watson, and Higham works also have good maps.

In addition to the boundaries and capitals of the contemporary nations of Southeast Asia, you are asked to know and to be able to place on an outline map:

Geographical items

Burma: Irrawaddy, Salween, Sittang Rivers; Arakan Range, Tennasserim Range and Coast, Gulf of Martaban, Mergui Archipelago, areas inhabited by the Chin, Shan, Kachin, and Karen peoples. Vietnam, Cambodia, Laos: Mekong, Song Koi, and Song Bo (rivers), Ailao and Mu Chia Passes, Tonlé Sap, Plaine des Jarres, Chaine des Cardomomes, Central Highlands, delta areas, Plaine des Joncs. Thailand: Chao Phraya (river), Three Pagodas Pass, Khorat Plateau, Isthmus of Kra, Gulf of Siam, Phuket. Malaysia and Indonesia: Penang, Straits of Malacca, Sumatra, Java, Bali, Sulawesi, Kalimantan, Timor, Maluku; Musi, Solo, and Barito rivers; Java, Banda, and Arafura seas; Makassar and Sunda Straits; mountainous areas; areas of Javanese, Sundanese, Madurese, Buginese, Minangkabau, Acehnese, Iban, and Dayak peoples. Philippines: Luzon, Mindanao, Mindoro, Cebu, Leyte; Mindoro Straits; Sulu Sea and Archipelago; Corderilla Central.

Historical Sites or Settlements

Siem Reap, Angkor, Dong-son, Battambang, Thanh-long, Bassac (Champassac), Oc Eo, Lopburi (Lavo), Ayuthia, Phitsanoluk, Sukhothai, Sawankulok, Haripunjaya (Lamphun), Nagara Sri Dharmaraja, Ligor, Takuapa, Pagan, Srikshetra,

Prome, Mandalay, Moulmein, Mergui, Pegu, Vijaya, Malacca, Pasai, Jambi, Palembang, Yogyakarta, Surabaya, Kediri, Ternate, Ambon; Chenla, Funan, Champa, Nanchao, Majapahit, Khmer Empire, Srivijaya, Mataram, Mon Kingdom, Pyu Kingdom, Taruma, Singosari.

Written assignment:

Undergraduates may choose to write a brief paper (approximately 10 pages, or 2,500-3,000 words) on any topic agreed upon with the instructor; this paper should exhibit the student's research and writing skills, and will be graded on accuracy, style, and originality. The paper is entirely optional.

Graduates may choose to prepare a research paper of approximately 20 pages (5,000-6,000 words) on a subject to be agreed upon by the student and the instructor. Those who take this option may be excused from the mid-term examination. The paper will be graded on investigative depth, accuracy, style, and originality; it is intended to give the student a chance to display research and writing skills on a carefully limited topic. Again, the paper is entirely optional.

Examinations and grading:

Examinations for this course follow a pattern which tests both factual knowledge and conceptual understanding. The mid-term and final examinations are structured in the following manner: a question worth 25 points requiring identification (in two sentences only) of five out of eight items (persons, places, events); a question worth 30 points requiring an informative response to a direct inquiry about a particular topic and/or period covered by the course; a question worth 45 points requiring a thoughtful essay of fact and opinion in reaction to a pair of quotations, generally but not always taken from the readings for the course. The first and second questions test specific knowledge; the third question tests general and comparative knowledge, at the same time as calling for a display of informed opinion.

Grading for undergraduates: mid-term examination: 40%; final examination: 60%. With paper option: mid-term, 30%; final, 40%; paper, 30%. For graduates: mid-term: 40%; final, 60%. With research paper option and mid-term: mid-term, 25%; final 35%; research paper, 40%. With research paper option and no mid-term: final, 40%; research paper, 60%.

Policies:

Absences: The student is responsible for material covered during class time; consistent attendance is highly recommended, and any consequences of absence from class are the responsibility of the student.

Academic Dishonesty: The Ohio University code of student conduct prohibits all forms of academic dishonesty, and empowers the instructor to lower the grade of any student engaged in course-related dishonesty. Students are responsible for understanding thoroughly the accepted definition of "academic dishonesty" (including, for example, plagiarism) at Ohio University. In this course, any student found writing examinations or preparing papers in a dishonest fashion will receive an "F" for the course, will not be given the option of withdrawing, and may be referred to the Judiciaries office.

SOUTHEAST ASIA 1750-1942:

CONFLICT AND CHANGE

William H. Frederick
Ohio University

Bentley 306
MTWTh 3-4 PM

PURPOSE:

The second installment of a three-part survey of Southeast Asian history, this course attempts to introduce the highlights of the region's past during a period of great difficulty and intensity, a time during which Southeast Asians sought to control an internal current of change and, at the same time, to maintain their independence in the face of rapidly increasing European threats. The goal of the course is to highlight and examine patterns of transition — evolutionary as well as revolutionary — in the societies and cultures of Southeast Asia, laying particular emphasis on the development of a modern Southeast Asian world view in the 20th century. Colonialism, both in general and in specific, receives considerable attention, but European activities, viewpoints, and materials are intentionally subordinated to Southeast Asian perspectives and sources. European colonial policies, for example, are examined in a generalized fashion, while Southeast Asian ideas about and reactions to them are analyzed in considerable detail. In keeping with the effort to understand indigenous views and interpretations of the period, the writings of Southeast Asians themselves — ranging from fiction to political statement — are used as sources wherever this is practical. Finally, the course is designed to avoid a country-by-country approach to its subject and to promote, instead, a truly region-wide vision of the Southeast Asian experience in the pre-World War Two era.

TEXTS:

The works listed in this section are assigned — many of them only in part — as reading for the course. All students are required to complete the portions listed under "REQUIRED" in each section; the materials tagged "SUGGESTED" are, well, suggested . . . especially for graduates.

Items marked with an asterisk (*) are available for purchase at the College Book Store, 50 S. Court St. (594-3505). A copy of all items is available in the Reserve Room at Alden Library, but purchasing the texts is the more practical way to proceed.

Adas, Michael, "'Moral Economy' or 'Contest State'?: Elite Demands and the Origins of Peasant Protest in
      Southeast Asia," *Journal of Social History* 13, 4 (1980), pp. 521-546.
Bastin, John and Harry J. Benda, *A History of Modern Southeast Asia* (Englewood Cliffs: Prentice-Hall, 1968). [pp. 1-14;
      33-49; 91-122.]
Benda, Harry J. and John A. Larkin, *The World of Southeast Asia* (New York: Harper & Row, 1967). [pp. 53-102;
      102-119; 119-132; 160-203.]
Cady, John F. *Southeast Asia, Its Historical Development* (New York: McGraw-Hill, 1964).
Emmerson, Donald K., "'Southeast Asia': What's in a Name?" *Journal of Southeast Asian Studies* 15, 1 (1984),
      pp. 1-21.
Hall, D. G. E., *A History of South East Asia* 4th edition (New York: St. Martin's Press, 1981.
Hall, D. G. E. (ed.), *Michael Symes: The Journal of his Second Embassy to the Court of Ava in 1802* (London:
      Allen & Unwin, 1955). [pp. ix-lxxix; documents 4, 14, 20, 22.]
Htin Aung, Maung (trans.), *Epistles Written on the Eve of the Anglo-Burmese War* (The Hague: Martinus Nijhoff,
      1968). [Letters 3, 4, 10, 11, 14, 17.]

*Kartini, R. A., *Letters of a Javanese Princess* (New York: Norton, 1964; reprint edition Lanham: American Universities Press and the Asia Society, 1988) [Original edition, 1911.] [pp. 7-26;31-112.]

*Ma Ma Lay, *Not Out of Hate* (Athens: Ohio University Monographs in International Studies, 1991).

Moffat, Abbot Low, *Mongkut, the King of Siam* (Ithaca: Cornell University Press, 1961)

Multatuli [E. Douwes Dekker], *Max Havelaar* (New York: London House and Maxwell, 1967) [Original edition, 1860]. [pp. 62-77; 95-113; 255-320.] {There are many editions and several translators of this famous work.}

*Nguyen Du, *The Tale of Kieu* (New York: Random House, 1973) [2nd edition, New Haven: Yale University Press, 1983]. [pp. ix-xviii; 3-29; 125-142.]

*Orwell, George, *Burmese Days* (New York: Harcourt, 1985) [Original edition, 1934].

Reid, A. J. S., *Southeast Asia in the Age of Commerce* Vol. 1 (New Haven: Yale University Press, 1988) [pp. 1-10.]

Rizal, José, *The Lost Eden* (New York: Norton, 1968). [pp. ix-xviii; 114-161.]

Rizal, José, *The Subversive* (New York: Norton, 1968). [pp. 256-299.]

Solheim, Wilhelm, "'Southeast Asia: What's in a Name?' Another Point of View," *Journal of Southeast Asian Studies* 16, 1 (1985), pp. 141-147.

Sukarno, *Indonesia Accuses!* (Kuala Lumpur: Oxford, 1976). [pp. xvi-lxxi; 5-17; 32-41; 94-112.]

*Steinberg, D. J. (ed.), *In Search of Southeast Asia* 2nd edition (Honolulu: University of Hawaii Press, 1987).

Wyatt, David K. and Alexander Woodside (eds.), *Moral Order and the Question of Change: Essays on Southeast Asian Thought* (New Haven: Yale University Southeast Asian Studies, 1982).

OUTLINE AND ASSIGNMENTS:

- *Tuesday, January 7*
  Introduction to the course

- *Wednesday, January 8 - Monday, January 13*
  I. SOUTHEAST ASIA'S HISTORY BEFORE 1750.

  REQUIRED: Reid, pp. 1-10; Steinberg, pp. 1-95 [Cady, Ch. 1, and Hall, Chs. 1-22 cover similar ground]; Bastin and Benda, pp. 1-14; Benda and Larkin, pp. 53-102.
  SUGGESTED: Emmerson; Solheim; Wyatt and Woodside, pp. 78-103.

- *Tuesday, January 14 - Wednesday, January 29*
  II. SOUTHEAST ASIA, 1750-1820: CHANGES AND CONTINUITIES.

  REQUIRED: Steinberg, pp. 99-170 (start reading this, and continue in next section) [similar ground is covered in Hall, Chs. 23-31; and in Cady, 281-302, 322-336, 406-409, and Ch. 11]; Benda and Larkin, pp. 102-119. Nguyen Du, entire.
  SUGGESTED: Hall (Symes), pp. ix-lxxix and documents 4, 14, 20, and 22. Wyatt and Woodside, pp. 9-52.

- *Thursday, January 30 MID-TERM EXAMINATION (1 hour)*

- *Monday, February 3 - Thursday, February 13*
  III. SOUTHEAST ASIA, 1820-1890: GENESIS AND SPREAD OF THE COLONIAL PATTERN.

  REQUIRED: Steinberg, pp. 97-170 (finish this, which should have been started in the previous section) [Hall, Chs.

32-41, covers similar ground]; Bastin and Benda, pp. 33-49; Benda and Larkin, pp. 119-132; Multatuli, pp. 62-77, 95-113, 255-320; Moffat, Chapters 1, 2, 3, 8, and Appendix IV.
SUGGESTED: Maung Htin Aung, Letters 3, 4, 10, 11, 14, and 17; Wyatt and Woodside, pp. 53-77, 104-150, 151-273.

● *Monday and Tuesday, February 17 and 18*
  IV. INTERLUDE: INDIGENOUS VOICES.

  REQUIRED: Kartini, entire.
  SUGGESTED: Rizal, *Lost Eden*, pp. ix-xviii; *Subversive*, pp. 256-299. Wyatt and Woodside, pp. 244-337.

● *Wednesday, February 19 - Thursday, March 5*
  V. SOUTHEAST ASIA, 1890-1940: THE STRUGGLE FOR SURVIVAL.

  REQUIRED: Steinberg, pp. 173-345 (you may also want to look at the roughly equivalent sections of Hall and Cady); Bastin and Benda, pp. 91-122; Benda and Larkin, pp. 160-203; Orwell, entire; Ma Ma Lay, entire.
  SUGGESTED: Adas; Sukarno, pp. xvi-lxxi, 5-17, 32-41, 94-112.

● *Friday, March 6 - Friday, March 13*

  Showing of the films "The King and I" (1956) [Color, 133 mins. D: Walter Lang. Yul Brynner, Deborah Kerr, Rita Moreno, etc.] and "Max Havelaar" (1976) [Color, 176 mins. D: Fons Rademakers. Peter Faber, Sacha Bultuis, Elang Mohamad, Adenan Soesilaningrat.] Screening times will be announced later.

  Note: These films are assigned with the specific purpose of encouraging you to compare historical knowledge of a period with "popularized" versions reflected, in this case, in mass cinema productions. Please take care to prepare thoroughly for watching these films by reviewing your class notes on 19th Century Thailand and Indonesia, and the readings on King Mongkut (Moffat, Chapters 1, 2, 3, 8, and Appendix IV) and the novel *Max Havelaar* (pp. 62-77; 95-113; 255-320). A portion of the final examination will concern the topics treated by the films, and the issues raised.

● *Tuesday, March 17 at 12:20 P.M   FINAL EXAMINATION   (2 hours)*

MAP ASSIGNMENT:

It is always a good idea to know where things are, and where they were in the past; maps help give history a down-to-earth quality it may otherwise lack. As part of the the final examination, you will be asked to fill in, on a blank map of Southeast Asia, a selection of 10 out of 13-15 items from the following list. You will be provided with practice maps at the beginning of the quarter; everything else is up to you. Good sources of information are: *Atlas of South-East Asia* D. G. E. Hall, intro. (New York: MacMillan, 1964), and R. Ulack and G. Pauer, *Atlas of Southeast Asia* (New York: MacMillan, 1988), held behind the desk in the Southeast Asia Collection, 1st floor of Alden library, but other similar publications may serve the purpose. Be sure, however, that you use relatively up-to-date materials.
  You will need to know, first of all, *the boundaries and capital cities of all the modern nations of Southeast Asia.* These are: Burma (Myanmar), Thailand, Laos, Cambodia, Vietnam, Malaysia, Singapore, Brunei, Indonesia, and The Philippines. In addition, you should be acquainted with the following locations:
  GEOGRAPHICAL ITEMS: Burma (Myanmar): Irrawaddy, Salween, and Sittang Rivers; Arakan Range, Tennasserim

Range and Coast, Gulf of Martaban, Mergui Archipelago, Andaman and Nicobar Islands; areas inhabited by the Chin, Shan, Kachin, and Karen peoples. *Vietnam, Cambodia, and Laos*: Mekong, Red R., Black R., Ailao and Mu Chia passes; Tonlé Sap, Plaine des Jarres, Chaine des Cardomômes, Central Highlands, delta areas. *Thailand*: Menam Chao Phraya (river), Three Pagodas Pass, Khorat Plateau, Isthmus of Kra, Gulf of Siam, Phuket. *Malaysia and Indonesia*: Penang, Straits of Malacca, Sumatra, Java, Bali, Sulawesi, Kalimantan, Timor, Maluku (islands); Musi, Solo, and Barito rivers; Java, Banda, and Arafura seas; Makassar, Sunda, and Malacca straits; mountainous areas (indicate areas of volcanic activity); areas of Javanese, Sundanese, Buginese, Madurese, Minangkabau, Acehnese, Iban, and Dyak peoples. *Philippines*: Luzon, Mindanao, Mindoro, Cebu, Leyte (islands); Mindoro Straits; Sulu Sea and Archipelago; Corderilla Central.

    Cities and/or historical sites: *Burma (Myanmar)*: Pegu, Pagan, Ava, Mergui, Mandalay; *Thailand*: Ayuthia, Chiengmai, Nakhon Si Thammarat, Thonburi, Nakhon Ratchasima, Phitsanoluk; *Laos*: Luang Prabang, Vientiane; *Vietnam*: Hue, Haiphong, Saigon-Cholon (Ho Chi Minh), Thanh Hoa, Yen Bai, Da Nang (Tourane); *Malaysia*: Ipoh, Johor Baru, Kota Kinabalu (Jesselton), Kuching, Georgetown, Melaka, Sandakan; *Indonesia*: Medan, Palembang, Bandung, Yogyakarta, Surabaya, Den Pasar, Banjarmasin, Ujung Pandang (Makassar); *Philippines*: Manila, Davao, Cebu, Iloilo, Zamboanga.

WRITTEN ASSIGNMENT:

Undergraduates may choose to write a brief paper (approximately 10 pages, or 2,500-3,000 words) on a topic agreed upon with the instructor. The paper should exhibit the student's research and/or writing skills, and will be graded on accuracy, style, and originality. The paper is entirely optional. See section on grading, below, concerning special arrangements for those who elect to do a paper.

    Graduates may choose to prepare a research paper of approximately 20 pages (5,000-6,000 words) on a subject to be agreed upon by the student and the instructor. Those who take this option may be excused from the mid-term examination, if they wish. The paper will be graded on investigative depth, accuracy, style, and originality; it is intended to give the student a chance to display research and/or writing skills on a carefully limited topic. Graduate students in the Department of History who are majoring or minoring in Southeast Asia are expected to take the paper option. See the section on grading for special arrangements for those who elect to do a paper.

EXAMINATIONS AND GRADING:

Examinations in this course follow a pattern which tests both factual knowledge and conceptual understanding.

    The mid-term examination (1 hour) is structured in the following manner: 1) a section worth 30 points consisting of identification questions (people, places, terms) drawn from reading and the lectures; 2) a question worth 30 points requiring an informative response, using material from both readings and lectures, to a direct inquiry about a particular topic and/or period covered by the course; 3) a question worth 40 points requiring a thoughtful essay of fact and opinion in reaction to a pair of quotations, generally but not always taken from the assigned readings. The first and second questions test specific knowledge (the first question also tests the thoroughness with which reading assignments have been completed); the third question tests ability to use specific, general, and comparative knowledge in the formation of educated opinions.

    The final examination (2 hours) is structured similarly, except that there is a 10-point map question, and the questions numbered 1-3 above are worth 20, 30, and 40 points, respectively.

    There are separate tests for graduate and undergraduate students.

    Grading for undergraduates: mid-term examination: 40% final examination: 60%. With paper option: mid-term, 30%; final, 40%; paper, 30%. For graduates: mid-term: 40%; final, 60%. With research paper and mid-term: mid-term, 25%; final 35%, research paper, 40%. With research paper option and no mid-term: final, 50%; research paper, 50%.

Modern History of Southeast Asia

I.   Introduction: Geography of Southeast Asia - a quick historical survey up to 1800 - European contacts in the region 1511-1800.

Establishment of Konbaung (Burma), Chakri (Thailand) and Nguyen (Vietnam) dynasties.

II-III-IV. Nature and causes of Western expansion in the 19th century - distinction in policies and situations in the two halves of the century, economic and non-economic factors in the era of "new imperialism."

Case studies of Western expansion: Britain in Burma and Malaya; France in Indo-China; the Netherlands in the Indonesian Islands.

V.   Thailand in the 19th and 20th centuries - Thailand's geo-political position; Mongkut and Chulalongkorn's reign; Anglo-French rivalry - Thai efforts to establish complete independence - coup d'etat of 1932 - political developments to 1939.

VI.   (a) Nationalism in Southeast Asia - Discussion of the factors responsible for the rise of nationalist movements - nature of the elite - economic factors. (b) Nationalism in the Philippines vs. Spanish and American colonial rule - U.S. administration of the Philippines to 1939.

VII-VIII. (a) Nationalism and communism in individual countries of Southeast Asai. (b) Impact of Japanese Occupation on Nationalist Movements during World War II.

IX-X. Independence - Southeast Asia - Problems and Performance - The Vietnam Conflict - Emergence of communist states in Indochina.

TEXT: D.R. SarDesai, Southeast Asia, Past and Present, Boulder, Colorado, Westview Press, 1989. (Second edition).

OTHER USEFUL SURVEYS:

   D.G.E. Hall, A History of South-East Asia, New York, 1964 (Third Edition).
   Cady, John F., Southeast Asia: Its Historical Development, New York, 1964.

ATLAS: D.G.E. Hall, ed., Atlas of South-East Asia, Amsterdam, 1962.

BIBLIOGRAPHY:

   K.G. Tregonning, Southeast Asia: A Critical Bibliography, Tucson, Arizona, 1969.

Required Reading:

Week I -- SarDesai, ch. I and pp. 70-82

Weeks II, III, IV -- SarDesai, pp. 83-125

Week V -- SarDesai, pp. 126-136

Weeks VI, VII, VIII -- SarDesai, pp. 137-196

IX, X -- SarDesai, pp. 197-299

Recommended Reading:

Weeks II, III, IV --

Burma and Malaya

Adas, M. The Burma Delta: Economic Development and Social Change on an Asian Rice Frontier, 1852-1941. Madison, Wisc., 1971.

Allen, G.C. and Audrey G. Donnithorne. Western Enterprise in Indonesia and Malaya: A Study in Economic Development. London, 1957.

Aung, Htin. The Stricken Peacock, Anglo-Burmese Relations 1752-1948. The Hague, 1965.

Bastin, John. The Native Policies of Sir Stamford Raffles in Java and Sumatra. Oxford, 1967.

Benda, Harry J. "Political Elites in Colonial Southeast Asia, An Historical Analysis," Comparative Studies in Society and History. VII (1975), pp. 233-251.

Cady, John F. A History of Modern Burma. Ithaca, N.Y., 1958.

Chai, Hon-chan. The Development of British Malaya, 1896-1909. Kuala Lumpur, 1964.

Cowan, C.D. Nineteenth Century Malaya. London, 1961.

Emerson, Rupert. Malaysia, A Study in Direct and Indirect Rule. New York, 1937.

Ennis, Thomas E. French Policy and Developments in Indo-China. Chicago, 1936.

Furnivall, J.S. Colonial Policy and Practice. Cambridge, 1948.

Galbraith, John S. "The 'Turbulent Frontier' as a Factor in British Expansion."
Comparative Studies in Society and History, II, 2 (1960), pp. 157-162.

Lim, Chong-Yah. Economic Development of Modern Malaya. Kuala Lumpur, 1967.

Parkinson, C. Northcote. British Intervention in Malaya, 1867-1877. London, 1959.

SarDesai, D.R. British Trade and Expansion in Southeast Asia, 1830-1914. New Delhi,
1977.

Singhal, D.P. The Annexation of Upper Burma. Singapore, 1960.

Tarling, Nicholas. British Policy in the Malay Peninsula and Archipelago, 1824-1871.
Kuala Lumpur, 1968.

Trager, Frank. Burma From Kingdom to Republic. New York, 1966.

Wright, Harrison. The "New Imperialism." Boston, 1975, 2nd ed.

French Indochina

Buttinger, Joseph. The Smaller Dragon. New York, 1958.

Cady, John F. The Roots of French Imperialism in Eastern Asia. Ithaca, 1954.

Fall, Bernard B. The Two Vietnams. New York, 1967.

Osborne, Milton E. The French Presence in Cohin-China and Cambodia: Rule and
Response, 1859-1905. Ithaca, N.Y., 1969.

Priestley, H.I. France Overseas, A Study of Modern Imperialism. New York, 1938.

Thompson, Virginia. French Indochina. New York, 1937.

Woodside, Alexander. Vietnam and the Chinese Model. Cambridge, Mass., 1971.

Dutch East Indies

Boeke, J.H. The Structure of the Netherlands Indian Economy. New York, 1942.

Day, Clive. Policy and Administration of the Dutch in Java. New York, 1904, reprinted
Kuala Lumpur, 1966.

Multauli (E.D. Dekker). Max Havelaar. New York, 1969.

Vandenbosch, Amry. The Dutch East Indies. Berkeley, 1942.

Vlekke, Bernard. The Story of the Dutch East Indies. Cambridge, Mass., 1945.

Vlekke, Bernard. Nusantara, A History of East Indian Archipelago. Cambridge, Mass., 1943.

Wilson, Greta, ed. Regents, Reformers and Revolutionaries: Indonesian Voices of Colonial Days. Honolulu, 1978.

Week V --

Griswold, A.B., King Mongkut of Siam, New York, 1961.

Thompson, Virginia. Thailand, the New Siam. New York, 1941.

Vella, Walter R. The Impact of the West on the Government of Thailand. Berkeley, 1955.

Vella, Walter R. Siam Under Rama III, Locust Valley, N.J., 1957.

Vella, Walter R. Chaiyo! The Role of King Vajiravudh and the Development of Thai Nationalism. Honolulu, 1978.

Wyatt, David K. The Politics of Reform in Thailand. New Haven, CT, 1969.

Weeks VI, VII, VIII --

(a) Nationalism and Communism in Southeast Asia

Aung, Htin. The Stricken Peacock, 1752-1948, The Hague, 1965.

Brimmell, J.H. Communism in Southeast Asia. London, 1959.

Emerson, Rupert. From Empire to Nation. Cambridge, 1962.

Emerson, Rupert. "Paradoxes in Asian Nationalism," Far Eastern Quarterly, XIII, 2 (Feb. 1954), 131-142.

Holland, William L. Asian Nationalism and the West. New York, 1953.

Kennedy, J. Asian Nationalism in the Twentieth Century. London, 1963.

Scalapino, Robert A., ed., The Communist Revolution in Asia. New Jersey, 1965.

Singhal, D.P. "Nationalism and Communism in Southeast Asia," Journal of Southeast Asian History, III, 1 (March, 1962), 56-66.

Trager, Frank N. Marxism in Southeast Asia. Stanford, 1959.

Von der Mehden. Religion and Nationalism in Southeast Asia. Madison, Wisc., 1963.

(b) Nationalism in Burma

Butwell, Richard, U Nu of Burma, Stanford, 1963.

Moscotti, Albert D. British Policy and the Nationalist Movement in Burma, 1917-1937. Honolulu, 1973.

Sarkisyanz, E. Buddhist Backgrounds of the Burmese Revolution. The Hague, 1965.

Smith, Donald E. Religion and Politics in Burma. Princeton, N.J., 1965.

Trager, Frank N. Burma From Kingdom to Republic. Princeotn, N.J., 1965.

(c) Nationalism in Indonesia

Kahin, George, M. Nationalism and Revolution in Indonesia. Ithaca, N.Y., 1952.

McVey, Ruth. The Rise of Indonesian Communism. Ithaca, N.Y., 1965.

Palmer, Leslie. Communists in Indonesia. New York, 1973.

Vandenbosch, Amry. "Nationalism and Religion in Indonesia," Far Eastern Survey, XXI, (1952), pp. 181-185.

Van der Kroef, Justus M. "Prince Diponegero, Progenitor of Indonesian Nationalism," Far Eastern Quarterly, VII (Aug., 1949), pp. 424-450.

Wilson, Greta, ed. Regents, Reformers and Revolutionaries: Indonesian Voices of Colonial Days. Honolulu, 1978.

(d) Nationalism and Communism in Vietnam

Chesneaux, Jean. The Vietnamese Nation. Sydney, 1966.

Devillers, Philippe and Jean Lacouture. End of a War: Indochina, 1954. New York, 1969.

Duiker, William J. The Rise of Nationalism in Vietnam, 1900-1941. Ithaca, N.Y., 1976.

Hammer, Ellen. The Struggle for Indochina. New York, 1954.

Huynh, Kim Khanh. Vietnamese Communism, 1925-1945. Ithaca, N.Y., 1986.

Lam, Truong Buu. Patterns of Vietnamese Response to Foreign Intervention, 1858-1900, New Haven, 1967.

Lancaster, Donald. The Emancipation of French Indochina. (London, 1961), (reprinted, N.Y. 1975).

Marr, David. Vietnamese Anti-colonialism, 1885-1925. Berkeley, 1971.

Pike, Douglas. History of Vietnamese Communism, 1925-1976. Stanford, 1978.

(e) Nationalism in the Philippines

Agoncillo, Theodore A. The Revolt of the Masses. The Story of Bonifacio and the the Katipunan. Manila, 1965.

Coates, Austin. Rizal, Philippine Nationalist and Martyr, Kuala Lumpur, 1968.

Friend, Theodore. Between Two Empires. The Ordeal of the Philippines, 1929-1946. New Haven, Conn., 1965.

McCormick, Thomas. "Insular Imperialism and the Open Door: The China Market and the Spanish American War," Pacific Historical Review, XXXII (1963), pp. 155-169.

Rizal, Jose. Noli Me Tangere (The Lost Eden), translated by Leon Ma Guervero, Bloomington, Indiana, 1961.

Taylor, George. The Philippines and the United States, Problems of Partnership, New York, 1971.

(f) Japan and Southeast Asian Nationalism

Agoncillo, Teodoro, The Fateful Years: Japan's Adventure in the Philippines, 1941-1945. Manila, 1965.

Anderson, Benedict R. Some Aspects of Indonesian Politics Under the Japanese Occupation, 1944-45. Ithaca, N.Y., 1961.

Benda, Harry. The Crescent and the Rising Sun, Indonesian Islam Under the Japanese Occupation, 1944-45. The Hague, 1958.

Cheah, Boon Kheng. Red Star over Malaya. Resistance and Social Conflict during and after the Japanese Occupation, 1941-1946, Singapore, 1983.

Christian, John and Ike Nobutake, "Thailand in Japan's Foreign Relations," Pacific Affairs, XV, 2 (June, 1942), pp. 195-221.

Elsbree, William H. Japan's Role in Southeast Asian Nationalist Movements. Cambridge, Mass., 1953.

Nu, Thakin. Burma Under the Japanese. New York, 1954.

Silverstein, J. ed. Southeast Asia in World War II. New Haven, 1966.

Weeks IX, X

Anand, R.P. and P.V. Quisumbing. ASEAN: Identity, Development and Culture. Honolulu, 1981.

Barron, John and Paul Anthony. Murder of a Gentle Land: The Untold Story of Communist Genocide in Cambodia. New York, 1977.

Chan, Heng Chee. The Dynamics of One Party Dominance: The PAP at the Grassroots, Singapore, 1976.

Crouch, Harold. The Army and Politics in Indonesia. Ithaca, N.Y., 1978.

Duiker, William. The Communist Road to Power in Vietnam. Boulder, 1981.

Fall, Bernard B. The Two Vietnams: A Political and Military Analysis. New York, 1967 (third edition).

Fitzgerald, Frances. Fire in the Lake. New York, 1972.

Harrison, James P. The Endless War. Fifty Years of Struggle in Vietnam. Riverside, N.J., 1981.

Kahin, George M. Intervention: How America Became Involved in Vietnam. N.Y., 1986.

Karnow, Stanley. Vietnam: A History. N.Y., 1983.

Kiernan, Ben. How Pol Pot Came to Power: A History of Communism in Kampuchea, 1930-1975. London, 1985.

Lacouture, Jean. Ho Chi Minh. London, 1968.

Lev, Daniel S. Transition to Guided Democracy. Ithaca, 1966.

McAlister, John and Paul Mus. The Vietnamese and their Revolution. New York, 1970.

McDonald, Hamish. Suharto's Indonesia. Honolulu, 1981.

Morell, David and Chai-Anan Samudavinija. Political Conflict in Thailand: Reform, Reaction, Revolution. Cambridge, Mass., 1981.

Nguyen, Van Canh. Vietnam Under Communism, 1975-1982. Palo Alto, 1983.

O'Neil, Robert. General Giap. New York, 1969.

Osborne, Milton. Politics and Power in Cambodia, the Sihanouk Years. Canberra, 1973.

Ponchaud, Francois. Cambodia Year Zero. New York, 1977.

Rotter, Andrew J. The Path to Vietnam: Origins of American Commitment to Southeast Asia. Ithaca, N.Y., 1987.

Silverstein, J. Burma: The Politics of Stagnation. Ithaca, 1978.

"Symposium on Vietnamese Communism," Asian Survey. September 1972.

Tham, Seong Chee. Malays and Modernization: A Sociological Interpretation. Singapore, 1977.

Woodside, Alexander. Community and Revolution in Modern Vietnam. Boston, 1976.

C. M. Wilson
Zulauf 613
Tel. 753-6824
Office Hours:
MW 1-2:00

Department of History
Northern Illinois University
History 343: Southeast Asia since 1800
Fall Semester, 1991

Required reading: All of the required reading materials are available at the reserve desk in Founders Library. Please check the list in the notebook under History. The following titles are also available in the bookstore;

Current History. Southeast Asia, March 1990.
Kartini, Letters of a Javanese Princess.
Lat, Mat Som.
Marr, Vietnamese Tradition on Trial, 1920-1945.
Steinberg, In Search of Southeast Asia.

Please handle all library materials with care. PLEASE DO NOT DAMAGE LIBRARY MATERIALS! PLEASE DO NOT WRITE IN OR UNDERLINE LIBRARY MATERIALS! Remember that other students need to use these materials. The library does not have the funds to replace damaged items. Please xerox copies of anything that you want for your own use.

Examinations: There will be two midterm examinations and a final. All examinations will consist of essay questions. A choice of essays is always offered. NO MAKE UP EXAMINATIONS WILL BE GIVEN.

The map work and paper are required.

Grades: There are five grade units for the course, the two midterm examinations, the paper, and the two sections of the final. The average of the four highest grades will be your course grade. The map quiz will be an "add on". You will be graded on how good your work is. 90-95 is A; 80-89 is B; 70-79 is C; 60-69 is D; 50-59 is F. "No show" is 40.

Note: All students are expected to their own work. This is especially important on examinations and papers.

Please make every effort to stay ahead in your reading. You will get more out of the course and will do better on your examinations if you come to class prepared.

August 26   Introduction. Video: "Bali, Masterpiece of the Gods."

August 28   Traditional Political Culture.
                  (Steinberg, Introduction and Chs. 1-4).

September 4   Religion and Economic Life.
                  (Steinberg, Chs. 5-6.)

September 9   Buddhism in Southeast Asia: Burma.
                  (Steinberg, Chs. 7 & 12.)

September 11	Buddhism in Southeast Asia: Thailand and Cambodia. (Steinberg, Chs. 13-14.) Map work due.
September 16	Vietnam: The Confucian State. (Steinberg, Chs. 8 & 15.)
September 18	Island Southeast Asia: Political Fragmentation. (Steinberg, Chs. 9, 16 & 17.) **Map Quiz.**
September 23	Java and the Javanese. (Steinberg, Chs. 10 & 18. Please start reading Kartini.)
September 25	Growing up in Java under Dutch Rule. (Kartini. <u>Letters of a Javanese Princess</u>, all.)
September 30	**FIRST MIDTERM EXAMINATION!** (Two essay questions.)
October 2	Spain and the Philippines. (Steinberg, Chs. 11 & 19.)
October 7	Western Ideas in Southeast Asia. (Steinberg, Chs. 20-21.)
October 9	A Changing Southeast Asia. (Steinberg, Chs. 22-24.)
October 14	The Philippines and the United States. (Steinberg, Ch. 25.)
October 16	Burma under Great Britain. (Steinberg, Ch. 26.)
October 21	Indonesia and the Dutch. (Steinberg, Ch. 27.) Please start reading Marr, <u>Vietnamese Tradition on Trial</u>
October 23	Indochina under the French. (Steinberg, Chs. 28 & 31. Marr, Chs. 1-3)
October 28	Vietnamese question their culture. (Marr, Chs. 4-8.)
October 30	**SECOND MIDTERM EXAMINATION!** (Two essay questions.)
November 4	Modernization in the Malay States and Thailand (Siam). (Steinberg, Chs. 29 & 30.)

November 6	War in Indochina: Vietnam, Laos and Cambodia. (Steinberg, Chs. 32-34, Marr, Chs. 9 & 10.)
November 11	Modern Burma and Thailand. (Steinberg, Chs. 35 & 36.)
November 13	Modern Malaysia, Singapore and Brunei. (Steinberg, Ch. 37. Lat, Mat Som, All)
November 18	The Republic of Indonesia. (Steinberg, Ch. 38.) **Book reports are due. Penalty date November 20.**
November 20	The Republic of the Philippines. (Steinberg, Ch. 39.)
November 25	Southeast Asia Today. (Current History, All.)
December 2	Summary and Review. (Steinberg, Ch. 40.)
December 4	In reserve for the final examination or, if the final is rescheduled, a film will be shown.
TO BE ANNOUNCED!	**FINAL EXAMINATION!** 1 hour and 50 minutes. Part I. Comprehensive question (one hour). Part II. Two shorter essay questions.

SOUTHEAST ASIA SINCE 1942:

DEFINING NEW STATES AND SOCIETIES

William H. Frederick	Bentley Hall 132
Ohio University	MTWTh 11 AM-12 Noon

PURPOSE:

The third and final installment of a survey of Southeast Asian history, this course attempts to introduce the highlights of the region's recent past, a time during which war, rebellion, and revolution made their mark, and in which Southeast Asians, having entered a new period of independence, attempted to construct new social, political, and economic patterns. The emphasis in the course is upon studying prominent events, persons, and circumstances in order to illustrate general principles or theses about the region as a whole. Wherever possible, a comparative approach is used. A major aim is to see as much as possible of Southeast Asia's contemporary experience from indigenous points of view. The primary goal of the course, beyond conveying a body of basic information, is to offer a series of reasonable -- and reasonably even-handed -- opinions on the nature of Southeast Asia today and its likely role in the world of the future. In keeping with the aim of understanding indigenous views and interpretations, the writings of Southeast Asians themselves, ranging from fiction to political statements, are used as sources wherever this is practical. Finally, the course is designed to avoid the constraints of a country-by-country approach, and to promote instead a comparative and truly region-wide vision of Southeast Asia from the Japanese occupation down to the present.

TEXTS:

The works listed in this section are assigned -- many of them, of course, only in part -- as reading for the course. All students are required to complete the portions listed under "REQUIRED" in each section; the materials tagged "SUPPLEMENTARY" are required for graduates and suggested for undergraduates who wish to achieve a superior grade in the course. Items marked with an asterisk (*) are available for purchase at the College Book Store, 50 S. Court St. (594-3505). Other items are on reserve in the Reserve Reading Room at Alden Library, 3rd floor. There will inevitably be pressure on the Reserve Room facilities, so please take care to plan your work well, and to be considerate of others in the class, who must work within the same limitations as you. If you have any difficulty with the reserve reading system, please report them immediately.

Ahmad, Shahnon, *No Harvest But A Thorn* Translated and introduced by Adibah Amin. (Kuala Lumpur: Oxford University Press, 1972). PL5139/S55/R313/1972x

Anderson, Benedict R., and Ruchira Mendiones (ed. and trans.), *In the Mirror. Literature and Politics in Siam in the American Era* (Bangkok: Duang Kamol, 1985). PL4208/15/1985x

Cady, John F., *The History of Post-War Southeast Asia* (Athens: Ohio University Press, 1974). DS511/C25/1974x

Khamsing Srinawk [Lao Khamhawn], *The Politician and Other Stories.* Translated by Damnern Garden. Edited and annotated by Michael Smithies (Kuala Lumpur: Oxford University Press, 1973). PL4209/K49/P6x

*K'tut Tantri, *Revolt in Paradise* Reprint edition (New York: Griffin, 1991).

*Lansing, J. Stephen, *Priests and Programmers; Technologies of Power in the Engineered Landscape of Bali* (Princeton: Princeton University Press, 1992.

Lubis, Mochtar, *The Indonesian Dilemma* Revised English edition. Translated by Florence Lamoureux. (Singapore: Graham Brash, 1983). HN703.5/L8313/1983x

*Luong, Hy V. *Revolution in the Village. Tradition and Transformation in North Vietnam, 1925-1988* (Honolulu: University of Hawaii Press, 1991).

Mahathir bin Mohamad, *The Malay Dilemma* (Singapore: Times Books International, 1970). DS595/M26/1970

Mihardja, Achdiat K. *Atheis* Translated by R.J. Maguire (St. Lucia: University of Queensland Press, 1972). PL5089/M5/A8/1972x

McCoy, Alfred W. (ed.), *Southeast Asia Under Japanese Occupation* (New Haven: Yale U. Southeast Asia Studies, 1980). DS518/S68x

Osborne, Milton, *Southeast Asia, An Illustrated Introductory History* Expanded edition (Sydeney: Allen and Unwin, 1988). DS525/O8/1988x

Reflections on Rebellion. Stories from the Indonesian Upheavals of 1948 and 1965 Translated by William H. Frederick and John McGlynn (Athens: Ohio University Monographs in International Studies, 1983). PL5088.2/E5/R44/1983

Reid, Anthony J. S., and Akira Oki (eds.), *The Japanese Experience in Indonesia: Selected Memoirs of 1942-1945* (Athens: Ohio University Monographs in International Studies). DS643.5/J37/1986

Reynolds, Craig J. *Thai radical discourse. The real face of Thai feudalism today* (Ithaca: Cornell University Southeast Asia Program, 1987). DS568/R49/1987x

*Samruam Singh [Surasingsamruam Shimbanao] Voices from the Thai Countryside Ed. and trans. Katherine A. Bowie (Madison: University of Wisconsin Center for Southeast Asian Studies, 1992).

Scott, James C. *Weapons of the Weak. Everyday Forms of Peasant Resistance.* (New Haven: Yale University Press, 1985). HD1537/M27/S36/1985x

Silverstein, Josef (ed.), *Southeast Asia in World War II: Four Essays* (New Haven: Center for Southeast Asian Studies, Yale University, 1966). D767/S56

*Steinberg, David Joel (ed.), *In Search of Southeast Asia* 2nd edition (Honolulu: University of Hawaii Press, 1987). DS525/I48/1987

*Takeyama Michio, *The Harp of Burma* Translated by Howard Hibbett (Rutland: Tuttle, 1966). PL839/a58/H3/1966x

Taruc, Luis, *Born of the People* (New York: International Publishers, [1953]). DS686.2/T3/A3

Von der Mehden, Fred. *Southeast Asia, 1930-1970* (New York: Norton, 1974). DS518.1/V66/1964

Wijaya, Putu. *Bomb. Indonesian Short Stories.* Edited by Ellen Rafferty and Laurie J. Sears (Madison: Center for Southeast Asian Studies, University of Wisconsin, 1988). PL5089/W54/A6/1988x

OUTLINE AND ASSIGNMENTS:

● *Tuesday, March 31*

Introduction to the course.

○ *Wednesday, April 1 FILM*: "Indonesia: Unity with Diversity." Shown during class time at the Preview Room, Learning Resources Center, 2nd floor of Alden Library. Please be prompt, as the film will start at 5 minutes past the hour.

○ *Thursday, April 2 FILM*: "Malaysia: Sparrow with Sparrow, Raven with Raven." Shown during class time at the Preview Room, Learning Resources Center, 2nd floor of Alden Library. Please be prompt, as the film will start at 5 minutes past the hour.

● *Monday, April 6 - Tuesday, April 7 (2 lectures)*

I. Southeast Asia before 1942.

REQUIRED: *Steinberg, Chapters 23-31; Von der Mehden, Ch. 1.

● *Wednesday, April 8 - Wednesday, April 15 (5 lectures)*

II. The Japanese Occupation, 1942-1945.

REQUIRED: *Takeyama, entire; *Steinberg, review the portions of Chapters 23-31 which concern the early Japanese period; Chapter 32; the portions of chapters 33-39 which concern the Japanese period. Osborne, Chapter 9. McCoy, introduction.

SUPPLEMENTARY: McCoy: pages 16-32, 91-190, and 267-302. Reid and Oki: pages 159-288, 297-395. Silverstein, choose 2 chapters on countries of your choice.

● *Thursday, April 16 - Wednesday, April 29 (8 lectures)*

   III. The Colonial Aftermath, 1945-1950.

   REQUIRED: *Steinberg, Chapters 33-39, portions appropriate to this period; K'tut Tantri, entire; *Reflections*, first two stories; Von der Mehden, Ch. 3; Osborne, Chapters 10 and 11.
   SUPPLEMENTARY: Mihardja, entire; Taruc, entire.

O *Thursday, April 16 FILM:* "Harp of Burma." Shown during class time at the Preview Room, Learning Resources Center, 2nd floor of Alden Library. Please be prompt, as the film will start at 5 minutes past the hour, and will run to about 12:30.

●● *Thursday, April 30 Mid-term examination (1 bour)*

● *Monday, May 4 - Thursday, May 14 (7 lectures)*

   IV. Trials of Independence: 1950-1965.

   REQUIRED: *Steinberg, Chapters 33-39, portions appropriate to this section; *Reflections*, last two stories; Osborne, Chapter 12; Luong, first half. [Appropriate sections of Cady may be reviewed for this period.]
   SUPPLEMENTARY: Mahathir, entire; Khamsing, selections; Anderson and Ruchira Mendiones, selections.

O *Monday, May 11 FILM:* "The Masked Dance [of Thai Politics]." Shown during class time at the Preview Room, Learning Resources Center, 2nd floor of Alden Library. Please be prompt, as the film will start at 5 minutes past the hour.

● *Monday, May 18 - Thursday, June 4 (9 lectures)*

   V. Devising New States and Societies, 1965-present.

   REQUIRED: Finish with *Steinberg, Chs. 33-39, and read Ch. 40; Osborne, Chapter 13; Luong, last half; Samruam Singh, entire; Lansing, entire. [Appropriate sections of Cady may be reviewed for this period.]
   SUPPLEMENTARY: Reynolds, entire; Lubis, entire; Ahmad, entire.

O *Monday, May 18 FILM:* "Tongpan." Shown during class time in the Preview Room, Learning Resources Center, 2nd floor of Alden Library. Please be prompt, as the film is scheduled to begin at 5 pat the hour, and run until about 12:30.

O *Monday, June 1 FILM:* "Philippines: No Choice But Change." Shown during class time at the Preview Room, Learning Resources Center, 2nd floor of Alden Library. Please be prompt, as the film will start at 5 minutes past the hour.

●● *Thursday, June 11, at 12:20 PM Final Examination (2 bours)*

FILMS:

   Several films and videos will be shown during the Quarter. Dates and places of some showings are listed in the schedule above; others may be announced during class. These materials are to be treated as visual texts; you are expected to attend, and are responsible for the information and ideas presented in them.

MAP ASSIGNMENT:

It is always a good idea to know where things are, and where they were in the past; maps help give history a down-to-earth quality it may otherwise lack. As part of the final examination, you will be asked to fill in, on a blank map of Southeast Asia, a selection of 10 out of 13-15 items from the following list. You will be provided with practice maps at the beginning of the quarter; everything else is up to you. Good sources of information are: *Atlas of South-East Asia* D. G. E. Hall, intro. (New York: MacMillan, 1964) [G2368/D5/1964], and R. Ulack and G. Pauer, *Atlas of Southeast Asia* (New York: MacMillan, 1988) [G2360/U4/1989], held behind the desk in the Southeast Asia Collection, 1st floor of Alden library, but other similar publications may serve the purpose. Be sure, however, that you use relatively up-to-date materials.

In addition to the boundaries and capitals of the contemporary nations of Southeast Asia, you will need to know:

Geographical items

Myanmar (Burma): Irrawaddy, Salween, and Sittang Rivers; Arakan Range, Tennasserim Range and Coast, Gulf of Martaban, Mergui Archipelago, Andaman and Nicobar Islands; areas inhabited by the Chin, Shan, Kachin, and Karen peoples.

Vietnam, Cambodia, and *Laos*: Mekong, Song Hong (Red R.), Song Da (Black R.); Ailao and Mu Chia passes; Tonlé Sap, Plaine des Jarres, Chaine des Cardomômes, Central Highlands, delta areas.

Thailand: Menam Chao Phraya (river), Three Pagodas Pass, Khorat Plateau, Isthmus of Kra, Gulf of Siam, Phuket.

Malaysia and *Indonesia*: Penang, Straits of Malacca, Sumatra, Java, Bali, Sulawesi, Kalimantan, Timor, Maluku (islands); Musi, Brantas, Solo, and Barito rivers; Java, Banda, and Arafura seas; Makassar, Sunda, and Malacca straits; mountainous areas (indicate areas of volcanic activity); areas of Javanese, Sundanese, Buginese, Madurese, Minangkabau, Acehnese, Iban, and Dayak peoples.

Philippines: Luzon, Mindanao, Mindoro, Cebu, Leyte (islands); Mindoro Straits; Sulu Sea and Archipelago; Corderilla Central.

Cities and/or historical sites:

Pegu, Pagan, Ava, Mergui, Mandalay, Ayuthia, Chiengmai, Luang Prabang, Hue, Haiphong, Saigon-Cholon [Ho Chi Minh City], Songkhla, Ipoh, Johor Baru, Kota Kinabalu [Jesselton], Kuching, Medan, Bandar Sri Begawan [Brunei Town], Sandakan, Palembang, Bandung, Yogyakarta, Surabaya, Banjarmasin, Ujung Pandang [Makassar], Manila, Davao, Cebu City.

WRITTEN ASSIGNMENT:

Undergraduates may choose to write a brief paper (approximately 10 pages, or 2,500-3,000 words) on a) an events or series of events of the past 10 years in a single Southeast Asian nation; or b) a Southeast Asian personality (active chiefly in the period since 1942) of historical significance. The paper should exhibit the student's research and/or writing skills, and will be graded on accuracy, style, and originality. The paper is entirely optional. See section on grading, below, concerning special arrangements for those who elect to do a paper.

Graduates may choose to prepare a research paper of approximately 20 pages (5,000-6,000 words) on a) three or more selected book-length studies concerning Southeast Asia since 1942; b) an event or series of events of the past 10 years in a single Southeast Asian nation, or, comparatively, in several nations in the region; or c) a subject to be agreed with the instructor. Those who take this option may be excused from the mid-term examination, if they wish. The paper will be graded on investigative depth, accuracy, style, and originality; it is intended to give the student a chance to display research and/or writing skills on a carefully limited topic. The paper is highly recommended for regular students in the History Department graduate program. See the section on grading for special arrangements for those who elect to do a paper.

NB: Students, graduates as well as undergraduates, who choose to write a paper for the course *must* so inform the instructor *no later than* the class preceding the mid-term examination.

223

EXAMINATIONS:

Examinations in this course follow a pattern which tests both factual knowledge and conceptual understanding. There are separate examinations for undergraduate and graduate students, similar in structure but varying in degree of difficulty.

The mid-term examination (1 hour) is structured in the following manner: 1) a section worth 30 points consisting of brief identifications -- people, events, concepts -- based on the reading material; 2) a question worth 30 points requiring an informative response, using material from both readings and lectures, to a direct inquiry about a particular topic and/or period covered by the course; 3) a question worth 40 points requiring a thoughtful essay of fact and opinion in reaction to a pair of quotations, generally but not always taken from the assigned readings. The first and second questions test specific knowledge (the first question also tests the thoroughness with which reading assignments have been completed); the third question tests ability to use specific, general, and comparative knowledge in the formation of educated opinions.

The final examination (2 hours) is structured similarly, except that there is a 10-point map question, and the questions numbered 1-3 above are worth 20, 30, and 40 points, respectively.

GRADING:

For undergraduates: mid-term examination: 40% final examination: 60%. With paper option: mid-term, 30%; final, 35%; paper, 25%.

For graduates: mid-term: 40%; final, 60%. With research paper and mid-term: mid-term, 25%; final 35%, research paper, 40%. With research paper option and no mid-term: final, 50%; research paper, 50%.

ABSENCES:

The student is responsible for all material covered during class time. Attendance is highly recommended. A voluntary sign-in sheet is passed around the class each day, but there is no formal penalty for individual absences. Any consequences of absence from class, such as missing announcements, assignments, and course material, are the responsibility of the student.

POLICY ON ACADEMIC DISHONESTY:

The Ohio University code of student conduct defines and prohibits all forms of academic dishonesty, and empowers the instructor to lower the grade of any student engaged in course-related dishonesty. (Students are responsible for understanding how the university defines "plagiarism," "cheating," and other forms of academic dishonesty.) In this course, any student found writing examinations or preparing papers in a dishonest fashion will receive an "F" for the course, will not be given the option of withdrawing, and may be referred to University Judiciaries for disciplinary action.

OFFICE HOURS:

Bentley 84 (593-4341), MTWTh 10-11 and by appointment. Please make appointments in person after class, with the History Department secretary, or by calling 593-7139.

Department of History
Northern Illinois University
History 446: Thailand
Spring Semester, 1989

Constance M. Wilson
Zulauf 613
Tel. 753-6824
Office Hours: MW 1-2 p.m.

Required Reading:

All of the required books and data papers are available at the reserve desk
in the library.

The following titles are also in the bookstore:

    Engel. LAW AND KINGSHIP IN THAILAND DURING THE REIGN OF KING
        CHULALONGKORN.

    Girling, THAILAND: POLITICS AND SOCIETY.

    Ishii, SANGHA, STATE, AND SOCIETY: THAI BUDDHISM IN HISTORY.

    Wyatt, THAILAND: A SHORT HISTORY.

Because of the complications of the copyright law, the reserve desk has
asked faculty to reduce the number of articles placed on reserve. All of
the periodical articles used in the course are available in the library.

Bound volumes of ASIAN PERSPECTIVES will be found on the first floor of
Founders Library, the JOURNAL OF THE SIAM SOCIETY is located in the stacks
of the Donn V. Hart collection on the fourth floor.

If you cannot locate an article, please let me know. I usually have
duplicate copies available.

Please handle all library materials carefully. Do NOT write in or mark
library books. The library is seriously handicapped by a shortage of funds.
If materials are lost or damaged, it may not be possible for the library to
replace them.

Also, please return materials to the reserve desk as soon as possible. Try
not to keep materials out for the full 24 hour period. Some materials exist
in only one or two copies. Your fellow students will appreciate this!

Examinations:

There will be two midterm examinations and a final. A choice of essay
questions will always be offered. Undergraduates will be graded separately
from graduate students.

Other Comments:

Each student is expected to do his or her own work with special reference to
maps, papers, and examinations.

January 23.   Geography and Ethnolinguistic Groups.

                Films: Ka Rorn: Southern Village; Harvest at Nong Lub.

January 30.   Prehistory; Early History: Dvaravati, Funan and Chenla.

                Wyatt, THAILAND, Chs. 1 & 2.
                Stargardt, "Hydraulic Works and South East Asian Politics",
                pp. 23-48; and Srisakra, "Political and Cultural Continuities
                at Dvaravati Sites", pp. 229-238 in Marr and Milner,
                SOUTHEAST ASIA IN THE 9TH TO 14TH CENTURIES.
                White, DISCOVERY OF A LOST BRONZE AGE: BAN CHIANG. pp. 12-
                49, 54-93. (Be familiar with the types of artifacts found at
                Ban Chiang, the specific details given in the catalogue about
                these artifacts are not necessary).

                Recommended: ASIAN PERSPECTIVES, Vol. XIII, articles by
                Gorman, Bayard and Solheim; Vol. XXV, No. 1, (Memorial volume
                for Chet Gorman).

February 6.   Angkor: The Largest of the Early Empires.

                Mabbett, "Kingship in Angkor", JOURNAL OF THE SIAM SOCIETY,
                Vol. 66, Pt. 2, (July 1978) p. 1-51.
                Groslier, THE ART OF INDOCHINA, Chs. 3-11, Map II, Plan of
                Angkor. (Read primarily for information on art and
                architecture, note the complex system of irrigation canals
                presented in the map.)

February 13.   Lanna Thai, Sukhothai and Lan Sang (Lang Chang).

                Wyatt, THAILAND, Chs. 3 and 4.
                Stratton and Scott, THE ART OF SUKHOTHAI: THAILAND'S GOLDEN
                AGE, All.
                Smith, RELIGION AND LEGITIMATION OF POWER IN THAILAND, LAOS,
                AND BURMA, articles by Andaya, Swearer and Sommai, and
                Reynolds, pp. 2-33, 166-93.

February 20.   FIRST MIDTERM EXAMINATION! Two essay questions, map quiz.
                6-7:15p.m.

                Ayutthaya (Ayudhya).

                Wyatt, THAILAND, Ch. 5.
                Charnvit, THE RISE OF AYUDHYA: A HISTORY OF SIAM IN THE
                FOURTEENTH AND FIFTEENTH CENTURIES, All.
                Skinner, CHINESE SOCIETY IN THAILAND, Ch. 1.

February 27:   Bangkok: Economic Development and Social Change.

                Wyatt, THAILAND, Ch. 6.
                Akin, THE ORGANIZATION OF THAI SOCIETY IN THE EARLY BANGKOK
                PERIOD, All.

Skinner, CHINESE SOCIETY IN THAILAND, Chs. 2-5 (There is no
need to be involved in the detailed arguments over the
validity of population data, a knowledge of general
population trends is adequate, pay more attention to economic
and social life).

March 6.   Bangkok: The Modernization of the Thai State.

Wyatt, THAILAND, Chs. 7 and 8.
Engel, LAW AND KINGSHIP IN THAILAND IN TEH REIGN OF KING
CHULALONGKORN, All.

Recommended: Tej Bunnag, THE PROVINCIAL ADMINISTRATION OF
SIAM 1892-1915: THE MINISTRY OF THE INTERIOR UNDER PRINCE
DAMRONG RAJANUBHAB; and
Ramsey, "The Development of a Bureaucratic Polity: The Case
of Northern Siam".

March 20.   A Buddhist Society.

Films: Temple of Twenty Pagodas; Siam-People of Thailand;
Children of Bangkok.

Ishii, SANGHA, STATE, AND SOCIETY: THAI BUDDHISM IN HISTORY.
All.

March 27.   Modern Thailand: The Military and Politics.

Wyatt, THAILAND, Chs. 9 and 10.
Girling, THAILAND, All (The first chapter is largely review,
concentrate on chapters 2-7).

April 3.   SECOND MIDTERM EXAMINATION! Two essay questions. 6-7:15 p.m.

Modern Thailand: Society and Culture.

Skinner: CHINESE SOCIETY IN THAILAND, Chs. 6-9 (Again,
concentrate on economic, social and political life).
Phillips, MODERN THAI LITERATURE, Part I, pp. 3-67, and your
choice of the literary selections.

April 10.   Modern Thailand: Minorities.

Race, "The War in Modern Thailand", MODERN ASIAN STUDIES,
Vol. 8, No. 1, (1974) pp. 85-112.

Choose one of the following titles:
Forbes, THE MUSLIMS OF THAILAND, South East Asian Review,
    Vol. 13, 1988.
Geddes, MIGRANTS OF THE MOUNTAINS: THE CULTURAL ECOLOGY OF
    THE BLUE MIAO (HMONG NJUA) OF THAILAND.
Keyes, ETHNIC ADAPTATION AND IDENTITY: THE KARENS ON THE
    THAI FRONTIER WITH BURMA.

Poole, THE VIETNAMESE IN THAILAND: A HISTORICAL
PERSPECTIVE.

April 17.   Laos: The Landlocked Kingdom.

Archaimbault, "Religious Structures in Laos", JOURNAL OF THE
SIAM SOCIETY, Vol. 52 (April 1964) pp. 57-74.
Adams and McCoy, LAOS: WAR AND REVOLUTION, articles by
Whitmore, Adams, McCoy, and Thee, pp. 53-138.
Stuart-Fox, CONTEMPORARY LAOS, pp. 17-75 (articles by Brown,
Norindr, and Christie, a knowledge of the main political
institutions will be adequate); 148-162 (Lafont); 220-305
(Stuart-Fox, Thayer, van der Kroef, and Chiou).

Recommended: Any of the papers in Joel M. Halpern's Laos
Project Series.

April 24.   Cambodia/Kampuchea: The Tragic Kingdom.

Chandler, "Cambodia's Relations with Siam in the Early
Bangkok Period: The Politics of a Tributary State", THE
JOURNAL OF THE SIAM SOCIETY, Vol. 60 (January 1972) pp. 153-
70.
Osborne, POWER AND POLITICS IN CAMBODIA, pp. 12-117.
Kiernan and Chanthou Boua, PEASANTS AND POLITICS IN
KAMPUCHEA, 1942-1981. pp. 227-304. "Pol Pot and the
Kampuchean Communist Movement".

May 1.   Current Events and Review.

Institute of Southeast Asian Studies, SOUTHEAST ASIAN AFFAIRS
1988, pp. 123-149 (Porter and Gunn); pp. 269-294 (Kusuma and
Ruangthong).

May 8.   FINAL EXAMINATION! 6-7:50 p.m.
Part I.   Comprehensive question (one hour).
Part II. Two short essay questions (fifty minutes).

Department of History
Northern Illinois University
History 449: Malaysia and Indonesia
Spring Semester 1990

C. M. Wilson
Zulauf 613: Tel. 753-6824
Office Hours:
1:00 - 2:00 MW

Required reading.

All of the required books and data papers are available at the reserve desk in the library. The following titles are also available at the bookstore.

Andaya and Andaya, **A HISTORY OF MALAYSIA.**
Geertz, **NEGARA: THE THEATRE STATE IN NINETEENTH-CENTURY BALI.**
Legge, **SUKARNO.**

Because of the complications created by the copyright law, the reserve desk has asked the faculty to reduce the number of periodical articles placed on reserve. All of the articles assigned in the course are available in the library. The **JOURNAL OF ASIAN STUDIES and PACIFIC AFFAIRS** are located on the first floor of Founders Library. **INDONESIA** can be found on the fourth floor, in the Donn V. Hart Collection.

If you cannot locate an article, please let me know.

Please handle library materials carefully. The library is faced with a serious shortage of funds. If materials are lost or damaged, it cannot replace them. If you need a copy of anything, please use the available copiers.

Special assignments.

The map work is required. Instructions are on a separate sheet.

Each student is expected to write a paper. Instructions are contained in another handout. Undergraduates are expected to hand in a paper of 10-12 double-spaced, typed pages; graduate students should turn in 15-20 double-spaced, typed pages.

Examinations.

There will be two midterm examinations and a final. Examinations will consist of essay questions; a choice of essays is always offered. Undergraduates will be graded separately from graduate students. Please note that the final examination will be on May 2.

Other comments.

Each student is expected to do his or her own work, especially with respect to examinations, papers and maps.

January 17	Introduction. Geography.
January 22	Prehistory.

Taylor, "Madagascar in the Ancient Malayo-Polynesian Myths," in Hall and Whitmore, EXPLORATIONS IN EARLY SOUTHEAST ASIAN HISTORY: THE ORIGINS OF SOUTHEAST ASIAN STATECRAFT, pp. 25-52. (Concentrate on trade and cultural exchanges, don't worry about the linguistic details.)

Macknight, "Changing Perspectives in Island Southeast Asia," in Marr and Milner, SOUTHEAST ASIA IN THE 9TH TO 14TH CENTURIES, pp. 215-27.

January 24	Srivijaya.

Andaya and Andaya, Ch. 1.

McKinnon, "Early Politics in Southern Sumatra: Some Preliminary Observations Based on Archaeological Evidence." INDONESIA, October 1985, pp. 1-36.

January 29 & 3Q	Central and East Java.

Holt, ART IN INDONESIA, Part I.

de Casparis, "Some Notes on Relations between Central and Local Government in Ancient Java," and, Christie, "Negara, Mandala, and Despotic State: Images of Early Java," in Marr and Milner, SOUTHEAST ASIA IN THE 9TH TO 14TH CENTURIES, pp. 49-93.

Johns, "The Role of Structural Organization and Myth in Javanese Historiography," JOURNAL OF ASIAN STUDIES, 24, no. 1, (1964) pp. 91-99.

February 5	Islam in Southeast Asia.

Johns, "Islam in Southeast Asia: Reflections and New Directions," INDONESIA, April 1975, pp. 33-55.

February 7	The Rise of Melaka.

Andaya and Andaya, Ch. 2.

February 12	Indonesian Culture.

Holt, ART IN INDONESIA, Part II.

Recommended: Anderson, MYTHOLOGY AND THE TOLERANCE OF THE JAVANESE.

February 14	FIRST MIDTERM EXAMINATION (two essay questions plus map quiz)

February 19   The Arrival of the Europeans.

                     Meilink-Roelofsz, ASIAN TRADE AND EUROPEAN INFLUENCE IN
                     THE INDONESIAN ARCHIPELAGO..., chs. 8-11.

February 21   The Dutch in the Netherlands East Indies.

                     Ricklefs, A HISTORY OF MODERN INDONESIA, chs. 10-13.

February 26   Independent Bali.

                     Geertz, NEGARA: THE THEATRE STATE IN NINETEENTH-CENTURY
                     BALI, pp. 3-136.

February 28   Responses to Dutch Rule in the Netherlands East Indies.

                     Please read one of the following:

                     Graves, THE MINANGKABAU RESPONSE TO DUTCH COLONIAL RULE
                     IN THE NINETEENTH CENTURY. All.

                     van der Kraan, LOMBOK: CONQUEST, COLONIZATION AND
                     UNDERDEVELOPMENT, 1870-1940. All.

March 5 & 7   Nationalism and Revolution in Indonesia.

                     Dahm, HISTORY OF INDONESIA IN THE TWENTIETH CENTURY,
                     Chs.2-5. pp. 38-142.

                     Mrazek, "Tan Malaka: A Political Personality's Structure
                     of Experience," INDONESIA, October 1972, pp. 7-49.

                     Legge, SUKARNO, Chs. 1-9, pp. 1-239.

March 19   Sukarno and Independent Indonesia.

                     Legge, SUKARNO, Chs. 10-15, pp. 240-409.

March 21 & 26   Modern Indonesia.

                     Crouch, THE ARMY AND POLITICS IN INDONESIA, chs. 10-
                     Conclusion.

                     Bryan Evans III, "The Influence of the United States Army
                     on the Development of the Indonesian Army (1954-1964),"
                     INDONESIA, April 1989, pp. 25-48.

                     SOUTHEAST ASIAN AFFAIRS 1989. Articles on Indonesia.

                     Frederick, "Rhoma Irama and the Dangut Style: Aspects of
                     Contemporary Indonesian Popular Culture," INDONESIA,
                     October 1982, pp. 103-30.

March 28   SECOND MIDTERM EXAMINATION (two essay questions).

231

April 2	The Malay States: Out of the Old, the New.

April 2   The Malay States: Out of the Old, the New.

                   Andaya and Andaya, chs. 3 & 4.

April 4 & 9   Indigenous Malay Political Systems.

                   Please read one of the following studies:

                   Andaya, B., PERAK, THE ABODE OF GRACE....

                   Andaya, L., THE KINGDOM OF JOHOR, 1641-1728.....

                   Gullick, J.M., INDIGENOUS POLITICAL SYSTEMS OF WESTERN
                   MALAYA.

                   Trocki, C., THE PRINCE OF PIRATES.

April 11 & 16   British Rule and Malay Nationalism.

                   Andaya and Andaya, chs. 5 and 6.

                   Roff, THE ORIGINS OF MALAY NATIONALISM, chs. 3-7.

April 18 & 23   Modern Malaysia.

                   Andaya and Andaya, ch. 7 and Conclusion.

                   Bedlington, MALAYSIA AND SINGAPORE: THE BUILDING OF NEW
                   STATES, chs. 1-5.

                   SOUTHEAST ASIAN AFFAIRS 1989, Articles on Malaysia.

                   Essays by Jackson, Leigh and Peacock in Jackson and
                   Rudner, ISSUES IN MALAYSIAN DEVELOPMENT, pp. 273-304,
                   339-95.

                   Negata, "Religious Ideology and Social Change: The
                   Islamic Revival in Malaya," PACIFIC AFFAIRS, Fall 1980,
                   pp. 405-39.

April 25   Singapore.

                   Bedlington, chs. 6-9.

                   SOUTHEAST ASIAN AFFAIRS 1989, Articles on Singapore.

April 30   Brunei. Review

                   Bedlington, ch. 10.

                   SOUTHEAST ASIAN AFFAIRS 1989, Article on Brunei.

May 2   FINAL EXAMINATION
                   PART I: Comprehensive.
                   Part II: Two essay questions.

PENNSYLVANIA STATE UNIVERSITY

HISTORY 173: Vietnam at War
Course Syllabus

Mr. Duiker
Spring 1992

Week 1: (Reading Assignment: None)

A. Introduction to the Course. Procedures and Requirements.

B. A Brief Outline of Vietnamese History. Origins of the
Vietnamese People. Vietnam Under Chinese Rule. The Rise of
Dai Viet.

C. Key Issues in Vietnamese Foreign Policy. The Historical
Relationship With China. The "March to the South."

Week 2: (Reading Assignment: None)

A. Dynamics of Traditional Society. The Political Culture.
Confucianism and Buddhism. Economy and Society.

B. The French Conquest. Early European Penetration of Southeast
Asia. The Formation of French Indochina.

C. Vietnam Under Colonial Rule. The French Colonial System. The
Impact of Colonial Policies. France's "Mission Civilisatrice:"
A Balance Sheet.

Week 3: (Reading Assignment: Duiker, Chapters 1-3.)

A. The Rise of Vietnamese Nationalism. Prenationalist
Traditionalism. The Rise of Modern Nationalism.

B. Ho Chi Minh and the Origins of Vietnamese Communism. The World
of Ho Chi Minh. The Revolutionary Youth League. The Formation
of the Indochinese Party.

C. Film. (PBS 1: "The Roots of War")

Week 4: (Reading Assignment: Duiker, Chapters 4-6, pp. 127-144;
Herring, pp. 3-20.)

A. The August Revolution. World War II and the Formation of the
Vietminh Front. The Days of August. The Return of the French.

B. The Franco-Vietminh Conflict, 1946-1950. The Ho-Sainteny
Agreement. The Fontainebleau Conference. Incident at
Haiphong. People's War. The "Bao Dai Experiment."

C. Indochina Enters the Cold War. Traditional U.S. Foreign Policy
in Asia. Roosevelt and Indochina. The Cold War and Southeast
Asia.

Week 5: (Reading Assignment: Duiker, pp. 145-162; Herring,
          pp. 20-38.)

A. Study Group 1. January 1950: Should the U.S. Aid the French?

B. Film. (PBS 2: "The First Vietnam War, 1946-1954")

C. The Road to Geneva. America Aids the French. The Navarre Plan.
   Decision at Dien Bien Phu.

Week 6: (Reading Assignment: Duiker, pp. 162-172; Herring,
          pp. 39-55.)

A. First Midterm Examination.

B. The Geneva Conference. Goals of Participants. Division at the
   Seventeenth Parallel. Neutralization of Indochina. The
   Political Declaration: Legal Implications and Realities.

C. America Takes Charge. The Establishment of the Diem Regime.
   Crisis in Saigon.

Week 7: (Reading Assignment: Duiker, pp. 172-203; Herring,
          pp. 55-86.)

A. Study Group 2. July 1955: Should the U.S. Support National
   Elections?

B. Sink or Swim with Ngo Dinh Diem. The "Winston Churchill of
   Asia." The View From Hanoi. Return to Revolutionary War.

C. Film. (PBS 3: "America's Mandarin")

Week 8: (Reading Assignment: Duiker, pp. 203-221; Herring,
          pp. 86-107.)

A. Kennedy and the Crisis in Indochina. The Eisenhower Legacy.
   Khrushchev and the People's War. Crisis in Laos.

B. Study Group 3. November 1961: The Debate Over Counter-
   insurgency.

C. The Fall of the Diem Regime. Counter-insurgency in Action. The
   Viet Cong. The Buddhist Crisis. Coup in Saigon. Was Kennedy
   Leaving Vietnam?

Week 9: (Reading Assignment: Duiker, pp. 221-240; Herring,
          Chapter 4.)

A. Study Group 4. October 1963: Should We Run a̱ Coup?

B. Film. (PBS 4: "LBJ Goes to War")

C. Lyndon Johnson's War. The Tonkin Gulf Incident. Musical Chairs
   in Saigon. The Pleiku Incident.

(Reading Assignment: Duiker, pp. 240–263; Herring, Chapter 5.)

    A. Study Group 5. February 1965: Should We Take the Plunge?

    B. Film. (PBS 5: "America Takes Charge, 1965–1967")

Week 11: (Reading Assignment: Duiker, pp. 263–273; Herring, Chapter 6.)

    A. A View From Hanoi. Hanoi and its Allies. Psychomilitary Strategy.

    B. Second Midterm Examination.

    C. The Tet Offensive. Toward the "Decisive Hour." The TV War. Lyndon Johnson's Dilemma.

Week 12: (Reading Assignment: Duiker, pp. 273–280.)

    A. Film. (PBS 7: "Tet 1968")

    B. Study Group 6. March 1968: Should We Fight or Negotiate?

    C. The Road to Negotiations. Background to Paris. Fighting and Negotiating.

Week 13: (Reading Assignment: Duiker, pp. 280–300; Herring, Chapter 7.)

    A. Nixon and Vietnamization. Nixon's Plan to End the War. Operation Marco Polo. COSVN and Cambodia.

    B. Study Group 7. March 1970: What Should We Do About the Sanctuaries?

    C. Peace is at Hand. Cambodia and Kent State. The Secret Talks. The Eastern Offensive. Breakthrough. The Paris Agreement.

Week 14: (Reading Assignment: Duiker, Chapter 12; Herring, pp. 257–269.)

    A. The Final Drama. War and Peace. The Ho Chi Minh Campaign. "A War that is Finished."

    B. Film. (PBS 12: "The End of the Tunnel, 1973–1975")

    C. Study Group 8. April 1975: Can We Save Saigon?

Week 15: (Reading Assignment: Duiker, Chapter 13; Herring,
          pp. 269–281.)

A. Vietnam in Postwar Regional Politics. "Special Relationship" in
   Indochina. War with China. Hanoi and the Collapse of the Cold
   War.

B. A Revolution in Crisis. Building Socialism in Vietnam.
   Perestroika, Hanoi-style. Whither the Revolution?

C. Study Group 9. Debating the Lessons of Vietnam.

FINAL EXAM.

Required Reading:

William J. Duiker. The Communist Road to Power in Vietnam.
    Boulder: Westview Press, 1981.

George Herring. America's Longest War: The United States and
    Vietnam, 1950-1975. New York: Knopf, 1986.

Study Group Assignments:

Participants in study group projects will be expected to attend a
group session to work out policy recommendations and then present a
group report to the class.

Roger Dingman   History 344
University of Southern California   Summer, 1992

THE VIETNAM WAR

This course is designed to provide a broad overview of the
Vietnam War.   It focuses on the causes, conduct, and
consequences of the conflict as it affected both Americans
and Vietnamese.   By analyzing the processes by which
governments and individuals made decisions during the war, it
attempts to provide a framework for understanding the
conflict's place in the larger history of American relations
with the peoples and nations of East Asia.

REQUIRED READING MATERIALS

George Herring. America's Longest War. 2nd ed. Knopf, 1986

Andrew Rotter, Light at the End of the Tunnel. St. Martin's
                Press, 1991

Lewis B. Puller, Jr., Fortunate Son. Grove Weidenfeld, 1991

REQUIRED WRITTEN WORK

Each course participant will complete three quizzes, a course
project, and the final examination.   Quizzes will test
comprehension of basic factual materials.   The final
examination, which will be comprehensive, will test both
factual knowledge and the ability to draw broad conclusions
about material presented in the course.
All participants will prepare their own 12-15 page cartoon
history of the Vietnam War.   This project will require the
location, collation, interpretation, and synthesis of primary
contemporary materials.
NO MAKEUP quizzes or examinations will be given.

GRADING

Evaluation of performance in the course will be on a 1000-
point scale.   Points will be allocated as follows:
Quizzes: 150; Project: 250; Course discussion: 250;
Final exam: 350.

May 13	Introduction: America and Vietnam, 1898 - 1954 Readings: Rotter, Introduction Herring, ch.1
14	War without War, 1954 - 1963 Readings: Herring, ch.2-3 Rotter, pp.1-3, 5-7, 15
May 18	QUIZ 1 Decisions for War, 1964-65 Readings: Herring, ch.4 Rotter, pp.16, 17, 35
20	Lyndon Johnson's Wars: Fighting and Talking, 1966-1969 Readings: Herring, ch.5-6 Rotter, pp.18-25
21	Nixon's War, 1969-1973 Readings: Herring, ch.7 Rotter, pp.11-14
25	Memorial Day
27	QUIZ 2 Opponents of War Readings: Rotter, pp.31-33 Puller, ch.1-2
28	National and International Impacts Readings: Herring, ch.8 Rotter, p.36
June 1	PROJECT PRESENTATIONS Reading: Puller, ch.3-4
3	QUIZ 3 Personal Impacts (1) Readings: Rotter, pp.37-39 Puller, ch.5-6
4	PROJECT DUE IN CLASS Personal Impacts (2) Reading: Puller, ch.7-10
8	Vietnam: "Lessons" and Legacies Readings: Rotter, pp.26-30 Puller, Epilogue
9	COMPLETED FINAL EXAMINATION DUE

NEW YORK UNIVERSITY
GRADUATE SCHOOL OF LIBERAL STUDIES

THE AMERICAN WARS IN VIETNAM, 1945-1991

G65.1190
PROFESSOR A. TOM GRUNFELD   THURSDAYS, 6:10-7:50PM

This course is designed to examine the role that the United
States played in Vietnam (and in Cambodia and Laos) during the
years 1945 to the present. We will explore the historical
context of these events in both Vietnamese and American history.
We will also investigate some of the vexing questions raised by
American involvement in Southeast Asia such as: how and why was
the United States involved? Why was the war as prolonged as it
was? Did the United States have alternatives to all-out war?
What was the American legacy in Vietnam, as well as in America?

Required Readings:

Marilyn Young, The Vietnam Wars, 1945-1990 (HarperCollins)
Graham Greene: The Quiet American (Penguin)
Truong Nhu Tang, A Vietcong Memoir. An Inside Account of the
Vietnam War and its Aftermath (Harcourt Brace Javonovich)
Le Ly Hayslip: When Heaven and Earth Changed Places (Doubleday)
Selected articles and excerpts from other books.

Suggested Readings

Marvin E. Gettleman, ed., et. al. Vietnam and America. A
Documentary History (Grove Press)
Jonathan Schell, The Real War (Pantheon)
James Williams Gibson, The Perfect War. The War We Couldn't Lose
and How We Did (Vintage)

Class Requirements:

1. attendance and participation

2. EITHER 2 short papers (5-10 pages) discussing two of the
central issues raised in the readings and class discussions; OR
1 longer (15-20 pages) research paper on a major issue. Both
papers must utilize primary sources. Topics MUST be approved by
instructor.

3. Final examination

239

<u>Class Schedule</u>:

September 5:   Vietnamese culture and tradition
            Readings: Gettleman, et. al. <u>Vietnam. A Documentary</u>
                    <u>History</u> [on reserve]

September 12:   Resistance to the French and an end to colonialism
            Film: "Vietnam. A Television History," Part I
            Readings: Young, Chap. 1
                    Truong, Chap. 1-4

September 19:   The beginnings of U.S. foreign policy in Asia
            Film: "Vietnam. A Television History", Part II
            Readings: Young, Chap. 2-3
                    William Appleman Williams, "The Roots of
                    Intervention, 1776-1945" in <u>America in</u>
                    <u>Vietnam. Documentary History</u> [on reserve]

September 26:   America gets cautiously involved
            Readings: Graham Greene
                    David G. Marr, "The Rise and Fall of
                    'Counterinsurgency': 1961-1964" [on reserve]
                    Le, Chap. 1-5

October 3:   America gets seriously involved
            Readings: Young, Chap. 4-5
                    Truong, Chap. 5-7

October 10:   Lyndon Baines Johnson goes to war, I
            Readings: Young, Chap. 6-7
                    Truong, Chap. 8-10

October 17:   Lyndon Baines Johnson goes to war, II
            Readings: Young, Chap. 8-9
                    Truong, Chap. 10-14

October 24:   The Nixon/Kissinger war
            Readings: Young, Chap. 11-12
                    Le, Chap. 6-10

October 31:   Cambodia (Kampuchea) and Laos
            Readings: Cohen, "Cambodia and Laos," in <u>Vietnam.</u>
                    <u>Anthology & Guide to a Television History</u>
                    [on reserve]

November 7:   Homefront USA
            Readings: Young, Chap. 10

November 14:   The Vietnamization of the war
            Readings: Young, Chap. 13
                    Truong, Chap. 15-17

November 21:   The war finally ends
            Readings: Young, Chap. 14
                      Truong, Chap. 18-23
                      Le, Chap. 11-14

November 28:   Thanksgiving/No class.

December 5:   Lessons for today and tomorrow
            Film: "Thanh's War"
            Readings: Young, Chap. 15
                      Richard Nixon: "How We Won the War"
                      [on reserve]

December 12:   Wrap Up.
            Readings: Young, Epilogue
                      Truong, Chap. 24
                      Le, Epilogue

December 19: Final Examination

HISTORY 197/201T   Professor D.R. SarDesai
                                                             Spring Quarter, 1992

The following topics will be discussed in the seminar. Each of you will write 2 papers of
about 4-5 pages on any of the seven topics. Each of you will be a formal discussant of a
paper on any two occasions. The grade will be 30 points each for the two papers, 15 points
for each performance as a discussant and 10 points for your general participation in the
classroom discussions. The schedule for papers will be prepared on the first day of classes.
The papers may be revised and submitted to me by the class meeting in the 9th week, except
those who are scheduled to present their papers in the first instance in the 9th week. For
them the due date will be the class meeting of week 10. All papers will be due on the
Monday of the week in which they will be presented to the class. Papers should be
submitted to the History Department Library by 10 A.M. on Monday.

TOPICS:

1.   Communist and Nationalist Movement in Vietnam, 1920-1954.

2.   The Leadership of the DRV; Role of Guerrilla Warfare in Communist strategy
      in Vietnam; relations between the DRV and the NLF.

3.   U.S. and the Conflict in Vietnam, Cambodia and Laos Phase I...1954-1964.

4.   -do- Phase II...1965-1975.

5.   Communist Governments in Vietnam and Cambodia since 1975 - Political leadership
      and factions - Domestic Policies: Economic and Social.

6-7. Communist Governments in Vietnam and Cambodia - International relations -
      Moscow, Beijing, Hanoi relations - Interstate conflicts: Vietnam-Cambodia and
      Vietnam-China wars - ASEAN and the Communist states of Southeast Asia.

REQUIRED: D.R. SarDesai, Vietnam: Struggle for a National Identity, Boulder,
               Colorado: Westview Press, 1992.

               Gary R. Hess, Vietnam and the United States, Boston, Twayne
               Publishers, 1990.

Topic 1. VIETNAM - Communist and Nationalist Movement, 1920-1954

Chaliand, Gerard. The Peasants of North Vietnam. Baltimore, 1969.

Chen, King C. Vietnam and China, 1938-1954. Princeton, 1969.

Duiker, William J. The Comintern and Vietnamese Communism. Athens, Ohio University, Southeast Asia Program, 1975.

_____. The Rise of Nationalism in Vietnam, 1900-1941. Ithaca, N.Y., 1976.

Duncanson, Dennis J. Government and Revolution in Vietnam. London, 1968.

Fall, B.B. Street Without Joy. New York, 1964.

Fall, B.B. The Two Vietnams, A Political and Military Analysis. New York, 1963, 1967, 1970.

Fall, B.B. Hell in a Very Small Place: The Siege of Dien Bien Phu, Philadelphia, 1967.

Fall, B.B. The Viet-Minh Regime: Government and Administration in the Democratic Republic of Vietnam. Ithaca, N.Y., 1956.

Fitzgerald, Frances. Fire in the Lake. New York, 1972.

Foreign Language Pub. House. Breaking Our Chains: Documents on the Vietnamese Revolution. Hanoi, 1958.

Gurtov, Melvin. The First Vietnam Crisis. New York, 1967.

Hammer, Ellen. The Struggle for Indo-China 1940-1955. Stanford, 1955.

Hoang, Van Chi. From Colonialism to Communism. New York, 1965.

Ho Chi Minh. On Revolution, trns., by B.B. Fall. New York, 1967.

Ho Chi Minh. Prison Diary. 3rd ed., Hanoi, 1966.

Honey, P.J. Communism in North Vietnam. Cambridge, Massachusetts, 1964.

Honey, P.J. ed., North Vietnam Today: Profile of a Communist Satellite. New York, 1962.

Huynh, Kim Khanh, Vietnamese Communism, 1925-1945. Ithaca, 1975.

Lacouture, Jean. Vietnam Between Two Truces. New York, 1966.

Lancaster, Donald. The Emancipation of French Indo-china. London, 1961.

McAlister, John T. Vietnam, The Origins of Revolution. New York, 1969.

McAlister, John T. and Paul Mus. The Vietnamese and Their Revolution. New York, 1970.

Ngo Vinh Long. Before the Revolution: The Vietnamese Peasants Under the French. Cambridge, Massachusetts, 1973.

Nguyen Khac Huyen. Vision Accomplished? New York, 1971.

O'Ballance, Edgar. The Indo-china War, 1945-54, A Study in Guerrilla Warfare. London, 1964.

Patti, Archimedes, Why Vietnam? Berkeley, 1980

Pike, Douglas. A History of Vietnamese Communism, 1925-1976. Stanford, 1978.

Popkin, Samuel. The Rational Peasant. Berkeley, 1979.

Raskin, Marcus G. and Fall, B.B. eds., The Vietnam Reader. New York, 1965.

Roy, Jules. Battle of Dien Bien Phu, New York, 1965.

Sacks, Milton. Political Alignments of Vietnamese Nationalists. Washington, Department of State, No. 3708, 1949.

_____. "Marxism in Vietnam," in Frank Trager, ed. Marxism in Southeast Asia. Stanford, 1959.

Swearingen, Rodger and Hammond Rolph. Communism in Vietnam, A Documentary Study, Chicago, 1967.

Truong, Chinh. The August Revolution. Hanoi, 1958.

Truong, Chinh and Vo Nguyen Giap. The Peasant Question, 1937-1938, trans., Ithaca, N.Y. Cornell University data paper, No. 94, 1974.

Vo, Nguyen Giap. Unforgetable Days. Hanoi, 1975.

Vo, Nguyen Giap. People's War, People's Army. New York, 1962.

Woodside, Alexander B. Community and Revolution in Vietnam. Boston, 1976.

Topic 2 COMMUNISM IN VIETNAM (DRV, Viet Cong, NLF, Guerrilla Warfare):

I.

Bodard, Lucien. The Quicksand War. Boston, 1967.

Burchett, Wilfred. Vietnam, The Inside Story of the Guerrilla War. New York, 1965.

Carver, George A. "The Faceless Viet Cong." Foreign Affairs, 44 (1966), pp. 347-72.

Devillers, Philippe and Jean Lacouture. End of War. New York, 1969.

Duiker, William. The Communist Road to Power in Vietnam. Boulder, Colorado, 1981.

Lewis, John Wilson, ed. Peasant Rebellion and Communist Revolution in Asia. Stanford, 1974.

McGarvey, Patrick, ed. Visions of Victory: Selected Vietnamese Communist Military Writings, 1964-1968. Stanford, 1969.

Mangold, Tom. The Tunnels of Cu Chi. London, 1985.

O'Ballance, Edgar. The Indochina War, 1945-1954, A Study in Guerrilla Warefare. London, 1964.

Pike, Douglas. The Viet Cong. Boston, 1967.

Porter, Gareth. Vietnam: The Definitive Documentation of Human Decision. 2 vols., Stanfordville, N.Y., 1979.

Shaplen, Robert. The Lost Revolution. New York, 1965.

Tanham, George K. Communist Revolutionary Warfare, the Viet Minh in Indochina. London, 1962.

Thompson, Robert. Defeating Communist Insurgency. New York, 1966.

Truong, Nhu Tang. Journal of a Viet Cong, London, 1986.

Turley, William, ed. Vietnamese Communism in Comparative Perspective. Boulder, Colo., 1980.

U.S. State Department. A Threat to the Peace. Washington, D.C. 1961.

Vo Nguyen Giap. People's War, People's Army: The Viet Cong Insurrection, Manual for Underdeveloped Countries. New York, 1962.

II. Biographical

Das, S.R. Mohan. Ho Chi Minh, Nationalist or Soviet Agent? Bombay, 1950.
Fischer, Ruth. "Ho Chi Minh: Disciplined Communist," Foreign Affairs. (Oct. 1954).
Foreign Languages Pub. House. Days with Ho Chi Minh. Hanoi, 1962.
Lacouture, J. Ho Chi Minh, London, 1968.
O'Neill, Robert. General Giap. New York, 1969.
Sainteny, Jean. Ho Chi Minh and his Vietnam; A Personal Memoir. Chicago, 1970.
Shaplen, Robert. "The Enigma of Ho Chi Minh," The Reporter. XII, Jan. 27, 1955.

Topics 3 and 4. U.S. and the Conflict in Vietnam, Cambodia and Laos, 1954-1975:

Blaufarb, Douglas. The Counterinsurgency Era. New York, 1977.
Blum, Robert M. Drawing the Line: The Origins of American Containment Policy in East Asia. New York, 1982.
Cooper, Chester L. The Lost Crusade: America in Vietnam. Greenwich, Conn., 1972.
Currey, Cecil B. Self-Destruction: Disintegration and Decay of the United States Army during the Vietnam Era. New York, 1981.
Dacy, Douglas C. Foreign Aid, War and Economic Development: South Vietnam, 1955-1975. Cambridge, 1986.
Elliott, David. NLF-DRV Strategy and the 1972 Spring Offensive. Ithaca, N.Y.: Cornell University, International Relations of East Asia (IREA) project, 1974.
Fall, Bernard. The Two Vietnams. New York, 1970.
_____. Vietnam Witness, 1953-1966. New York, 1966.
Fishel, Wesley (ed.) Vietnam: Anatomy of a Conflict. Itasca, Ill., 1968.
Fitzgerald, Frances. Fire in the Lake. New York, 1972.
Gaddis, John. Strategies of Containment. New York, 1982.
Gettleman, Marvin E. (ed.) Vietnam: History, Documents, and Opinions on a Major World Crisis. New York, 1965.
Goodman, Allan. The Lost Peace. America's Search for a Negotiated Settlement of Vietnam War. Stanford 1978.
Harrison, James P. The Endless War: Fifty Years of Struggle in Vietnam. New York, 1982.
Herrington, Stuart. Silence was a Weapon: The Vietnam War in the Villages. San Rafael, Calif., 1982.
Hilsman, Roger. To Move a Nation. New York, 1969.
Hoopes, Townsend. The Limits of Intervention. New York, 1969.
Joiner, Charles A. The Politics of Massacre: Political Processes in South Vietnam. Philadelphia, 1974.

Kahin, George McT. Intervention: How America Became Involved in Vietnam. New York, 1986.

Karnow, Stanley. Vietnam, A History, the First Complete Account of Vietnam at War. New York, 1983.

Kattenburg, Paul. The Vietnam Trauma in American Foreign Policy, 1945-1975, New Brunswick, 1980.

Kelley, Gail P. From Vietnam to America: A Chronicle of the Vietnamese Immigration to the United States. Boulder, Colo., 1977.

Kissinger, Henry. The White House Years. Boston, 1979.

Kolko, Gabriel. Anatomy of a War: Vietnam, the United States and the Modern Historical Experience. New York, 1985.

Kurland, Gerald, ed. Misjudgment or Defense of Freedom? The United States in Vietnam. New York, 1975.

Lacouture, Jean. Vietnam: Between Two Truces. New York, 1966.

Lewy, Guenther. America in Vietnam. New York, 1978.

Nguyen, Cao Ky. Twenty-Years and Twenty-Days. New York, 1976.

Nguyen Khac Vien (ed.) Tradition and Revolution in Vietnam. Berkeley, Calif., and Washington, 1974.

Oberderfor, Donald. Tet! New York, 1971.

The Pentagon Papers (Senator Gravel Edition, 4 vols.) Boston, 1971.

Pike, Douglas. Viet Cong. Cambridge, Mass., 1966.

Podhoretz, Norman. Why we Were in Vietnam. New York, 1982.

Porter, Gareth. A Peace Denied. Bloomington, 1975.

Porter, Gareth. Vietnam: The Definitive Documentation of Human Decision. 2 vols. Stanfordville, N.Y., 1979.

Race, Jeffrey. War Comes to Long An. Berkeley and Los Angeles, 1972.

Rotter, Andrew J. The Path to Vietnam: Origins of American Commitment to Southeast Asia. Ithaca, 1987.

Sansom, Robert L. The Economics of Insurgency in the Mekong Delta of Vietnam. Cambridge, Mass., 1970.

Scigliano, Robert. South Vietnam: Nation Under Stress. Boston, 1963.

Shaplen, Robert. The Lost Revolution. New York, 1966.

Shawcross, William. Sideshow: Kissinger, Nixon, and the Destruction of Cambodia. New York, 1979.

Sihanouk, Norodom. My War with the CIA. Harmondsworth, 1973.

Snepp, Frank. A Decent Interval. New York, 1977.

Stanton, Shelby L. The Rise and Fall of an American Army, U.S. Ground Forces in Vietnam, 1965-1975, San Rafael, Calif., 1985.

Stettler, Russell (ed.) The Military Art of People's War. New York, 1970.

Summers, Jr., Harry G. On Strategy: A Critical Analysis of the Vietnam War. Nobato, Calif., 1982.

Tanham, George. Communist Revolutionary Warfare. New York, 1967.

Terzani, Tiziano. Giai Phong! The Fall and Liberation of Saigon. New York, 1976.

Thompson, Robert. No Exit from Vietnam. New York, 1969.

Thompson, Robert. Defeating Communist Insurgence. New York, 1966.
Tran Van Don. Our Endless War: Inside Vietnam, San Rafael, Calif., 1978.
Turley, William S. The Second Indochina War. A Short Political and Military History. Boulder, Colo., 1986.
Van Tien Dung. Our Great Spring Victory. New York, 1977.
Warner, Denis. Not With Guns Alone. London, 1977.
Westmoreland, William, C. A Soldier Reports. New York, 1976.

Topics 5, 6, 7 Vietnam and Cambodia since 1975

Albin, David A. and Marlowe Hood, eds. The Cambodian Agony. Armonk, 1987.
Barron, John and Anthony Paul. Murder of a Gentle Land; The Untold Story of Communist Genocide in Cambodia. New York, 1977.
Basu, Sanghamitra. Kampuchea as a Factor in the Sino-Soviet Conflict, 1975-1984. Calcutta, 1987.
Becker, Elizabeth. When the War was Over; The Voices of Cambodia's Revolution and Its People. New York, 1986.
Brzezinski, Zbignew. Power and Principle, Memoirs of the National Security Advisor, 1977-1981. New York, 1983.
Carney, Timothy M., ed. Communist Party in Kampuchea, Documents and Discussion, Ithaca, 1977.
Chanda, Nayan. Brother Enemy; The War after the War, A History of Indochina since the Fall of Saigon. San Diego, 1986.
Chandler, David P., Ben Kiernan, Chanthou Boua, eds. Pol Pot Plans the Future: Confidential Leadership Documents from Democratic Kampuchea, 1976-1977. New Haven, 1988.
Chang, Pao-min, Kampuchea between China and Vietnam, Singapore, 1985.
Chang, Pao-min, The Sino-Vietnamese Territorial Dispute. New York, 1986.
Dellinger, David T. Vietnam Revisited; From Covert Action to Invasion to Reconstruction. Boston, 1986.
Duiker, William J. China and Vietnam; The Roots of Conflict. Berkeley, 1986.
Duiker, William J. Vietnam Since the Fall of Saigon. Athens, 1985.
Etcheson, Craig. The Rise and Demise of Democratic Kampuchea. Boulder, CO, 1984.
Fforde, Adam. The Agrarian Question in North Vietnam, 1974-1979. Armonk, 1989.
Hayslip, Le Ly. When Heaven and Earth Change Places; A Vietnamese Woman's Journey from War to Peace. New York, 1989.
Hildebrand, George C. Cambodia; Starvation and Revolution. New York, 1976.
Jackson, Karl D., ed. Cambodia, 1975-1978; Rendezvous with Death. Princeton, 1981.
Kelley, Gail Paradise. From Vietnam to America: A Chronicle of the Vietnamese Immigration to the United States. Boulder, Colorado, 1977.

Kiernan, Ben. How Pol Pot Came to Power: A History of Communism in Kampuchea, 1930-1975. London, 1985.

Kiljunen, Kimmo, ed. Kampuchea: Decade of the Genocide. London, 1984.

Klintworth, Gary. Vietnam's Withdrawal from Cambodia. Canberra, 1987.

Leifer, Michael. Cambodian Conflicts: The Final Phase? London, 1989.

Long, Robert Emmet, ed. Vietnam Ten Years After. New York, 1986.

McGregor, Charles. The Sino-Vietnamese Relationship and the Soviet Union. London, 1988.

Ngor Haing S. Surviving the Killing Fields: The Cambodian Odyssey, London, 1988.

Nguyen Khac Vien. Southern Vietnam, 1975-1985. Hanoi, 1985.

Picq, Laurence. Beyond the Horizon: Five Years with the Khmer Rouge. New York, 1989.

Pike, Douglas Eugene. Vietnam and the Soviet Union: Anatomy of an Alliance. Boulder, Colorado, 1987.

Ponchaud, Francois. Cambodia, Year Zero. New York, 1977.

Porter, Gareth. "Vietnamese Policy and the Indochina Crisis," in David W.P. Elliot, ed. The Third Indochina Conflict, Boulder, Co. 1981.

Pradhan, P.C. Foreign Policy of Kampuchea. New Delhi, 1985.

Ross, Robert S. The Indochina Tangle: China's Vietnam Policy, 1975-1979. New York, 1988.

Schanberg, Sydney Hillel. The Death and Life of Dith Pran. New York, 1985.

Shawcross, William. The Quality of Mercy: Cambodia, Holocaust and Modern Conscience, New York, 1984.

Sibler, Irwin. Kampuchea: The Revolution Rescued. Oakland, 1986.

Socialist Republic of Vietnam. Vietnam Ten Years After. Hanoi, 1985.

Stuart-Fox, Martin. The Murderous Revolution: Life and Death in Pol Pot's Kampuchea. Chippendale, 1985.

Tan Teng Lang. Economic Debates in Vietnam: Issues and Problems in Reconstruction and Development (1975-84), Singapore, 1985.

Thrift, Nigel and Dean Forbes. The Price of War: Urbanization in Vietnam, 1954-1985. London, 1985.

Tran Van Don. Our Endless War: Inside South Vietnam. Novato, CA, 1978.

Turley, William S., ed. Confrontation or Coexistence: The Future of ASEAN-Vietnam Relations. Bangkok, 1985.

Turley, William S. "The Khmer War: Cambodia after Paris," Survival, XXXII, 5 (September-October, 1990), pp. 437-453.

Vickery, Michael. Kampuchea: Politics, Economics, and Society. London, 1986.

Vickery, Michael. Cambodia, 1975-1982. Boston, 1984.

Yang Sam, Khmer Buddhism and Politics form 1954 to 1984. Newington, 1987.

"THE STRUCTURE OF
SOUTHEAST ASIAN HISTORY" REVISITED

William H. Frederick
Ohio University

Bentley 24, MW 7-9PM
Spring 1992

PURPOSE:

This colloquium is an advanced class in Southeast Asian history. Its aim is to survey a generous selection of the major works published on selected topics in Southeast Asian history since approximately 1960, and in doing so to assess the changing "structure" of the field. A secondary purpose of the course is to hone research and writing skills, though this is neither a research or writing course in the way, for example, a proseminar might be; the research and writing are intended not to produce a major piece of academic work, but to serve and inform in every way possible intelligent analysis and discussion of the topics chosen. Much emphasis will be placed upon developing analytical judgement and understanding how such judgement functions in and informs (or misinforms) modern historical study. The basic operating principle is that all students in the course share and critique each other's ideas freely, contributing to discussions and behaving like good academic colleagues. The papers which students produce, however, must of course reflect their own ideas, opinions, basic research, and writing.

TEXTS:

Except for the general work *In Search of Southeast Asia*, which is available at the College Bookstore, there are no texts of the usual sort for this course. All students will read the original article to which the title of the course refers, but beyond that the reading is individual. Students will survey the bibliographic resources for the topic and area chosen in each of five sections, and will describe and evaluate for class colleagues one or more works in each section. This collection of papers becomes a text of a kind, and forms the basis for discussion. Copies of all written work are to be shared with all members of the colloquium.

OUTLINE AND ASSIGNMENTS:

M, March 30 INTRODUCTION to the colloquium.

Initial reading.
Since Harry J. Benda's classic article, "The Structure of Southeast Asian History: Some Preliminary Observations" *Journal of Southeast Asian History* 3 (1962) pp. 106-138, there has been no substantive attempt to "revisit" the subject of the overall structure of Southeast Asian history. This class will attempt to begin to remedy the situation, and the obvious place to start is Benda's article. Please read this piece very thoroughly and critically. Be prepared to discuss it from a number of perspectives. Be prepared, also, to evaluate the article and argue its strong and weak points. Finally, why has no one written a sequel in 30 years?

INTRODUCTION to Topic 1:

The Shape and Structure of Southeast Asian History

Some Bibliographic Suggestions:

Aung-Thwin, Michael. "Spirals in Early Southeast Asian and Burmese History," *Journal of Interdisciplinary History* XXXI, 4 (Spring 1991), pp. 575-602.

Bastin, John and Harry J. Benda. *A History of Modern Southeast Asia.* Englewood Cliffs: Prentice-Hall, 1968.

Benda, H. J. and John A. Larkin. *The World of Southeast Asia.* New York: Harper and Row, 1967.

Cady, John F. *Southeast Asia: Its Historical Development.* New York: McGraw Hill, 1964.

Cowan, C. D. and O. W. Wolters (eds.) *Southeast Asian history and historiography: essays presented to D. G. E. Hall.* Ithaca: Cornell University Press, 1976.

Emmerson, Donald K. "Issues in Southeast Asian history: room for interpretation -- A review article." *Journal of Asian Studies* 40 (1980), pp. 43-68.

Hall, D. G. E. *A History of Southeast Asia.* Fourth Edition. New York: St. Martin's Press, 1981.

Hall, D. G. E. "The integrity of Southeast Asian history." *Journal of Southeast Asian Studies* 4 (1974), pp. 159-168.

Hall, D. G. E. "Looking at Southeast Asian history." *Journal of Asian Studies* 19 (1959-60), pp. 268-281.

Hall, D. G. E. (ed.). *Historians of Southeast Asia.* London: Oxford University Press, 1961.

Hall, D. G. E. "On the study of Southeast Asian history." *Pacific Affairs* 33 (1960), pp. 268-281.

McCloud, Donald G. *System and Process in Southeast Asia. The Evolution of a Region.* Boulder: Westview, 1986.

Neher, Clark D. *Southeast Asia in the New International Era.* Boulder: Westview, 1991.

O'Connor, Richard A. *A theory of indigenous Southeast Asian urbanism.* Singapore: Institute of Southeast Asian Studies, 1983.

Owen, Norman G. (ed.), *Death and disease in Southeast Asia* Singapore: Oxford University Press, 1987.

Reid, Anthony J. S. and David Marr (eds.). *Perceptions of the Past in Southeast Asia.* Singapore: Heinemann, 1979.

Sharp, Lauriston. "Cultural continuities and discontinuities in Southeast Asia." *Journal of Asian Studies* 22 (1962), pp. 3-11.

Smail, John R. W. "On the possibility of an autonomous history of modern Southeast Asia." *Journal of Southeast Asian History* 2 (1961), pp. 72-102.

Steinberg, David Joel, et al. *In Search of Southeast Asia. A Modern History.* Revised Edition. Honolulu: University of Hawaii Press, 1987.

Vickers, Adrian. "Writing indonesian history: poststructuralism and perceptions..." *Asian Studies Association of Australia Review* 10, 1 (1986), pp. 15-21.

Wheatley, Paul. *Nagara and Commandery.* Chicago: University of Chicago, Department of Geography, 1983.

Wolters, O. W. *History, culture, and region in Southeast Asian perspectives.* Singapore: Institute of Southeast Asian Studies, 1982.

ASSIGNMENT 1. Topic 1 Paper.

First: As a supplement to the list presented above, prepare a short (no more than 2 pages or 25 items), briefly annotated (1 or 2 sentences) bibliography of additional items relevant to Topic 1 (and to the work on which you will write your paper in this section). Bibliographic sources will be discussed in class, but you will need to be both selective and creative. Prepare sufficient copies for everyone in the class.

DUE: M, April 6.

Second: Choose *at least* one book or two articles (consideration in grading will be given for papers that cover more than the minimum number of items) relevant to the topic, and write a brief (1250-2500 words) paper on this material. Include information on the author as well as the work itself, and analyze and evaluate the contents rather than simply report on them descriptively. (Follow — as exactly as possible — the format laid out on the accompanying explanatory sheet.) Prepare sufficient copies for everyone in the class.

DUE: F, April 10 at 4 PM in Bentley 110.

W, April 1   Choosing of items to be read during the quarter.

M, April 6   DISCUSSION of Topic 1 (including Benda article) and bibliographies.

W, April 8   Tutorials

F, April 10   Pick up copies of Topic 1 papers in Bentley 110, and read them.

M, April 13   COLLOQUIUM on Topic 1.

W, April 15   INTRODUCTION to Topic 2:

Early States and Societies (Before c. 1300 CE)

Some Bibliographic Suggestions:

Aung-Thwin, Michael. *Pagan, The Origins of Modern Burma.* Honolulu: University of Hawaii Press, 1985.

Aung-Thwin, Michael. *Irrigation in the Heartland of Burma: Foundations of the Pre-Colonial Burmese State.* DeKalb: Northern Illinois University Center for Southeast Asian Studies, 1990.

Barrett Jones, Antoinette M. *Early Tenth Century Java from the Inscriptions.* Verhandelingen KITLV, 107. Dordrecht: Foris, 1984.

Bellwood, Peter. *Prehistory of the Indo-Malaysian Archipelago.* Sydney: Academic Press, 1985.

Hall, Kenneth R. *Maritime Trade and State Development in Early Southeast Asia.* Honolulu: University of Hawaii Press, 1985.

Hall, Kenneth R. and John K. Whitmore (eds.). *Explorations in Early Southeast Asian History: The Origins of Southeast Asian Statecraft.* Ann Arbor: University of Michigan Center for South and Southeast Asian Studies, 1976.

Higham, Charles. *The Archeology of Mainland Southeast Asia.* Cambridge: Cambridge University Press, 1989.

Holmgren, Jennifer. *Chinese colonisation of Northern Vietnam. Administrative geography and political development in the Tongking Delta, first to sixth centuries A.D.* Canberra:

Australian National University, 1980.

Kulke, Harmann. *The Devaraja Cult*. Ithaca: Cornell University Southeast Asia Program, 1978.

Mabbett, Ian W. "The 'Indianization' of Southeast Asia: Reflections on the Prehistoric Sources," *Journal of Southeast Asian Studies*, 8, 1 (1977), pp. 1-14, and 8, 2 (1977), pp. 143-166.

Marr, David G. and A. C. Milner. *Southeast Asia in the 9th to 14th Centuries*. Singapore: Institute of Southeast Asian Studies, with the Research School of Pacific Studies, Australian National University, 1986.

Naerssen, F. H. van and R. C. de Iongh. *The Economic and Administrative History of Early Indonesia*. Leiden: E. J. Brill, 1977.

Reid, Anthony J. S. and Lance Castles (eds). *Pre-colonial State Systems in Southeast Asia*. Monographs of the Malaysian Branch of the Royal Asiatic Society, No. 6. Kuala Lumpur: MBRAS, 1975. [Reprint, 1979.]

Setten van der Meer, N. C. van. *Sawah Cultivation in Ancient Java: Aspects of Development during the Indo-Javanese Period, Fifth to Fifteenth Century*. Canberra: Australian National University Press, 1979

Smith, R. B. and W. Watson (eds.) *Early Southeast Asia*. Oxford: Oxford University Press, 1979.

Taylor, Keith W. *The Birth of Vietnam*. Berkeley: University of California Press, 1983.

White, Joyce C. *Ban Chiang. Discovery of a Lost Bronze Age*. Philadelphia: University of Pennsylvania Museum with the Smithsonian Institution, 1982.

Wolters, O. W. *Early Indonesian Commerce. A Study of the Origins of Srivijaya*. Ithaca: Cornell University Press, 1967.

ASSIGNMENT 2. Topic 2 Paper.
First: Bibliography.
DUE: April 20.
Second: Paper on Topic 2.
DUE: April 24, 4 PM.

M, April 20   DISCUSSION of bibliographies and of Topic 2.

W, April 22   Individual tutorials.

F, April 24   Pick up copies of Topic 2 papers and read.

M, April 27   COLLOQUIUM on Topic 2.

W, April 29   INTRODUCTION to Topic 3:

The Classical Age (c. 1450-1750)

Some Bibliographic Suggestions:

Andaya, Barbara Watson. *Perak: The Abode of Grace*. Kuala Lumpur: Oxford University Press, 1979.

Andaya, Leonard Y. *The Heritage of Arung Palakka: A History of South Sulawesi in the*

Seventeenth Century. The Hague: M. Nijhoof, 1981.

Andaya, Leonard Y. *The Kingdom of Johor, 1641-1728*. Kuala Lumpur: Oxford University Press, 1975.

Chaudhuri, K. N. *Trade and Civilization in the Indian Ocean. An Economic History from the Rise of Islam to 1750*. Cambridge: Cambridge University Press, 1985.

Graaf, H. J. de and Th. G. Th. Pigaud. *Chinese Muslims in Java in the 15th and 16th centuries*. Clayton, Victoria: Monash University Centre for Southeast Asian Studies, 1984.

Kasetsiri, Charnvit. *The Rise of Ayudhya: A History of Siam in the Fourteenth and Fifteenth Centuries*. Kuala Lumpur: Oxford University Press, 1976.

Koenig, William J. *The Burmese Polity, 1752-1819: Politics, Administration, and Social Organization in the Early Kon-baung Period*. Ann Arbor: University of Michigan Center for South and Southeast Asian Studies, 1990.

Lieberman, Victor B. *Burmese Administrative Cycles. Anarchy and Conquest, c. 1580-1760*. Princeton: Princeton University Press, 1984.

Meilink-Roelofsz, M. A. P. *Asian Trade and European Influence in the Indonesian Archipelago between 1500 and about 1630*. The Hague: M. Nijhoff, 1962.

Pigeaud, Th. G. Th. *Java in the Fourteenth Century; A Study in Cultural History*. 5 Vols. The Hague: M. Nijhoff, 1962.

Rabibhadana, Akin. *The Organization of Thai Society in the Early Bangkok Period*. Ithaca: Cornell University Southeast Asia Program, 1969.

Rafael, Vicente. *Contracting Colonialism. Translation and Christian Conversion in Tagalog Society under Early Spanish Rule*. Ithaca: Cornell University Press, 1988.

Reid, Anthony J. S. *Southeast Asia in the Age of Commerce, 1450-1680. Vol. I: The Lands Below the Winds*. New Haven: Yale University Press, 1988.

Reid, Anthony J. S. "The Structure of Cities in Southeast Asia: Fifteenth to Seveteenth Centuries," *Journal of Southeast Asian Studies* 11, 2 (1980) pp. 235-250.

Scott, William H. *Prehispanic Source Materials for the Study of Philippine History*. Manila: University of Santo Thomas Press, 1968

Slametmuljana. *A Story of Majapahit*. Singapore: Singapore University Press, 1976.

Taylor, Jean Gelman. *The Social World of Batavia. European and Eurasian in Dutch Asia*. Madison: University of Wisconsin Press, 1983.

ASSIGNMENT 3. Topic 3 Paper.
First: Bibliography.
DUE: May 4.
Second: Paper on Topic 3.
DUE: May 8, 4 PM.

M, May 4   DISCUSSION of bibliographies and of Topic 3.

W, May 6   Individual tutorials.

F, May 8   Pick up copies of Topic 3 papers and read.

M, May 11   COLLOQUIUM on Topic 3.

The Modern Colonial Era (c. 1850-1940)

Some Bibliographic Suggestions:

Adas, Michael. *The Burma Delta: Economic Development and Social Change on an Asian Rice Frontier, 1852-1941.* Madison: University of Wisconsin Press, 1974.

Ahmat, Sharom. *Tradition and Change in a Malay State: A Study of the Economic and Political Development of Kedah, 1878-1923.* Luala Lumpur: Malaysian Branch of the Royal Asiatic Society, 1984.

Alatas, Hussein Syed. *The Myth of the Lazy Native: A Study of the Image of the Malays, Filipinos and Javanese from the 16th to the 20th centuries.* London: F. Cass, 1977.

Batson, Benjamin A. *The End of the Absolute Monarcy in Siam.* Singapore: Oxford University Press, 1984.

Bunnag, Tej. *The Provincial Administration of Siam 1892-1915.* Kuala Lumpur: Oxford University Press, 1977.

Cheah Boon Kheng. *The Peasant Robbers of Kedah, 1900-1929: Historical and Folk Perceptions.* Singapore: Oxford University Press, 1988.

Elson, Robert E. *Javanese Peasants and the Colonial Sugar Industry: Impact and Change in an East Java Residency, 1830-1940.* Singapore: Oxford University Press, 1984.

Geertz, Clifford. *Negara. The Theater State in Nineteenth-Century Bali.* Princeton: Princeton University Press, 1980.

Gullick, J. M. *Malay Society in the Late Nineteenth Century: The Beginnings of Change.* Singapore: Oxford University Press, 1987.

Hong Lysa. *Thailand in the Nineteenth Century: Evolution of the Economy and Society.* Singapore: Institute of Southeast Asian Studies, 1984.

Ileto, Reynaldo C. *Pasyon and Revolution: Popular Movements in the Philippines.* Quezon City: Ateneo de Manila Press, 1979.

Ingleson, John. *In Search of Justice: Workers and Union in Colonial Java, 1908-1926.* Singapore: Oxford University Press, 1986.

Kartodirdjo, Sartono. *Protest Movements in Rural Java: A Study of Agrarian Unrest in the 19th and Early 20th Centuries.* Singapore: Oxford University Press, 1973.

Keeton, C. L. *King Thibaw and the Ecological Rape of Burma.* Delhi: Manohar, 1974.

Khin Yi. *The Dobama Movement in Burma (1930-1938).* Ithaca: Cornell University Southeast Asia Program, 1988.

Larkin, John A. *The Pampangans. Colonial Society in a Philippine Province.* Berkeley: University of California Press, 1972.

Lim Teck Ghee. *Peasants and Their Agricultural Economy in Colonial Malaya, 1874-1941.* Kuala Lumpur: Oxford University Press, 1976.

May, Glenn A. *Battle for Batangas; A Philippine Province at War.* New Haven: Yale University Press, 1991.

Ngo Vinh Long. *Before the Revolution: The Vietnamese Peasants Under the French.* Cambridge: MIT Press, 1973.

Ni Ni Myint. *Burma's Struggle Against British Imperialism, 1885-1895.* Rangoon: Universities Press, 1983. 2nd edition, 1985.

Owen, Norman G. *Prosperity Without Progress: Manila Hemp and Material Life in the Colonial Philippines.* Berkeley: University of California Press, 1984.

Pham Cao Duong. *Vietnamese Peasants Under French Domination, 1861-1941.* Berkeley: University of California Center for South and Southeast Asian Studies, 1985.

Pringle, Robert. *Rajahs and Rebels: The Ibans of Sarawak under Brooke Rule, 1841-1941.* Ithaca: Cornell University Press, 1970.

Roff, William R. *The Origins of Malay Nationalism.* New Haven: Yale University Press, 1964. 2nd edition, Kuala Lumpur: Penerbit Univeristi Malaya, 19??

Shiraishi, Takashi. *An Age in Motion. Popular Radicalism in Java, 1912-1926.* Ithaca: Cornell University Press, 1990.

Tai, Hue-Tam Ho. *Millenarianism and Peasant Politics in Vietnam.* Cambridge: Harvard University Press, 1983.

Talib, Shaharil. *After Its Own Image: The Trengganu Experience, 1881-1941.* Singapore: Oxford University Press, 1984.

ASSIGNMENT 4. Topic 4 Paper.
First: Bibliography.
DUE: May 18.
Second: Paper on Topic 4.
DUE: May 22, 4 PM.

M, May 18   DISCUSSION of bibliographies and of Topic 4.

W, May 20   Individual tutorials.

F, May 22   Pick up copies of Topic 4 papers and read.

T, May 26   COLLOQUIUM on Topic 4. (NOTE: This class will be held in Bentley 83.)

W, May 27   INTRODUCTION to Topic 5:

War and Revolution (c. 1940 - c. 1960)

Some Bibliographic Suggestions:

Anderson, Benedict R. O'G. *Java in a Time of Revolution: Occupation and Resistance, 1944-1946.* Ithaca: Cornell University Press, 1972.

Cheah Boon Kheng, *Red Star over Malaya: Resistance and Social Conflict During and After the Japanese Occupation of Malaya.* Singapore: Singapore University Press, 1983.

Colbert, Evelyn. *Southeast Asia in International Politics, 1941-1956.* Ithaca: Cornell University Press, 1977.

Cribb, Robert. *Gangsters and Revolutionaries.* Honolulu: University of Hawaii Press. 1991.

Frederick, William H. *Visions and Heat. The Making of the Indonesian Revolution.* Athens: Ohio University Press, 1989.

Friend, Theodore. *The Blue-Eyed Enemy. Japan Against the West in Java and Luzon, 1942-1945.* Princeton: Princeton University Press, 1988.

Kerkvliet, Benedict J. *The Huk Rebellion: A Study of Peasant Revolt in the Philippines.* Berkeley: University of California Press, 1977.

Lockhart, Greg. *Nation in Arms. The Origins of the People's Army of Vietnam.* Sydney: Allen & Unwun, 1989.

Lucas, Anton. *One Soul, One Struggle. Region and Revolution in Indonesia.* Sydnay: Allen & Unwin, 1991.

Maung Maung, U. *Burmese Nationalist Movements, 1940-1949.* Honolulu: University of Hawaii Press, 1991.

McCoy, Alfred W. (ed.). *Southeast Asia Under Japanese Occupation.* New Haven: Yale University Southeast Asia Studies, 1979.

Said, Salim. *Genesis of Power. General Sudirman and the Indonesian Military in Politics, 1945-1949.* Singapore: ISEAS, 1991.

Short, Anthony. *The Communist Insurrection in Malaya, 1948-1960.* London: Muller, 1975.

Silverstein, Joseph (ed.). *Southeast Asia in World War II: Four Essays.* New Haven: Yale University Southeast Asia Studies, 1966.

Smail, John R. W. *Bandung in the Early Revolution, 1945-1946: A Study in the Social History of the Indonesian Revolution.* Ithaca: Cornell University Modern Indonesia Project, 1964.

Steinberg, David J. *Philippine Collaboration in World War II.* Ann Arbor: University of Michigan Press, 1967.

Taylor, Robert H. *The State in Burma.* Honolulu: University of Hawaii Press, 1987.

Woodside, Alexander B. *Community and Revolution in Vietnam.* Boston: Houghton Mifflin, 1976.

ASSIGNMENT 5. Topic 5 Paper.
First: Bibliography.
DUE: June 1.
Second: Paper on Topic 5.
DUE: June 5, 4 PM.

M, June 1   DISCUSSION of bibliographies and of Topic 5.

W, June 3   Individual tutorials.

F, June 5   Pick up copies of Topic 5 papers and read.

M, June 8   COLLOQUIUM on Topic 5.

ABOUT THE PREPARATION OF WRITTEN ASSIGNMENTS:

All written assignments are to be presented in neatly typed form, with an internally consistent format and attention to details such as spelling, grammar, typographical accuracy, and proper methods of citation of sources. On matters of style, follow the standards established in *The Chicago Manual of Style* 13th edition (Chicago: University of Chicago Press, 1982). Copies of this work are available in the library, but you should own one if you are serious about academic writing. Remember that neatness and accuracy do affect how readers evaluate your work, like it or not.

EXAMINATION:

There is no written examination.

GRADING:

The grade is based primarily upon the written work presented to the class. The bibliographic assignments will be worth 5 points, and the written assignments 15 points, for a total of 20 points for each of 5 topic assignments. Class participation may account for an indeterminate portion of the grade, but no more than 15%.

Bibliographies will be evaluated on the basis of selection, range, and appropriateness of annotations. Papers will be evaluated — in roughly equal measure — on thoroughness, depth of analysis, originality, and quality of writing.

POLICY ON ACADEMIC DISHONESTY:

The Ohio University code of student conduct defines and prohibits all forms of academic dishonesty, and empowers the instructor to lower the grade of any student engaged in course-related dishonesty. (Students are responsible for understanding how the university defines "plagiarism," "cheating," and other forms of academic dishonesty.) In this course, any student found writing examinations or preparing papers in a dishonest fashion will receive an "F" for the course, will not be given the option of withdrawing, and may be reported to the Judiciaries office.

OFFICE HOURS:

Bentley 84 (593-4341), MTWTh 10-11 PM and by appointment.

Rhoads Murphey, University of Michigan
ASIAN STUDIES 111/ HISTORY 151   The Civilization of South Asia.   Fall, 1991

This is an introduction, within an historical framework, to the origins, evolution, character, and contemporary problems of civilization in India. South Asia, a label now since 1947, includeswhat is now Pakistan, India, Bangladesh, Nepal, and Sri Lanka, but all remain part of the greater Indian tradition. We are dealing with about a fifth of the world's population, and its oldest living civilization. The treatment here can thus be only an introduction, but with an effort to look at the Indian experience from several points of approach.

Reading is about equally divided between a text, Stanley Wolpert's A NEW HISTORY OF INDIA, 3rd. edition, which you should find easy and pleasant reading; two short novels (like Wolpert, in paperback), which help to put you into the modern Indian scene: Kushwant Singh, Train to Pakistan and R.K. Narayan, Waiting for the Mahatma; and acourse pack available at Dollar Bill Copy on Church Street which samples a wide variety of sources and rounds out the treatment. Wolpert's bibliography at the end of his book gives a further guide, and I would be glad to supplement that on particular topics. The India field has been much studied in English, given the long and close Western involvement, and the literatur about it is immense. The best single guide is Maureen Paterson, South Asian Civilizations: A Bibliographic Synthesis (Chicago, 1982).

Total reading is kept modest so that you can reflect on and absorb what you read. Assignments (below) are arranged mainly to precede the class sessions in which the topics will be discussed; please read them accordingly. Several breaks or easy periods are built in, but no week is burdensome. There will be a midterm and a final exam, but no other exams or papers, although there may be occasional quizzes in the weekly sections, to reward you for paying attention to both the assigned readings and the leatures.

The following schedule is intended to be firm but not rigid. Circumstances and student preferences may suggest some flexibility as the term goes on.

Fri. Sept. 6   Introduction, and Images of India

Mon Sept. 9   India in Cultural and Geographic Context

    Readings: Jawarlahal Nehru, "The Quest"; W.N. Brown, "The Content of Cultural Continuity"; from A.L. Basham, The Wonder That Was India -- all in Course Pack -- and Wolpert, A New History of India, pp. 3-23.

Wed. Sept. 11 Beginnings: The Indus Civilization (c. 3000-c.1800 B.C.)

    Readings: From F. Watson, A Concise History of India, pp. 26-29 --Course Pack

Fri. Sept. 13   Continued

    Readings: Wolpert, pp. 24-26

Mon. Sept. 16   The Coming of the Aryans (c. 1800-1000 B.C.)

    Readings: From R. Tirtha, Society and Development in India, pp. 140-51 --Course Pack

Wed. Sept. 18   Caste: Origins and Evolution

    Readings: Wolpert, pp. 37-54

Fri. Sept. 20   Vedic India and the Growth of a Hybrid Culture, 1500-500 B.C.

   Readings: Wolpert as above; selections from Bhagavad Gita --Course Pack

Mon. Sept. 23   Hinduism, Jainism, and Buddhism

   Readings: Wolpert, pp. 55-70

Wed. Sept. 25   The Mauryan Empire, 326-184 B.C.; Connections East and West

   Readings: Wolpert pp. 70-103

Fri. Sept. 27   Kushan and Guptan India, 100B.C.-550 A.D.

   Readings: Wolpert pp. 104-125

Mon. Sept. 30   The Coming of Islam, 900-1526 A.D.

   Readings: finish the above

Wed. Oct. 2   Discussion and Review

   Readings: Wolpert pp. 126-34 and 149-67

Fri. Oct. 4   Mughal India, 1526-1707

   Readings: Wolpert pp. 168-66

Mon. Oct. 7   Mughal India, continued

   Readings: as above

Wed. Oct. 9   The Mughal Legacy

   Readings: Wolpert pp. 135--86

Fri. Oct. 11   The Coming of the Europeans, 1498-1750

   Readings: Wolpert, pp. 187-200

Mon. Oct. 14   The Rise of the British Raj, 1600-1756

   Readings: Wolpert, pp. 201-38

Wed. Oct. 16   The Building of the Colonial Empire, 1757-1856

   Readings: Wolpert pp. 239- 49 and 265-300

Fri. Oct. 18   Film: The Delhi Way   HAND OUT MIDTERM EXAM

   Readings: take a breather, and review

Mon. Oct. 21   The Colonial System, 1657-1919

   Readings: Wolpert, pp. 250-64 and 301-28

Wed. Oct. 23   The Indian Nationalist Movement, 1886-1947

    Readings: R.K. Narayan, Waiting for the Mahatma, entire

Fri. Oct. 25   The Colonial Period Evaluated

    Readings: D. Kopf, "British Orientalism", "Education", "The Hindu Revival", and
    R. Kipling, selected verse and "The Bridge Builders" --all in Course Pack

Mon. Oct. 28   Evaluation of Colonialism, continued

    Readings: M.D. Morris, "Toward a Reinterpretation.." and "Values as Obstacles"-- C.P.

Wed. Oct. 30   Gandhi, Nehru, and Independence

    Readings: Rudolph on Gandhi (Course Pack)   and Wolpert, pp. 329-49

Fri. Nov. 1   Partition: Its Roots and Consequences

    Readings: Kushwant Singh, Train to Pakistan, entire, and Narayan,"All Avoidable Talk"
                                                   (Course Pack)

Mon. Nov. 4   The Kashmir Issue, and War with China

    Readings: Wolpert, pp. 351-370

Wed. Nov. 6   Regionalism in South Asia

    Readings: Tirtha, pp. 111-27   (Course Pack)

Fri. Nov. 8   The Language Issue

    Readings: as above, plus tables and maps in Course Pack

Mon. Nov. 11   Pakistan, 1947-1991

    Readings: Wolpert pp. 371-407

Wed. Nov. 13   Bangladesh, 1971-1991

    Readings: finish the above, and review

Fri. Nov. 15   Film: North Indian Village

    Readings: as above

Mon. Nov. 18   Ceylon (Sri Lanka), 1948-1991

    Readings: as above

Wed. Nov. 20   Slides of South Asia

    Readings: as above

Fri. Nov. 22   Economic Development in South Asia, 1600-1991

    Readings: Tirtha, pp. 88-109 (on population) --Course Pack

Mon. Nov. 25   Agriculture and the Village

    Readings: Tirtha, pp. 112-27 and 194-241 (Course Pack)

Wed. Nov. 27   Industrialization and Resource Base

    Readings: Tirtha, pp. 266-314 (Course Pack)

Fri. Nov. 29   Thanksgiving holiday--don't eat too much!

Mon. Dec. 2   Urbanization and its Problems

    Readings: Wolpert pp. 407-16

Wed. Dec. 4   The Nation-state in South Asia

    Readings: Wolpert, pp. 417-35

Fri. Dec. 6   The Future, and some Conclusions

    Readings: review

Mon. Dec. 9.   Same continued

Wed. Dec. 11   Discussion and review. Hand out of final exam

Columbia University
History G9496y
Spring 1991

David Lelyveld

Seminar: Modern South Asia

The seminar will concentrate on the subaltern studies project and three other recent efforts to reformulate the central concerns of nineteenth and twentieth century South Asian history: feminist history, the analysis of colonial discourse, and the perspective of world capitalism. We will want to know how these orientations confront each other and earlier approaches to historical research and exposition. Most of the readings deal with what is today India, but students are encouraged to shift the focus of discussion to other parts of South Asia, notably Pakistan, Bangladesh, Sri Lanka, and Nepal.

Members of the seminar will do a minimal common core of readings, which are marked below with an asterisk (*). Each student will be asked to introduce one of the class sessions on the basis of the other readings listed for the week, and to lead a discussion that will attempt to connect the historiographic orientation under consideration to a specified empirical problem. (If the number of members in the seminar warrants a collective arrangement of a small groups, rather than individual presentations, this will be worked out in the first meeting). In addition, there wil be a research paper or historiogrphic essay of about 3500 to 5000 words (normally 15-20 pages) related to the class presented in class or on another topic to be discussed with me early in the term. The final version of the paper will be due May 1st.

Required course readings will generally be available for purchase at Barnard Book Forum or on reserve in the College Library in Butler [CR]. In some cases they will be made available through the South Asia Institute office, 1128 International Affairs Building, or distributed in class. It will be necessary to share.

My office is 405 Lewisohn, and the best time to see me without an appointment is 4:00 to 5:00 everyday but Wednesday, the day of the seminar itself. The phone number is 854-2881.

Basic Bibliographic and Reference Aids:

Maureen L. P. Patterson, ed. <u>South Asian Civilizations: A Bibliographic Synthesis</u> (University of Chicago Press, 1981)

<u>Bibliography of Asian Studies</u> (1978-1985)

Carol Sakala, <u>Women of South Asia: A Guide to Resources</u> (Millwood. NY: Krauss International, 1980)

Joseph E. Schwartzberg, ed. <u>A Historical Atlas of South Asia</u> (University of Chicago Press, 1978)

Sumit Sarkar, Modern India, 1885-1947 (Delhi: Macmillan, 1983)
Course Outline

January 16 - Introduction: Historiographic Agendas

January 23 - Historiography and Nationalism

          *Ainslie T. Embree, India's Search for National
          Identity (New York: Knopf, 1972), ch. 1. [Students who
          have not read all of this book are advised to do so].

          *Partha Chatterjee, Nationalist Thought and the
          Colonial World: A Derivative Discourse (London: Zed,
          1986), chs. 1, 2, 6 [CR].

          R.C. Majumdar, "Nationalist Historians," in C. H.
          Philips, ed. Historians of India, Pakistan and Ceylon
          (London: Oxford University Press, 1961), pp. 416-28.

          Anil Seal, "Imperialism and Nationalism in India," in
          John Gallagher, Gordon Johnson and Anil Seal, eds.
          Imperialism and Nationalism in India (Cambridge:
          Cambridge University Press, 1973), pp. 1-27.

          Gyan Prakash, "Writing Post-orientalist Histories of
          the Third World: Perspectives from Indian
          Historiography," Comparative Studies of Society and
          History 32 (1990), pp. 383-408 [Butler periodicals].

          Homi Bhabha, "DissemiNation: time, narrative, and the
          margins of the modern nation," in his, ed. Nation and
          Narration (London: Routledge, 1990).

January 30 - The Subaltern Studies Project

          *Antonio Gramsci, "Notes on Italian History" in
          Selections from the Prison Notebooks, ed. and trans. Q.
          Hoare and G.N. Smith (New York: International
          Publishers, 1971), pp. 52-55 (and continuation of note
          to p. 57).

          *Veena Das, "Subaltern as Perspective," Subaltern
          Studies VI, 310-324 [CR].

          *Ranajit Guha, "Some Aspects of the Historiography of
          Colonial India," SS I, 1-8 [Also in Selected Subaltern
          Studies (New York: Oxford, 1988) [CR].

          ------------, "The Prose of Counter-insurgency,"
          SS II,   [Also in Selections] [CR]

----------, "Dominance without Hegemony and its Historiography," SS VI, 210-309 [CR].

February 6 - 1857 and Resistance: Models of and Models for

Ranajit Guha, Elementary Aspects of Peasant Insurgency (Delhi: Oxford, 1983), *1-76, [+77-277, 333-39] [CR].

Eric Stokes, The Peasant and the Raj (Cambridge University Press, 1978), 120-39 [CR]. (Also available in Past and Present, no. 48 [August 1970] in Butler Stacks).

Eric Stokes, The Peasant Armed, ed. by C.A. Bayly, pp. 1-16, 119-42, 214-243 [CR].

Gautam Bhadra, "Four Rebels of Eighteen Fifty-Seven," in SS IV, 229-75. [Reprinted in Selections] [CR].

February 13 - Varieties of Resistance and Historiographic Context

*Walter Hauser, Review of Guha, Elementary Aspects in Journal of Asian Studies 45 (1985-86), 174-77 [Lehman]

*Sumit Sarkar, "The Conditions and Nature of Subaltern Militancy: Bengal from Swadeshi to Non-Cooperation, c. 1905-22," SS III, 271-320 [CR].

Sumit Sarkar, 'Popular' movements and 'middle class' leadership in late Colonial Inida (Calcutta: K.P. Baghchi, 1983)[CR].

Rosalind O'Hanlon, "Recovering the Subject: Subaltern Studies and Histories of Resistance in Colonial South Asia," Modern Asian Studies 22 (1988), 189-224 [Lehman]

Gyanendra Pandey, "Peasant Revolt and Indian Nationalism: The Peasant Movement in Awadh, 1919-1922," SS I, 143-97. [Reprinted in Selections] [CR].

David Arnold, "Rebellious Hillmen: The Gudem-Rampa Risings, 1839-1924," SS I, 88-142 [CR].

Ramachandra Guha, "Forestry and Social Protest in British Kumaon, c. 1893-1921," in SS IV 54-100 [CR].

February 20 - Beyond insurrection: subaltern consciousness

*Dipesh Chakrabarty, "Trade Unions in Hierarchical Culture: The Jute Workers of Calcutta, 1920-50, SS III, 116-52 [CR].

[Dipesh Chakrabarty, Rethinking Working Class History: Bengal 1890-1940 (Princeton University Press, 1989)] [CR].
*Partha Chatterjee, "Caste and Subaltern Consciousness," SS VI, 169-209.

Jan Breman, Of Peasants, Migrants and Paupers: Rural Labour Circulation and Capitalist Production in West India (Delhi: Oxford University Press, 1985), pp. 49-76, 115-58, 361-79, 402-432.

February 27 - Subaltern religious consciousness and communalism

*Gyanendra Pandey, "Rallying Round the Cow: Sectarian Strife in the Bhojpuri Region, c. 1888-1917," SS II, 60-129 [CR].

Sumit Sarkar, "The Kalki-Avatar of Bikrampur: A Village Scandal in Early Twentieth Century Bengal," SS VI, 1-53 [CR].

Partha Chatterjee, "Agrarian Relations and Communalism in Bengal," SS I, 9-38 [CR].

Gyanendra Pandey, "'Encounters and Calamities': The History of a North Indian Qasba in the Nineteenth Century," SS III, 231-270. [Reprinted in Selections] [CR].

Nita Kumar, The Artisans of Banaras: Popular Culture and Identity, 1880-1986 (Princeton University Press, 1988), pp. 40-82, 201-236, [237-43] [CR].

Sandria B. Freitag, Collective Action and Community: Public Arenas and the Emergence of Communalism in North India (Berkeley: University of California Press, 1989), pp. 99-174, 197-248 [CR].

March 6 - Sources and Forms of Historical Exposition

*Shahid Amin, "Gandhi as Mahatma: Gorakhpur District, Eastern UP, 1921-2," in SS III, 1-61. [Also in Selections] [CR].

Bernard S. Cohn, "The Pasts of an Indian Village," in his An Anthropologist among the Historians (Delhi: Oxford University Press, 1987), pp. 88-99 [CR].

Nicholas Dirks, The Hollow Crown: Ethnohistory of an Indian Kingdom (Cambridge University Press, 1987), ch. 1.

Gyan Prakash, Bonded Histories: Genealogies of Labor Servitude in Colonial India (Cambridge University Press, pp. [1-12], 34-81, 192-217 [CR].

Paul Greenough, Prosperity and Misery in Modern Bengal: The Famine of 1943-1944 (New York: Oxford University Press, 1982), pp. 147-182 [CR].

Akaler Sandhaney (In Search of Famine), Film by Mrinlal Sen (Calcutta: Seagull Books, 1983).

March 13 - Subaltern Studies and Feminist Perspectives

*Sumanta Banerjee, "Marginalization of Women's Popular Culture in Nineteenth Century Bengal," in Kumkum Sangari and Sudesh Vaid, eds. Recasting Women: Essays in Colonial History (Rutgers University Press, 1990), pp. 127-79 (hitherto RW) [CR].

Kumkum Sangari and Sudesh Vaid, "Recasting Women: An Introduction," RW, pp. 1-26 [CR].

Gayatri Chakravorty Spivak, "A Literary Representation of the Subaltern: Maheshweta Devi's 'Stanadayini,'" SS V, 91-134, [252-76] [CR].

Ranajit Guha, "Chandra's Death," SS V, 166-202 [CR].

Nirmala Banerjee, "Working Women in Colonial Bengal: Modernization and Marginalization," RW 269-301 [CR].

Prem Chowdhry, "Customs in a Peasant Economy: Women in Colonial Harayana," RW, 302-36 [CR].

Vasantha Kannabiran and K. Lalitha, "That Magic Time: Women in the Telangana People's Struggle," RW, pp. 180-203 [CR].

[Stree Shakti Sangatha [Lalita K. et al, eds.], 'We Were Making History...': Life Stories of Womken in the Telangana People's Struggle (Delhi: Kali, 1989)]

March 27 - History of women and encompassing discourses

*Susie Tharu and K. Lalita, Women Writing in India (New York: Feminist Press, 1991), vol. I, pp. 1-37, 41-64, 145-186

Lata Mani, "Contentious Traditions: The Debate on Sati in Colonial India," RW, pp. 88-126 [CR]

Partha Chatterjee, "The Nationalist Resolution of the Women's Question," RW, pp. 233-253 [CR]

Uma Chakravarti, "Whatever Happened to the Vedic Dasi? Orientalism, Nationalism and a Script for the Past," RW, pp. 27-87 [CR]

April 3 - Colonial Knowledge and South Asian Histories

*Bernard S. Cohn, "The Command of Language and the Language of Command," SS IV, 276-329 [CR]

Bernard S. Cohn, An Anthropologist among the Historians, pp. 136-171, 224-54, 632-82 [CR]

Shahid Amin, "Approver's Testimony, Judicial Discourse: The Case of Chauri Chaura," SS V, 166-202, 277-89 [CR]

Shahid Amin, "Editor's Introduction," William Crooke, A Glossary of North Indian Peasant Life (reprint ed., Delhi: Oxford University Press, 1989), pp. xviii-xlii.

David Washbrook, "Law, State and Agrarian Society in Colonial India, Modern Asian Studies 15 (1981), 649-722 [Lehman].

David Lelyveld, Aligarh's First Generation: Muslim Solidarity in British India (Princeton University Press, 1978), pp. 3-20, 204-261 [CR]

Gauri Viswanathan, Masks of conquest: Literacy and British Rule in India (New York: Columbia University Press, 1989), pp. 1-21, 118-41

Ronald Inden, Imagining India (Oxford: Blackwell, 1990), pp. 7-21, 36-48, 49-84, 162-212

Benita Parry, "Problems in current theories of colonial discourse," Oxford Literary Review 9 (1-2) (1987), pp. 27-58 [Butler Stacks]

Gayatri Chakravorty Spivak, "Can the Subaltern Speak?" in Cary Nelson and Lawrence Grossberg, Marxism and the Interpretation of Culture (Urbana: University of Illinois Press, 1988), pp. 271-313

April 10-17 - Beyond Consciousness: World Systems and Modes of Production

*David Washbrook, "South Asia, the World System, and World Capitalism," _Journal of Asian Studies_ 49 (1990), pp. 479-508 [Lehman current periodicals].

*Frank Perlin, "Disarticulation of the World: Writing India's Economic History," _Comparative Studies of Society and History_ 30 (1988), pp. 379-387 [Lehman and Butler].

Irfan Habib, "Studying a Colonial Economy - without Perceiving Colonialism"; and Dharma Kumar, "The Dangers of Manichaeism" in _Modern Asian Studies_ 19 (1985), 355-86 [Lehman].

David Washbrook, "Progress and Problems: South Asian Social and Economic History," _Modern Asian Studies_ 15 (1981), pp. 57-96 [Lehman].

K.N. Chaudhuri, "Foreign Trade and Balance of Payments (1757-1947)," in Dharma Kumar and Meghnad Desai, eds. _The Cambridge Economic History of India_, Vol. II (Cambridge University Press, 1982), pp. 804-877

Hamza Alvi, "India: Transition from Feudalism to Capitalism," _Journal of Contemporary Asia_ 10 (1980), pp. 359-399 [Lehman]

Alice Thorner, "Semi-feudalism or capitalism: the contemporary debate on classes and modes of production in India" in Jacques Pouchepadass, ed. _Caste et Classe en Asie du Sud_ (Paris: Editions de l'Ecole des Hautes Etudes en Science Sociales, 1982), pp. 19-72 [Lehman]

April 17, 24 and May 1 - Presentations and Reformulations

University of Washington
HSTAS 503/SISSA 590
Seminar: History of India

David Lelyveld
Fall 1991

Islam, Language, and Nationalism
in Modern South Asia

This course will deal with reading, writing and other forms of
memory and communication and their social and technological
development in the lives of South Asian Muslims. We will explore
the relation of these developments to changing patterns of
political community, including the role of the British analysis
of language, the introduction of printing, the political context
of linguistic standardization, linguistic nationalism, and mass
communications.

The course will demand individual reading assignments and class
participation. Readings that are marked with an asterisk will be
read by all of us before the class meets. The other readings on
this list will be assigned to one or more students who will take
responsibility for presenting and commenting on them in class.
Most of these readings will be available in photocopies or will
be on reserve. Suggested additional readings are indicated in
brackets. The following books will be available for purchase:

> Benedict Anderson, Imagined Communities, revised ed.
> (London: Verso, 1991)
>
> Bernard Lewis, The Political Language of Islam (Chicago:
> University of Chicago Press, 1991)
>
> Amrit Rai, A House Divided: The Origin and Development of
> Hindi/Hindavi (Delhi: Oxford University Press, 1984)
>
> Michael C. Shapiro and Harold F. Schiffman, Language and
> Society in South Asia (Delhi: Motilal Banarsidas, 1981)

In addition to class participation, there will be three essay
assignments of about 1200 words each and a map exercise, all of
which will be described in separate hand-outs. Students who wish
to substitute a research paper for the essay assignments should
discuss their proposals with the instructor by the end of
October. All work must be handed in by the assigned dates.
Students are invited to meet regularly with me out of class
hours, especially before they are due to make class
presentations. My office will be 324 Thomson; the phone number is
543-4999. Regular office hours will be announced, and I will be
generally available at other times as well.

Course Outline

I. Orientations (October 2)

[Jack Goody, _The Logic of Writing and the Organization of Society_ (Cambridge: Cambridge University Press, 1986]
[Raymond Williams, _Marxism and Literature_ (Oxford: Oxford University Press, 1977), pp. 21-44.

[Michel Foucault, _The Order of Things_ (New York: Vintage, 1973), pp. 17-45, 78-124, 280-307]

[M. M. Bakhtin, _Speech Genres and Other Late Essays_ (Austin: University of Texas, 1986), pp. 60-102]

[Karl W. Deutsch, _Nationalism and Social Communication_, 2nd ed. (Cambridge, MA: M.I.T. Press, 1966) pp. 41-46, 86-106, 223-230]

II. Religion, Language and Nationalism (October 9)

*Benedict Anderson, _Imagined Communities_, chs. 1-3, 5-11.

Paul R. Brass, _Language, Religion Politics in North India_ (Cambridge: Cambridge University Press, 1974), pp. 3-14, 403-434.

John J. Gumperz, _Language in Social Groups_ (Stanford: Stanford University Press, 1971), pp. 97-150.

III. The Linguistic Situation in Modern South Asia: An Overview (October 16)

*Michael C. Shapiro and Harold F. Schiffman, _Language and Society in South Asia_ (Delhi: Motilal Banarsidas, 1981), pp. 1-15, 70-87, 116-49, 150-93, 207-209, 215-22, 238-60.

*Joseph Schwartzberg, _A Historical Atlas of South Asia_, pp. 65-66, 217, 100-102, 234-35. (Start the map assignment, due November 6)

*Amrit Rai, _A House Divided_, pp. 1-35.

Murray B. Emmeneau, "India as a Linguistic Area," in Dell Hymes, ed. _Language in Culture and Society_ (New York: Harper & Row, 1964), pp. 642-653

IV. Speech. Memory, Reading and Writing in Pre-Colonial South Asia (October 23)

*Amrit Rai, _A House Divided_, pp. 37-116.

Madhav M. Despande, _Sociolinguistic Attitudes in India:_

An Historical Reconstruction (Ann Arbor: Karoma, 1979),
pp. 1-21, 57-103.

Daniel H.H. Ingalls, "The Brahman Tradition," in Milton
Singer, ed. Traditional India: Structure and Change, pp.
3-9.

R. G. Bhandarkar, "Relations between Sanskrit, Pali, the
Prakrits and the Modern Vernaculars," [1883] in J. F.
Staal, ed. A Reader on the Sanskrit Grammarians, pp.94-
101.

[Luigi Nitti-Dolci, The Prakrita Grammarians, tr. P. Jha
(Delhi: Motilal Banarsidas, 1972)]

Jeremiah P. Losty, The Art of the Book in India (London: The
British Library, 1982), pp. 5-17

[Erich Auerbach, Literary Language and its Public in Late
Latin Antiquity and in the Middle Ages (Princeton, 1965),
pp. 237-338]

V. Islam, Language and South Asia (October 30)

*Bernard Lewis, The Political Language of Islam (Chicago:
University of Chicago Press, 1991), pp. 1-116.

*Amrit Rai, A House Divided, pp. 116-225.

Abu'l Fazl, A'in Akbari [c. 1600] (Blochmann trans.) I,
ch. 34, pp. 102-113; II, chs, 10-13, pp. 268-74; ch. 25,
pp. 288-89; ch. 30 pp. 606-682.

Rajendralala Mitra, "On the origin of the Hindvi language
and its relation to the Urdu dialect," Journal of the
Asiatic Society 33 (1865), pp. 489-518.

Annemarie Schimmel, Calligraphy and Islamic Culture, pp.
77-114.

Abdul Halim Sharar, Lucknow: The Last Phase of an Oriental
Culture, tr. E.S. Harcourt and Fakhir Hussain (London: Paul
Elek, 1975), pp. 76-108, 198-201.

William Adam, One Teacher, One School [Reports on the
State of Education in Bengal, (1835, 1838)], ed. J. Di
Bona (New Delhi: Biblia, 1983), pp. 6-16, 187-260.

David Shulman, "Muslim Popular Literature in Tamil: The
Tamimancari malai," in Yohanan Friedmann, ed. Islam in Asia,
vol. I (Jerusalem, 1984), pp. 174-207.

[Jacques Berque, _Cultural Expression in Arab Society_ Today (Austin: University of Texas, 1978), pp. 32-47]
FIRST ESSAY - due October 30

__VI__ The Colonial Analysis of South Asian Languages
(November 6)

*Joseph Schwartzberg, _A Historical Atlas of South Asia_ (see map assignment).

*John Gumperz, _Language in Social Groups_, pp. 1-11

*Amrit Rai, _A House Divided_

John Gilchrist, _The Stranger's Infallible East-India Guide_ (3rd. ed., 1820), pp. i-xxx.

Christopher Rolland King, "The Nagari Pracharini Sabha (Society for the Promotion of the Nagari Script and Language) of Benares, 1893-1914: A Study in the Social and Political History of the Hindi Language," (Ann Arbor: University Microfilms, 1974), pp. 41-76.

G. A. Grierson, _The Linguistic Survey of India_ [1903], vol. I, pp. 1-31.

H. H. Risley, _The People of India_ [Second ed., 1915], pp. 6-13, 28-29, 286-290.

R.A. Singh, "Inquiries into the Spoken Languages of India, from early times to the Census of 1901," _Census of India, 1961_, vol. I, pt.XI-C(i), pp. 117-20, 141-49, 178-89, 234-38, 310-41.

Bernard S. Cohn, "The Command of Language and the Language of Command," in Ranajit Guha, ed. _Subaltern Studies IV_, pp. 276-329.

David Washbrook, "'To each a language of his own': language culture, and society in colonial India," in Penelope J. Corfield, ed. _Language, History and Class_ (Oxford: Basil Blackwell, 1991)

MAP EXERCISE - Due November 6

__VII__ Education, Standardization, Printing and the Role of English
(November 13)

*T.W. Clark, ed. _The Novel in India_ (Berkeley, 1970), 9-20, 102-178.

C. R. King, "The Nagari Pracharini Sabha," pp. 77-105, 201-225.

Report of the Indian Education Commission [1883], pp. 55-62, 83-85, 124-129, 148-151, 198-199, 210-11, 229-30, 272-273, 338-340, 521-522.

Selections from the Records of the Government of the North-Western Provinces, 1868-1874, vol. III (1867), pp. 385-394, 460-483; vol. IV (1868), pp. 111-166.

Frances W. Pritchett, Marvelous Encounters: Folk Romance in Urdu and Hindi (New Delhi: Manohar, 1985), pp. 20-36.

C.M. Naim, "How Bibi Ashraf Learned to Read and Write," Annual of Urdu Studies 6 (1987), pp. 99-115.

Kathryn Hansen, "Sultana the dacoit and Harischandra: Two popular drams of the Nautanki tradition of North India," Modern Asian Studies 17 (1983), pp. 313-31.

Krishna Kumar, "Quest for Self-Identity: Cultural Consciousness and Education in Hindi Region, 1880-1950," Economic and Political Weekly, vol. 225, no. 23 (June 9, 1990), pp. 1247-55.

[Ellen E. McDonald, "The Modernizing of Communication: Vernacular Publishing in Nineteenth Century Maharashtra," Asian Survey, 8 (1968), pp. 589-606]

[Gauri Viswanathan, Masks of Conquest: Literary Study and British Rule in India (New York: Columbia University Press, 1989), 1-44, 94-169]

[Raymond Williams, The Long Revolution (New York: Harper & Row, 1961), pp. 214-29]

[Jurgen Habermas, The Structural Transformation of the Public Sphere: An Inquiry into a Category of Bourgeois Society (Cambridge, Mass.: M.I.T. Press, 1989), pp. 1-5, 19-88]

VIII Hindi/Urdu/Hindustani, Religion and Nationalism (November 20, 27)

*G.A. Grierson The Linguistic Survey of India, IX, 42-65.

*Amrit Rai, A House Divided, pp. 226-89.

C. Shackle and R. Snell, <u>Hindi and Urdu Since 1800: A Common Reader</u> (London:SOAS, 1990), pp. 1-20, [23-94; if there are members in the class with an adequate background, a special session will be held to examine the rest of this book, including some of the sample texts, pp. 83-180].

Sayyid 'Abdu'l Latif, <u>The Influence of English Literature on Urdu Literature</u> (London, 1924), pp. 31-105.

Barbara Metcalf, <u>Islamic Revival in British India</u>, pp. 215-34.

David Lelyveld, <u>Aligarh's First Generation</u>, pp. 68-101, 204-12, 217-38, 300-13; "Eloquence and Authority in Urdu: Poetry, Oratory and Film," in Katherine P. Ewing, ed. <u>Shari'at and</u> <u>Ambiguity in South Asian Islam</u>, pp. 98-113.

C. R. King, "The Nagari Pracharini Sabha," pp. 106-148, 226-42, 355-444.

Suniti Kumar Chatterji, <u>Indo-Aryan and Hindi</u> (Ahmedabad: Gujarat Vernacular Society, 1942), pp. 133-235.

Ravi Shankar Shukla, <u>Lingua Franca for India (Hind)</u> (Lucknow: Oudh Publishing House [1947]), pp. 1-40.

SECOND ESSAY - due November 27

<u>IX</u> Language and Nationalism (December 4)

*M. K. Gandhi, <u>Our Language Problem</u>, ed. by A. T. Hingorani.

*Paul Brass, <u>Language, Religion and Politics in North India</u>, pp. 50-116.

Francis Robinson, <u>Separatism among Indian Muslims</u>, pp. 33-83, 133-43.

Victor Kiernan, "Introduction," <u>Poems by Faiz</u> (London: George Allen & Unwin, 1971), pp. 21-44.

C.M. Naim, "The consequences of Indo-Pakistani War for Urdu language and literature," <u>Journal of Asian Studies</u> 28 (1968), pp. 269-83.

Aijaz Ahmad, "Some Reflections on Urdu," <u>Seminar</u> 39 (July 1989), pp. 23-29.

C. Shackle, "Rival linguistic identities in Pakistan

Punjab," in Peter Robb and David Taylor, eds. <u>Rule, Protest, and Identity</u> (London:SOAS, 1978), pp. 213-34.

[Ranajit Guha, <u>Elementary Aspects of Peasant Insurgency in Colonial India</u>, pp. 28-76]

[Shahid Amin, "Gandhi as Mahatma: Gorakhpur District, Eastern U.P. 1921-2," in Ranajit Guha, ed.<u>Subaltern Studies III</u>, pp. 1-59]

[Eugene F. Irschik, <u>Politics and Social Conflict in South India</u>, pp. 275-310]

Mass Communications, Imperialism and the Nation (December 11)

*Ashis Nandy, "The Political Culture of the Indian State," <u>Daedalus</u> vol. . 118, no. 4 (Fall, 1989), pp. 1-26.

[Homi Bhabha, "DissemiNation: time, narrative, and the margins of the modern nation," in his, ed. <u>Nation and Narration</u> (London: Routledge, 1990]

*Schwartzberg, <u>A Historical Atlas of South Asia</u>, pp. 103-105, 236-37, 109, 240, 117, 244, 77-78, 224-25.

*[Lionel Fielden], <u>Report on the Progress of Broadcasting in India</u> [1939], pp. 1-10, 17-57, 71.

[Lionel Fielden, <u>The Natural Bent</u>, pp. 126-216]

Lelyveld, "Transmitters and Culture: The Colonial Roots of Indian Broadcasting," <u>South Asia Research</u> 10, no. 1 (Spring, 1990).

Shukla, <u>Lingua Franca</u>, pp. 320-34.

Durga Das, ed. <u>Sardar Patel's Correspondence, 1945-50</u>, vol. IV (Ahmedabad: Navajivan Publishing House, 1972), pp. 60-91.

[S. Theodore Baskaran, <u>The Message Bearers: Nationalist Politics and the Entertainment Media in South India, 1880-1945</u>, pp. 67-150]

[Erik Barnouw and S. Krishnaswamy, <u>Indian Cinema</u> (2nd ed.) 1980)]

[P. C. Chatterji, <u>Broadcasting in India</u>, pp. 58-164]

The Image of the Nation: A Film Anthology (time and place to be arranged)

THIRD ESSAY - due December 11

University of Washington
History 498H
SISSA 490

Fall 1991
David Lelyveld

Colloquium: Islam in South Asia

In this course we will examine what it has meant to be Muslim in South Asia, with special attention to the relations of Islam to non-Muslim religious traditions of the subcontinent and the ways that twentieth century Muslims and others have understood the history of Islam in India.

You are asked to write four short (about 1000 word) essays, as noted in the course outline below, plus one ungraded exercise. One of the papers should include, as an appendix, a map exercise (see attachment to this reading list). You should keep up with the readings so that you are prepared to summarize and comment upon them during class discussions. Supplementary readings will be divided among us: individual students will be asked to prepare class presentations based on these readings and you will want to refer to some of them for your essay assignments. As far as possible, readings will be on reserve (marked with asterisk) or in photocopies that I will make available. The following books will be available for purchase:

> Ainslie T. Embree, ed. Sources of the Indian Tradition (revised ed.), Volume I.
> _____, Alberuni's India
> Nikki Keddie, ed. An Islamic Response to Imperialism: Political and Religious Writings of Sayyid Jamal ad-Din "al-Afghani"
> Muhammad Iqbal, The Reconstruction of Religious Though in Islam
> Patricia Jeffrey, Frogs in a Well (not required)
> Akbar S. Ahmed, Discovering Islam (not required)
> Salman Rushdie, Shame (not required)
> Jawaharlal Nehru, The Discovery of India (not required)

All work must be handed in by the assigned dates. Students are invited to meet regularly with me out of class hours, especially before they are due to make class presentations. My office will be 324 Thomson; the phone number is 543-4999. Regular office hours will be announced, and I will be generally available at other times as well.

Course Outline

I. Perspectives and Background

September 30 - Ayodhya 1990

    Video: "Newstrack" (December, 1989)

    *Newspaper clippings on Ayodhya controversy - to be

276

distributed. Ungraded exercise, due October 7.
Supplementary Readings:
        van der Veer 1987: 283-301

October 2 - Looking Backward: The Partition of India

        *Muhammad Ali Jinnah, "Presidential Address ... All India
        Muslim League ... March 1940," pp. 12-15 (hand-out).

        *Jawaharlal Nehru, The Discovery of India (New York: Anchor,
        1960), pp. 129-47,162-64, 166-76 (hand-out).

        *Sir Reginald Coupland, The Indian Problem, 1837-1935, pp.
        28-36 (hand-out).

        Supplementary Readings:
                *Aziz Ahmad 1964: 263-76; Robinson 1983: 185-203.

UNGRADED EXERCISE: Notes on Ayodhya (due October 7)

October 7 - The Essential and the Variable

        *Clifford Geertz, Islam Observed, (Chicago: University of
        Chicago Press, 1971), pp. 1-22.

        Supplementary Readings:
                [For a brief, somewhat personal introduction to the
                history of Islam by a contemporary Pakistani
                anthropologist, see Akbar S. Ahmed, Discovering Islam
                (London: Routledge & Kegan Paul, 1988). See also Fazlur
                Rahman, Islam [revised ed.], pp. 1-67, 85-116, 128-149,
                167-180. Students with limited background on Indic
                civilization may wish to read Embree, ed. Sources of
                the Indian Tradition, vol. I., pp. 201-378].

                *Roff 1987: 31-52

II. Islam in India: The Era of First Encounters

October 9 - The Coming of Muslims and Islam to India

        Chach-Nama [Tarikh-i Hind wa Sind] in H.M. Elliot and
        John Dowson, The History of India as Told By Its Own
        Historians: The Muhammadan Period. Vol. I (London:
        Trubner, 1867), pp. 131-211.

        Supplementary Readings:
                *Aziz Ahmad 1964: 73-100; *Ikram 1964: 2-85;
                Maclean 1989: 22-82; Friedmann 1975: 233-45;

Friedmann 1984: 23-35.
October 14 - Muslim Perceptions of Indian Civilizations

A. Embree, ed. Alberuni's India, pp. v-xix, I: 3-8, 17-32,
59-124, 228-29; II: 13-14, 145-46, 161-63.

Supplementary Readings:
Thapar 1971: 408-436.

October 16 - Conversion: The appeal of Islam
*Sources of the Indian Tradition, pp. 440-46.

Supplementary Readings:
Hardy 1979: 68-99; Eaton 1985: 106-23.

FIRST PAPER: Why Hindus might be attracted to Islam; why Muslims
might be drawn to aspects of Hinduism. (Due October 16)

III. Sunni Islam and Dissenting Traditions in India

October 21 - Piety and Authority

*Sources, pp. 381-440

Supplementary Readings:
*Ikram 1964: 134-208; *Aziz Ahmad 1964: 3-21;
*Asher 1988: 79-97.

October 23 - Sufi, Shi'i and Messianic Movements

*Sources, pp. 447-463.

Supplementary Readings:
Zaehner 1969: 86-109; *Schimmel 1975: 344-402;
*Eaton 1978: 19-39, 107-174; Qureshi 1986: 79-131;
*Nanji 1988: 63-76; Rizvi 1965: 68-105.

October 30 - Hindu-Muslim Syncretisms and Orthodox Resistance

*Sources, pp. 447-463.

Supplementary Readings:
*Roy 1983: 141-206; *Rafiuddin Ahmed 1988: 114-42;
*Aziz Ahmad 1964: 119-166, 182-217; *Metcalf 1990: 79-
172; *Dale 1980: 24-32, 63-91; *S. Bayly 1989: 104-150,
187-215; Rizvi 1965: 202-329; C.A. Bayly 1985: 177-
203; *Cole 1988: 13-35, 145-172, 223-250.

History 498H/SISSA 490

SECOND PAPER: The achievements and limits of syncretism. (Due
November 4).
IV - The Reproduction of Tradition: Family and Schooling

November 4 - Learning to be a Muslim

*Barbara Metcalf, Perfecting Women, pp. 39-78, 163-203.

Supplementary Readings:
        Eickelman 1978: 485-516; *Robinson 1984: 152-183;
        *Ajmal 1984: 241-251; *Lelyveld 1978: 35-56.

November 6 - Women and Islam

Read either:
*Mrs. Meer Hassan Ali, Observations on the Mussalmauns of
India [1832] (Reprint ed., Karachi, 1974), pp. 163-
227; or *Barbara Metcalf, Perfecting Women, pp. 241-314.

Supplementary Readings:
        Papanek 1973: 289-325; Jeffery 1979: 1-55, 119-176;
        *Vreede de Stuers 1968: 41-101

November 11-13 - Solidarity: Ritual and "Caste"

Jaffur Shurreef, Qanoon-e-Islam, or the Customs of the
Mussalmans of India, tr. G.A. Hercklots (London, 1832),
pp. 41-48.

*Barbara Metcalf, Perfecting Women, pp. 79-161.

Supplementary Readings:
        *Kumar 1988: 40-62, 83-110, 201-27; S. Bayly 1986: 35-
        74; Metcalf 1990 [B]: 85-107; Lindholm 1986: 61-73;
        *Fusfeld 1988: 205-19; *Cole 1988: 95-137.

THIRD PAPER: Hierarchy and Egalitarianism - Person and Group
(due November 18).

V. Imperialism, Apologetics, Resistance and Nationalism

November 18 - Muslims and British Rule

*W. W. Hunter, The Indian Musalmans: Are They Bound in
Conscience to Rebel Against the Queen? [1871] (Reprint
ed. Delhi, 1969), pp.1-35, 100-137.

Supplementary Readings:
        *Lelyveld 1978: 3-34; *Hardy 1972: 31-115; *Pandey

279

1990: 23-108; *Cole 1988: 251-82.

November 20 - Forms of Resistance

*Nikki R. Keddie, ed. An Islamic Response to
Imperialism: Political and Religious Writings of Sayyid
Jamal ad-Din "al-Afghani", pp. (3-35), 73-84, 130-180.
Supplementary Readings:
    Muin-ud-din Ahmad Khan 1965: 1-115; Pearson 1979: 75-
    166; *Dale 1980: 50-60, 119-52, 194-218.

November 25 - Apologetics and New Institutions

*Stephen Hay, ed. Sources of the Indian Tradition (revised
ed., 1988), vol. II, pp. 9-15, 173-191, 205-212.

Muhammad Iqbal, The Reconstruction of Religious
Thought in Islam (Reprint ed., Lahore, 1965), pp. 1-27, 95-
145.

Supplementary Readings:
    *Aziz Ahmad and von Grunebaum 1970: 25-129;
    *Ameer Ali 1922: 122-187; Douglas 1988: pp. 27-96, 189-
    252; *Metcalf 1982: 87-137, 264-347; *Lelyveld 1978:
    56-101, 253-261; *Gilmartin 1984: 221-240; Fyzee 1964:
    47-52, 460-68.

November 27 - Islam and Modern Politics

*Hay, Sources, vol. II, pp. 191-204, 222-42, 379-411.

*Muhammad Iqbal, The Reconstruction of Religious
Thought in Islam pp. 146-180.

Supplementary Readings:
    *Hardy 1972: 116-146, 168-197, 222-255; Aziz Ahmad
    1967: 156-185, 195-223; Hasan 1979: 134-184; *Freitag
    1988: 115-145; *Gilmartin 1988: 146-68; Minault 1982:
    111-207; Shaikh 1991: 204-26.

December 2 - Law and the Modern State

*Pakistan [Munir Commission], Report of the Court of
Inquiry under Punjab Act II of 1954 to Enquire into
the Punjab Disturbances of 1953 (Lahore, 1954), pp.
183-235.

Supplementary Readings:
    Fyzee 1965: 169-98;Carroll 1983: 205-222;

Kishwar 1986: 4-13; Jai 1986; Naseem 1988: 1-25.

December 4 - Modern Politics and Islam

*Barbara Daly Metcalf, "Islamic Arguments in Contemporary Pakistan," in Roff, ed. Islam and the Political Economy of Meaning, pp. 132-59; (see also readings for September 30).

Supplementary Readings:
*Pandey 1990: 233-61; *Brass 1974: 119-274; Ewing 1983: 251-268; Mayer 1981: 481-502.

December 9-11 - Islam and the Modern World

*Geertz 1971: 90-118.

Supplementary Reading:
Salman Rushdie, Shame; Naipaul 1981: 85-222; Naim 1988: 57-65; Smith 1957: chs. 1, 5-6, 8.

FOURTH PAPER: Private and Public Religion in Contemporary Life
(due December 11).

Rhoads Murphey, University of Michigan
HISTORY 396, 010   Fall, 1987

Vasco da Gama to Pearl Harbor: The West in Asia, 1498-1941

This is a colloquium ("talking together"),a discussion course in which we all read
things and talk about them in weekly sessions. Since we meet only twice (and sometimes
only once) a week, there is plenty of time to read widely and unhurriedly. The total is
decidedly modest -- 1200 pages for the entire term --and much of it is candy. Please read
each week's assignments carefully and analytically before we meet so that you can discuss
it intelligently. The importance of faithful attendance is obvious; I will hope not to have
to remind you of this, or to penalize you for breaching this basic rule of any colloquium.
This is also an ECB course (for those who register for it as such). There are four short
(5 page) papers (essays), growing out of the readings and/or discussions, which must be
submitted seriatim according to the dates given on the assignment sheet included in the
course pack, so as to allow time for necessary feedback. The reason for this is equally
obvious, and paper due dates must be observed. It makes no sense for me to accept late
papers under this system, or to accept them in a bunch late in the term. Please don't make
an issue of this; just do it!, following the dates given. The four essays take the
place of an examination and are the sole basis of grades (except for absenteeism and
lateness), but we may also want to schedule some/individual oral presentations, another
useful skill to acquire.

The literature in this field is, as you might imagine, immense. I have tried to put
together a varied sample of it, but can include only the tiniest teaser. There is lots
more, including tons of "My Years in X" kinds of books, much of it fascinating, which you
may want to explore sometime, if not right now. I will hand out lists of more titles, again
only the smallest sample, as a sort of beginner's guide. Some of the best books included
in the course pack are out of print, but in any case there are far too many for you to
buy or to scramble for as single library copies. The course pack solution is a godsend for
a course like this, and also a colossal steal at the price, when you consider the time and
hassle saved -- a job I did for you in various libraries during the dog days of last
summer. This way you needn't even get out of bed --except, of course, to attend class, and
sit up at your typewriter. This bargain is waiting for you at Dollar Bill Copying on
Church Street, and combines general surveys and other secondary works with personal reminis-
cences and "flavor" readings, including a bit of poetry and some primary snippets. Much
of it is pure pleasure, and even so averages much less than 100 pages a week, a sort of
standard amount, though you may find some weeks easier going than others. Sansom, Parry,
Fieldhouse, Edwardes, Fairbank-Reischauer, and to some extent Murphey are all general
surveys, but each with a different pitch and focus and with relatively little overlap.
Fairbank-Reischauer is the most detailed and standard account of events in East Asia.
Feel free to read the rest of it for a more complete survey of China, Japan, Korea,
Vietnam, and Thailand in the 19th. and 20th. centuries, as well as the rest of the other
books I have selected bits from. For India the most convenient survey of the period since
da Gama is Stanley Wolpert, A New History of India, for Southeast Asia,David Steinberg, ed.,
In Search of Southeast Asia.   The teaser samples in the course pack should whet your
appetite for more — but in any case, this is meant to be a pleasurable learning
experience.   Enjoy!

R. Murphey

Course Pack Contents and Assignments

Week of

Sept. 14 R. Murphey, The Outsiders, 1-35. J.H. Parry, Establishment of the European
Hegemony, 8-38, 80-92, and 134-48.

Sept. 21 G. Sansom, The Western World and Japan, 3-13, 66-73, 88-98, 105-113, 136-39,
162-64. D.K. Fieldhouse, The Colonial Empires, 142-73. M. Edwardes, Asia in
the European Age, 19-23, 106-115. J.K. Fairbank and E.O. Reischauer, East Asia:
The Modern Transformation, 10-35.

Sept. 28 Fairbank and Reischauer, Mod. Transf., 35-77. C.R. Boxer, Fidalgos in the Far
East, 4-7, 72-83, 123-38. Murphey, The Outsiders, 36-79.

FIRST ESSAYS DUE Tues. Sept. 29

Oct. 5 P.J. Marshall, East Indian Fortunes, 214-19, 662-67. M. Collis, The Great Within ,
264-65, 274-77, 288-93. Fieldhouse, Colonial Empires, 177-80, 190-201, 271-86.
Murphey, Outsiders, 80-98. M. Collis, Foreign Mud, 20-69, 80-95, 114-19.

Oct. 12 W.L. Langer, The Diplomacy of Imperialism, 67-96. Fieldhouse,"The New Imperialism
74-97, 357-62. Fairbank etc. Mod. Transf., 408-16, 440-68, 483-87.

Oct. 19 Fairbank etc., Mod. Transf., 720-55. J.G. Butcher, The British in Malaya, 50-75,
76-37, 97-112.

SECOND ESSAYS DUE October 20 (Tuesday)

Oct. 26 Geoffrey Moorhouse, India Britannica, 82-148, 194-219. Kipling, selected verse.

Nov. 2 David Kopf, "British Orientalism...", 131-42. M. Edwardes, Bound to Exile, 24-35,
46-7, 54-5, 86-7, 90-91, 158-59. Kipling, "The Bridge Builders", 3-47. Jim Corbett
My India, iv-9, 14-16, 17 (stet)-28, 132-51.

Nov. 9 JK. Fairbank, ed., The Missionary Enterprise, 1-5, 249-82, 360-73. J.C. Thomson e
al., Sentimental Imperialists , 44-60. J.G. Lutz, Christian Missions, 13-33.

THIRD ESSAYS DUE, Tuesday Nov. 10

Nov. 16 Murphey, Outsiders, 99-176.

Nov. 23 Carl Crow, Foreign Devils in the Flowery Kingdom, 9-46, 152-65. George Kates,
The Years That Were Fat, 8-27, 76-81, 158-59.

Nov. 30 Murphey, Outsiders, 177-234. J.R. Levenson, Revolution and Cosmopolitanism, 21-4

Dec. 7 (Note that this is the anniversary of the Japanese attack on Pearl Harbor in
1941, which marks the effective end of Western colonialism in Asia, a process
completed in stages after the war, Malaysia not until 1957, Vietnam 1954--or197
It thus appropriately marks also the end of this course, which concludes with
the following readings: Sansom, Western World and Japan, 275-80, 287-91, 305-08
Thomson, Sentimental Imperialists, 61-79, 121-33. K.M. Panikkar, Asia, 306-32.
More verse, and farewell.

FOURTH ESSAYS DUE TUESDAY, DECEMBER 8

WITTENBERG UNIVERSITY

EAST ASIA AND THE WEST—SYLLABUS

History 160
Jim Huffman, teacher
Spring, 1991

Rudyard Kipling said it, and thousands have repeated it: "East is East; West is West, and never the twain shall meet."

Did he know what he was talking about? Certainly East and West have met! They have clashed, fought, studied each other, cursed each other, worked together and exerted massive influence on each other. But is that what Kipling meant? Have they really met each other, studied each other, come to understand each other? Or CAN they even meet that way? And what happens if they do?

These are the basic questions of this course. We will look at Japanese, Chinese and Philippine interactions with Westerners in two eras, attempting to understand what impact East and West had on each other--and what the impact has to say about our world today.

Instructor. The course is taught by Jim Huffman. His office is Room 122 Leamer Hall; his office hours are:

Monday	2:30 to 4:00
Tuesday	12:00 to 3:00
Wednesday	2:30 to 4:00
Thursday	By Appointment
Friday	2:30 to 4:30

Phone numbers are: office--7846; home--399-9728. Please feel free to contact him about matters of any kind (before 9 p.m., please).

Goals. We will attempt, specifically, to:

1. Learn the nature of the major events and trends of East-West interaction during two epochs, 1500-1750 and 1750-1900.
2. Confront the value questions raised by these developments, especially the questions inherent in cultural interaction.
3. Hone our critical skills, both oral and written.
4. Enjoy ourselves!

Requirements. The following are required:

1. Attendance at (and discussion in) class sessions. Each unexcused absence over two absences of any kind will result in a three-point deduction.

2. A five-page critical essay on one of the assigned books. It should include a discussion of one important cultural concept that appears in the book--describing how that concept

284

is treated by the author, then critiquing/analyzing it from your own experiences and reading. The "critique" portion should be at least half of the essay.

Page numbers should be cited for all direct references to the book; your essay must begin with a full citation of the book, and it should be typed (double spaced) on white paper. This essay is due on the day that the book is listed in the class schedule below. You should, however, indicate to the instructor by April 1 which book you intend to discuss.

3. A journal of your thoughts about the class. In it, you should focus on the ideas that provoke and stimulate you in class and, particularly, in your readings. It will be graded for the quality and intensity of thought, not for the quality of the writing. Journals should be kept in a looseleaf notebook and brought to class daily, since three or four will be collected each day on a random basis. For a C, you must write at least three solid entries a week. (The journal also should include a one-page summary of each reading, written by the day when that reading is due; this summary is in addition to regular journal entries.)

4. A paper and a 35-minute, oral debate presentation. You are to: 1) Choose (on April 1) one of the debate topics and individuals listed on the last page of this syllabus. 2) Do a research paper of five to seven pages, focusing on that person's likely ideas about some aspect of the debate topic. 3) Take part in the debate.

NOTE: The paper should follow standard research-paper format and will be due two class sessions prior to your debate. Debate participants are asked to appear in costume and to take on the persona of their individual. Members of each debate should meet several times to prepare their session, making sure that all sides of the issue will be well represented and that the session will be lively. Each debate should last thirty minutes. It also should be FUN! (A bibliography of at least six sources will be due May 3.)

5. Four quizzes, over the terms used in lectures. Your knowledge of terms will be expected to be cumulative during each of the two halves of the class.

6. Two tests—a midterm and a final.

Grading. Requirements will be rated on the following scale. Students will be informed of any changes. Plus or minus points may be given in the categories marked "credit."

Attendance/discussion	credit
Quizzes	40 (10 each)
Critical essay	50
Debate	50
Paper	50
Journal	50
Reading summaries	credit
Tests	200 (100 each)

NOTES. 1. Students should be aware of the Wittenberg policy on academic honesty; violations (including cheating and plagiarism) will result in severe penalties.

2. Late work will be assessed a five percent penalty the first day and an additional percent each day thereafter. No papers will be accepted after the final exam.

285

3. Major papers are to be typed, in proper style, on white paper. One-page papers and journals may be handwritten (neatly).

4. No makeup tests or quizzes will be given; if the student has an excused absence for a test, her/his term grade simply will be based on the remainder of course work.

Required Readings. Each should be completed by the day listed in the Class Schedule below.

Spence, Jonathan. The Question of Hu. Random, 1990.

Endo Shusaku. The Samurai. Random, 1984.

Pruitt, Ida. Daughter of Han. Stanford, 1967.

Bain, David. Sitting in Darkness. Penguin, 1986.

Fukuzawa Yukichi. The Autobiography of Yukichi Fukuzawa. Columbia, 1966.

Class Schedule The following schedule is tentative. Lecture topics may be shifted and changed. Due dates, however, are solid unless a change is announced. (NOTE. The following books, which have been placed on overnight reserve at the library, should be useful in providing a historical context for the lectures: 1. Paul H. Clyde and Burton Beers, The Far East. Prentice-Hall, 1975. 2. John Fairbank and Edwin Reischauer, East Asia--Tradition and Transformation and East Asia-The Great Tradition. Houghton-Miflin. 3. Edward L. Farmer, et al. Comparative History of Civilizations in Asia, 2 vols. Addison-Wesley Publishing, 1977.)

PLAYING BY ASIAN RULES, 1500-1750

Week One (3-25).   THE NATURE OF EAST ASIAN SOCIETY

M.	Introduction
W.	Fan Yuan: Chinese Journalism
F.	no class

Week Two (4-1).

M.	Traditional China	debate, essay topics
W.	"100 Herbs," AV Theater I	
Th.	6:30, "Rickshaw Man," at Huffmans'; 3 hours	
F.	Traditional Japan, Philippines	

Week Three (4-8).   WESTERNERS IN EAST ASIA

M.	Missionaries in China	
M.	3:45, East Asia colloquium	
W.	no class	
F.	Merchants in China	Spence

286

Week Four (4-15).

M.	Traders and Priests in Japan	quiz
W.	Japan "Handles" the West	
F.	"Yojimbo," 1:10-3:10, AV I	Endo

Week Five (4-22).

M.	Disc: Endo and Spence	
W.	Spain in the Philippines	quiz
W.	7:15 p.m., Review Session (optional)	
F.	Midterm	

PLAYING BY WESTERN RULES, 1750-1900

Week Six (4-29). DIFFERENT COUNTRIES, DIFFERENT APPROACHES

M.	Technology and New Western Attitudes	
W.	Opium and War in China	Pruitt
F.	No class	biblio. due

Week Seven (5-6).

M.	China's Responses
M.	3:45, E.A. colloquium (required)
W.	Debates: Opium, Christianity
F.	Disc: Pruitt

Week Eight (5-13).

M.	The Philippine Struggle	Bain
W.	"Bloody, Blundering Business," AV Theater I	quiz
F.	Deb: America's Philippine Policy Disc: Bain	

Week Nine (5-20).

M.	America's Challenge to Japan	
W.	Japan's Response	
F.	Deb: Japan's Imperialism Disc: Fukuzawa Yukichi	Fukuzawa

Week Ten (5-27).   SUMMING IT UP

      M.   Deb: Japan v. China
      W.   Disc: Two Eras, Two Histories   quiz
      F.   Review

Week Eleven (6-3).

      M.   1:30, Final Test

DEBATE TOPICS

1. Opium: Does the West Have a Right to Sell It?

Lord Napier	William Jardine
Queen Victoria	Ci Xi
Qian-long emperor	Lin Ze-xu
Kang Xi emperor	Charles Elliot
John Hu	

2. Missions: What is the Right Approach?

Peter Parker	Maria Taylor
Kang-xi	Ci Xi
Timothy Richard	a Boxer
Hong Xiu-quan	Matteo Ricci
Father Velasco	Tokugawa Ieyasu
John Hu	

3. What Should America Have Done in the Philippines?

Apolonia de la Cruz	Theodore Roosevelt
Jose Rizal	Emilio Aguinaldo
Mark Twain	David Bain
William McKinley	Lazaro Segovia
Frederick Funston	

4. Did Japan Have a Right to Become Imperialist?

Queen Victoria	Kang You-wei
E. H. House	Tokutomi Soho
Fukuzawa Yukichi	Czar Nicholas II
Frederick Funston	Empeor Meiji
Li Hong-zhang	

5. Why Japan Fared Better than China

Ito Hirobumi	Ci Xi
Emperor Meiji	Emilio Aguinaldo
Sun Yat-sen	Meiji
Li Hong-zhan	Jose Rizal
John Hu	

UNIVERSITY OF SOUTHERN CALIFORNIA

SOCIAL SCIENCES 396
AMERICA'S ASIAN WARS

Professor Roger Dingman
Spring Term 1991

Tuesdays & Thursdays 11 - 1215
Houston-205

I. Course Objectives

America has just fought its fifth Asian war in this
century. This course seeks to explain how and why Americans have
so often come into conflict with Asians. It will analyze the ways
in which those wars have been fought so as to illuminate the
processes by which American foreign and military policies are
shaped. The course also seeks to demonstrate the ongoing
importance of Asia in American life by examining the economic,
social, and cultural consequences of these conflicts.

II. Course Schedule

DATE	TOPIC	READINGS
Mar 19	A. Course Introduction: Death and Distance	
	B. To the Philippines: Imperialism, Idealism, & Unintended Consequences	TSP, pp 106-120, B, 9-101
21	A. War as Adventure, 1899-1901 1899-1901	B, 154-198 244-55, 273-94, 318-28, 344-50, 361-74
	B. Adaptation & Atrocities, 1902	
26	A. The Burdens of Success 1902-41	TSP, ch 11
	B. America & Japan:Cooperation to Conflict, 1919-1939	& pp 176-89 D, chs 1-3
28	QUIZ ONE	
	A. No MAGIC: The Road to Pearl Harbor, 1940-1941	D, ch 4 TSP, 190-97
	B. Race & War: Guadalcanal	TSP, 198-202 D, chs 8-9
Apr 2	A. Pacific Endgame: Hiroshima	D, ch. 11
	B. From Enmity to Alliance	TSP, 203-16
4	A. Midterm Examination	
	B. The Origins of the Korean War: Commitment & Miscalculation	TSP, 217-38

289

    9   A. Korea: the Accordian War, 1950-1951   RD, pp.50-79
        B. Atomic Bombs, Honor, and Eisenhower's   RD, pp. 79-91
           Peace, 1951-1953

    11 A. Korea: the Costs of "Limited" War
        B. Lines that Would Not Hold: America in   TSP, 253-67
           Southeast Asia, 1950 - 63   R, 1-25, 31-
                                                    47, 68-72,
                                                    239-52,379-97

    16 QUIZ 2
        A. Vietnam: The Noble Crusade, 1961-8   R, 283-310,514
                                                     -26, 137-64,
        B. Vietnam: Nixon's War   R,315-43,436-53

    18 A. Vietnam: Peace with Honor?   R, 457-74,
                                                     493-503,
                                                     550-578

        B. Reflections on America's Asian Wars:
            From Manila to Kuwait, 1898-1991
        C. Course paper due in class

    To be arranged: FINAL EXAMINATION

III. Required Reading Materials

    (TSP) Thomson, James D., Stanley, Peter, and Perry, John C.,
          Sentimental Imperialists chs 7-8, 11, 13-18

    (B)   Bain, David H., Sitting in Darkness, chs. 1, 3, 6,
          8, 10, 12, 14

    (D)   Dower, John W., War Without Mercy, chs 1-4, 89-, 11

    (RD) Dingman, Roger, "Atomic Diplomacy during the Korean
          War, 1950-1953," International Security 13 (Winter
          1989), pp. 50-91   (xeroxed)

    (R)   Rotter, Andrew, Light at the End of the Tunnel
          pp 1-25, 31-47, 68-72, 125-35, 137-64, 239-252, 283-
          310, 315-43, 436-74, 493-503, 550-578

IV. Required Written Work

    Each course participant will complete two short quizes, a
mid-term, and a final examination. In addition, a short paper
(5-7 pages, typewritten, double-spaced) on a topic approved by
the instructor will be required.

V. Grading

    Evaluation of participants' performance will be as follows:

    Quizzes   10%
    Midterm exam   20%
    Class participation   20%
    Course paper   20%
    Final examination   30%

V. Office Hours

    Your instructor is here to help you learn. Please feel
    free to come in to discuss class work, topics of special
    interest, papers, grades, etc. during regular office hours or
    at other times by prior aarrangement.

    WHERE: Lowell Heiny Hall 240   (Social & Behavioral Sciences)

    WHEN: Tuesdays & Thursdays   1:30 — 3,   and by prior
                arrangement

    TELEPHONE: 248-1316

University of Cincinnati

WOMEN IN ASIA PRIOR TO 1800:   INDIA AND CHINA   AUTUMN QUARTER, 1989-90
History 15-075-531   Barbara N. Ramusack

Office: 360 McMicken. Office telephones: 556-2140 or 556-2144.
Office Hours: MWF 11:00 a.m.-noon, MW 2:00-4:00 p.m. and by appointment.

TEXTS: Cyril Birch, ed.   Stories from a Ming Collection.
        R. K. Narayan. The Ramayana.
        Jonathan Spence. The Death of Woman Wang.
        M. Strobel and C. Johnson-Odim. Restoring Women to World History.
        *Denotes that material will be handed out in class.
        #Denotes reading required only for graduate students.
        All other material will be on reserve in the Langsam Library.

Sep 20-25: Introduction. Studying Women in Cross-Cultural Perspective.
                 Strobel and Johnson-Odim, pp. 1-30.

Sep 27:   India: The Historical Context.
                 Begin to read Ramusack, pp. 1-16, in Strobel and Johnson-Odim.
                 Begin to read The Ramayana.

Sept 29:   India: Women as Daughters and Daughters-in-law.
                   "Dadi's Family."
                   Two page typed commentary on this film is due Oct 2.
Oct 2:   India: Women as Wives-Marriages, Divorce, Widowhood.
                   *Selections from the Laws of Manu.
                   *Selections from The Qur'an.
                   B. F. Musallam. Sex and Society in Islam, pp. 10-38.
Oct 4:   India: Women as Mothers.

Oct 6:   India: Women's Sexuality, as Lovers and as Courtesans.
                   J. A. B. van Buitenen. Tales of Anicent India.
                   "The Red Lotus of Chastity" and "The Tale of Two Bawds."

Oct 9:   India: Women in Religion, As Divinites and As Devotees.
                   David Kinsley. Hindu Goddesses. Parvati, pp. 35-54,
                   Radha, pp. 81-94, Durga, pp. 95-115.
                   #Sita, pp. 65-80 and Kali, pp. 116-131.
Oct 11:   "Wedding of the Goddess."
Oct 13:   Islam.
Oct 16:   Devotional Worship: Bhakti and Sufism.

Oct 18:   India: Women in Politics.

Oct 20-23: India: Women in Literature, as Doers and as Portrayed.
                   Kalidasa, "Sakuntala and the Ring of Recollection," in
                   Barbara S. Miller, ed. Theater of Memory.
                   J. S. Hawley and M. Jergensmeyer. Songs of the Saints of
                   India. Mirabai, pp. 119-140.

Oct 25:   India: Women in the Visual Arts.

Oct 27:   Mid-Quarter Examination. Bring blue book and pen to class.

                                  292

Oct 30:   China: The Historical Context.
           Begin to read Sievers, pp. 64-87 in Strobel and Johnson-Odim.
           Begin to read Spence, The Death of Woman Wang.

Nov 1:   China: Women as Daughters.
Nov 3:   "Small Happiness."
           Two page typed commentary on this film is due Nov 6.

Nov 6:   China: Women as Wives-Marriage, Divorce, Widowhood.
                    Pan Chao, "Lessons for Women" in Nancy Lee Swann,
                    Pan Chao, Foremost Woman Scholar of China, Chapter 7.

Nov 8:   China: Women as Mothers.
           Charlotte Furth, "Concepts of Pregnancy, Childbirth and Infancy
           in Ch'ing Dynasty China," Journal of Asian Studies, 46, 1,
           (February 1987), pp. 7-37.

Nov 10:   Veterans Day Holiday.

Nov 13:   China: Women's Sexuality, as Lovers and as Courtesans.
           "The Pearl Sewn Shirt" in Birch, Stories from a Ming Collection.

Nov 15-17: China: Women in Religion, as Divinities and as Devotees.
           Theresa Kelleher. "Confucianism," pp. 135-161 and
           Barbara Reed. "Taoism," pp. 161-182 in Arvind Sharma, ed.,
           Women in World Religions.
           #Kathryn Tsai, "The Chinese Buddhist Monastic Order for Women,"
           in Guisso and Johannesson, eds., Women in China.

Nov 20:   China: Women in Politics.
           #Priscilla Ching Chung, "Power and Prestige: Palace Women in the
           Northern Sung," in Guisso and Johannesson, eds., Women in China.
           RESEARCH PAPERS ARE DUE.

Nov 22:   China: Women in Literature, as Doers and as Portrayed.
           "The Lady Who Was a Beggar" and "The Fairy's Rescue," in Stories
           from a Ming Collection.

Nov 24:   Thanksgiving Holiday.

Nov 27:   China: Women in the Visual Arts.

Nov 29:   Cross-Cultural Historiography.
           *Uma Chakravarti and Kumkum Roy. "In Search of Our Past: A
           Review of the Limitations and Possibilities of the Historiography
           of Women in Early India." Economic and Political Weekly, 23
           (April 20, 1988), WS 2-WS 10.

Dec 1:   Review.

Dec 4:   Final Examination. 1:30 - 3:30 p.m.

University of Cincinnati

WOMEN IN ASIA: CHINA AND INDIA
History 15-075-532

Winter Quarter 1989-1990
Barbara N. Ramusack

Office: 360 McMicken
Office Hours: MWF 11:00-Noon and 2:00-3:00 p.m. and by appointment.
Office telephones: 556-2140 and messages may be left at 556-2144.

Texts:

Emily Honig and Gail Hershatter. Personal Voices: Chinese Women
in the 1980s. (Optional for purchase, on reserve in Langsam.)
Rokeya Sakhawat Hossain. Sultana's Dream and Selections from the
Secluded Ones.
Maxine Hong Kingston. Woman Warrior: Memoirs of a Girlhood among
Ghosts.
Ono Kazuko. Chinese Women in a Century of Revolution, 1850-1950.
Restoring Women to History. General Introduction and Section on Asia.

This course provides an overview of continuity and change in the roles
and conditions of women in South Asia and China from about 1800 to the present. We will focus on how class and gender create different life possibilities for women; explore the relationships between individual life history, the development of consciousness, and historical events; and analyze
personal documents and fictional writing by Asian women as historical sources.

Students are evaluated on the basis of participation in class discussions
of assigned materials and so all readings should be completed by the date
listed. Written work includes a book review for which the bibliographies in
Restoring Women to History are a primary source, a mid-quarter and a final
examination. Graduate students will do either a research paper or a review
essay to obtain graduate credit. Topics for these papers should be selected
in consultation with the professor. The course grade will be divided as follows: 20% for class participation, 20% for the mid-quarter examination, 20%
for a book review, and 40% for the final examination.
*Indicates that title is on reserve in Langsam.

January 3: Colonialism, Imperialism, and Asian Women.
Chandra Mohanty, "Under Western Eyes: Feminist Scholarship
and Colonial Discourse," Feminist Review 30 (Autumn 1988).
Restoring Women to History, Introduction, pp. 1-30.

January 5: Overview of Modern Chinese History.
Restoring Women to History, Sievers, sections on China in
pp. 87-112.

January 8: Chinese Women in Rebellion and Reform Movements.
Ono. Chapters 1-3.

January 10: Chinese Women in Revolution.
Ono. Chapter 4.

January 12: Chinese Women as Wives and Mothers before 1949.

Ono. Chapters 5 and 7.

January 15: Martin Luther King Holiday. No classes.

January 17: Chinese Women and Work before 1949.
Ono. Chapters 6 and 7.

January 19: Chinese Women and the 1949 Revolution.
Ono. Chapter 8.

January 22: Chinese Women and Marriage after 1949.
*Honig and Hershatter. Chapters 3 & 5.

January 24: Chinese Women and Political Activity:
Empress Tz'u Hsi and Chiang Ch'ing.

January 26: Chinese Women and Work after 1949.
Honig and Hershatter. Chapter 7.

January 29: Feminism and Women in China.
Honig and Hershatter. Chapter 9.

January 31: "Small Happiness."

February 2: Mid-Quarter Examination.

February 5: Overview of Modern South Asian History.
Restoring Women to History, Ramusack, pp. 17-32.

February 7: British Administrators, Indian Reformers, and Indian Women.
*Lata Mani. "Contentious Traditions: The Debate on Sati in
Colonial India." In Kumkum Sangari and Sudesh Vaid (eds.),
Recasting Women: Essays in Colonial History, pp. 88-126.

February 9: Educational Opportunities for Indian Women:
By Whom, What Content, and for What Ends.

February 12: British Memsahibs, Feminists, and South Asian Women.
*Barbara Ramusack. "Cultural Missionaries, Maternal
Imperialists, and Feminist Allies," Women's Studies
International Forum (July 1990). (Graduate students only.)
SUBMIT A BIBLIOGRAPHICAL CITATION OF THE TITLE OF THE BOOK
THAT YOU HAVE SELECTED FOR YOUR REVIEW.

February 14: Women, Indian Nationalism, and Mahatma Gandhi.
*Madhu Kishwar. "Women and Gandhi." Economic and Political
Weekly, (October 5, 12, 1985), 1691-1702 and 1753-1758.

February 16: South Asian Women, Purdah, and Religion.
Discussion of Sultana's Dream and The Secluded Ones.

February 19: Indian Women Organizations and the Franchise.
            *Geraldine Forbes. "Votes for Women: The Demand for Women's
            Franchise in India, 1917-1937." In Vina Mazumdar (ed.),
            Symbols of Power.

February 21: Indian Women and Changing Conditions of Work.
            *Nirmala Banerjee. "Working Women in Colonial Bengal:
            Modernizationa and Marginalization." In Sangari and
            Vaid (eds.), Recasting Women, pp. 269-301.

February 23: Urban and Rural Indian Women: Legal Rights, Physical Health,
            and Reproductive Roles after 1947.
            *Selections from Toward Equality.

February 26: Pakistan: Women in an Islamic Republic.
            BOOK REVIEWS AND PAPERS ARE DUE.

February 28: South Asian Women and Economic Development Programs.
            Joan P. Mencher and Deborah D'Amico, "Kerala Women as Labourers
            and Supervisors: Implications for Women and Development," pp.
            255-266, and Malavika Karlekar, "A Study of Balmiki Women in
            Delhi," pp. 324-340. In Dube, Leacock and Ardener (eds.)
            Visibility and Power: Essays on Women in Society and
            Development. Delhi: Oxford University Press, 1986.
            Hanna Papanek. "To Each Less Than She Needs, From Each More
            Than She Can Do: Allocations, Entitlements, and Value." Pp.
            162-181 in Irene Tinker (ed.) Persistent Inequalities: Women
            and World Development. (New York: Oxford University Press,
            1990).

March 2: "No Longer Silent." Or "Kamala and Raje."

March 5: Feminism and South Asian Women.
            Read two articles from Manushi.
            TWO PAGE CRITIQUE OF "No Longer Silent" IS DUE.

March 7: Chinese American Women.
            Discussion of Woman Warrior.

March 9: Feminism and Women's History.
            Sharon Sievers. "Six (or more) Feminists in Search of a
            Historian." Comment: Janet Afary, "Some Reflections on
            Third World Feminist Historiography." Asuncion Lavrin,
            "Comments on Sharon Sievers' Six (or more) Feminists in
            Search of a Historian," Journal of Women's History, 1, 2
            (Fall 1989), 134-157.

March 15: Final Examination. 8:00 a.m. - 10:00 a.m.

THE UNIVERSITY OF ARIZONA

HISTORY/WOMEN'S STUDIES/EAST ASIAN STUDIES 489/589
WOMEN IN EAST ASIA

SYLLABUS

Fall Semester, 1991   Professor Gail Bernstein

OFFICE HOURS: Tuesday and Thursday, 3:30-5:00 and by appointment, Social
              Sciences Building, Room 131

OFFICE TELEPHONE: 621-1336 (main office of History Department)
                  621-5486 (private office)

BOOKS TO PURCHASE

Bernstein, Gail Lee, Recreating Japanese Women (University of California/
                     Berkeley paperback, 1991)

_____, Haruko's World (Stanford University Press paperback, 1983)

Pruitt, Ida,   Old Madame Yin: A Memoir of Peking Life (Stanford University
                      Press paperback, 1979)

Wolf, Margery, and Witke, Roxanne, Women in Chinese Society (Stanford University
                      Press paperback, 1975)

Wolf, Margery,   Revolution Postponed : Women in Contemporary China (Stanford
                      University Press paperback, 1985)

BOOKS ON RESERVE

Copies of all required reading will be placed on reserve in the Reserve Reading
Room of the Main Library. In addition, the following background history texts
will also be on reserve: Reischauer, Edwin O. and John Fairbank, East Asia, the
Great Tradition and East Asia, the Modern Transformation

COURSE DESCRIPTION

This course satisfies the "Non-Western" requirement of the Core Curriculum.
It also satisfies the "Institutions, Societies and Individuals" requirement.
Although there is no prerequisite, it will help to have had courses in East
Asian studies, History, or Women's Studies, or to have lived in East Asia.
Obviously, few, if any, students will be perfectly prepared to handle all the
material in this course, and so we must help each other. An open sharing of
experiences, material from other relevant courses, and ideas will be encouraged.

Students are expected to attend all class meetings and to come prepared to
contribute to classroom discussion of the lecture material and reading assignments. Because the class meets only once a week and that weekly session will
consist of audio-visual materials as well as lectures and discussions, ATTENDANCE
IS IMPERATIVE.Students who do not attend regularly may receive administrative drops.

297

History 489
SCHEDULE OF LECTURES AND READING ASSIGNMENTS

August 28   INTRODUCTION: East Asian Society and Women's Studies

- Wolf and Witke, "Introduction," Women in Chinese Society
- Michelle Rosaldo, "Woman, Culture, and Society: a Theoretical
  Overview," ON RESERVE IN MAIN READING ROOM

TRADITIONAL PERIOD: FROM ANCIENT TIMES TO CIRCA 1800

September 4   CHINA   Women in the Family

- Arthur Wolf, "The Women of Hai-shan: A Demographic Portrait,"
  Women in Chinese Society
- Marjorie Toply, "Marriage Resistance in Rural Kwangtung,"
  Women in Chinese Society
- Marjorie Wolf, "Women and Suicide in China," Women in Chinese Society
- Begin reading Ida Pruitt, Old Madame Yin

September 11   Ideology and Sexuality

- Emily Ahern, "The Power and Pollution of Chinese Women,"
  Women in Chinese Society

- Joanna Handlin, "Lu Kun's New Audience, the Influence of Women's
  Literacy on Sixteenth-Century Thought," Women in Chinese Society
- Continue reading Old Madame Yin
- Vivien Ng, "Ideology and Sexuality: Rape Laws in Quing China,"ON RESERVE

September 18   Women as Rulers, Warriors, Concubines,   Matriarchs, and Widows

- Finish Old Madame Yin
- Susan Mann, "Widows in the Kinship, Class, and Community Structures of
  Qing Dynasty China," ON RESERVE

September 25   JAPAN   Women in the Family

- Gail Bernstein,"Introduction,' Recreating Japanese Women, pp. 1-
  bottom of p. 6
- Kathleen Uno, "Women and Changes in the Household Division of Labor,"
  Recreating...
- Review Rosaldo, "Woman, Culture and Society" and compare it with Uno.

October 2   Farm Women and the Economy

- Anne Walthall, "The Life Cycle of Farm Women in Tokugawa Japan,"
  Recreating...

  FILM: "Four Families," Part II:Japan and Canada

October 9   Women Rulers, Preachers, Artists, and Entrepreneurs

               -Jennifer Robertson, "The Shingaku" Woman", Recreating...
               -Patricia Fister, "Female Bunjin," Recreating...
               -Joyce Lebra, "Women in an All-Male Industry," Recreating ...

WOMEN IN THE MODERN PERIOD: 1800-1945

October 16   Reform and Revolution in East Asia: Women in Political Movements

               -Mary Rankin, "The Emergence of Women at the End of the Ch'ing,"
                 Women in Chinese Society
               -Gail Bernstein, "Introduction," Recreating, pp. 6-14.
               -Sharon Nolte and Sally Hastings, "The Meiji State's Policy toward
                 Women," Recreating...

               FILM: "China: the Social Revolution" (17 min.)

October 23   Defining the New Woman
               -Sharon Sievers, "The Early Meiji Debate on Women," ON RESERVE
               -Laurel Rodd, "Yosano Akiko and the "New Woman'" Recreating ...
               -Margit Nagy, "Middle-Class Working Women," Recreating...
               -Yi-Tsi Feuerwerker," Women as Writers in the 1920s and 1930s,"
                 Women in Chinese Society
               -Lu Hsun, "My Views on Chastity," ON RESERVE
October 30   Industrialization and Factory Girls

               -Barbara Molony, "Activism Among Women in the Taisho Cotton
                 Textile Industry," Recreating
               -Miriam Silverberg, "The Modern Girl as Militant," Recreating
               -Yoshiko Miyake, "Doubling Expectations, Recreating

WOMEN IN CONTEMPORARY EAST ASIAN SOCIETIES: 1945-PRESENT

November 6 JAPAN   The Contemporary Japanese Family

               -William Hauser, "Women and War," Recreating...
               -Gail Bernstein, Haruko's World, Part 1 and Part 2

               FILM: "The Japanese"

November 13   The Changing Position of Women in Contemporary Japan
               -Suzanne Vogel, "The Professional Housewife," ON RESERVE
               -Compilation of student journal/scrapbook

November 20 CHINA   Women in the Chinese Communist Revolution

               -Delia Davin,"Women in the Countryside of China," Women in Chinese Society
               -Roxane Witke, "Chiang Ch'ing's Coming of Age," Women in Chinese Society
               -Margery Wolf, Revolution Postponed , ch. 2 , 3, and 5

	November 27	Women in the People's Republic of China
		-Margery Wolf, Revolution Postponed, ch. 6-8, 10,11
		ROUNDTABLE DISCUSSION WITH WOMEN FROM THE PEOPLE's REPUBLIC OF CHINA
	December 4	Farm Women in China and Japan Today
		-Margery Wolf, Revolution Postponed, ch. 4 and 9
		-Gail Bernstein, Haruko's World, Part 3
		FILM: "Small Happiness: Women of a Chinese Village"
	December 11	TO BE ANNOUNCED

COURSE ASSIGNMENTS

100   Take-home essay examination: seven doublespaced, typewritten pages on a question to be distributed two weeks before due date. Due: Oct. 16th, at beginning of class.

100   Take-home essay examination: seven doublespaced, typewritten pages on questions distributed two weeks before due date. Due: Dec. 11. This essay will be returned on the day of the regularly scheduled final examination, Dec. 20th.

100   Paper of no more than seven doublespaced pages on a topic of the student's choice, with the approval of the instructor. Due Nov. 6 at start of class.

A journal or scrapbook of clippings and information on the position of contemporary Japanese women, drawn from newspapers and magazines read between the start of this class and November 13th. Students may choose to focus on one topic (divorce, employment, childcare, etc.) or on one source (N.Y. Times, Japan Times, Newsweek, etc.) Come prepared on Nov. 6th with at least two doublespaced, typed pages of information to share with other members of the class.

GRADING POLICY

The term grade will be based on a judicious weighing of the student's performance on the three papers, the journal, and classroom discussions. Attendance is required for all class meetings; students who do not regularly attend may be administratively dropped. All assignments must be turned in on time; in order to preserve equal standards for everybody, I will have to penalize late papers. Students should come prepared to discuss assigned readings for that week. If you have difficulties keeping up with the coursework, feel free to contact me during office hours. If you are ill or if an emergency prevents you from attending class or turning in your assignments on time, contact me immediately. You can leave messages for me in my mailbox or call the main office.

GRADUATE STUDENTS: SEE ME ABOUT ADDITIONAL OR OPTIONAL COURSEWORK

This course is planned to run on a discussion basis as much as
possible. Such an approach is usually more rewarding for everyone
concerned, but it does require that everyone has read and thought
about the books to be discussed rather that to try to pick it up in
classroom sessions. Total reading has been planned with this in
mind, and will be scheduled so as to makes it easy for everyone to
keep ahead, as above. The readings can of course be only samples,
and such choices are never easy. The course focuses on Asian-Western
interactions and Asian-Western perspectives on that interaction,
directly and indirectly, as seen through works of fiction, primarily
novels. There is no pretense to deal with Asian fiction as a whole,
or with Asian-centered Western fiction. In the interest of keeping
the reading load easily manageable, many appropriate books have
(reluctantly) been left out, as has traditional Asian literature.
Some use will be made of films as an adjunct to the course,
primarily films which come along in one or the other of the film
series on campus and which fit the above prescriptions for fiction;
time will be provided for discussions of these films, in a way
which can be left flexible to adjust to expressed student interest.
There will be no exams, and instead one short essay (5 typed pages)
on some aspect of the reading from each of the four areas, due at
the end of each section.   NOTE DUE DATES BELOW AND KEEP TO THEM.

Good fiction is an excellent means to understanding a culture,
including the perspective of an insider. Our aim in this course is
the better understanding of major Asian cultures and their
interaction with the modern West. There will thus be some attention
to the context of each work as well as to its particular
perspectives and its merits as literature.

These are the books we will read, in this order:

INDIA

Rudyard Kipling, Two Tales and Kim. Try to read also samples of The
Jungle Book (try "Red Dog"), "The Miracle of Purun Bhagat", "The
Courting of Dinah Shadd", "The Reincarnation of Krishna Mulvaney"'
"The Bridge Builders", "The Mark of the Beast", and as many others
as possible in copies of Kipling's stories available to you in
bookstores or libraries.

E. M. Forster, A Passage to India

Kemala Markandaya, Nectar in a Seive

R. K. Narayan, The Guide

Kushwant Singh, Train to Pakistan

INDIA PAPERS DUE Monday, Feb.10

CHINA

Robert van Gulick. The Chinese Bell Murders

Pearl Buck. The Good Earth

Lu Hsun. Stories (various editions, but please try to read all the
    stories, including "Ah Q")

Chen Jo-Shi. The Execution of Mayor Yin

    CHINA PAPERS DUE March 9

SOUTHEAST ASIA

Joseph Conrad. An Outcast of the Islands

George Orwell. Burmese Days

Graham Greene. The Quiet American

    Other materials - short stories - will be handed out in ditto
    or xerox form

    SOUTHEAST ASIA PAPERS DUE April 6

JAPAN

Junichiru Tanizaki. Some Prefer Nettles

Yukio Mishima. Death in Midsummer (stories)

Shusaku Endo. When I Whistle

    Other materials will be handed out

    JAPAN PAPERS DUE April 22

OTHER READINGS, CRITICAL, REFERENCE, AND OTHER

General:

Shakespeare. The Tempest

Strunk & White. The Elements of Style. 3rd ed., 1979

R. Murphey. The Outsiders. Chs.1-5 (pp.1-79) and ch.8 (pp.131-155)

G. Amirthanayagam, ed.. Asian and Western Writers in Dialogue

M. Prasad. ed.. Indian-English Novelists

A. Nandy. The Intimate Enemy: Loss and Recovery of Self Under
    Colonialism

R. Winks & J. Rush. Asia in Western Fiction

Ahmed Ali, Twilight in Delhi

G. C. Roadarmel, A Death in Delhi

John Masters, Bhowani Junction (a novel set in India on the eve of Independence)

T. W. Clark, The Novel in India

Angus Wilson, The Strange Ride of Rudyard Kipling

R. J. Lewis, E. M. Forster's Passage to India

M. E. Derrett, The Modern Indian Novel in English

Benita Parry, Delusions and Discoveries: `Studies on India in the British Imagination

A. J. Greenberger, The British Image of India: The Literature of Imperialism

Meenakshi Mukherjee, Indian Novels in English: The Twice-Born Fiction

Rumer Godden, Two Under the Indian Sun (plus her many novels)

Philip Mason, Kipling: The Glass, the Shadow, and the Fire

Chas. Allen, ed., Plain Tales from the Raj (personal reminscences of old India Hands)

Paul Scott, The Raj Quartet, Staying On

R. S. Singh, Indian Novel in English

G. P. Sharma, Nationalism in Indo-Anglican Fiction

Jim Corbett, My India (delightful personal accounts by a "colonialist")

Leonard Woolf, The Village in the Jungle

R. K. Narayan--all his novels and stories, especially The Vendor of Sweets
David Rubin, After the Raj: British Novels of India since 1947

SOUTHEAST ASIA

Anthony Burgess, The Long Day Wanes

Maria Dermout, The Ten Thousand Things

Rufus Hendon, Indonesian Short Stories

Philip Jenner, Southeast Asian Literature in Translation (a bibliography)

Multatuli, Max Havelaar

George Orwell, Shooting an Elephant and Other Stories

A. Teauw, Modern Indonesian Literature

Botan, Letters from Thailand

Pramoedya Toer, This Earth of Mankind (a novel by the author of "Revenge").
H.P. Phillips, ed., Modern Thai Literature

JAPAN

Y. Kawabata, Snow Country, Sound of the Mountain (a major novelist, died 1975).

G. B. Peterson, Moon in the Water: Understanding Tanizaki, Kawabata, and Mishima

Makoto Ueda, Modern Japanese Writers and the Nature of Literature

Miyoshi Mano, Accomplices of Silence: The Modern Japanese Novel

Pierre Loti, Madame Chrysanthemum

George Sansom, The Western World and Japan

Osamu Dazai, The Setting Sun--a bitter and ironic novel of Japan in the last years
of the 1940's--the ashes of war.

J. Tanizaki, The Makioka Sisters (another fine novel).

K. Tsuruta and T. E. Swann, Approaches to the Modern Japanese Novel

N. M. Lippit, Reality and Fiction in Modern Japanese Literature

J. T. Rimer, Modern Japanese Fiction and Its Traditions

Irena Powell, Writers and Society in Modern Japan

CHINA

Cyril Birch, Anthology of Chinese Literature (2 volumes).

John Hersey, A Single Pebble (a novellette).

C. T. Hsia, History of Modern Chinese Fiction

L. O. Lee, The Romantic Generation of Modern Chinese Writers

Andre Malraux, Man's Fate (a novel set in 1927 Shanghai).

V. I. Semarov, trans. C. Allen, Lu Hsun and His Predecessors

J. Spence, The Death of Woman Wang

Mao Tun, Midnight, Spring Silkworms (two novels).

Robert van Gulick, more Judge Dee Stories--Murder in Canton, The Chinese Gold Murders

William Lyell, Lu Hsun's Vision of Reality

William Jenner, Modern Chinese Stories

Richard McKenna, The Sand Pebbles (a superb novel of China in the 1920's).

Han Kai-yu and Ting Wang, eds., Literature of the People's Republic of China
    Indiana, 1980. (a representative anthology).

Perry Link, Stubborn Weeds: Chinese Literature after the Cultural Revolution

Perry Link, ed., People or Monsters? Stories from China after Mao

Pa Chin, Family (an outstanding novel of generational and personal tensions in
    a China stirring towards revolution).

Liang Heng, Son of the Revolution (a recent vivid personal account of life
    during and after the Cultural Revolution).

Leo Lee, ed., Lu Xun (Lu Hsun) and His Legacy

Leo Lee, Voices from the Iron House: A Study of Lu Hsun

Lee, Yee, The New Chinese Realism: Writings from China after the Cultural Revolution

FILMS

Films, many of them excellent, have been made based on many of the novels used in this course. They include the following: The Man Who Would Be King, Kim, A Passage to India, The River, The Good Earth, Outcast of the Islands, Allmayer's Folly, Lord Jim, The Quiet American, Snow Country, The Sand Pebbles, Bhowani Junction, and probably others I am not aware of. Unfortunately once commercial films are a year old they seldom reappear, but you may be able find some occasionally on late television. By all means see as many as you c ; all of the above are well done. There is another genre of Western films which deals in Western stereotypes about Asia: adventure tales and melodramas, such as Marlene Dietrich's Shanghai Express, several films by the ubiquitous John Wayne and Charlton Heston as U.S. military figures holding back the yellow hordes, dashing adventures like Lives of a Bengal Lancer, and so on. These are often fun and also worth considering as powerful makers of Western images of Asia, however inaccurate or prejudiced. More recently a new genre has emerged illustrated by the films of Bruce Lee, showing Asians as superhuman figures, e.g., as karate experts righting the wrongs of the world. There is of course also a spate of war movies. Here it is interesting to notice the change from the hate message of war and immediate post-war years, showing all Japanese as fiends, to films of more recent years which at least make an effort to be more even-handed. The best example here is probably the really remarkable film Tora, Tora Tora, American-made, about the Japanese attack on Pearl Harbor, where the Japanese emerge almost as heroes. During the war and post-war years, the Chinese, then our allies against Japan, were of course shown as heroes, and it is illuminating to compare this with the popular and film images of China after 1949. By far the best film job on China so far is The Sand Pebbles, which quite faithfully follows McKenna's book and is almost as even-handed and well-rounded as he is. Incidentally, references in the book to the "gearwheel" and the "gearwheel flag" may puzzle some readers: the film version makes it clear that this is the sunburst symbol of the Nationalist Party (Kuomintang) and its flag, which in the late 1920's and 1930's formed the first effective central government after the fall of the old dynasty in 1911, and commanded the movement of Chinese nationalism, as a genuinely revolutionary party—hence the image which McKenna gives it, through Cho-jen and others—an accurate image for those years.

In general, it seems sensible to take any chance you may get to see Western films about Asia, both for whatever merits they may have and as image-makers for the Western perception of Asia. But of course the total of Asian-made films about Asia is far, far greater. India alone produces more films than any country in the world, most of them never seen outside India (and most of them not very interesting to a Western audience, quite apart from language problems). But a few superb Indian films do get fairly frequent showings in this country, most notably the incomparable films of Satyajit Ray, including the Apu Trilogy (Pather Panjali, The World of Apu, Aparajito), The Target, The Music Room, Devi, and many more. Grab any chance you get to see any one of Ray's films.

The Japanese are also major film makers, and turn out many of the finest films in the world according to most film critics. Here the output of high quality is so great that it is really impossible to pick and choose, even in terms of leading directors, of whom there are many. This is not to say that all Japanese films are great, or that you will like any one of them, but most which you would get a chance to see in this country will at least be worth looking at, and most will be very, very good. The output includes both films set in traditional Japan (e.g., Rashomon, perhaps the best known Japanese film in this country) and in the contemporary urbanized and Westernized culture. Some are occasionally shown on U.S. television, especially on the PBS stations.

Practically no Southeast Asia-made and very few Chinese-made films make it to this country, but from time to time you may have a chance to see one of them on PBS.

Some better known Western films, such as The Bridge on the River Kwai or The Ugly American (far better as a movie than the book of the same title) are mainly about Westerners and their adventures rather than about Asia or Asians, but are good theatre and well done. See whatever you get a chance to see! On films in general, feel free also to write one or more of your papers on relevant films you have seen, analyzing them and/or comparing them with what you are reading.

René Goldman, University of British Columbia

Asian Studies 405
COMMUNIST MOVEMENTS IN EASTERN ASIA
Spring Term 1992
Course Outline and Reading List

In the Spring Term the course has as its main objective the study of Chinese Communism in the past 50 years, the evolution of some of the CCP's policies, the relationship between rulers and ruled, the culture of present-day China and China's relations with the world. These policies, as well as the policies that will not be discussed in class, constitute interesting subject matters for the writing of research papers. In addition, there will be several survey lectures on the history of the Communist movements of Japan, Vietnam, and Korea. The latter may also constitute subject matter for the writing of research papers. Remember that source materials included also articles in scholastic journals. Consult the instructor when in doubt.

Although more books are being listed here than those which are either required or recommended reading, this is not intended to be an exhaustive reading list. It lists nevertheless sources that are important for the writing of papers on almost any subject; it is strongly recommended that you read at least one of the books marked with an asterisk* under each heading.

COURSE TEXTBOOKS

(R) Stephen Uhalley, Jr. A History of the Chinese Communist Party.
Lowell Dittmer. China's Continuous Revolution: 1949-1981.
Richard Thornton. China: A Political History: 1917-1980 (Westview).
*Jonathan Spence. The Gate of Heavenly Peace (Penguin).
* Maurice Meissner. Mao's China and After: A History of the People's Republic .
Craig Dietrich. People's Chine: a Brief History.
Laszlo Ladanyi. The CCP and Marxism: 1921 - 1949.
Jan W. Mabbett. Modern China: The Mirage of Modernity (1985).
Jacques Guillermaz. The Chinese Communist Party in Power: 1940-1976.
P'eng Shu-tse. The Chinese Communist Party in Power (Monad/Pathfinder).

ASSIGNMENTS

One book report before the mid-term break AND and one book report after the mid-term break but before March 31, or one term paper.

Year-end examination.

COLLECTIONS OR DOCUMENTS

Winberg Chai. Essential Works of Chinese Communism (Bantam).
Franz Schurmann and Orville Schell. The China Reader, Vol. 3- Communist China and
        Vol. 4 - People's China.
Theodore Ch'en, edit. The Chinese Communist Regime: Documents and Commentary.
Stuart R. Schram. The Thought of Mao Tse-tung.

READINGS ON VARIOUS SUBJECTS

Ideology, Leadership, Politics

Arif Dirlik and Maurice Meisner, ed. Marxism and the Chinese Experience.
Lucian Pye. The Mandarin and the Cadre: China's Political Cultures.

Alan Liu. How china is Ruled.

Franz Schurmann. Ideology and Organization in Communist China.

Stuart R. Schram. La "Revolution Permanente" en Chine.

Stuart R. Schram. Mao Tse-tung; The Political Thought of Mao Tse-tung.

John B. Starr. Ideology and Culture: An Introduction to the Dialectics of Contemporary Chinese Politics.

James R. Townsend. Political Participation in Communist China; Politics in China.

Benjamin Schwartz. Communism in China: Ideology in Flux. (1968).

A. Doak Barnett. Cadres, Bureaucracy, and Political Power in Communist China.

Frederic Teiwes. Politics and Purges in China.

*Martin King Whyte. Small Groups and Political Rituals in China (California).

Frederic Wakeman, Jr. History and Will: Philosophical Perspectives of Mao Tse-tung's Thoughts.

Ezra F. Vogel. Canton Under Communism: Programs and Politics in a Provincial Capital.

Vivienne Shue. The Reach of Government.

Economy

*Anita Chan, et al. Chen Village: The Recent History of a Peasant Community in Mao's China.

Mark Selden. The Political Economy of Chinese Socialism.

Peter Nolan. The Political Economy of Collective Farms.

S. Feuchtwang, et., edit. Transforming China's Economy in the Eighties (2 vols.).

Stephen Endicott. Red Earth: Revolution in a Sichuan Village.

Barry M. Richman. Industrial Society in Communist China (Vintage, 1972).

Vivienne Shue. Peasant China in Transition (U. of Calif., 1980).

Evelyn Rawski. China's Transition to Industrialism (Michigan, 1980).

Jan Prybyla. The Chinese Economy: Problems and Policies (S. Carolina, 1980).

Doak Barnett. China's Economy in Global Perspective (Brookings, 1981).

Ramon Myers. The Chinese Economy: Past and Present (1980).

*Jurgen Domes. Socialism in the Chinese Countryside (1980).

*Wm. Hinton. Fanshen and Shenfan.

The People's Liberation Army and Its Role in Chinese Politics

*Ellis Joffe. The Chinese Army after Mao (Harvard, 1987).

Ellis Joffe. Party and Army: 1949-1964 (1965). .

John Gittings. The Role of the Chinese Army (Oxford, 1967).

Samuel Griffith. Peking and People's Wars (Praeger).

*Monte Bullard. China's Political/Military Evolution. Party and Military, 1960-1984.

China's Foreign Policy

Samuel Kim. China, the U.N., and World Order.

John K. Fairbank. Images and Policies in Chinese-American Relation.

R. Blum. The U.S. and China in World Affairs.

Akira Iriye, edit. U.S. Policy Toward China.

Chalmers Johnson. Autopsy on People's War.

Neville Maxwell. India's China War.

Shih Chih-yu. The Spirit of Chinese Foreign Policy: A Psychocultural View.

Educational Policies

Stewart Fraser. Chinese Communist Education: Records of the First Decade.

*Stewart Fraser, Edit. Education and Communism in China: An Anthology of
    Commentary & Documents.
Thomas Bernstein. Up to the Mountains and Down to the Villages.

Anthologies of Miscellaneous Chapters on the People's Republic of China

Roderick McFarquhar, ed. China Under Mao.
Stuart R. Schram, Ed. Authority, Participation, and Cultural Change in China.
Doak Barnett, ed. Chinese Communist Politics in Action.
John M. Lindbeck. China: Management of a Revolutionary Society.
John W. Lewis. Party Leadership and Revolutionary Power in China.

Personal Accounts: Overview Presentations

*John Fraser. The Chinese: Portrait of a People.
David Bonavia. The Chinese.
*Fox Butterfield. China: Alive in the Bitter Sea.
*Simon Leys. Chinese Shadows: Broken Images.
Michael Frolic. Mao's People: Sixteen Portraits of Life in Revolutionary China.
Nigel Harris. The Mandate of Heaven: Marx and Mao in Modern China.
Richard Bernstein. From the Centre of the Earth: the Search for Truth about China.
Simon de Beaufort. Yellow Earth, Green Jade: Constants in Chinese Political Mores.
Dennis Bloodworth. Mao Tse-tung and the Ironies of Power.

COURSE SCHEDULE

JANUARY

I. The Yan'an (Yenan) Period

1. Maturation of Mao Zedong's political thought. The "Sinicization of Marxism-Leninism." Mao's On Practice, On Contradiction, On the New Democracy and other writings. Liu Shao-chi's How to be a Good Communist.

2. Communist controlled areas in the countryside of North China. Their administration and land policy.

3. Ideological work in the Border Areas. The Party Rectification Campaign of 1942. Mao's Talks at the Yenan Forum on Literature and the Arts.

4. CCP-KMT Relations during the War; the 7th Contress of the CCP (1945). Power of the CCP at the end of World War II.

5. The Final Civil War (1946-1949).

Readings:
*Spence, Chapters. 10 and 11 and **Lerner, pp. 170-179.
Mark Selden. The Yenan Way in Revolutionary China.
Hsu Yung-ying. A Survey of the Shenkanning Border Area (IPR).
*Edgar Snow. Red Star Over China, Random Notes on Red China, and Journey to
    the Beginning.
Helen Foster Snow. Inside Red China.
Harrison Forman. Inside Red China.
*Boyd Compton. Mao's China: Party Reform Documents: 1942-44.
Barbara Tuchman. Stilwell and the American Experience in China.
John Service. The Amerasia Papers—Some Problems in the History of U.S.-China
    Relations.
*Suzanne Pepper. Civil War in China: The Political Struggle, 1946-1949.
*Jack Belden. China Shakes the World.
*John Melby. The Mandate of Heaven.
A. Doak Barnett. China at the Eve of the Communist Takeover. Communist
    China: The Early Years (1949-1955).
Chester Ronning. A Memoir of China in Revolution.
A.S. Whiting. China Crosses the Yalu: the Decision to Enter the Korean War.
D. Gillin and R. Myers, Edit. Last Chance in Manchuria: the Diary of Chang Kia-
    ngau

II. "Liberation" and the Period of Reconstruction: 1949-1952

1. Land Reform

V.D. Lippit. Land Reform and Economic Development
*John Wong. Land Reform in the P.R. of China.
*Wm. Hinton. Fanshen.
*C.K. Yang. Chinese Communist Society: The Family and the Village.
Tai Hung-chao. Land Reform and Politics: A Comparative Analysis (1975).
Chen Yuan-Tsung. The Dragon's Village (N.Y., 1980).

2. Initial Relations with the U.S.S.R.: "Leaning to one side:; the Korean War (1950-1953); Soviet aid.

3. The "Three Anti-Five Anti" campaigns.

4. Government, Party and Mass Organizations.

III. The Period of the First Five-Year Plan (1953-1957)

1. The surge of industrialization.

2. Collectivization of agriculture. Mutual aid teams, cooperatives, and collectives.

Readings:
Chao Kuo-chun. Agrarian Policies in Mainland China.
Articles by Walker and Bernstein in China Quarterly, Nos. 26 and 31.
Franz Schurmann. Ideology and Organization, pp. 404-474.

3. The Socialization of Trade, Industry, and Handicrafts.

Readings
Kuan Ta-t'ung. The Socialist Transformation of the Capitalist Industry and Commerce in China (Peking).
Communist China, 1955-1959: Policy Documents with Analysis.

4. The 1956 "Thaw". The "Hundred Flowers" campaign for the encouragement of science and scholarship.

5. The Rectification campaign of 1957 and the "Anti-Rightist" campaign.

Readings
Roderick MacFarquhar. The Hundred Flowers Campaign and the Chinese Intellectuals.
Theordore Ch'en. Thought Reform of the Chinese Intellectuals.
Robert J. Lifton. Thought Reform and the Psychology of Totalism.
Merle Goldman. Literary Dissent in Communist China.
Rene Goldman. "Peking University," pp. 199-238 in Stewart Fraser. Education & Communism in China.
Dennis J. Doolin. "Communist China: The Politics of Student Opposition."

FEBRUARY

I.

1. The 1958 turning point--the "Mass Line" and "Red and Expert" issues. The "Great Leap Forward." Power Struggle: The Peng Dehuai Affair.

2. The People's Communes before and after 1960.

Readings:
Gargi Dutt. Rural Communes of China (London, 1967).
S.J. Burki. A Study of Chinese Communes (1965).
F. Schurmann. Ideology and Organization, pp. 464-500.
Wheelwright and McFarlane. The Chinese Road to Socialism.
Union Research Institute. The Case of Peng Te-huai: 1959-1968.

3. The Xth Plenum (September 1962). Training successors of the Revolution. Mao's concern over the future of China.

   Readings:
   *Richard Baum. Prelude to Revolution: Mao, the Party, and the Peasant Question, 1962-1966 (Columbia, 1976).
   J.D. Simmonds. "China: Evolution of a Revolution, 1959-1966."
   R. Baum and F. Teiwes. The Socialist Education Movement of 1962-1966.
   Ridley and Ch'en. Rural People's Communes in Lienchiang County.

4. Cultural Policies of the Chinese Communists. From Mao's Talks at the Yenan Forum on Literature and the Arts (1942) to the Cultural Revolution.

   Readings:
   Ralph C. Crozier, edit. China's Cultural Legacy and Communism (Praeger, 1970).
   Merle Goldman. Literary Dissent in Communist China.
   Joe Huang. Heroes and Villains in China.
   Hsu Kai-Yu. The Chinese Literary Scene (Pelican Books, 1975).

5. The "Struggle between Two Lines" and the outbreak of the "Great Proletarian Cultural Revolution." The XIth Plenum CCP (August 1966)--Formation of the Red Guards.

6. The "January Revolution" in Shanghai. Formation of the "Three-in-One" revolutionary alliances and seizure of power by the "Revolutionary Committees": 1967-1968.

7. Rise and Fall of Lin Biao. The IXth Congress of the CCP (April 1969) and the aftermath of the Cultural Revolution.

   Readings on the Cultural Revolution:
   *Chen Jo-hsi. The execution of Mayor Yin and Other Stories from the Great Prolitarian Cultural Revolution.
   *Cheng Nien. Life and Death in Shanghai.
   *Liang Heng and J. Shapiro. Son of the Revolution.
   *Yang Chiang. Six Chapters of Life in a Cadre School.
   Union Research Institute. CCP Documents on the Great Proletarian Cultural Revolution (Hong Kong, 1968).
   Victor Nee. The Cultural Revolution at Peking University.
   K. H. Fan. The Chinese Cultural Revolution: Selected Documents.
   *Ken Ling. The Revenge of Heaven.
   H.C. Chuang. Evening Chats at Yenshan or The Case of Teng To.
   Clive Ansley. The Heresy of Wu Han (Toronto University Press, 1971).
   David and Nancy Milton. The Wind Will Not Subside.
   Richard Solomon. Mao's Revolution and the Chinese Political Culture.
   William Hinton. "Hundred Day War" The Cultural Revolution at Tsinghua University," (Monthly Review, 1972).
   Lowell Dittmer. Liu Shao-ch'i and the Chinese Cultural Revolution: The Politics of Mass Criticism (Berkeley, 1975).
   *Simon Leys. The Chairman's New Clothes.

8. The Cultural Revolution and the Sino-Soviet Conflict: turning point in the history of the World Communist Movement.

Readings:
Herbert Ellison. The Sino-Soviet Conflict: A Global Perspective.
Donald Zagoria. The Sino-Soviet Dispute: 1958-1961 (Princeton).
*David Floyd. Mao Against Khrushchev (Praeger).
Edward Crankshaw. The New Cold War: China vs. Russia.
Edgar Snow. China, Russia, and the U.S.A..
Klaus Mehnert. Peking and Moscow.
*O. Edmund Clubb. China & Russia: The "Great Game."

9.   The Xth Congress of the CCP (1973) and the Anti-Confucian Campaign–Rise and Fall of the "Gang of Four."

10.   The "April 5th Movement and the Death of Mao Zedong."

11.   The brief reign of Hua Guofeng.

12.   China After Mao. Human Rights. The Chinese Democratic Movement and its suppression. The Massacre at Tiananmen.

Readings:
Andrew Nathan. Chinese Democracy.
David Goodman. Beijing Street Voices.
*Michael S. Duke. The Iron House.
Yi Mu, comp. Crisis at Tiananmen.
Amnesty International. Political Imprisonment in the People's Republic of China (1978).
Amnesty International. China Report (1984).
Rene Goldman. "Old Wine in New Bottles" , in Chen and Shyu, edit. China Insights, and "Commentary on the Amnesty International Report."

SOME SUGGESTED TOPICS FOR TERM PAPERS
AND CLASSROOM PERESENTATIONS

1. Bunking and de-bunking China under Communism: Compare the varying and changing images of China provided by different authors = e.g. Han Suyin, Felix Greene, Simon Leys, John Fraser, Edger Snow, Fox Butterfield, or others.

2. Land Reform policies (1946-1952).

3. The collectivization of agriculture (mid-1950's).

4. The People's Communes and their evolution.

5. The Great Leap Forward (1958-1960) and its consequences.

6. The "Great Proletarian Cultural Revolution" and its consequences.

7. "Radicals" vs. "Conservatives" in the CCP leadership: Mao's relationship to them; the "Gang of Four" vs. Deng Xiaoping.

8. Study of a leading figure in the CCP: Zhou Enlai, Zhu De, Deng Xiaoping, Liu Shaoqi, Lin Biao, Mao Zedong, etc.

9. CCP Educational Policies.

10. The industrialization of China.

11. CCP Cultural Policies.

12. Sino-Soviet relations.

13. China's foreign policy, or relationship with any particular country or area.

14. The people's Liberation Army.

15. Women in China.

16. Any other East Asian Communist movement.

Some Journals and Publications

China Quarterly
Pacific Affairs
Journal of Asian Studies
Problems of Communism
Modern Chinese History
Asian Survey
Beijing Review, etc.
Far Eastern Economic Review (and its annual Asia Yearbook).

UNIVERSITY OF INDIANA

HISTORY J475: SEMINAR IN HISTORY
Topic: *TRINITY: Birth of the Atom Bomb*

Spring 1991   T 2:30-4:15 pm
G. M. Wilson   Ballantine 137

The story of how America created the bomb and used it to defeat Japan and
end World War II is one of the truly compelling dramas in recent world history.
The story has a hero (Robert Oppenheimer), a middleman (General Groves), a cast
of thousands (mostly physicists and soldiers), and an outcome that changed the
world. Not only did the war end as a direct result; modern science and
technology entered a new stage that has shaped our present. There are numerous
biographies, even a novel and a movie as well as two plays, that treat this
episode. Yet the genesis of the atomic bomb is a story known only dimly.

Part of the problem arises from the fact that this is science, and we
assume science must be hard to understand. It is hard, to be sure. But the
process is so important that it repays study, and so relevant to our world that
it commands our attention. Another part of the problem concerns the
institutional arrangements and human actors, for they too are complex and hard
to understand. In fact, however, these were ordinary people who just happened
to run into an extraordinary assignment. They and their great achievement were
jerry-built; with study, we ought to be able to grasp it, and them as well.

The outcome of this seminar will be a *seminar paper* using *primary sources*
(=contemporary materials and memoirs) to explicate an aspect of the process by
which the atomic bomb was fashioned and put to use in World War II. Secondary
sources will also be employed. The seminar paper should be 12 word-processed
pages long (double-spaced); it will count for 50% of your final grade. What you
write about is up to you, but given your instructor's strengths it may be well
for you to consider writing a biographical study of one of the persons who
figured in the making of the bomb: e.g., Lawrence, Fermi, Szilard, Teller, or
Kistiakowsky, among the scientists; Groves or Nichols, among the military brass;
Kitty Oppenheimer or Haakon Chevalier, among the kindred souls.

Your seminar paper topic and its source base can be determined later. In
the early going we will collectively do a set of readings and discuss them in
class. The object is to create a shared context for appreciating the process
through which nuclear weapons came into being. (Discussion in class will count
25% of the final grade.) There will also be a takehome midterm exam (worth
25%), followed by a draft problem paper and a bibliographic essay, neither of
which will be formally graded (but note that they both count toward fulfilling
the COAS Intensive Writing requirement). The total required writing will be
5,000 to 7,000 words, depending on how long your final paper turns out to be.

Texts to Buy. The following paperbacks are available for you to purchase. The
other assigned readings are on 3-hour reserve in UGLi under "Wilson J475." Be
sure to read them **before** the dates when they will be discussed.

Alperovitz, Gar. *Atomic Diplomacy*. Penguin, 1985 (1965).
Fussell, Paul. *Thank God for the Atom Bomb*. Ballantine, 1990.
Groves, Leslie R. *Now It Can Be Told*. DaCapo, 1983 (1962).
Hersey, John. *Hiroshima*. Vintage, 1989 (1946).
Major, John. *Oppenheimer Hearing*. Scarborough House, 1983.
Rhodes, Richard. *The Making of the Atomic Bomb*. Touchstone, 1986.
Smith, Martin Cruz. *Stallion Gate*. Ballantine, 1986.

Tuesday:

Jan 8   INTRODUCTION - Film: *The Beginning or the End?* (1947).

Jan 15   WHAT IS IT THAT THEY DID?
Rhodes. *Making of the Atomic Bomb*. chs. 1-2.
Fussell. *Thank God for the Atom Bomb*. pp. 1-22.
Richard P. Feynman. *Surely You're Joking, Mr. Feynman*. pp. 83-115.

Jan 22   TRINITY AS A TELECOMMUNICATIONS TRIUMPH
Film: *The Day after Trinity* (1980).

Jan 29   MODERN PHYSICS AND U.C.-BERKELEY
Thomas S. Kuhn, *The Structure of Scientific Revolutions*. 2nd ed..
chs. 1-2, 4-5, 10.
Daniel Kevles, *The Physicists*. chs. 14-15, 20-21.

Feb 5   MANHATTAN DISTRICT AND LOS ALAMOS
Rhodes, *Making of the Atomic Bomb*. chs. 13-14.
Groves, *Now It Can Be Told*. to be announced

Feb 12   TRINITY BASE
Rhodes, *Making of the Atomic Bomb*. chs. 16, 18.

Feb 19   POTSDAM, HIROSHIMA, NAGASAKI (midterm exams handed out)
Rhodes, *Making of the Atomic Bomb*. ch. 19. epilogue.
R. J. C. Butow, *Japan's Decision to Surrender*. prologue & chs. 7-8.
Hersey, *Hiroshima*. entire.

Feb 26   DISCUSSION OF MIDTERM EXAM

Mar 5   SCIENCE AND MORAL RESPONSIBILITY (midterm exams turned in)
J. Robert Oppenheimer, *Science and the Common Understanding*. t.b.a.
Groves, *Now It Can Be Told*, t.b.a.

Mar 12   [spring break]

Mar 19   MAKING THE "SUPER": FROM THE A-BOMB TO THE H-BOMB
Freeman Dyson, *Disturbing the Universe*. chs. 5-9.
Alperowitz, *Atomic Diplomacy*. preface & chs. 4-7.

Mar 26   PRESENTATION OF RESEARCH TOPICS (bibliographical essays due)

Apr 2   HEROES AND VIPERS: OPPENHEIMER AS A SECURITY THREAT
Haakon Chevalier, *Oppenheimer: The Story of a Friendship*. pp.
vii-43, 104-172.
Philip Stern, *The Oppenheimer Case: Security on Trial*. chs. 3, 5-6,
8, 13.
Major, *Oppenheimer Hearing*. passim.

Apr 9   THE OPPENHEIMER CASE AS A LITERARY ARTIFACT
Heinar Kipphardt, *In the Matter of J. Robert Oppenheimer*. scan.
Smith, *Stallion Gate*, entire.

Apr 16 & 23   ORAL REPORTS ON STUDENT TOPICS (final papers due April 26)